NICHOLAS BARBON
DEVELOPING LONDON, 1667–1698

NICHOLAS BARBON
DEVELOPING LONDON, 1667–1698

by
Frank Kelsall and Timothy Walker

LONDON TOPOGRAPHICAL SOCIETY
Publication No. 186
2022

Edited by Sheila O'Connell

LONDON TOPOGRAPHICAL SOCIETY
312 Russell Court
Woburn Place
London WC1H 0NG
2022

ISBN
978-0-902087-73-6

PRODUCED IN GREAT BRITAIN BY
SCORPION CREATIVE

CONTENTS

ACKNOWLEDGEMENTS

The authors are grateful to the London Topographical Society for agreeing to publish this, the first, biography of Nicholas Barbon. We have gained enormously from Sheila O'Connell, the LTS editor, and from the work of Linda Fisher, the copy editor, and Steve Hartley, the designer, especially for his precise work on the maps showing Barbon's developments.

We have benefitted from the resources of many libraries and archives, including the British Library, the British Museum, London Metropolitan Archives, National Archives, the Bodleian Library, London Library and the Museum of London. Many archivists have helped us locate records, including Middle Temple, Inner Temple, All Souls College, Oxford, Camden Local Studies and Archives Centre, the City of Westminster Archives Centre, Lincolnshire Archives, Bedfordshire Archives, and Aidan Haley at the Devonshire Collection, Chatsworth. The Utrecht University Library kindly tracked down a copy of Barbon's doctoral thesis in the Staatsbibliothek zu Berlin – Preußischer Kulturbesitz. Ashley Baynton-Williams has been very helpful in providing detailed images of early maps.

We have also benefitted from countless conversations about the book's subject matter and would like to thank Barrie Cook, Peter Guillery, Robin Harcourt-Williams, Richard Hewlings, Richard Kleer and Robert Thorne for their helpful comments.

Finally, we want to thank our wives, Anna and Diane, for having put up with the long gestation period of this book and for their continuing encouragement.

NOTE ON DATING, INFLATION AND CURRENCY

It was only in 1752 that Britain adopted the Gregorian calendar with the year starting on 1 January. In Barbon's time the year started on 25 March, and this can sometimes cause confusion. We have translated dates in January, February and March to correspond with what modern readers would understand as the relevant year.

It is difficult to make meaningful comparisons of costs, prices or purchasing power over a period of some 350 years, but the National Archives and Bank of England calculators indicate that £1,000 in 1680 was the equivalent of between approximately £115,000 and £155,000 today.

Pre-decimalization currency converts as follows: 1 penny (d.) = 0.4 p; 12d. = 1 shilling (s.). = 5 p; 20s. = £1.

CHAPTER I
INTRODUCTION

Property speculators have often been vital elements of the reinvention of cities but have never drawn much praise. This was just as true in the seventeenth century when arguably London saw its first property speculation. There were then few large-scale developers active over long periods. Most of them were either financiers, including those who collected taxes for the government, or already active in the building industry, such as carpenters, bricklayers or suppliers of building material. One, however, was radically different. Although a Londoner by birth, he was an outsider; indeed, his lack of membership of any livery company meant he was not a freeman of the City and could be — and was — described as a 'foreigner'. He was a medical doctor with no background in building of any kind, limited ready access to finance, no legal training, and with a father only recently released from imprisonment in the Tower of London for treason. His name was Nicholas Barbon.

Barbon played a key role in the development of London after the Great Fire and for the rest of the seventeenth century. He is described variously by historians as the greatest speculative builder of the age, the principal developer responsible for the growth of the London brick terrace and an inventor of what became the classic London town house. At the same time, he has been called an indefatigable designer of financial schemes, an unscrupulous financial manipulator of genius, a wealthy and unscrupulous businessman who refused to pay his debts, as well as sometime slumlord and schemer extraordinaire.[1] Not everyone at the time disapproved. A few months before Barbon's death in 1698, the MP Sir John Lowther, who himself had done business with him, wrote that Barbon had invested 'not less than £200,000 in building; for which [...] he deserves more of the public than any subject in England'.[2] A few years later, Edward Hatton would describe him as 'a very great builder'.[3] Despite continued accusations of jerrybuilding, many of his houses survive to this day.

He also wrote on the controversial economic subjects of his time, and some claim this is his most important contribution. His writings have been praised by Marx, Keynes and Schumpeter.[4] Others call him an economist of prophetic perspicacity, one of the important forerunners of the monetary analysis which came to maturity during the eighteenth century and one of the earliest defenders of free trade, and cite his work as among the first stimulus, perhaps trickledown, arguments in favour of luxury consumption.[5] As suggested by these comments, economic historians have traditionally analysed seventeenth-century writers in terms of how close they come to modern economic ideas, but economics was not then a separate intellectual subject.[6] In any case, Barbon arguably was not writing about economics as we know it but about political economy. As we shall see, the politics was very important, and radical.

However, there was more to Barbon than being an economically literate property developer. As well as his building development, he was, in the parlance of the day, a 'projector'. A character in a Ben Jonson play labels projectors as 'Why one, sir, that projects ways to enrich men or to make them great',[7] but Defoe is more supportive, seeing them as, potentially at least, producing a public good. He defines an honest projector as 'he who, having by fair and plain principles of sense, honesty and ingenuity brought any contrivance to a suitable perfection, makes out what he pretends to'.[8] Apart from building, Barbon's projects extended to banking and insurance. His provision of the first fire insurance in England in 1682 means that he is widely regarded as the father of fire insurance, where some argue his best work was done.[9] In 1696, he promoted one of the first banks, ostensibly based on land but actually little different from the newly created Bank of England, with which it would have been in competition. Success was frustrated by the recoinage crisis, but it did some business, closing three years later, not long after his death. Other projects included the promotion of a company to provide water from the Thames with an innovative pump for which he had secured a patent, and he followed this up with another proposal for fire insurance, for the first time including the insurance of household goods.

His insurance and banking projects were controversial and undertaken in competition with others, both at the conceptual stage and when he tried to put them into operation. They provoked pamphlet wars, with the various sides of the argument producing hard-hitting material promoting their case and rubbishing their opponents. Barbon's father had been a prominent lay preacher, adept at stirring up crowds with his radical preaching, and Barbon inherited his father's skills and enthusiasm for controversy, albeit he never ventured into theological issues. Like his father, he had the ability to enthuse crowds and often worked through public meetings, both for his projects and his property development. His client, Roger North, saw him manage Middle Temple lawyers as well as groups of creditors or potential tenants, and captured this skill: 'He was an exquisite mob master, and knew the arts of leading, winding, or driving mankind in herds as well as any that I ever observed.'[10]

Nevertheless, and despite his many claims to fame, this is the first full biography devoted to him, perhaps in part because relatively little personal material remains and there is no portrait to allow us to judge his character for ourselves.[11] The chief exception is a striking pen picture by Roger North written with a certain wry appreciation of his faults as well as his strengths. But perhaps the most important reason is that those who have written about him subsequently have concentrated on (or indeed only been interested in) one part of his activities. Historians of architecture, London, insurance and economics have concentrated on their own area with only brief references to his other activity. This loses the benefit from looking at his life as a whole, for Barbon himself certainly did not separate his various activities.

London

Barbon's career was intimately linked with London, which he was to describe as 'the largest, richest, chiefest City in the world for trade'.[12] It was changing dramatically in the seventeenth century when its population almost trebled to some 575,000, almost eight times what it had been in 1550 and over ten times its size in 1500. By 1700, and despite both Great Fire and Plague, it was the largest city in Europe, with twenty times the population of Bristol, the next largest English city, itself smaller than Southwark, one of London's suburbs.[13] This new population needed somewhere to live and the fields that circled the City were rapidly developed; by 1700, almost ninety per cent of Londoners were outside the old City walls. Defoe described London early in the eighteenth century:

> New squares, and new streets rising up every day to such a prodigy of buildings, that nothing in the world does, or ever did, equal it, except old Rome in Trajan's time [...] It is the disaster of London, as to the beauty of its figure, that it is thus stretched out in building, just at the pleasure of every builder, or undertaker of buildings, and as the convenience of the people directs [...] this has spread the face of it in a most straggling, confus'd manner, out of all shape, uncompact, and unequal.[14]

London dominated England. Not only was it the centre of government and the Court but, by 1700, eighty per cent by value of imports to England from overseas entered through the port of London.[15] Much of this was raw materials for manufacture — London was a major manufacturing centre — but much was semi-luxury consumables from Europe, Levant, North America, the West Indies, the East Indies and China. These included goods like spices, wine, sugar, tobacco, coffee and tea, which had become virtually essentials for those with the money to spend on them, and a range of textiles including the Indian calicoes which had become all the rage, as well as a wide variety of silks. Many of these imports were rapidly re-exported to the rest of Europe, increasing London's role as a trade centre. These new products changed patterns of consumption and provided an enormous economic stimulus.

Young people came from all over the country to find work, to be apprenticed and, for some, to make their fortune. The diversity of London's population reinforced its role in promoting change. Huguenots had fled persecution in France, bringing artisan skills in silk and clock-making as well as high finance; Dutch, Flemish and Jews came, bringing their tastes, fashions and religions with them. London accepted this spread of cultures and created a market unique in its size, range and affluence, providing vast opportunities for the entrepreneur. These opportunities were enhanced by the development of a sophisticated financial market that caught up with and eventually surpassed that in the Netherlands and would enable the growth of the navy as well as supporting an English army in Continental Europe.

Not everyone welcomed these changes. The operations of less restrained markets began to disrupt what had been the natural order of a relatively static society and challenged long-held views about the role of consumption. Frugality was often still viewed as a virtue: many frowned on conspicuous consumption of things that were fashionable rather than necessary.[16] As in all ages, nimbyism was prevalent. There were plenty of Londoners who preferred to keep the fields around the City as they were rather than have them built on, or did not want competition from retailers outside the City who were not constrained by its regulations. Many from outside London argued that it was too big and sucked in resources that should be available for the rest of the country.

New building in London was therefore not just a matter of construction. It affronted many vested interests and raised many wider political and economic questions. Contrary to what many have believed, London's development in the later part of the seventeenth century was not largely due to aristocrats. Apart from one or two cases, while they may have sold or leased the land, they did not develop it themselves. As Defoe indicates, apart from building regulation designed to increase uniformity, reduce the risk of fire and attempt to restrict suburban sprawl, there was little or no 'town planning'. Often, development was taken on by a wide variety of private individuals investing relatively small single amounts to provide in due course an income or a settlement for their children.[17] There were essentially no banks, and larger-scale developers had to create the means to finance their operations, frequently using middlemen such as goldsmiths or scriveners. A further complication was the difficulty of establishing unambiguous title to urban property, potentially casting doubt on the security of any loans. Rich merchants preferred to invest cash surplus to their business in joint stock companies; little more than four per cent of their investment was in urban property, which would have included their own residence. When they did invest in property, it was usually outside London, which required less management time and could give them at least local status.[18]

Nicholas Barbon

Nicholas came from a family of radical Puritans. His grandfather was a Northamptonshire vicar expelled from his parish in 1605 because of his puritan views. His father, a younger son born in 1596, was sent to London and apprenticed to a strongly puritan member of the Leathersellers' Company. He too became a Leatherseller at the end of his apprenticeship. This was Praise God Barbon, a radical Puritan merchant and lay preacher who, nominated to be an MP by Oliver Cromwell in 1653, gave his name to the 'Barebones Parliament'. He preached at great length to excited crowds in his warehouse just off Fleet Street and conducted lengthy theological arguments by pamphlet, particularly about the rights and wrongs of child baptism. The building, which at some time may have also served as the family home, was regularly attacked by opponents who tried to shout down his sermons. Although ridiculed for preaching while supposedly an uneducated leatherseller, Praise God's father, an Oxford graduate and former fellow of Magdalen College, would have ensured him an education, not least in theology. Praise God became a rich and successful merchant, holding a variety of elected posts in both his parish and in the governance of the City of London as a whole. A public and vocal opponent of the Restoration, he was sent to the Tower of London for treason in 1661 and only released after a few months on the grounds of ill health. He lived a further seventeen years, becoming increasingly committed to his millennial convictions about Jesus Christ's imminent return to this world.

Nicholas's family clearly held radical opinions and were not afraid to express them forcefully, even in the face of violent opposition. They thought for themselves and were not bound by conventional views, and it was into this environment that Nicholas was born in about 1638, his only surviving sibling being a brother born some ten years later. He was well educated, getting his first degree from Oxford University early in 1659, where he had been admitted as an 'armiger' rather than a 'pleb', ostensibly reflecting an entitlement to a coat of arms. In his later economic and polemical writing he would, as did many of his contemporaries, use Latin tags and classical references. Prevented from remaining at Oxford by his father's status as a known opponent of the monarchy, he completed his education in the Netherlands, studying first at Leyden and then qualifying as a doctor at the University of Utrecht in 1661 with a doctoral thesis on malaria. Returning to London, he was made an Honorary Fellow of the Royal College of Physicians in December 1664 and so was able to practise medicine. He was one of the few doctors who did not leave London during the Plague but rather volunteered to help, producing ideas of his own on how best to deal with the epidemic. His father's main house and associated warehouse were burnt down in the Fire of London and Nicholas discovered the opportunities for making money from redevelopment. He never looked back and, although he always described himself as 'Doctor', he never practised medicine again.

Barbon and Development

Barbon began with a number of small developments, replacing buildings that had been burnt in the Fire of London, and followed with a major, controversial, and financially very rewarding redevelopment of Essex House on the Strand. This also provided him with his first property deal with lawyers, in this case the Middle Temple, and he became well acquainted with Roger North, who acted as client on their behalf. During the rest of his career, he redeveloped at least another six large aristocratic houses and a number of green field sites, as well as pulling down areas of poor housing and replacing them with more desirable homes. He started with very little capital and was arguably overtrading for all his career.[19] As for many property developers in later centuries, this influenced the type of building he put up and he was always alert to the possibility of providing a market on his land, or even an Exchange, the seventeenth-century equivalent of a shopping mall. His major innovation came from the way he financed his development, which North described:

> He was the inventor of this new method of building by casting of ground rents into streets and small houses, and to augment their number with as little front as possible, and selling the ground to workmen by so much per foot front, and what he could not sell build himself. This has made ground rents high for the sake of mortgaging, and others following his steps have refined and improved upon it ... [20]

It is important to recognize that his innovation was financial, not architectural. Barbon was not an architectural innovator and he rarely, if ever, used architects, who were few and far between and generally were not involved in London's domestic houses, other than those of a substantial nature. Maximizing the value of ground rents for a site naturally led to terrace housing, but while a degree of uniformity was imposed by the building requirements introduced within the City after the Fire of London, Barbon's approach of letting the sites in a terrace to a large number of builders inevitably led to some variation in the individual houses. He also preferred to leave the interior decoration to the person who bought or lived in the house to decide, rather than spending money on what might need to be changed.

He also developed an extremely successful legal strategy by using the law courts as a means of delaying payments and reducing the eventual interest payable, constructing complicated layers of leases and subleases to frustrate creditors' access to his property under development. Much of the ensuing litigation is recorded in over two hundred law cases which, despite the exaggerations and misstatements inherent in claims or counterclaims, give a real insight into his approach. Notes from these cases by one of the present authors provided material for Elizabeth McKellar in her study of building in seventeenth-century London, but we have used them to concentrate on Barbon's own activity.[21] For example, detailed analysis of the parties to the disputes demonstrate that, despite his reputation for late payment, investors, including sophisticated goldsmiths and scriveners, who often acted as advisers to potential smaller-scale property investors, continued to advance him money for new deals and many builders and craftsmen worked for or with him on a number of occasions.

Involvement in Politics

The last part of the 1670s saw repeated attempts in Parliament to restrict building in London suburbs, and for the first time Barbon entered the political arena, albeit anonymously, as was then usual for merchants and businessmen. He published pamphlets demonstrating that the rate of new building was far lower than claimed by opponents of development and used the official records of births and deaths to refute exaggerated claims about London's population. These short pamphlets were written to influence parliamentarians, as was a further one attacking proposals to tax new houses. They were, however, serious attempts to find relevant factual information and use it to argue his case, building perhaps on his medical training in Leyden that stressed the need for evidence in making a diagnosis. In this he was in the company of those such as William Petty (also with medical training) who were developing what was then called 'political arithmetic', an attempt to use measurement and numerical arguments to answer questions about demography and national wealth.

Barbon realized that further arguments were needed to underpin his conviction that a growing and wealthy London was essential for England's well-being. These came in his first substantial economic writing, published in 1678, the twenty-two page long *A Discourse showing the great advantages that New Buildings and the Enlarging of Towns and Cities do bring to a Nation.* Unsurprisingly, this contains elements of special pleading, but he also introduces ideas that he would develop further in his later economic writing. Most controversial was his assertion that cities promoted 'emulation', the idea that everyone was trying to keep up with everyone else, copy what they did and buy what they bought; and, moreover, that these desires 'will not [...] be ever satisfied'.[22] He argued that this promoted riches and made the country wealthier. He developed this further in a later book, identifying the 'Wants of the Mind' in distinction from the wants of the body:

> The wants of the mind are infinite, Man naturally aspires, and as his mind is elevated, his senses grow more refined, and more capable of delight; his desires are inlarged, and his wants increase with his wishes, which is for everything that is rare, can gratify his senses, adorn his body and promote the ease, pleasure and pomp of life. [23]

Following his *Discourse showing the great advantages that New Buildings*, he would produce three substantial books over the next twenty years, writing about the most pressing economic issues of his time: money, trade, interest rates, support of luxury consumption and promoting London's contribution to the national economy, claiming, 'a Nation cannot increase without the Metropolis be inlarged'.[24] They were not academic tracts but were intended to engage with the politicians of the day and so were published, and republished, when the debates were at their height. He is sometimes viewed as writing solely in support of his own financial interests but, even if true, that was no different from any other of his contemporaries, and few present-day economists are completely independent of political views or other biases. He wrote from a different point of view to others. Some, such as John Locke, equated the interests of the landed gentry with those of the country; others were either financiers, the 'moneyed men' anathematized by many, or merchants, which in the parlance of the time meant international traders. Barbon's interests, as a property developer dependent on finance and on the well-being of London, were very different and no doubt influenced his very individual analysis. He made the point himself that merchants did not always understand trade: 'The Merchant, and other Traders who should understand the true Interest of Trade, do either not understand it, or else, lest it might hinder their private Gain, will not Discover it.'[25]

Barbon's support of 'emulation', the promotion of new fashion and competitive consumption as a way of providing jobs and increasing the country's wealth, raised political as well as moral issues. He practised what he preached and was described as often 'as fine and as richly dressed as a lord of the bedchamber on a birthday'.[26] He argued that more spending, at least by the well off, could be beneficial to the country, and 'Prodigality is a vice that is prejudicial to the Man, but not to Trade'.[27] Improvement was not merely possible but desirable, including the prospect of people improving their station in life or at least being better off than their parents and grandparents.[28] For Barbon, the operation of the market was of great importance — 'The Market is the best judge of value [...] Things are worth just so much as they can be sold for' — and he added a Latin tag to reinforce the point.[29] In his last work, he goes even further, saying, 'For things have no value in themselves; it is opinion and fashion brings them into use and gives them a value.'[30] Emphasis on the role of the market was controversial, but it reflected his approach to the development of London's housing. He would develop these ideas in his later publications which go much further than was necessary merely to promote his business interests.

Barbon saw increased trade as both a means to ensuring London's greatness and the route to increasing the power of the state internationally, stating baldly, 'The freer Trade is, the better the Nation will thrive.'[31] One of his contentions is that the writers of the past — he instances Livy and Machiavelli — were deficient in their descriptions of what was important to governments because they omitted to mention trade. He argued that trade did not only enrich government, 'the more every man earns, the more he consumes, and the King's revenue is increased', but also allowed the purchase from abroad of those commodities necessary to produce armaments: 'Trade is now become as necessary to preserve governments as it is useful to make them rich.'[32] His *Discourse of Trade* repeats a panegyric from his previous writing, envisaging England with a large empire managed by sea:

> not only to preserve its Antient Sovereignty over the Narrow Seas, but to extend its Dominion over all the Great Ocean: an Empire, not less Glorious, and of a much larger Extent, than either Alexander's or Caesar's.[33]

Much of his output was expressly designed to influence the votes of Members of Parliament, and he finally became one himself in 1690, purchasing enough houses in the rotten borough of Bramber to guarantee himself a seat. (Bramber is five miles north of Shoreham in West Sussex and later became the parliamentary seat of William Wilberforce.) Unsurprisingly, he was one of the MPs asked to investigate and report back to the House of Commons about the need for emergency repairs to the Chamber. Although he is often described as a Tory, he was viewed as a Whig when he first entered Parliament and his political leanings, like many of his contemporaries, varied with time and, no doubt, how he saw his interests best advanced. Being an MP was very valuable to him; some said it saved him over a thousand pounds a year since it allowed him to use parliamentary privilege to avoid any legal cases involving his debts.[34] Apart from protecting his finances, it also allowed him to remain in his country house, Osterley Park, the former home of Sir Thomas Gresham.

Barbon's intervention in the arguments on trade paved the way for his position on the contentious question exercising Parliament in 1695–96 of how to manage the recoinage that became necessary. This produced his *Discourse concerning coining the new money lighter.* In it he comprehensively demolished the idea, advocated by Locke among others, that only silver contributed to wealth, so that the purpose of trade was to increase the nation's stock of silver. For him money could take any form, it did not need to be silver, which for him had no intrinsic or permanent value, and he warned about adverse effects from the reduction in the money supply resulting from the effective revaluation proposed by Locke.[35] A variant of Locke's proposal was eventually implemented and, while stabilizing the currency, did indeed create considerable hardship.

Just as Barbon's promotion of the macroeconomic benefits of luxury consumption was a radical change from the past, so was his vision of the unit of account essentially being established by the authority of government, and changeable when necessary or to suit. He was the first writer to set this out clearly and systematically and reflected a more flexible view of society and economic activity, departing from ideas of inherent worth and the preservation of hierarchy to the vitality and disruption of the market.[36] His vision of man's infinite desire for new things naturally led to an emphasis on economic growth and required a monetary system fit for such a purpose.

Why Barbon is Important Today

Barbon's ability as 'the exquisite mob master' described by his client Roger North has continued to fascinate subsequent generations. Some view him as the archetypal rapacious property speculator and are only too eager to believe the stories about him, often created by his enemies, where his fault is to have operated for longer and more successfully than others, who played the same tricks when they could. His use of the leasehold system to finance development provided the basis for building in London for two centuries but, as this biography makes clear, he also made major contributions to economic and monetary thinking as well as to the development of insurance and banking. It is only by taking these together that one can draw a full picture of the man.

This is illustrated by the various sources, which often shed light on more than one area of his activity. The legal material contains many cases related to his fire insurance, shows in detail how it was financed and, for the first time, allows the evolution of what was effectively the share register of the insurance enterprise to be described. The pamphlets written about insurance contain new information about Barbon's other building activity as well as demonstrating how he used evidence to bolster his arguments. Some of the legal cases also shed new light on the saga of the land banks, with more information about the subscribers and the way that funds were collected.

While he rejected his father's theological views, having his own children baptized in his local parish church, every other aspect of his thinking confirmed his radicalism. He obtained his Oxford BA remarkably quickly, but then had no difficulty in moving on from classical traditions, preferring to use evidence rather than deferring to classical writers. His doctoral thesis moves on from Galen's theory of humours; his theory of man's infinite desires went against Aristotle, as did his approach to money. His support for consumption and the idea of constant improvement with movement between the classes was controversial, as was the way he often dealt with those opposing his developments. At the same time, he had an ability to take others' ideas and make them work in practice; he was not the first to propose a scheme of fire insurance or a land bank but, unlike others, he brought both his proposals to fruition.

Barbon was a public figure and well known in London; references to him appear in the diaries and letters of the time and, like many others, he was the subject of satirical verse. He knew and dealt with both Christopher Wren and Robert Hooke, including dining with them from time to time, and his eight years as an MP ensured that he knew all the leading politicians of his time. His forays into insurance and banking gave him good contacts with major financiers, while his extensive use of the law and his continued building work for the Inns of Court did likewise with the legal profession. As well as his building activity, he was known as one of the great projectors. Announcements of his death referred to him as 'famous', whether as a builder or projector.[37]

Historians of economics may differ about the extent to which he represented the end of the old approach rather than anticipating Adam Smith some hundred years earlier, and this was still being argued about in the correspondence columns of *The Times* 230 years later.[38] It has often been assumed that his economic writing was largely ignored, but Locke had a copy of Barbon's *A Discourse concerning coining the new money lighter* in his library and recent scholarship has shown that Barbon was a significant, but unacknowledged, influence on David Hume and possibly Adam Smith as well.[39] Some writers describe Barbon as a mercantilist, others as an anti-mercantilist, essentially because they use different definitions, and it is not clear whether it is a particularly useful classification. Barbon was neither a bullionist nor concerned about the balance of trade; he was generally in favour of free trade, while conceding that tariffs (but not prohibitions) might be useful on some occasions. He viewed the market as the best judge of value but did recognize a role for government in steering the economy, and was in favour of promoting employment.

Developing London required that he made the case for its growth, defending it against those who saw it as too big or too different from the rest of the country. A prosperous London would be built on openness to people, to trade and to vibrant markets. He supported tourism, immigration and the granting of nationality to immigrants. He argued passionately in favour of free trade and against those such as John Locke and the bullionists who saw the country's wealth measured only in the amount of silver bullion it possessed. He sought to remove puritanical brakes on economic appetites and the operation of markets by promoting consumer appetites and luxury as a means to fuller employment and to wealth creation: 'All men by a perpetual industry were struggling to mend their former condition; and thus the people grow rich which is the great advantage of a nation.'[40]

Barbon's argumentation was often vigorous and combative, and so was his conduct in building development. He confronted many vested interests; his builders engaged in battle with Gray's Inn; he was accused of pulling down houses over the heads of the lessees; and his use, or abuse, of the legal system was legendary, although at least some of the stories that grew up about him have been proved to be incorrect. The issues that Barbon was concerned with at the end of the seventeenth century seem eerily familiar to the present day. Is London too large, does it take too much of the country's wealth, should it allow so much redevelopment, why is it so different from the rest of the country? But he was not interested solely in issues confined to London; he argued for free trade, for greater openness to immigrants, for a more mobile society fuelled by economic growth and continual improvement in man's condition. It is well worth reflecting on how the seventeenth century dealt with the same problems that we face now. The study of Nicholas Barbon's life is a good way to do so.

CHAPTER II

EARLY LIFE AND FAMILY

Family Background

Although there is relatively little firm evidence, and much myth, about Nicholas Barbon's family and domestic relationships, it is possible to build up a convincing picture of his background which suggests some of the factors which may have influenced him. He certainly came from an educated family and his father was an affluent merchant.

The principal evidence for his parentage comes from his contemporary and associate, the lawyer and writer Roger North, who worked with Barbon on the reconstruction of the Temple after the fire in 1679 and got to know him well. North reported in his autobiography that Barbon's father was the prominent 'sectarian' Praise God Barbon and that he was actually christened 'Unless Jesus Christ had died for thee thou hast been damned'.[1]

Praise God Barbon was a London merchant and freeman of the Leathersellers' Company. He came from near Daventry in Northamptonshire where his father John, a former fellow of Magdalen College, had been vicar of Charwelton from 1593 until the Bishop of Peterborough removed him in 1605 for Puritan activities. Spelling was not standardized then and John is referred to as Barbone and Barebone as well as Barbon. It is not clear what John Barbon did after he was removed from office until his death in 1634, but he certainly continued to be active in Puritan circles and took part in one discussion on the future of the Church in Coventry at the house of Sir William Bowes called by his Presbyterian wife, Isabel, to consider whether to secede from the Church of England.

We do not know how many children he had but, as well as Praise God, there are a number of references to a Fear God Barbon, who also came from the Daventry area. It is suggested that the two names of Fear God and Praise God were chosen by John Barbon for his sons following the Elizabethan Prayer Book, which defines the first cause of marriage as 'the procreation of children to be brought up in the fear and [...] praise of God'.[2] In this case Fear God would probably have been the elder. This would be possible (just) since Barbon was married in August 1594 and Praise God was born in 1596. Fear God appears to have abandoned his father's Puritan ways since a series of bawdy poems collected by him has survived, with a note that he collected them 'for the mending of his hand in writing than worse to bestow his time'.[3] In 1626 he was a witness of the will of a Northamptonshire Puritan grandee, Sir Euseby Isham, and may have been involved in the management of his estate. He also appears to have been a servant of Sir Arthur Ingram, the financier and politician.

Northamptonshire had other Barbons. Euseby Barbon was a sufficiently important servant, perhaps a steward, of Sir Euseby Andrew to have been left £100 in Andrew's will. Andrew was the owner of Charwelton manor, a strong Calvinist and nephew of Euseby Isham.[4] Both Mary Barbon (Praise God's widowed mother) and Euseby Barbon were buried a few months apart at the small village church of Easton Neston, only fifteen miles from Charwelton; she may have gone to live with him after widowhood. Euseby's son, John Barbon had graduated from Exeter College, Oxford, in 1646 but was clearly a royalist, being expelled from the University in 1648 and not regaining a local parish until after the Restoration, when he produced treatises in support of the Book of Common Prayer and Episcopacy. His will written in 1685, two years before his death, 'hopes his generous kinsman Dr Nicholas Barbon will not suffer [his son] John Barbon, [a student at the Middle Temple] to want anything'.[5] This suggests that Euseby was related to Praise God's father, possibly a brother.

As we have seen, names could be spelt in many different ways, even in the same document. While Praise God Barbon usually signed himself 'Praise', he was regularly referred to as Praise God and seems to have accepted that. Equally, like his father, his surname was spelt as Barbon, Barebon and Barebone, and the last was not just used by his opponents but also in many official parliamentary documents, including Cromwell's summons to the Parliament that would be named after him. We shall refer to him as Praise God Barbon in this book.

Praise God did not go to university but, as was common for a younger son, was sent to London to be an apprentice; John Atwood, a Leatherseller, was chosen as the apprentice master. This may well have been attractive to his father, and indeed Praise God, since Atwood was a known supporter of Puritanism which resulted in his emigration to New England around 1635 together with his brother, also John Atwood. One of them rapidly became a magistrate in New Plymouth. Long before then Praise God had completed his apprenticeship and became himself a freeman of the Leathersellers' Company in January 1624. This did not necessarily mean that he dealt in leather goods, since a freeman of one livery company was permitted to trade in the goods of any other City company and many did so. John Atwood himself may have been a general merchant since he was an associate of James Sherley, one of the financiers of the *Mayflower*, and helped to sort out the arguments between the settlers and the merchants who had supplied them.

Barbon was beginning to establish himself in the Leathersellers by the early 1630s, being elected Warden for the yeomanry (that is, those not yet liverymen) in 1630; he went on to become a liveryman, the entry to City politics, in 1634. More importantly for him, he had joined the semi-separatist congregation founded in 1616 by Henry Jacob, and later led by John Lathrop and finally Henry Jessey. In May 1640 this congregation divided, on geographical as well as religious lines, and Barbon became the leader of the western group as well as one of the leading lay pastors in London. His premises, at the sign of the Lock and Key in Fleet Street near Fetter Lane and just outside the City proper, were large enough for him to preach to 150 or more people. He was preaching to such a group at the end of 1641, attacking both bishops and the Book of Common Prayer, when a hostile crowd of apprentices gathered and began smashing the windows and trying to break down the doors. In the end the constables arrived and a number of the congregation, including Barbon, were taken to Bridewell prison, although freed without charge. He took the precaution of being elected Constable by the parish to give him some authority in dealing with future violence.

This was not the last time his sermons would be the cause of affrays, and there were a number of scurrilous pamphlets with titles such as *The Discovery of a Swarme of Separatists, or a Leathersellers' sermon.* He had joined forces with another lay preacher, John Greene, a feltmaker, and Figure 1 is an example of the way they were represented by their opponents. It also tells another story, since this was the fourth time in six months that the same woodcut had been used on material attacking various Puritan preachers. It was not made originally for Praise God Barbon and would be used on another pamphlet a couple of days later with his name removed and a different title.

Fig.1. Illustration to John Taylor, ... *the last tumult in Fleetstreet, raised by the disorderly preachment, pratings, and pratling of Mr. Barebones the Leather-seller, and Mr. Greene the Feltmaker, on Sunday last the 19. of December*, early nineteenth-century copy of a pamphlet of 1641 (British Library, E.180.(26.) © Trustees of the British Museum, 1896,1230.8

Barbon was becoming well known, and his name, normally using the spelling *Barebone*, or referred to as Rawbone, was used to ridicule him, while his membership of the Leathersellers' Company was used to suggest that he was uneducated. Despite this, he was respected within his Company and had a number of apprentices, sometimes from Puritan families, and was elected auditor to the Wardens in 1644 and Third Warden in 1648. Further evidence of his commercial success is the size of his shop/warehouse which was large enough to hold crowds listening to him preach, and his house in Fetter Lane on which he paid tax in 1666 on eight hearths and for which his rent was £40 per annum, a large amount for the time. His wealth is indicated by his providing in 1649, in addition to three other prominent figures, a £500 surety for the new Master of the Mint, Dr Aaron Guerdon.[6]

Although violently opposed to the Prayer Book, bishops and the monarchy, Barbon was more pluralistic than many of his kind.[7] He was opposed to believers' or adult baptism, produced a number of pamphlets supporting the baptism of children, and even defended baptisms received in the Church of England. He argued that God 'causeth much profit to come out of the variations of his servants, the truth is the more sought into and discovered, and cometh to shine more fully afterward'.[8] This approach allowed him to participate in the political life of his own parish, St Dunstan in the West, where he was involved in a number of conflicts with a group of rich Presbyterian merchants, sometimes involving litigation in the court of the King's Bench. He continued to sit on the parish vestry until 1661 and was appointed an auditor of the churchwardens' accounts on a number of occasions.[9]

Following the purge of Presbyterians from the City government, his increased profile in both parish and livery company resulted in his being elected to the City government as a Common Councilman for St Dunstan in the West in 1649, and he was re-elected the next year when he served on the Committee of Safety. He was thus a natural choice for the independent churches to recommend, and for Cromwell to nominate, as one of the seven London MPs for the 1653 Nominated Parliament which now bears his name. It was in use not long after the Parliament assembled.[10] It seems that the combination of a pious first name, a surname that had already been the source of mockery, and membership of the Leathersellers, which made easier the task of representing him as uneducated and of low social status, was too good to miss.

In 1630 Barbon married Sarah, a member of the same separatist congregation, but whose surname is unknown. Their first three children all died young: sons Thomas and Praise were buried at St Bride's, Fleet Street, in 1634 and in 1636 during an outbreak of the Plague, while his daughter Sarai was buried at All Saints, Wandsworth, in 1635 (not as sometimes suggested in the Huguenot cemetery there which was not created until some fifty years later). There is no record of their baptism in the parish records, presumably because they were baptized in his separatist congregation. Another son, Stephen, was born about 1648 and lived long enough to become apprenticed to his father in 1664 but died in September 1665. Nicholas Barbon was born in 1638 or 1640 (he gave his age differently on different occasions); his will does not refer to any close Barbon relations, nor is there other evidence of siblings who lived to adulthood.

Praise God did not attempt to continue as an MP after the Barebones Parliament of 1653 was dissolved and was less involved politically for a time. He was again elected as a Common Councilman in 1657 and re-elected till 1660, opposing the City sending its compliments to General Monk. After the restoration of the Rump Parliament in May 1659, he was nominated to the London Militia Committee and for a short time was Controller of the Commissioners for Compounding. He did all he could to prevent the Restoration of the monarchy, publishing unfavourable anecdotes about Charles Stuart and others, and presenting a petition to the Rump Parliament urging that they 'use all possible endeavours to prevent the Commonwealth's adversaries in this their most dangerous stratagem'. This resulted in his windows being broken more than once by apprentices, as recorded by Samuel Pepys,[11] and a variety of both physical and verbal attacks on him, including his portrait called *The Picture of the Good Old Cause drawn to the Life* (Fig. 2).

Fig. 2. Praise God Barbon, engraving from a royalist broadsheet, *The Picture of the Good Old Cause drawn to the Life in the Effigies of Master Prais-God Barebone*, 1660.

Although Praise God Barbon took advantage of the general pardon of 1660, he continued to visit his friends in prison and was himself arrested, charged with treason and sent to the Tower at the end of 1661. He was kept a close prisoner there and only released seven months later on the petition of his wife that he was 'so ill that he must perish unless released'.[12] He was then aged sixty-six, an old man for those days. His millennial convictions began to strengthen and in *Good Things to Come*, published in 1675, he looked forward to the coming of Christ and his rule for a thousand years. He died in 1679 and was buried in the Nonconformists' cemetery at Bunhill Row.

During the Interregnum there had, of course, been no restrictions on the son of a prominent Puritan attending university. Nicholas Barbon studied at Oxford University matriculating in 1656 at Magdalen Hall, a well-known centre for Puritans, and took his BA early in 1659. He was already conscious of his status and described himself as 'armiger' rather than 'plebeian', which his cousin John Barbon had done a few years earlier. An armiger, or esquire, was entitled to a coat of arms, and a dictionary of arms from the 1670s explicitly ascribes one to Nicholas, shown in Figure 3, although the College of Heralds has no record of it being granted to anyone in the Barbon family.[13] Official records show it is associated with other family names and there is no record of him having used it.[14] It is not clear what such an entitlement would have been based on; given his age of either sixteen or eighteen at matriculation, it would have been on the basis of his father's position, and Cromwell's letter of appointment to the Barebones Parliament had indeed addressed him as 'esquire'.[15]

Barbon's choice of status had real implications. Only 7.5 per cent of his contemporaries at Magdalen Hall styled themselves as armiger, 14 per cent opted for the status of 'gentleman' and 3 per cent as noble. He would have been allowed more elaborate dress than others, lived better in college and dined with his peers rather than with those classified as 'plebs'; naturally, he would also have had correspondingly higher costs.[16] He would demonstrate all these characteristics later in life. He was unusual in taking his degree since most of those in the top social categories never bothered to do so. Of the twenty-three such in Magdalen Hall during Barbon's time, only four other than Barbon took their BA, three of whom went into the church. He graduated in around two and a half years, quicker than all but two of his contemporaries.

We do not know the detailed contents of Barbon's degree course, although he clearly had a good knowledge of Latin and classical history; to judge from his later writing, he probably also studied rhetoric. He next surfaces at the University of Leyden where he matriculated in the medical school in July 1661. It is not clear whether he had already started medicine at Oxford, but there would have been good reasons for going abroad. It took up to fourteen years to become a Doctor of Medicine at Oxford and no work with patients was required, the necessary study concentrating on reading the works of Hippocrates and Galen and commentaries on them. Even the famous physician Thomas Sydenham, himself a graduate of Magdalen Hall, is quoted as saying, 'Physick is not to be learned by going to universities [...] one had as good send a man to Oxford to learn shoemaking as practising physick.'[17] Leyden taught clinical medicine rather than its abstract philosophy or the approach of the classics, and its medical school was headed by the famous Sylvius who had made hospital visits central to the medical curriculum, involving his students in his daily rounds. Leyden also had the considerable advantage of a much quicker route to the degree of Doctor of Medicine. There had been a small group of English and Scottish people living in Leyden for some time, chiefly Puritans, and there was a steady stream of English-speaking matriculands, including a few in the medical school. Four had joined in the three years before Barbon.

Fig. 3. Arms attributed to Nicholas Barbon. Drawn by Timothy Walker

Numbers would, however, soon increase. Leyden welcomed students of whatever belief, but the English universities soon became closed to those who did not conform with the Anglican faith or were closely associated with those who did not.

More Englishmen matriculated at Leyden in 1661 than in the three previous years put together; six of them were medical students. This would become a well-worn path for Dissenters and their sons, many of whom went on to become distinguished doctors.[18] Given his father's continuing activity, it is hardly surprising that Nicholas was one of these and, indeed, if he wanted a doctor's degree, that would have been the only way of achieving it.

Many people studied at Leyden without bothering to matriculate, which only became necessary if one wanted to attend particular university lectures or, of course, to take a degree. It is possible therefore that Nicholas had been studying there for some time. In any case he soon moved to the University of Utrecht and was awarded his doctorate there on 17 December 1661, together with another student, Thomas Man (or Mennius) who had also matriculated at Leyden a few weeks before Nicholas. They were two of the first Englishmen to obtain their medical doctorate at Utrecht.

While Leyden was well established with an international reputation, Utrecht had only become a university twenty-five years before and was trying hard to attract students. Charging less for a degree and not demanding long periods of residences may well have been two ways of competing. Both of these would have been attractive to Barbon. There is some suggestion that his thesis was not subject to the usual disputation, but the thesis, which still exists, is cast in the normal form of a number of assertions to be tested in argument.[19]

The thesis yields much information about Barbon and the title page is shown in Figure 4. It is in Latin, and the subject, *De Febre Ardente*, is malaria. This was very topical since the cause of fevers was much argued about, as was the means of treating them. There had been a severe outbreak of malaria in England in 1661 and Cromwell's death in September 1658 is attributed, at least in part, to malaria and refusing to take the 'popish powder' medicine made from the South American cinchona bark containing quinine that was introduced to Europe by the Jesuits.[20] Nicholas dedicated his thesis

DISPUTATIO MEDICA
INAUGURALIS,
DE
FEBRE ARDENTE.
QUAM
Favente Deo Opt. Max.
Ex Authoritate Magnifici D. Rectoris,
D. JOHANNIS LEUSDEN,
L. A. M. Sacræ Linguæ in Illustri Academiâ Ultra-
jectinâ Professoris Celeberrimi.
NEC NON
Amplissimi Senatus Academici consensu, & Nobilissimæ Facultatis
Medicæ Decreto:
Pro Gradu Doctoratûs summisque in Medicinâ honoribus & privi-
legiis ritè consequendis,
Publicè sine præside ventilandam proponit
NICOLAUS BARBONE, Anglô-Brit.
Ad diem 5. Decemb. horâ locoque solitis.

ULTRAJECTI,
Ex Officinâ EVERHARDI ab EEDE, Bibliopol.
Anno cIↃ IↃ c LXI.

Fig. 4. Title page of Barbon's doctoral thesis.
Staatsbibliothek zu Berlin — Preußischer Kulturbesitz, Abteilung Historische Drucke, Shelfmark:Ah 9561

to 'the most learned and illustrious man' Dr Aaron Guerdon, Cromwell's appointment to be Master of the Mint, for whom Nicholas's father, Praise God, had put up a £500 bond. Guerdon had obtained his doctorate at the University of Reims in 1634 and had been chosen as tutor for the future 1st Earl of Shaftesbury shortly afterwards. He was appointed physician to the military hospital at the Savoy in 1642 and continued there during the Civil War, remaining active as a physician all his life. Even when he was Master of the Mint, he was ordered by the Rump Parliament in 1653 to examine and report on 220 sick soldiers.[21] Barbon claims in his thesis to have seen the success of Guerdon's medical treatments at the Savoy hospital, and this may have been what led him to medicine.

This brief history gives some pointers to Nicholas Barbon's background. He was too young to experience the violence of the early 1640s and was probably away from London during the attacks on his father's house in 1660/61, but the threat will still have been there. Despite Praise God's strongly held views, he was, perhaps surprisingly, prepared to tolerate other beliefs, and his son inherited an openness to ideas and a resistance to attempts to impose uniformity. Nicholas was brought up in an environment in which he would have been encouraged not to be afraid of thinking differently from the majority of the population and to defend this publicly in pamphlets or even in litigation, or to support likeminded individuals when threatened whether by the State or others. He was also used to his father playing an active role in public life, making real attempts to sway crowds and influence events and he inherited these skills. Roger North picked this up in commenting on Nicholas that:

> He was bred in the practices, as well as the knowledge of, working the people, under his father in the late times, [...] but that, with his much dealing in building, and consequently dealing with multitudes, he was an exquisite mob master and knew the arts of leading, winding, or driving mankind in herds as well as any that I have ever observed.[22]

His stay in the Netherlands enabled him to build further on these points. The Dutch approach to medical education encouraged him to look for evidence and learn from it, an approach favoured by Francis Bacon, and one which would underpin the work of the Royal Society. He was exposed to some of the leading European medical thinkers who were grappling with the consequences of Harvey's discovery of the circulation of the blood, which undermined the traditional Galenic theories of the causes of fever. Guerdon, like many other Puritan physicians, was strongly influenced by the 'iatrochemistry' put forward by Jan Baptist van Helmont which saw the blood as a mixture of different particles in corpuscular agitation; Barbon's thesis demonstrates a familiarity with these ideas as well as those of Paracelsus.[23]

The assertions in his thesis demonstrate his capacity to take up the latest scientific ideas and to reject the old ones in no uncertain terms. He even added two at the end which were unrelated to the rest of his arguments and attacked the pseudoscience of physiognomy, the supposed art of judging character from facial characteristics, which was promoted by the English doctor Sir Thomas Browne. Barbon wrote, 'Physiognomy has no relationship with the stars' and

> Although the lines on a face result from the movement of muscles, they are often caused by a person's feelings. They should not, therefore be despised but rather seen as caused by something altogether less significant.

We do not know how Barbon spent his time in the Netherlands, or indeed how long he spent there. While it is tempting to speculate on whether he took an interest in the Dutch approach to the development of cities, or of their building techniques and organization, there is no specific evidence of it.

CHAPTER III

FIRST STEPS IN BUILDING

Barbon did not start his building in London until the last years of the 1660s, but attitudes to new building in and around London had been forming for at least a century before. Such building was controversial for a number of reasons, many of which are still current in the twenty-first century. Nimbyism is not a new phenomenon. There are always those whose interests are threatened by new houses being built near them or on open space which has been used for other arguably desirable purposes. Redevelopment or reuse of existing buildings may import 'undesirables' to the area or cause it to be used more intensively. People are worried about the 'tone' of their neighbourhood being lowered and the value of their property being reduced accordingly, while others worry about losing business to new potentially more attractive locations. All these arguments were deployed in the seventeenth century in the same way as they are now.[1]

London in the Seventeenth Century

The Dissolution of the Monasteries under Henry VIII had stimulated a period of rapid growth in London by allowing more people into the City and providing the space on which to build for them. However, this additional space was used up by about 1570, and thereafter an increasing proportion of the population lived outside the walls. While the immediate extramural wards were under the City's jurisdiction, the ones further away were outside the control of the City government or the monopolies operated by the guilds. The City feared that these unregulated areas would give rise to plague, famine, plots and disorder; in addition, business moving outside its jurisdiction would face lower taxes and fewer controls, thereby jeopardizing the City's economy. Accordingly, the Lord Mayor and Aldermen wrote to the Privy Council in 1580 alerting them to the

> vast increase of new buildings and number of inhabitants within the City and suburbs of London, chiefly occasioned by the great move of people from all parts of the Kingdom to settle here; which was imagined would prove of dangerous consequence, not only to this great metropolis, but likewise to the Nation in general if not timely remedied.[2]

A proclamation from Queen Elizabeth followed, prohibiting any new building within three miles of the gates of the City with a series of penalties and fines for breaking this injunction, which expressed a fear that London building was causing houses elsewhere in the country to be empty 'to the decay of divers ancient good boroughs and towns'.

This last point was an important one. The population of London had doubled in the sixteenth century and grew during the seventeenth century from about 200,000 to almost 600,000, only 70,000 of whom lived inside the walls and so in the City itself. London's population grew faster than that of the country as a whole, forming 5 per cent of England's population in 1600 but 11 per cent in 1700. The next two biggest cities in 1700 were Bristol and Norwich with 29,000 and 20,000 respectively; Southwark, no more than a suburb of London, was larger than either of them.[3] Even at the end of the sixteenth century, London had seemed to many to be disproportionately large and to take far too much of the nation's resources, sucking the goodness out of other parts of the country and impoverishing them accordingly. The problem only became greater through the seventeenth century.

Against this background, it is not surprising that Queen Elizabeth's was only the first of many proclamations or Acts of Parliament over the next ninety years imposing a variety of geographical constraints of three, five or even seven miles from the gates of London. James I described London in 1607, perhaps reflecting on his rickety son, Charles, as like 'the head of a rickety child, in which an extensive flux of humour drained and impoverished the extremities, and at the same time generated distemper in the overloaded part'.[4]

Laws only work if they are enforced properly, and the suspicion grew that the Crown was more interested in using the regulations as a means of raising money by imposing fines with strict regulations for new buildings as to the thickness of walls, size of bricks and other important details. Even so, there were dissenting voices, and Sir Robert Cotton, when Commissioner for London's buildings in 1623, supposedly with the task of controlling new building, received a paper describing them as 'honourable and useful' and that London's consumer demand would benefit the whole country.[5]

The arguments continued, and in June 1642 a petition from the Mayor, Aldermen and Common Council of the City claimed:

> many great troubles and inconveniences have and do daily happen within the City of London through the multiplicity of new buildings on new foundations, dividing of houses, and converting of barns [...] By means whereof people of all conditions (as well as papists as others) from all parts of the Kingdom resort unto the City of London and parts adjacent and are there harboured, divers vagrants and ill-disposed people entertained, great dearth of victuals, fuel, and other necessaries increased, and the said City and suburbs and places adjacent grown so populous and especially of persons of desperate fortunes and small ability and the people resident can hardly be governed fed or provided for with water, fuel, and other necessaries.

In practice, building naturally slowed down during the Civil War. Thomas Hobbes had given 'immoderate greatness of a town' as one of the infirmities of a commonwealth, although this was principally because of its potential to furnish and equip an army.[6] Worries were still expressed about the size of London, particularly in relation to the rest of England. Some preferred the analogy of London as the spleen rather than the head, so the cleric Peter Heylin, who was a supporter of Archbishop Laud and so not well disposed to London, wrote,

> Great cities in the body of the state are like the spleen or melt in the body natural; the monstrous growth of which impoverisheth all its members, by drawing to it all the animal and vital spirits which should give nourishment to them.[7]

The problems were not solved, and returned under Cromwell. As late as 1656 he issued a proclamation prohibiting all further building in St James's Fields and the most draconian of all Acts of Parliament was passed in 1657. This forbade all new building on new foundations within a radius of ten miles and provided fines to be levied on all such built since 1620 and without four acres of land attached. There were also substantial exceptions, such as the Earl of Bedford's development at Covent Garden, which was excused £7,000 of fines, and in later years the amount of money actually raised by this Act was disputed.

Meanwhile, the future Charles II was receiving advice from Hobbes's patron, William Cavendish, Duke of Newcastle, that London was a 'great leviathan, that monster [...] that head so much too big for the body of [...] England', a statement harking back to James I.[8] This may have been behind the King issuing a proclamation in June 1661 forbidding any building on new foundations within two miles of any gate in London and Westminster. This was tempered by comments on the design of new building, which asserted that building of brick or stone was more beautiful than timber and forbidding jetties and overhanging windows. He also allowed himself to be persuaded by Henry Jermyn, Earl of St Albans, to make an exemption to allow the building in St James's Fields of 'houses fit for the dwellings of noblemen and other persons of quality'. This reinforced the effects of the Civil War and the deposition of Charles I which had begun to widen the geographical separation between those formerly associated with the Court and City merchants. St James's became the most fashionable suburb, a move westward from the previous favourite of Drury Lane, and led to the eventual creation of the West End. Taken together, it is not clear that these various royal decisions had any more effect than any of the previous proclamations or Acts of Parliament, but they were in any case overtaken in a few years by the Great Fire.

Arguments about London's population were put on a new footing in 1662 by the appearance of the first detailed demographic study when the Royal Society published John Graunt's review of London's population.[9] This was based on a detailed analysis of the Bills of Mortality, which recorded the burials in the City of London, and parishes around, together with the returns from parishes of details of baptisms. This kind of analysis was similar to the 'political arithmetic' being developed by Sir William Petty designed to provide a practical numerical basis for measuring such attributes of a country as we take for granted such as size, population of the country or cities, and the economy, and to answer questions of whether they were declining or growing. Graunt was able to show the error of the then current estimates of London's population, sometimes running as high as six or seven million. His estimate was 384,000. He was, however, still concerned about the size of London and, although qualifying his statement with a 'perhaps', echoed previous worries:

> London, the Metropolis of England, is perhaps a head too big for the body, and possibly too strong; that this head grows three times as fast as the body unto which it belongs, that is, it doubles its people in a third part of the time.

These concerns continued to be shared and there were repeated petitions for strict enforcement of the proclamations — with little effect.

Nicholas Barbon Returns to London

It is not known what Nicholas Barbon did immediately after qualifying as a doctor in the Netherlands in 1661. He may have thought it imprudent to return immediately after the Restoration, not least because of worries about further attacks on his father's house, although the Lock and Key in Fleet Street appears by then to have been more of a shop or warehouse, and Praise God lived in a large house with eight hearths higher up Fetter Lane in the nearby parish of St Andrew Holborn. It would surely also have been unwise to return during his father's imprisonment for treason for seven months in the Tower from November 1661. In the event, his younger brother, Stephen, became apprenticed to the family firm in October 1664 and this may have prompted Nicholas's return.

Late in 1664 the Royal College of Physicians offered the possibility of becoming an honorary fellow to those with doctorates in medicine. Although this did not confer the full range of rights and privileges, it did allow the new fellows to practise in London, a privilege otherwise confined to members of the College. The College probably took this step to make it easier for them to enforce limiting the practice of medicine in London to their members, although it had the added attraction of raising £20 and a piece of plate from all the honorary fellows. Eighty-four doctors became honorary fellows, the great majority of whom had Continental doctorates, mostly from Padua or Leyden. Nicholas Barbon and his colleague, Thomas Man, both took advantage of this and were admitted in December 1664; they were the only Utrecht graduates in the list. Aaron Guerdon and his brother Dennis became honorary fellows at the same time, taking the opportunity to legitimize their practice in London — Aaron had been prosecuted in the 1640s for practising without qualifications from the College.

There is little evidence that Barbon practised as a doctor, although he used the title for the rest of his life and may have attended family members.[10] Although his father's membership of the Leathersellers' Company entitled his sons to automatic membership of the Company, Nicholas had no interest in learning the business as his younger brother intended, and he was content to forego the status and benefits of being a freeman of the City of London. Lack of this status made him a 'foreigner', a charge that was made against him from time to time to suggest that he did not have the interests of the City of London at heart.

There was, however, one occasion on which he did undertake medical work, and that was during the Plague when his offer to work 'gratis' was accepted on 27 July 1665 and he was appointed by the Court of Aldermen to work in the parishes of St Dunstan in the West, St Bride, St Martin, Ludgate and St Anne Blackfriars, all near his father's Fleet Street property at the Lock and Key.[11] There would have been plenty of work for him in these parishes. A total of 1,417 died of the Plague that year in St Bride's and 665 in St Dunstan's. His brother Stephen died in September 1665, albeit not of the Plague. Volunteering to help may appear to be no more than any doctor would do but most had already left the City, including all the officials of the College of Physicians.[12] Unlike these more established doctors Barbon clearly threw himself into the crisis and tried to help. Two weeks after joining, he made some proposals for 'putting a stop to the further spreading of the infection' which were referred to a committee for a view on their reason and practicability. It is not clear exactly what work he did, but it will have familiarized him with the area after his absence abroad and this would prove useful later.

Deaths from the Plague peaked in August/September 1665, but it was only in February 1666 that it was considered safe enough for the King and his entourage to return. About 70,000 Londoners were officially identified as dying from the Plague, but most estimates of the total start at 100,000. What little infection may have lingered on, after the winter had reduced the number of rats which carried the fleas that transmitted the disease, was finished off by the Great Fire in September that year.

Both the Plague and the Fire changed the arguments about building and population, and the two events changed Barbon's life. The rest of this chapter shows how he first became involved in housing development. Although growing in number, the individual sites remained relatively small for some years and this chapter covers his early housing activities in the City up to 1672; these were confined to rebuilding on sites which had been destroyed in the Fire. As a result, he did not yet have to confront the worries already expressed about London's size, building in the suburbs, and nimbyism, nor about a new concern which saw the growth of London and expensive houses as another example of inappropriate conspicuous consumption.

The Great Fire and its Aftermath

The Great Fire resulted in the destruction of some 13,200 houses as well as many churches and other buildings.[13] As far as we know, Nicholas Barbon owned no property before the Fire, but one of those burnt belonged to his father: the Lock and Key on Fleet Street in the parish of St Dunstan in the West was almost the last building destroyed at the westernmost end of the Fire's reach. It was no more than three doors away from the church of St Dunstan in the West which the Dean of Westminster had saved by getting forty boys from Westminster School to extinguish the flames with numerous buckets of water. It is possible that Praise God's stock and furniture was then, like that of other local homeowners and tradesmen, stored in the church.

An extract from Hollar's map of the City after the Fire, shows the extent of the devastation (Fig. 5). The area between Fetter Lane and Shoe Lane in the parishes of St Bride's and St Dunstan's was completely destroyed, but Praise God's other house, higher up Fetter Lane in the parish of St Andrew Holborn survived.

Immediately after the Fire, several proposals for rebuilding the City with elegant town plans were produced by John Evelyn, Christopher Wren, Robert Hooke and others. A proclamation was issued

Fig. 5. Detail of *A map or groundplott of the City of London, with the suburbes thereof ... since the last sad accident of fire, the blanke space signifijing the burnt part*, detail of etching by Wenceslaus Hollar, 1666.

within a week setting out the principles that would be applied to the rebuilding, including the promise of a seven-year exemption on the hearth tax, worth some £150,000 in total.

A direction to the City authorities to undertake a complete survey of ownership of sites proved impossible to deliver, not least because of the myriad of leases and subleases with complicated covenants.[14] The complexities of sorting out land ownership with consequent inevitable delays to the rebuilding meant implementing overarching plans was impracticable. London remained its unplanned self and individuals got on with their own rebuilding — or failed to do so.

The enormity of the task facing the City can be illustrated by the fact that it was three months before the rubbish was cleared (some claimed it amounted to raising the ground level of London by four feet); the streets were staked out in December.[15] What with a severe winter and the logistical problems associated with producing the necessary bricks and other building materials, as well assembling the workforce, there was little rebuilding before the spring of 1667. By then Parliament had passed three Acts setting the framework for future activity, all of which proved very effective.

All the restored houses, and very many of those built in the extending suburbs, were of brick and without overhanging windows. Houses were to be of four different types, depending on the importance of the street and this too was generally observed. However, the brick houses and their improved construction took up more space than the wooden houses they replaced and, coupled with the widening of several streets, the 13,200 destroyed houses were replaced by only 9,000, encouraging building in the suburbs.[16]

One of the Acts also provided for a Fire Court to help unravel the conflicts between landlords and tenants, with their varying responsibilities — and capacity — for rebuilding, by enabling the overriding of all covenants and penalties in the leases. It even included a clause empowering the Lord Mayor and Aldermen to seize property that had not been rebuilt after three years, sell to someone who would build, and return the proceeds to the original owners. The Court was guided by what would make rebuilding happen quickest while awarding compensation to those who thereby lost rights.

This massive effort could not be accomplished by the existing workforce of freemen of the City and the Act enabled the breaking of the monopoly held by the guilds. The relevant Section provided that 'bricklayers, masons, plasterers, joiners, and other artificers, workmen and labourers to be employed in the said building' were allowed to work in the City with the same rights as freemen and, what is more, if they continued to do so for seven years, they acquired that right for life. This naturally stimulated craftsmen of all kinds to flock to London, again increasing demand for housing, although some of the more successful lived in the villages outside London and invested in houses there as well as in the suburbs.[17]

The Act provided that, before any rebuilding, the site had to be surveyed by one of the City surveyors to check the foundations and so confirm and mark the boundaries. Records still survive of the requests for such surveys as well as the detailed measurements from two of the surveyors, Peter Mills and John Oliver.[18] (Robert Hooke was the third surveyor, but his notebooks do not survive.[19]) The first request after the Act was in May 1667, eight months after the Fire, and, until December that year, there had been no more than 650 requests for such surveys.[20] A contemporary estimate is that some 800 houses had been rebuilt by the spring of 1668.[21]

Praise God was already seventy years old at the time of the Fire and spending more of his time on the millennialism of the Fifth Monarchist movement. The fact that he had taken on his younger son as an apprentice only two years before the Fire suggests that he was still in business, but he may not have had the energy for sorting out any new lease arrangements and then managing the rebuilding of his property as well as dealing with whatever stock and business that he had lost as a result of the Fire. It was a substantial house with seven hearths, typical of one occupied by a wealthy merchant, but the lease only had fourteen years left and there was a substantial rent to pay, £40 per annum. Reductions would be needed to make any rebuilding worthwhile.

This was exactly the situation that the Fire Court was set up to deal with and Praise God applied to it in March 1668. As a return for doing the rebuilding himself, he proposed a reduction of annual rent from £40 to £15 and asked for forty years to be added to his term of lease. It is perhaps significant that, probably at his son's instance, Barbon was represented by a lawyer at the hearing while the owner was not. In any case the Court found the proposals reasonable and ordered that the house be rebuilt at all convenient speed. Praise God applied a few days later for the survey but the results were recorded in Nicholas's name, the property being later assigned to him by his father. Within six months the rebuilding was complete, and the property leased at £60 p.a. with a down payment ('fine') of £105, a very profitable transaction.[22] This was the first of Barbon's involvements with the surveyors and the City records show that he would in due course request surveys in connection with twenty-six properties, last of these at the start of 1675.[23] Only one person made more requests: Richard Frith, the speculator who went on to develop much of Soho, made thirty-four requests to the City surveyors.

Barbon used the fine to purchase a nearby property in Fleet Street, and subsequently he raised a mortgage of £300 early in 1669 on the Lock and Key from Thomas Fountaine, a Lincoln's Inn lawyer, on which he paid six per cent interest. Other purchases followed, including two in Newport Market, but he also began to build up a portfolio of properties close to his father's former site. In 1669 and 1670, the vast majority of Barbon's requests were in his own parish of St Dunstan in the West or in the adjacent parish of St Bride's, suggesting that he was using his local knowledge and contacts to identify sites and sellers. They tended to be small, with no more than one or two houses on them.

The scale of the rebuilding required in London, coupled with the uncertainties and risks faced by the large numbers of individuals concerned, provided an opportunity that was seized by Nicholas Barbon. It is sometimes suggested that he turned to property speculation because he failed as a doctor, probably a reference to Roger North's comment 'he was bred a doctor of physic, but that failing he fell into that of building, and the Fire of London gave him means of doing and knowing much of that kind', but it seems more likely that it was a positive decision.[24] Unlike his father, he does not appear in any tax or other returns up to and including the 1666 Hearth Tax, made before the Fire, but it is hardly surprising that someone with the entrepreneurial drive that he subsequently exhibited should have identified the possibilities following the Great Fire. Nor was he the only man with medical qualifications to do so: others included a Dr Thomas Cox who built six houses on the west side of Bloomsbury Square before the Great Fire, Dr James Fairclough who seems to have started the development in College Hill, which Barbon purchased with a partner in 1676, and the great supporter of land banks, Dr Hugh Chamberlain. Speculation sometimes offered far more exciting possibilities than a solid professional career.

By the middle of 1669, Nicholas Barbon was becoming established as a successful developer and was able to contemplate settling down. He married on 27 January 1670. His bride was Margaret Hayes, the daughter of John Hayes of Hadley, Middlesex, who had died in 1661 and was well off with property in Devon, Hertford, Bedford, Middlesex and the City of London.[25] Margaret brought a dowry of £1,000. According to the application for a marriage licence, which allowed the service not to be advertised to the general public, Barbon described himself as about twenty-eight and from the parish of St Dunstan in the West. She was about twenty-three and they were married in her parish church, St Martin's in the Fields. Nicholas and Margaret had no surviving children. The records of St Bride's, Fleet Street, show that their son, John, was baptized on 26 November 1670 but buried five days later, while another male child was buried there in March 1674. There are no records of other children being born to them and no child is mentioned in Nicholas's will (his wife having died two months earlier), although he left a legacy of 20s. 'in full of all claims to my estate' to his cousin John Barbon, presumably the person that John Barbon senior had asked him to look after (see p. 9). No doubt that legacy was chosen carefully to demonstrate that he had indeed thought of his cousin but did not wish to leave him more than a token. Figure 6 shows Barbon's family tree.

His eldest sister-in-law, Bridget, had married Edmund Lenthall, the nephew of both the Speaker of the Rump Parliament, William Lenthall, and Sir John Lenthall who was notorious for his extortions as Keeper of the King's Bench prison. Edmund benefited from this by being appointed Marshall of the King's Bench prison, but he died shortly after in 1676. While it is tempting to think that Barbon gained some advantage from this connection in his future appearances at the King's Bench on debt-related issues, it seems unlikely. The only member of the Hayes family for whom there is extensive evidence that Nicholas kept in touch was his youngest sister-in-law, Rebecca, who lived in at least one of the houses he built and whom he chose as one of the executors of his will. He showed no sign of Nonconformism as an adult and his children were baptized in his parish church, the Anglican St Bride's, rather than in his father's congregation. He remembered the fact that his own baptism was not entered in any parish register when arguing that the number of births in London was underestimated because Dissenters were not included in parish records of baptisms.[26]

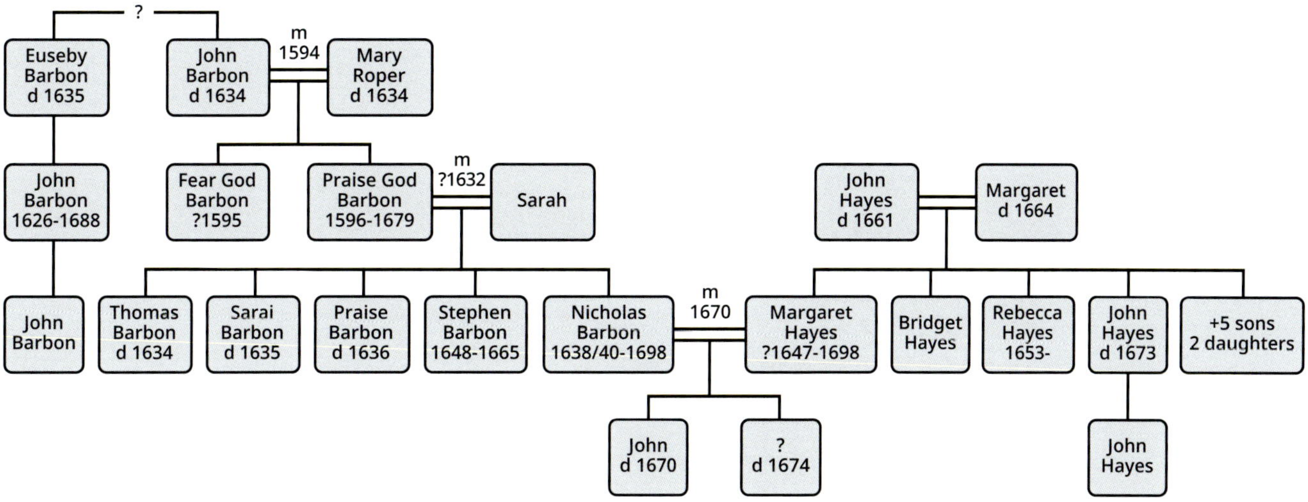

Fig. 6. Nicholas Barbon's family tree
Compiled by Timothy Walker

Crane Court and its Immediate Neighbourhood

In 1670 Barbon acquired a number of properties just north of his father's old warehouse, at the Lock and Key, around what was then called Two Crane Court (nowadays merely Crane Court) and the nearby Fleur de Lys Court and Red Lion Court. It was there that he built what was to be his own house, later No. 7 Crane Court, together with at least thirteen other buildings. Although much of Crane Court was in the parish of St Dunstan's, Barbon's house was in St Bride's parish, accounting for where his children were baptized and buried (Fig. 7).

Fig. 7. Crane Court and immediate environs, detail from Ogilby and Morgan's *Large and Accurate Map of London*, 1676

By permission of the British Library, Maps Crace Port. 2.61

At the time of the Fire, the sites at the top of Crane Court were owned by the Goldsmiths' Company and Barbon acquired a lease from them in 1669, purchasing the freehold in 1674. We know that he started work quickly because when the Company surveyed the property on 16 June the next year, they found Barbon's own house (later No. 7) was already built, as were two houses on the east (later Nos 5 and 6), while a house on the west (later No. 8) was under construction. Barbon's house was valued at a rent of £100 per annum and the other two completed ones at a rent of £60. His was a house designed to impress, and it did, with a lavish plastered ceiling, marble fireplaces, and the court before it paved with 'black marble and white purbeck stone, well rubbed, and of such a square and dimension as might be most durable as well as ornamental for the design proposed'.[27] Barbon had taken particular care to ensure that the court was attractive, ordering a pair of piers placed at the entrance from Fleet Street with necks and balls topped by a stone coping and a marble stone with golden letters. He also persuaded the occupiers of the eleven other houses looking onto the court to divide the costs equally between them, even though his was the largest house.[28] His friend Roger North described it as 'a capital messuage, where he lived as lord of the manor' while Strype called the court,

> a very handsome open Place with a Freestone pavement, and graced with good Buildings, well inhabited by Persons of Repute; the front House being larger than the rest, and ascended up large Stone steps.[29]

The first occupant of one of the Barbon houses was Samuel Vincent, who was his partner in a number of developments including the first fire insurance company, covered in Chapter VI. Barbon's houses in Crane Court had a distinguished future before them. He sold his own house in 1688 to Dr Edward Browne, a physician and Fellow of the Royal Society, who lived there until he died in 1708.[30] Isaac Newton identified it as a possible home for the Royal Society and, following approval of the building by Christopher Wren, the Society purchased it for £1,450, together with the neighbouring No. 8. The move was somewhat controversial with members of the Society at the time and extensive repairs were needed, costing £310, with a further £400 spent on a repository designed by Christopher Wren.[31] It remained the home of the Royal Society until 1782 when it was sold to the Scottish Corporation and remained their headquarters until destroyed by fire in 1877. Figure 8 shows a print of the top end of Crane Court from 1830 and Figure 9 is a watercolour from 1850. What is now No. 8 is on the left in these illustrations, while Nos 5 and 6, on the right, which also back on to Red Lion Court, have survived to this day although they too were damaged by fire as recently as 1971 and what remains is largely a reconstruction.

Fig. 8. Crane Court, 1830, etching by Charles John Smith

Image © London Metropolitan Archives (City of London), no. 1932

Some have suggested that these Barbon houses were designed by Christopher Wren but there is no evidence for that, although we have seen that he may have overseen the renovation of No. 7 in 1710 when the Royal Society acquired it. While Barbon certainly knew Wren in later years, and Hooke's diary records that they both had dinner with Wren in March 1675, it is unlikely that they knew each other well in 1670.[32] Neither is there evidence that Barbon ever used an architect, rather relying on skilled craftsmen. The houses are of a type that a skilled craftsman could easily have built; the stonework and fireplaces are certainly consistent with that assumption. Normally, speculative housing would not have elaborate decoration since the developer would not want to incur extra and possibly unnecessary expenditure, but Barbon was keen that his own house would be decorated. We know something of how the main room in Barbon's house looked from a nineteenth-century print of the Scottish Corporation headquarters (Fig. 10). Figures 11 and 12 below show some of the elaborate plaster work in Nos 5 and 6 Crane Court, presumably commissioned by the original occupiers.

In 1670 and 1671 Barbon continued to be active in the Crane Court area. Many of his early purchases were jointly with his wife, presumably using her dowry, with additional finance when needed from his previous mortgagee, Thomas Fountaine. He sold houses on quickly once they had been rebuilt.[33] Thus he bought an adjoining site in Fetter Lane, built two houses and sold them within nine months for £400, being sure to maintain his right to access a passage to Three Leg Alley, north of Crane Court, and to display the sign of the nearby Red Lion Inn, a property which he would sell later. Two more houses were sold for £200 and three for £510. Many of these were small, at least by modern standards, the last three being 15 feet deep and a combined 45 feet wide. Sites for shops with rooms over them in Three Leg Alley were bought, built on, and then sold in the same way. Some of his dealings were a little further away including in Shoe Lane and George Alley just off it, where he sold two houses for £100 to a charitable trust, and in Seacole Lane and Bear Alley, some of which land he sold to the City for £1,400 to widen the Fleet Ditch.[34] These are shown in Figure 13.

Fig. 9. Crane Court, 1850, watercolour by Thomas Colman Dibdin

Image © London Metropolitan Archives (City of London), no. 1927

The land ownership of a number of these sites had been very complicated and Barbon used the Fire Court to disentangle the various interests. Often the negotiation had been done before the appearance in the Court, but its endorsement of the deal resulted in the acquisition of an indisputable title to the property, of great importance in future transactions. He secured benefits such as increasing the length of the lease, reducing the ground rent, buying out minor interests and intermediate lessees, and ensuring that any rent payable for the period after the Fire was reduced to an absolute minimum. On one occasion,

Fig. 10. The main room of Barbon's house in Crane Court, later the meeting room of the Royal Society, wood engraving from the *Illustrated London News*, 1863

Image © London Metropolitan Archives (City of London), no. 318922

Figs 11 and 12 Interior views of Nos 5–6 Crane Court, photographs, 1969
Images © London Metropolitan Archives (City of London), nos 38973 and 39023

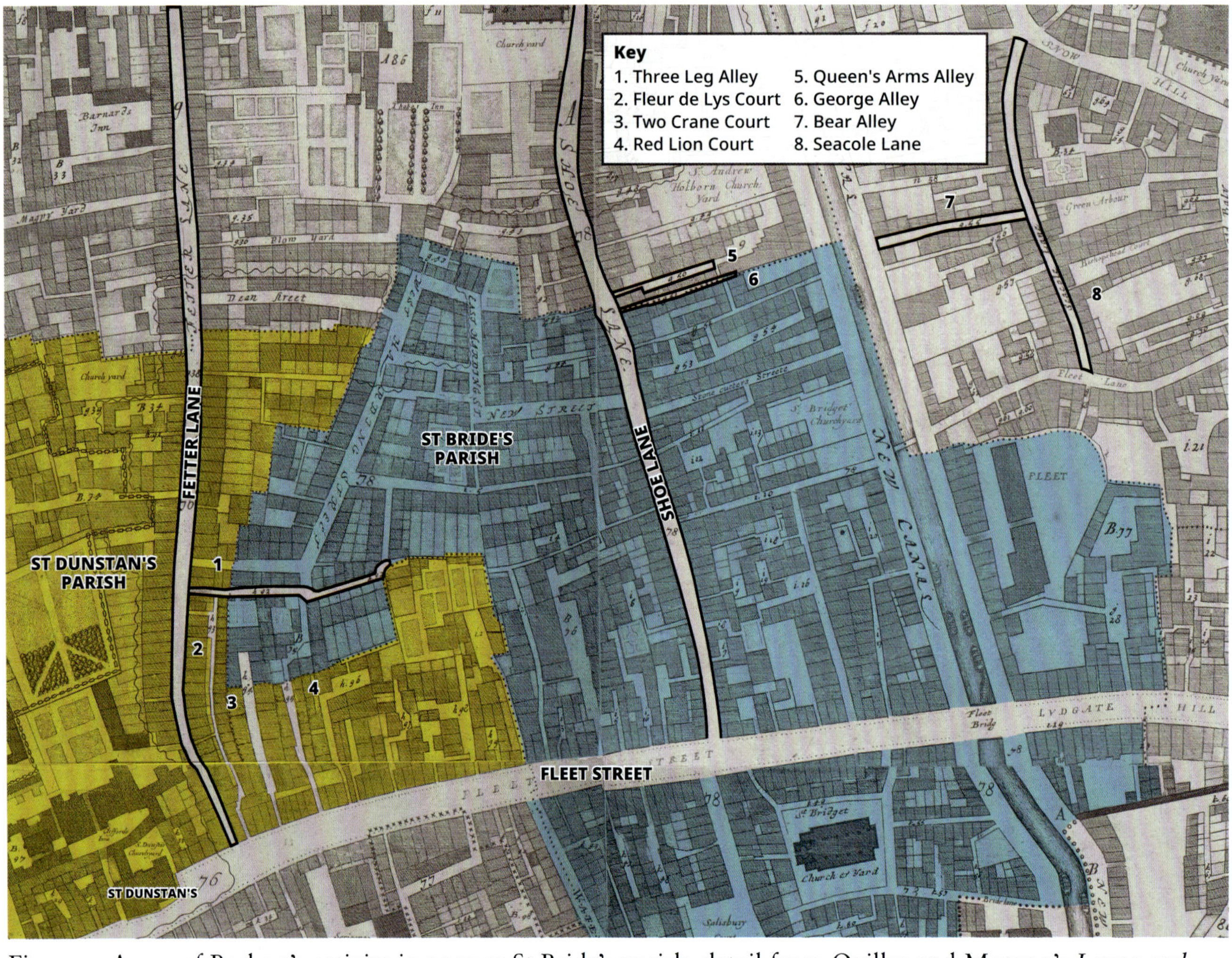

Fig. 13. Areas of Barbon's activity in or near St Bride's parish, detail from Ogilby and Morgan's *Large and Accurate Map of London*, 1676
By permission of the British Library, Maps Crace Port. 2.61

a couple of years later, he was able to use the provisions of the Rebuilding Act to purchase land which had not been rebuilt since the Fire. The City was empowered to issue a proclamation requiring such land to be built on, and if nothing happened, to arrange a valuation and sell to a willing buyer.

One interesting project of Barbon's was to build on a site near the Monument. The City Authorities asked Robert Hooke on 3 August 1670 to check that Barbon's proposals would not spoil the view of the Monument. Four months later Hooke confirmed that they did not, although it is not clear whether the proposal was implemented.[35] A later reference in Hooke's diary to a meeting with the Lord Mayor about 'Barbon's pillars' sheds no further light on the matter.[36]

Barbon's Developments Up to the Early 1670s

Up to 1672, Barbon's building had been very largely confined to Two Crane Court and its surroundings — he told one craftsman that he was building fourteen houses in the area — although there were a number of probably opportunistic purchases in other parts of the City. The houses in Two Crane Court, and particularly his, were substantial and he had gone to some lengths to make them and their surroundings attractive. This was not so for much of his other development. The properties had been small before the Fire and were so afterwards; he did not seek to redevelop them into larger, more expensive property. Some of them were in relatively unattractive streets — Strype describes Three Leg Alley as 'ordinary' and Fleur de Lys Court as 'of very small repute, being but meanly inhabited [...] It is of some note for the Mousetrap House, being the receptacle for lewd persons'.[37] However, Strype was writing some fifty years after Barbon built there and it may reflect a deterioration since Barbon's time when Dryden supposedly lived in a house in Fetter Lane backing onto Fleur de Lys Court from 1673–82.[38]

Many of the houses and shops that Barbon built at this time were sold for fifty to a hundred pounds, and few, if any, for over £200, corresponding to a rent of about £10 a year. While he may have kept some residual interest in these properties, the records of property transactions suggest that he did not keep them for long. Certainly, when he later bought the freehold of the Red Lion Inn from the Goldsmiths' Company as part of a package of property around Two Crane Court, he sold his entire interest in the Inn for £1,450 within five weeks. This rapid turnover will have made it easier to finance his activity and it is very noticeable that, apart from his appearances in the Fire Court, there are virtually no records of his being involved in litigation at this time, let alone arguments about not paying his debts. The only cases involve the mason who paved Two Crane Court and who had obtained a judgment in the Court of Common Pleas against Barbon who had retaliated with complaints in Chancery.[39] The sums involved were under £50 and appear to have been complicated by the death of the mason's partner and arguments about how the costs should be divided among the inhabitants of Two Crane Court. It is, however, apparent from later litigation that some of the mortgages and other financial arrangements that Barbon put in place in the early 1670s gave rise to problems later.

So far, Barbon's activity had been entirely within the City, although not necessarily within the old walls, and entirely concerned with rebuilding on sites which had been burnt down in the Fire. Clearly, this opportunity would not be continued indefinitely and, by the end of 1671, 95 per cent of the City's foundations had been staked out and confirmed.[40]

Substantial future building activity could only realistically be expected outside the City and in the suburbs. This was exactly where the demand was growing. The return of the Court to Westminster with the consequent demand for housing there from courtiers and office seekers saw the initial development of what was to become the West End. There was also pressure from those who had lost their homes and shops in the City itself and many moved to the area between the Cities of London and Westminster such as that between Drury Lane and St Martin's Lane. Merchants set up shop there and found it an attractive place to do business, free from the constraints of the City as well as avoiding living and working where there were still empty houses, or even streets, after the Fire with the attendant worries about crime and undesirables. The craftsmen needed for the large building programme also sought accommodation in the suburbs.

The main focus for domestic building in London moved from rebuilding in those parts that had been burnt or destroyed to building on green field or large redevelopment sites, largely outside the City walls. This naturally caused controversy and was by no means popular. It created problems for the Court who naturally wanted the housing near St James's to be confined to that appropriate for the aristocracy and others associated with the Court. Growth outside the City worried the City authorities who saw their economy threatened by retailing and other business moving away from their control and so becoming open to those who were not freemen of the City, the only people allowed to set up shop within its walls. It also reduced the pool of people eligible to take on the numerous roles in the governance of the City, which were expensive in both time and money.

The City's draft of the Rebuilding Act had included clauses not just prohibiting any building on new foundations within five miles of London at any time in the future, but also prohibiting all building on new foundations anywhere in England for seven years, 'unless the City be sooner fully rebuilt'. These had been struck out quickly. Both the Court and the City were also concerned about the possibility of undesirables of all kinds residing between Westminster and the City and bringing crime and disease. Christopher Wren finally petitioned for some control and this resulted in the King issuing a proclamation in April 1671 forbidding such building without his permission. The terms of the proclamation are given below as they capture the concerns well.

> Whereas in the fields commonly called the Windmill Fields, Dogfields, and those adjoining to So-Hoe and several other places about the suburbs of London and Westminster, divers small and mean habitations and cottages have been lately erected on new foundations and more are daily preparing, not only without any allowance from the King, but some against his express command signified by the Surveyor-General, which are likely to prove common nuisances by being used for the most noisome trades, and becoming a receptacle of a multitude of poor, to the damage of those parishes already too much encumbered, and by rendering the government thereof more unmanageable, but especially by choking up the air of the King's palaces and parks and endangering the infection if not the total loss of those waters which by many expenseful conduits are conveyed thence to the palace at Whitehall, whereof some decay is already perceived by the sergeant plumber, and more is feared: The King charges all persons to forbear erecting any more new buildings in the suburbs of London or Westminster, or to finish any already begun without a licence under the great seal, and if any disobey, all such buildings shall be abated and thrown down, and the offenders proceeded against with the utmost rigour of the law.[41]

The outcome illustrates well the difficulties faced in enforcement. In a few days, Wren became worried about houses being left unfinished with damage to both owners and craftsmen; some developers were approved, and within a year most of those who had been building were allowed to continue.[42] Although there were many subsequent attempts to introduce legislation or other controls to prevent new development in London or the suburbs, this proved to be the last time any was actually issued. The City continually returned to its attempt to prevent building in the suburbs, although the clauses proposed for the Rebuilding Act had been thrown out. Despite a few successes, the proclamation of 1671 proved largely ineffective, although petitions calling for more aggressive enforcement continued.[43]

The Crown's shortage of revenue necessitated the search for new taxes and so the possibility of using new buildings around London as a source of taxation was revisited a number of times in the 1670s, but it always failed. Apart from the difficulty of enforcement, many felt that it would not have the desired effect. William Petty himself asserted 'Buildings do not increase, until the People have already increased'.[44] And, indeed, the arguments against such building were not all on one side. As much as the City notables and guilds wanted to maintain the old system which had worked all too well by keeping 'foreigners' out when the City was an island surrounded by fields, others saw advantage in avoiding costs and constraints by setting up business outside the City controls. Even if the Court did not want to have craftsmen's houses near their own, they needed the craftsmen and servants who had to live somewhere. While some from the country believed that London was sucking the goodness — and money — away, others realized that the country benefited. Sir Thomas Clifford, MP for Totnes, commented in a debate in 1670:

> The bigger your city is the better will your land in Carlisle let. Do we not find a want of vending our commodities since the plague? The greatness of the city invites strangers. Is not more beef sold in Smithfield for it?[45]

Towards the end of 1671, the King's need for money to finance the war with the Dutch resulted in him approaching the main financiers and goldsmiths asking for a substantial loan; they declined. Three months later the Crown announced that it would prohibit certain payments from the Exchequer in respect of particular loans which turned out to be worth about £1,200,000.[46] In due course, five of the leading goldsmith banks went bust and nine others were seriously undermined but managed to survive.

Over ten thousand wealthy families lost out as the goldsmiths were unable to repay their deposits, including in many cases those that did not bear interest but had only been deposited for safe-keeping.

Barbon was not affected directly by this — he did not have surplus cash to deposit — but the Great Stop, as it was known, had the effect of removing a large amount of capital from the market and dampening down economic activity. It would have been surprising if house building in London were not adversely affected both by the reduction in capital available and by the reduced enthusiasm for investing, not least because the Stop was extended into 1674.

Although the vast majority of rebuilding was completed by the end of 1672, putting the lie to the inscription on the Monument to the Fire asserting that London was rebuilt within three years, the author of a contemporary pamphlet saw, 'with much reluctancy of spirit whole streets of houses new built within this City, standing uninhabited and no person so much as asks the price of any'.[47] He contrasted the situation with that outside the City both in Southwark and the 'outparishes' where 'they [were] inhabited as soon as built, and flourish in trade; many houses yielding better rents than those by the Royal Exchange'.[48] A return to the Guildhall in February 1673 gave the numbers of uninhabited houses in the City as 3,423, with 961 still unbuilt, and the next year a petition to Parliament gave the total of empty and unbuilt houses as still some 3,000 or almost one-sixth of the total in the City and Liberties.[49]

Only 60,000 of the 80,000 of those who had fled the Fire had returned and the emphasis moved from rebuilding to peopling the City.[50] The City Corporation issued an order that every Alderman should return with his family to the City on pain of heavy penalties, and extended that to Deputies and Common Councilmen. The author of the 1672 pamphlet argued that the solution was to allow anyone to become a freeman of the City (thereby allowing them to trade fully inside the City) by paying £1 and taking a house for twenty-one years or more. It was some time before the continued empty houses forced City authorities to implement such a radical move, and eventually they went further by giving up the entire £20 cost of becoming a freeman.[51]

Another set of solutions came from the author of a widely circulated pamphlet called the *Grand Concern of England*.[52] He started with the wildly exaggerated claim that 30,000 houses had been built in London during the last thirty or forty years which 'had they not been erected, those who inhabit them would have been in the country living an industrious and laborious life, improving their stocks, and thereby improving Gentlemen's lands and the Trade of the Nation'. He naturally called for controls, if not a ban, on building in or near London and went on to propose

> that a bound be put to the extravagant habits and expenses of all sorts of persons; that servants and handicraft tradesmen's expensive ways be reduced, and no foreign manufactures (except from Ireland) be suffered to be worn in England; but that importation and exporting them for sale be made a felony.

These proposals, limits on housing around London, controls on luxury consumption and bans on imports are all ones that Barbon would argue against in all his future economic writing. Some commentators have argued that he did no more than support his own economic interests, a fault they seem oddly unaware of in other economists, but Barbon was one of a number whose thinking drew on their direct experience of markets and in many ways anticipated later eighteenth-century writers.

In 1672, the Duke of Buckingham sold York House, his mansion on the Strand, for redevelopment to a large number of potential speculators whose plots were often disconnected and scattered across the site. This complication, coupled with the effect of the Great Stop on the availability of capital and economic activity generally as well as the war with the Netherlands, meant that the site was not laid out in streets until well into 1674.[53] Barbon did not participate in this development, despite many later assertions that he did. He continued with the properties that he already bought, but all in the City and none in the suburbs. He remained active in the Fire Court with his last request for staking on 1 January 1675, eighteen months before the last request overall in July 1696.[54]

Mincing Lane

While his earlier developments were all relatively small, and so not needing too much capital, Barbon did begin to put together a larger package in Mincing Lane near Fenchurch Street in the parish of St Dunstan in the East. He began collecting sites at the end of 1672, and John Bland, the lawyer who often acted as his agent, had another two. Some of these sites were for one house only, but early in 1673

Barbon identified another piece of land in Mincing Lane that was still not being built on and persuaded the City authorities to use their powers under the Rebuilding Act to issue a proclamation saying that the land would be valued and then sold if not built on in the next nine months. This they did; it was not built on, and Barbon went to the next stage of requesting a jury to carry out the valuation, purchasing it at their valuation of £1,400.[55] It was a large piece of land, almost fifty yards square and next to one owned by Bland, making it an important site. Sites for a further three smaller houses in Mincing Lane were acquired through two of his last visits to the Fire Court which extended the period of his lease by twenty years.

The houses that Barbon built on the large site that he had acquired through the Fire Court were substantial, being described as 'four fair large houses thereupon with three front houses, warehouses, coach houses and stables to every one of them'.[56] He sold the freehold of one of them to two merchants in early 1674 for £2,650 but there were continued arguments about finishing the work, the extent to which the customers had requested additional features and who should pay for them. According to the litigation that followed, the deals had been done in the Mitre tavern in Fenchurch Street and finalized in Garraway's coffee house so that may have led to the difficulty. The purchasers wanted the same marble fireplaces, carved oakwork on the stairs and dining room and a 'great gate of oak' that were in one of the other houses that had been sold. It is impossible now to know where the right was in this dispute which is a very recognizable one between builder and client, and was indeed mirrored by one brought at the same time across the road where the client had asked that the outside ornament should be made 'agreeable to the outward ornaments of the houses of the said Nicolas Barbon new built within his yard'.[57]

A different point that emerges from the complaint against Barbon's building was that

> such works done were so ill and inartificially done that the same were found to be new done and amended and repaired, several of the piers being cracked, the floors shrank, and the house in some place in danger of falling down [...] the vaults thereof are not tight, but are built so that the rain comes in to them, whereby the defendants cannot lay any goods in them.[58]

This may be a reference to the problems that Roger North identified when he wrote 'But [Barbon] had like to have lost his trade by slight building in Mincing Lane, where all the vaults for want of strength fell in, and houses came down most scandalously'.[59] The litigation quoted above was produced eighteen months after this house was supposedly finished and one would have expected a collapse to be included in the complaint if it happened, although there were clearly problems with the vaults. North may well be confusing Barbon's houses with another scandal in Mincing Lane five years earlier (well before any involvement of Barbon) when the Masters and wardens of the Carpenters', Bricklayers' and Masons' Companies were instructed by the Court of Aldermen to investigate why two new built houses in Mincing Lane collapsed, killing five or more people.[60]

Whatever the truth of this, it did not seem to have any repercussions for Barbon, and indeed Roger North was instrumental in getting Barbon hired to build new chambers for the Middle Temple while the litigation on the Mincing Lane house was still going on.

CHAPTER IV

REDEVELOPMENT OF LARGE HOUSES

The Peace of Westminster ended the war with the Dutch early in 1674 and a commercial boom followed for the next few years as the events of the Great Stop were left behind. As we have seen, the vast majority of the rebuilding in the City was complete, although there were still some open spaces that would come up for development in later years. Meanwhile the large aristocratic houses had become less attractive to their owners, whether through the need to realize cash, or because what we now know as the West End was becoming increasingly fashionable. The large houses off the Strand with their substantial grounds running down to the Thames were being vacated and redeveloped. York House, the former palace of the Duke of Buckingham, had already been sold to developers in 1672. Although Arundel House was not demolished until 1678, Milford Lane, the boundary road with its neighbour, Essex House, had already become full of alehouses and other more disreputable places and had been the subject of an Order in Council in 1634 because of its insanitary and crowded tenements (Fig. 14).[1]

There were still worries about suburban growth and in January 1674 the House of Commons returned to the issue.[2] Although the matter under formal consideration was a Bill concerning paving and maintaining the streets in London, the debate rapidly moved on to suburban expansion to which many were opposed, albeit for a variety of reasons. None were prepared to consider why tradesmen, and others, found it advantageous to move outside the City with its restrictive practices and high taxation and the subject was referred to a committee 'to bring in a bill for restraining any farther new buildings in all places within the Bills of Mortality, except the City of London and liberties thereof'. When it reported back in April, it generated more opposition, largely on the grounds of practicability, and the Committee it was referred to never reported.

Barbon's opportunity for a large development came with the death of the Duchess of Somerset, the sister of the Earl of Essex who had inherited Essex House in 1642. He seized the chance, and on 8 February 1675 contracted with the late Duchess's executors to buy the freehold of the house although payment was not to be made until the conveyance had been executed, a process that took a further eighteen months. He also bought an additional three associated tenements for a further £500. The large grounds gave him the first opportunity to try out his ideas about improving the building process and to test his ability to raise the necessary finance.

The recent debates in the House of Commons gave Barbon comfort in proceeding quickly and, unlike aristocrats such as the Earl of Exeter and the Duke of Buckingham, he did not follow the 1671 proclamation and petition the Privy Council for permission to develop. His plans must have been evident to others, because no more than sixteen days later the Middle Temple, who were neighbours to the site, petitioned the Privy Council against it saying that it

> for many ages past hath been a society consisting of divers of the nobility and principal gentry of His Majesty's kingdoms in which His Majesty's laws are studied, and have always enjoyed the benefit of a healthful open air westwards over the orchards and gardens belonging to Essex House which lie contiguous to the Middle Temple; that the petitioners are informed there is a treaty on foot to order to the building upon all the said gardens and orchards and turning the same into streets and setting up houses and wharves which if not prevented will turn to the great annoyance of the petitioners and decay if not ruin of the said society.[3]

The petitioners called for Barbon to be prohibited from building. Not to be outdone, the Lord Mayor and Aldermen of the City petitioned to the same effect a few days later. Although principally concerned with their revenues, they referred to the King's previous concern about

> the mischiefs and inconveniences daily arising to the said City from the multitude of new buildings erected in the outparts thereof, by which means the City is deprived of many thousands of their inhabitants and a vast number of new built houses within the same stand empty and unemployed; that besides these buildings erected upon new foundations, the houses of many noblemen situate in the Strand and other places near the

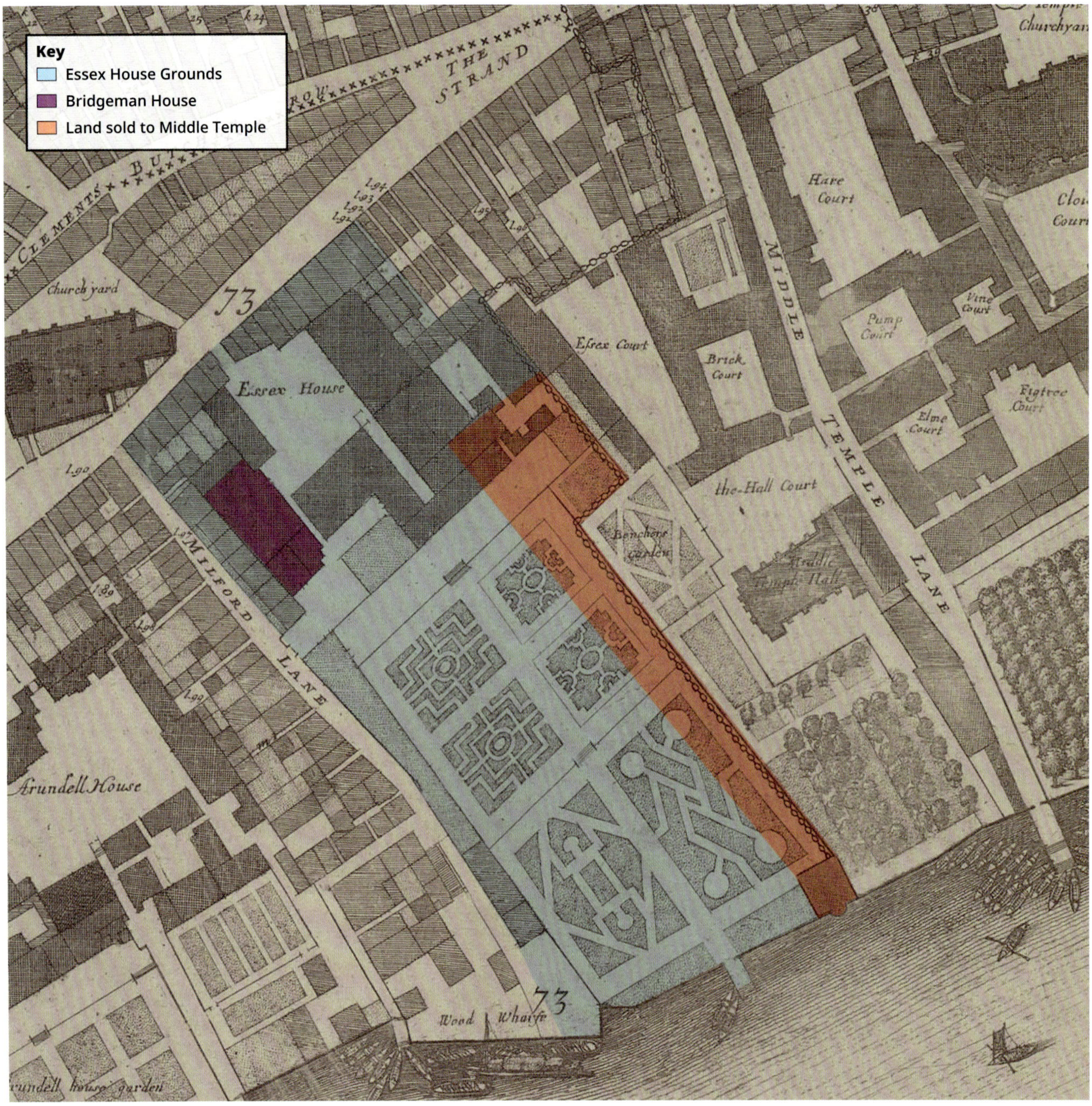

Fig. 14. Essex House and the Strand, detail from Ogilby and Morgan's *Large and Accurate Map of London*, 1676. By permission of the British Library, Maps Crace Port. 2.61

> said City are now converting into private hands and intended to be so employed, which, if permitted, will tend to the ruin of the said City already languishing under the great decay of their retail trade.[4]

At the same time the current Earl was using his personal influence with the King and his friends to prevent Barbon's development and to regain the house for his own use.[5] However, before the Privy Council had taken any action, Barbon had entered the gardens 'which he has absolutely destroyed and laid in it the foundation of the street which he designs'.[6] It was only after this, on 31 March 1675, that the Privy Council ordered Sir Christopher Wren, as Surveyor General, to forbid Barbon's workmen from proceeding.[7] In April Lord Ranelagh wrote to the Earl of Essex in a resigned tone:

> Barbon we have had before the Council twice, and the orders on his hearing were as large as care would allow them to be, my Lord Keeper and Lord Treasurer concerning themselves most heartily to recover the house for your excellency, but neither of them more earnest that way than the King himself. Notwithstanding

all, the Doctor goes on vigorously with his buildings, most of which he designs to finish by the latter end of next month, and I fear if the houses once get up a jury will not easily find it a nuisance.[8]

It does seem remarkable that Barbon could have achieved building at this speed since this would have meant that the demolition and new construction would have been completed in not much more than three months and there is evidence that many houses were not even completed by the end of the year.[9] By pressing on regardless and establishing 'facts on the ground', Barbon had been able to face down the Privy Council who knew that juries had been reluctant to require the demolition of well-built houses that were not causing trouble for others.

He used a different technique to deal with the Middle Temple, buying off the Society by offering them two pieces of land from the site which included a gate into what became Little Essex Street. He benefited from this not just by removing important opposition to his scheme but also by himself building two staircases of chambers on the transferred land, New Court and Garden Court. The first of these survives in close to its original form (Fig. 15). Although there were repeated issues about the state of the building of Garden Court, it lasted until 1883 when it was finally decided to rebuild rather than continue to prop it up. Figure 16 shows a watercolour of the building just before it was replaced.

At the same time, Barbon built on what became the alleyway Devereux Court. Next to New Court, his building was stuccoed at the end of the eighteenth century and eventually became Devereux Chambers, but other buildings in the alleyway were coffee houses. The first occupant of what is now No. 20 Devereux Court was the famous Grecian Coffee House, so called after its Greek owner. It was used by Opposition Whigs in the 1690s and members of the Royal Society in the first years of the eighteenth century. It still survives, remodelled as a pub (the Devereux Arms) in 1843. Figure 17 gives an impression of it in 1820.

Its neighbour, what is now No. 9 Devereux Court, also became a coffee house and was bought by Thomas Twining in 1706. Its success allowed him to expand into the Strand and Devereux Court became the home of the Twining family. It was rebuilt in 1952 after being bombed in the Second World War. Both this building and Devereux Chambers are now part of the Middle Temple. These are shown in Figure 21. Figure 18 shows how Devereux Court appeared in 1887, looking towards the gate into the Middle Temple.

Despite the suggestions that his buildings were not as substantial as they ought to have been, and even had cracks in them, Barbon established a good enough relationship with the Middle Temple to be asked in 1677 to knock down and rebuild the chambers on the west side of Essex Court forming what are now Nos 2–3 Essex Court (Fig. 19).[10] Since there was land available in New Court, the Middle Temple proposed that the new building should be larger than the one it replaced and required that 'it shall be built of brick and adorned with stone like Dr Barbon's building'.[11] He was also asked to create a passage between his two new buildings, arranged by using the ground-floor

Fig. 15. New Court, Middle Temple, 2022.
Photograph by Sheila O'Connell. Image used by kind permission of The Honourable Society of the Middle Temple

Fig. 16.
Garden Court, Middle Temple, 1883, watercolour by John Crowther. The building in the background is the former Middle Temple Library, bombed in the Second World War

Image © London Metropolitan Archives (City of London), no. 17990

Fig. 17.
The Grecian Coffee House, 1820, watercolour by Robert Blemmell Schnebbelie.

Image © London Metropolitan Archives (City of London), no. 21073

chambers vacated by the death of its resident. He would be involved yet again after a fire in 1679 and many of his lawyer associates over the next twenty years were members of the Middle Temple.

Rebuilding on the foundations of a single house that had been burnt or destroyed, or putting a new house where no building had been before, posed few difficulties once the site had been acquired either with a long lease or freehold. Developing a large house and grounds raised many more problems. The first was related to the actual assembly and acquisition of the site. It was rare for a large site not to contain a number of buildings, or sometimes parts of buildings, which had been leased for different periods and with a range of different rights of access or obligations to maintain. This meant that ownership of the head lease or freehold was not enough, raising all the difficulties of site acquisition that have faced property developers throughout the ages. The second issue was finance, and the scale of it, not just for the land purchase, but for the subsequent development and construction.

Barbon did not have substantial capital of his own and had to raise the large sums needed. His early developments in the City had only needed relatively small sums for short periods of time, which he appears to have had no difficulty in borrowing and repaying. He may also have been able to use his wife's portion of £1,000 to help the financing since her name often appeared on those transactions. Nevertheless, while the banking system was

Fig. 18. Devereux Court looking east towards Middle Temple, 1887, watercolour by John Crowther.
Image © London Metropolitan Archives (City of London), no. 17995

Fig. 19. Nos 2–3 Essex Court, Middle Temple, 2022.
Photograph by Sheila O'Connell. Image used by kind permission of The Honourable Society of the Middle Temple

still undeveloped in the 1670s, there was already a healthy market in property through a variety of leases as well as freeholds.[12] Many people were prepared to invest their surplus capital in the development of individual houses, while goldsmiths provided larger sums of money. Another source were the scriveners who prepared conveyancing and other documents, and increasingly found themselves involved in financing property deals and mortgages, whether directly or by acting as middlemen.

The purchase of the freehold of Essex House and its grounds was relatively straightforward, but this did not necessarily give Barbon control of the various other buildings on the site that had been constructed under leases. As with many of his later developments, some of the tenants of existing buildings on the site refused to vacate their property or allow him access as needed by his builders. This helped to complicate the financing of the enterprise by causing difficulty for the security given, or claimed to be given, by the leases. Barbon dealt with these issues in ways that would become familiar in the future: he either bought objectors out, ignored them, countered with litigation of his own, or went ahead leaving them to take legal action after the event, which was usually too late. This left behind a trail of litigation with substantial records remaining of the complaints and the answers to them, although rather less about court decisions, which may suggest that much of the litigation was tactical rather than designed to proceed to judgment.

The records shed much light on his behaviour and that of his partners and those with whom he dealt. While sometimes only one side of the argument is available, and both complaints and answers clearly have some hyperbole, they do provide a basis of factual material about the transactions as well as often giving life and colour to what would otherwise be rather dry financial matters. The extent of this litigation is a major change for Barbon; apart from his activity in the Fire Court, we know of only one piece of litigation in all his twenty-six earlier developments, and none begun by his clients or partners. Chapters XII and XIII will give a full analysis of Barbon's methods, but we begin here by describing the history of his first major development of the Essex House site in some detail using the records of at least ten disputes associated with it.

Barbon moved quickly to raise the funds, approaching a scrivener, John Adams, who put him in touch with two goldsmiths, Thomas Cooke and Nicholas Cary, who agreed to provide him with £13,000 on the security of the site, which he then mortgaged to them at the end of May 1675.[13] They put up about £8,000, but his failure to pay this back on time meant he had to refinance £5,000 from the prominent scrivener Sir Robert Clayton. There were then some arguments about how to structure the security for both sets of lenders, only finally sorted out after a court order for repayment.

The arguments about new building had not gone away and a petition was tabled at about that time:

> Proposals humbly offered [...] to suppress any more buildings near and about the Cities of London and Westminster [...] the mischiefs and inconveniences arising by the vast increase of new buildings near and about the Cities of London and Westminster are so notorious and evident, that both the City itself and all the countries in general feel at this day the smart and unhappy effects thereof. The Head swelling to too great a proportion, that it is at once become unwieldy and destructive to itself, and hath also left other parts of the Kingdom languishing and deprived of its due nutriment.[14]

In case this argument was not enough, the petition went on to suggest that a good source of revenue, 'several hundred thousand, if not a million pounds', might be found from taxing the houses built in 'defiance of successive orders in council and proclamations'. Yet another Bill was introduced into the House of Lords towards the end of November 1675 'to prohibit building on new Foundations in London, Westminster and the Suburbs', but it progressed very slowly through committee and Barbon moved to get on quickly with the construction of the various houses. He had no intention of doing all this himself and produced a plan of the site which he used as the basis of discussions with potential investors. A copy of what is at least an early draft of such a plan shows what he had in mind but must have been prepared before the deal with the Middle Temple as it makes no provision for Devereux Court or the cross street between Milford Lane and the Temple, and is rather optimistic about the width of the northern end of Essex Street, an optimism that would come back to haunt him.

His original plan (Fig. 20) allowed him to map out the various sites for development and persuade others to take them up. Equally importantly, it allowed him to estimate the ground rents based on how much per foot of frontage each house would let for, and from this the total value in ground rents was established. The site was divided into six plots, five of which had a stated frontage in feet, the sixth covering Bridgeman's house which was allowed to remain.

The ground rent per foot of frontage in Essex Street varied from 10s. to 15s. per foot, depending on the width of the road and whether the house had rear access to Milford Lane or Devereux Court. The value of the development could then be established by capitalizing this sum, usually at a figure of about twenty years' purchase, thereby allowing the money to be raised. He contracted with over thirty different investors, about half of whom were builders of some kind, and the others investors or people intending to live in the houses. In Essex Street Barbon let about three-quarters of the houses to other builders and took the rest for building at his own expense. These last houses were let to his agent, John Bland, lawyer and scrivener. Overall, there were seventy-nine houses, three wharves, and one stable. Leases were eventually signed by February 1676 and the ground rents added up to just over £1,000 per annum or up to £20,000 capital.

Roger North gives a description of this process that is so close to the methods used by Barbon in Essex Street that it is not difficult to believe that it was Essex House that he had in mind:

> He was the inventor of this new method of building by casting of ground rents into streets and small houses, and to augment their number with as little front as possible, and selling the ground to workmen by so much per foot front, and what he could not sell build himself. This has made ground rents high for the sake of mortgaging, and others following his steps have refined and improved upon it, and made a superfoetation of houses about London.[15]

Figure 21 shows the final layout.

Even before the conveyancing of the site had been completed, Barbon was approached by a potential purchaser for the developed site. Samuel Vincent, an excise farmer who wanted somewhere to put his money, was introduced to Barbon by John Hayes, sometimes described as an agent, sometimes as an adviser.[16] John Hayes, possibly Barbon's brother-in-law or a cousin of his wife Margaret, may well have been involved in advising her on her participation in a number of Barbon's transactions in the City. The result was that Vincent agreed to purchase the whole site on 16 February 1676, although the eventual conveyance took some time to finalize with some toing and froing about exactly what would be included. The final sum was £19,850 for everything 'now built or designed to be built according to a scheme or plot subscribed by both the parties'. It included £50 for Barbon's wife, and a commitment by Barbon to build 'an ornamental arch at the lower end of the street of the value of £150 by 1 August 1676'. It is not clear whether this had been in Barbon's original plan, but he agreed, and it had the advantage of blocking the view of the wharves along the riverside and making any traffic for the river go down Milford Lane rather than Essex Street itself. This is illustrated in Figure 22 of Milford Lane in 1853 with the delivery cart avoiding Essex Street on its way to the wharves and showing the backs of the houses in Essex Street. The arch still stands, although it was bombed in the Second World War and rebuilt subsequently. Figure 23 is a drawing from the mid-nineteenth century. By chance, a sketch of the river side of the arch appears as a detail in a print of the 1684 Frost Fair on the Thames and this is shown in Figure 24.

This deal allowed Barbon to pay off all his debts on the site and, according to Vincent, gave him a profit of some £5,000, as well as the £3,000 he had made from reuse or sale of the materials from Essex House.[17] Some of the timbers from the House can still be seen in the basements of Nos 32 and 34.[18]

Although many of the houses in Essex Street have survived, the vast majority have been either replaced or refronted, often more than once, and their interiors have also been modernized as leases fell in or to face the needs of new ways of living or of working. One whose exterior is perhaps the least changed is that of No. 19 Essex Street, shown in Figure 25.

Barbon's biggest problem, and one that continued for some time, was the other houses on the site. He had always intended to leave the substantial house of Sir Orlando Bridgeman, but there were six smaller houses fronting the Strand and he needed to demolish at least some to provide the access into the Strand for the houses in Essex Street. This access had been on the plan which Barbon used to persuade people to take leases to build the houses there and while he always denied that he had ever entered into a binding covenant for this purpose, the builders always maintained that he had committed himself and in particular to access 'open to the sky', that is more than the original narrow arched entry to Essex House itself. He managed to buy off some of the occupants but others complained that Barbon and his associates were trying to 'weary them out of possession' or had made 'diverse conveyances and insurances among themselves on purpose to perplex your orators and weary them out of their said leases'.[19]

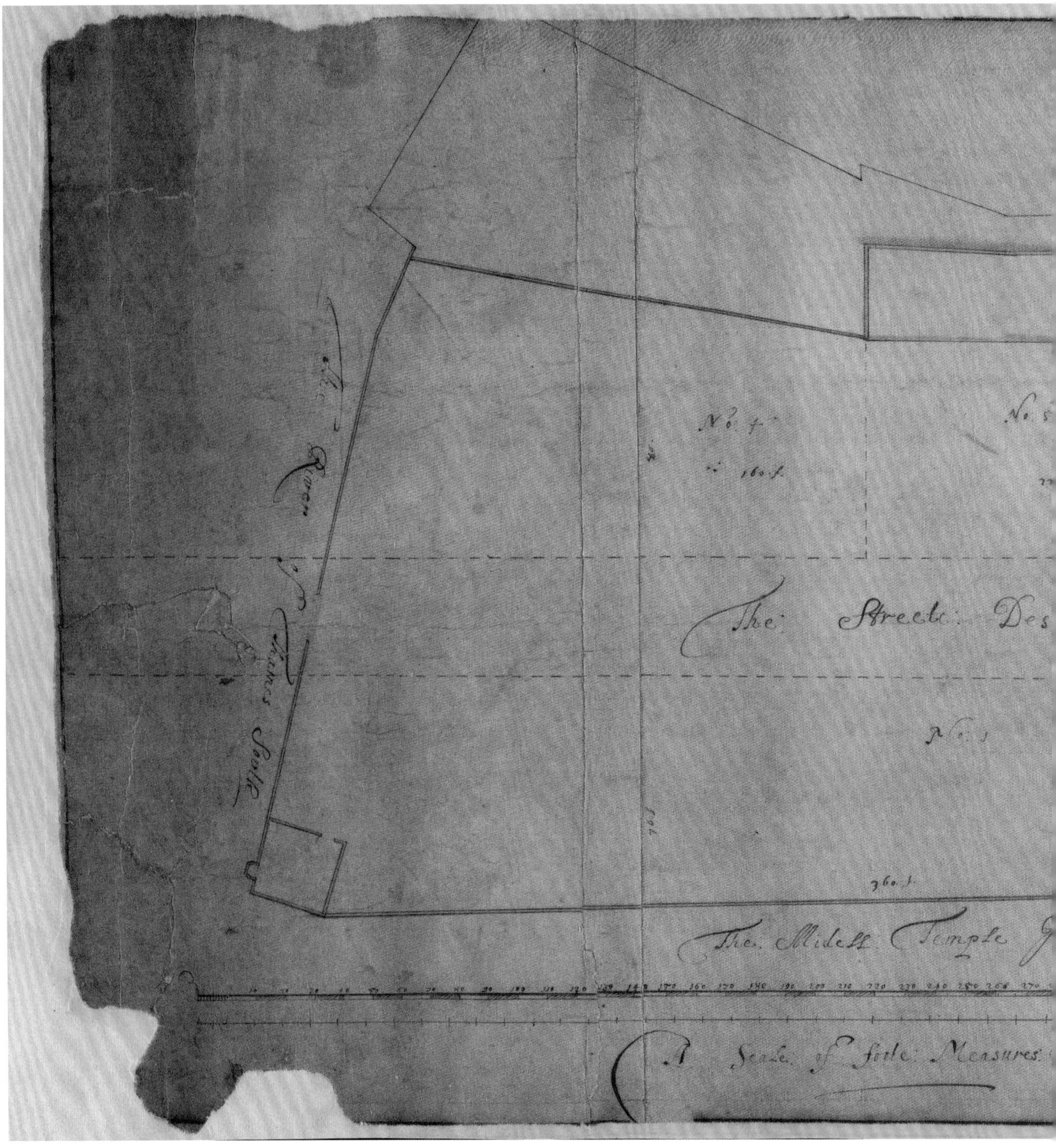

Fig. 20. Barbon's original plan for the Essex House development.

For two tradesmen tenants, Grice and Hanmer, who had their leases from a sublessee of the Duchess of Somerset, he found a loophole by purchasing the last eighteen months of the sublease and so voiding any supposed promises that had been made about a further lease at its expiry. The houses had complicated internal arrangements in that Hanmer's property ran both under and over some of Grice's rooms, and they tried to protect themselves by Hanmer giving a lease to Grice with a condition that possession could only be given up to Hanmer and expressly not to Barbon.[20] They then joined together to fund a lawsuit against Barbon in which Grice claimed that Barbon had threatened to 'untile the

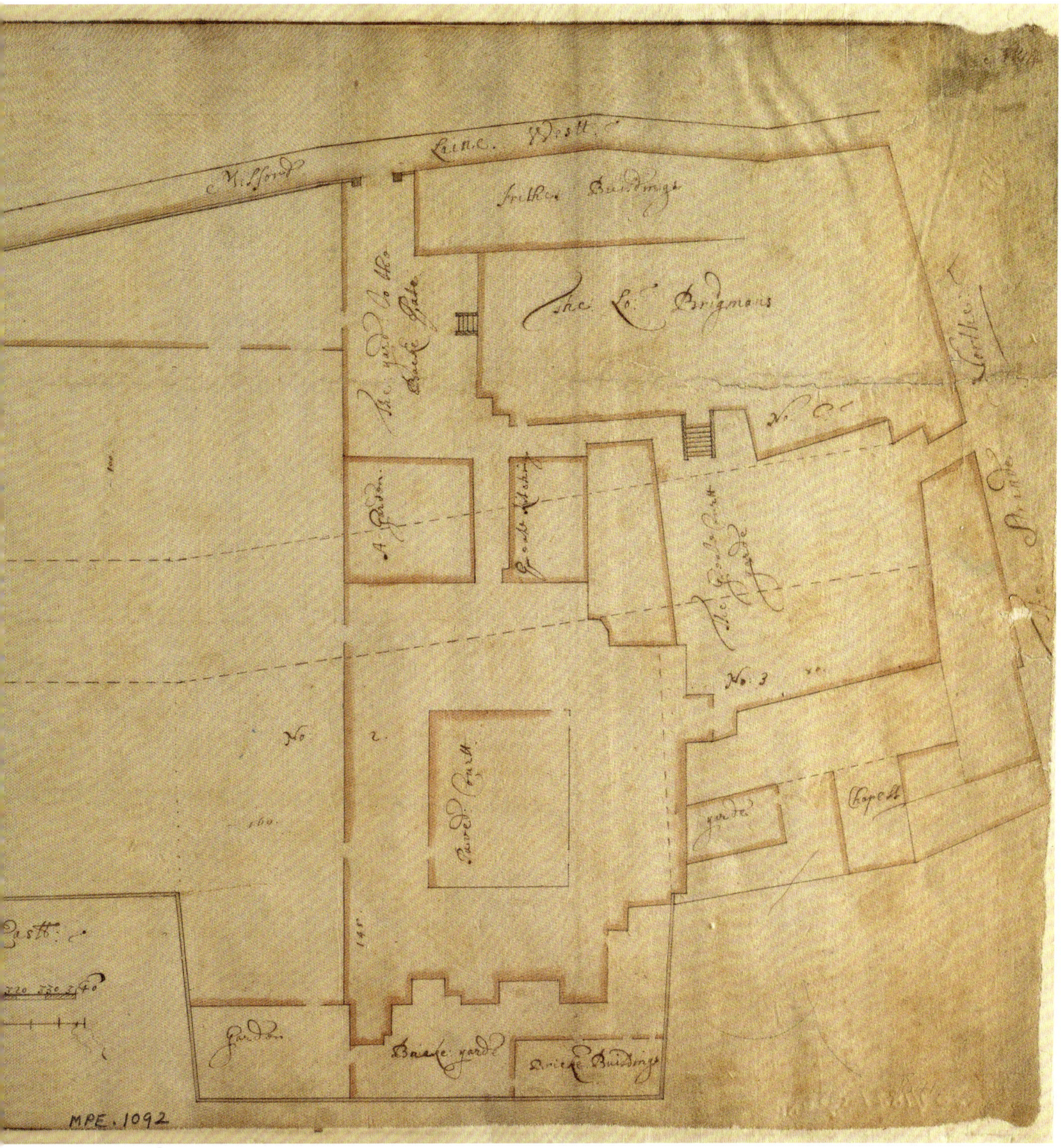

house and pull the same down over your orator's head'. Initially Grice won an injunction but Barbon claimed this was only through 'the neglect of this defendant's clerk or solicitor in not getting the [plea] filed in due time'. Grice subsequently withdrew his claim, giving possession to Barbon, who promptly pulled the house down and started a suit against Hanmer to eject him from two more houses, offering him 'by way of derision' the value of his future lease if anyone would buy it. This story must have been in Roger North's mind when he wrote of Barbon's approach:

> It mattered not a litigious knave did stand out, for the first thing he did was to pull the house down about their ears, and build upon the ground, and stand it out till their hearts ached, and at last they would truckle and take any terms for peace and a quiet life.[21]

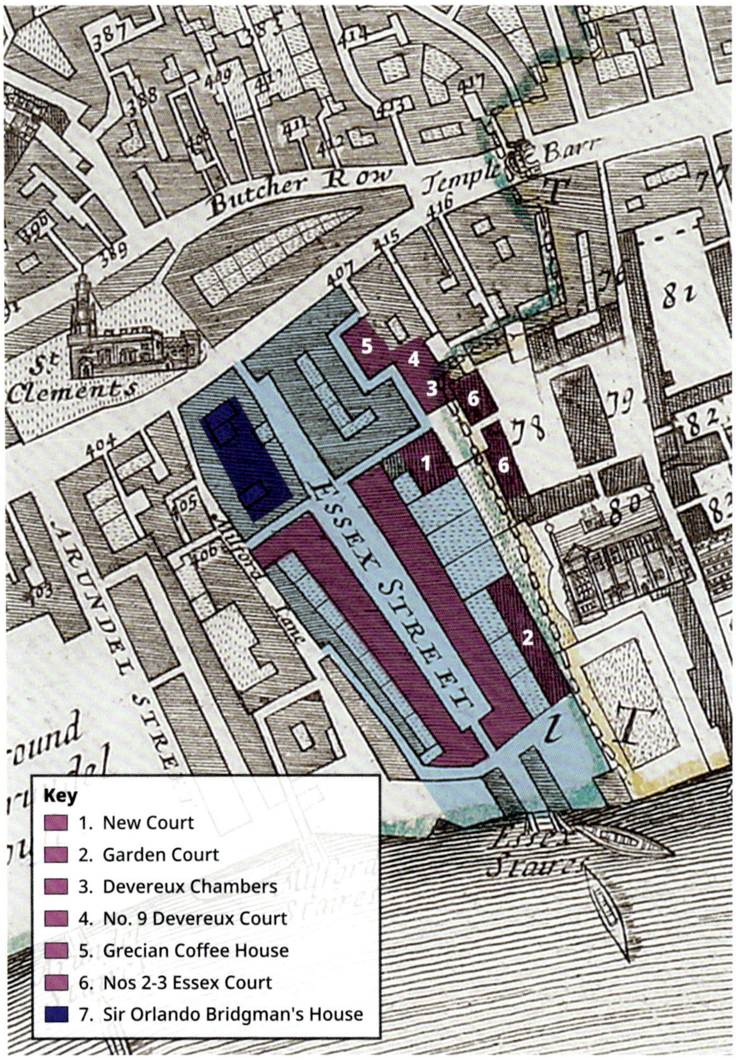

Fig. 21. Barbon's building in Essex House and Middle Temple as of 1677, detail from Morgan's *London &c. Actually Survey'd*, 1682. By permission of the British Library, Maps Crace Port. 2.58

The case did not end quite as happily for Barbon because he was pursued through the courts for some time, with judgments against him for compensation for loss of business for the various occupants. Even so he delayed paying — one complainant died and was no longer eligible — and he tried to pass on any obligation to the purchaser of the Essex House site, Samuel Vincent, thus promoting further litigation and making it even harder for those expecting compensation to receive it. Meanwhile, the final outlet to the Strand was smaller than that described on the original plan, but Vincent concluded that 'although not so convenient as the designed one would be, he does not think that the houses are very much injured by that'.[22]

Barbon had other arguments about his development. Dame Dorothy Bridgeman had difficulties with him, at first because his new buildings 'caused her house to be with great darkness much obscured', but also for a host of other reasons including his blocking the passage to her house for several months, stopping a watercourse that led to her cellars being filled with water and her goods ruined, building on her walls which were not party walls and for 'pulling off the tiles and lead from her house and converting the same to his or their own uses'. She had brought a number of actions for nuisance against Barbon and his workmen which for some time prevented building. Barbon countered by refusing to extend her lease on the property, persuading the executors for Essex House to sue for the redemption of her mortgage, and inciting occupants of the other tenements to start actions against her. Finally, all was resolved by Dame Dorothy and others dropping their actions and Barbon agreeing to extend her lease.[23]

This was not the only large development with which Barbon was engaged. The first was the redevelopment of Exeter House whose grounds ran down from Covent Garden to the Strand. Exeter House was the only great house where Barbon did not purchase the freehold. The Earl of Exeter had

Fig. 22. Delivery cart in Milford Lane, *c.* 1850, watercolour by Thomas Hosmer Shepherd.

Image © London Metropolitan Archives (City of London), no.308303

Fig. 23. Arch at bottom of Essex Street, watercolour by Thomas Hosmer Shepherd.

© Trustees of the British Museum, 1880,1113.2977

Fig. 24. Rear of the arch in Essex Street, detail from *A Wonderful Fair or a Fair of Wonders … on the River of Thames, in the time of the terrible frost, December 1684.*

By permission of the British Library, Maps K.Top.27.38.2

Fig. 25. No. 19 Essex Street, 2022.
Photograph by Timothy Walker

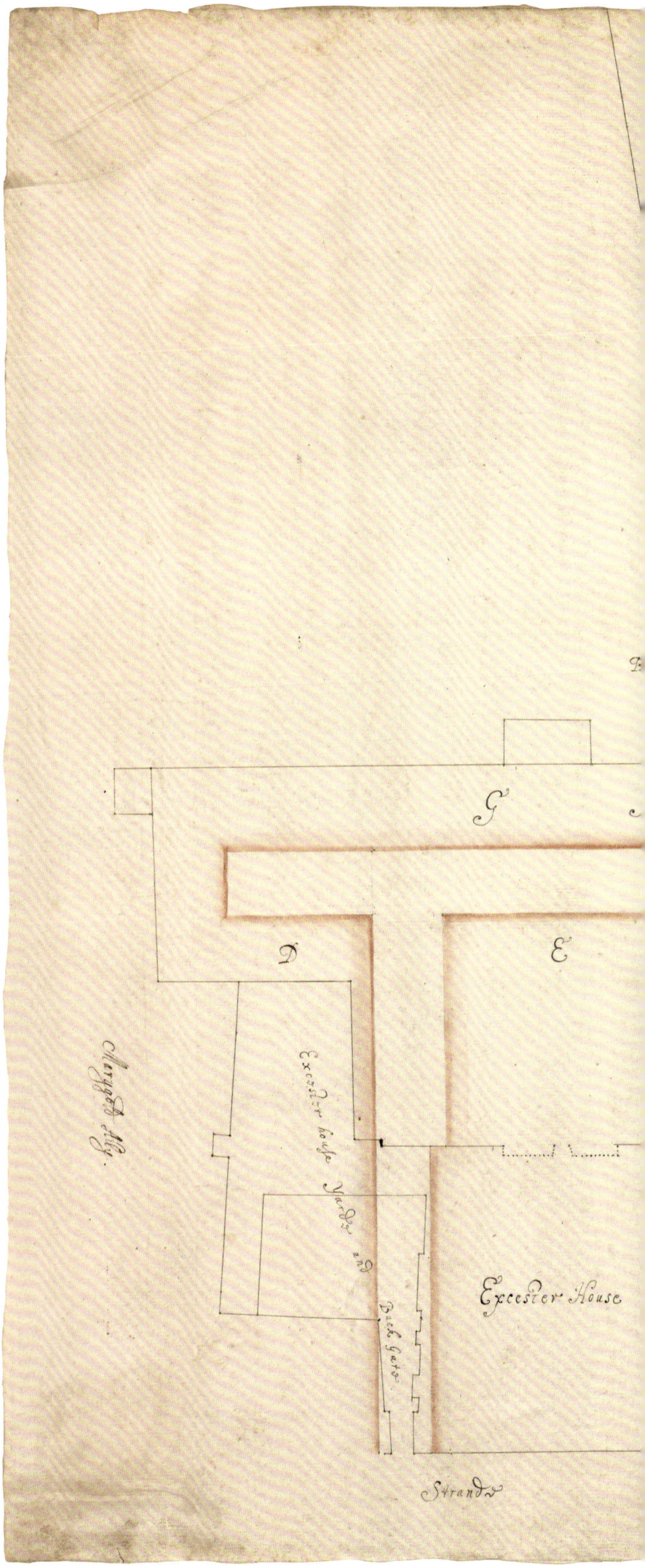

Fig. 26. Scheme approved by Wren for the development of Exeter House.

© The Warden and Fellows of All Souls College, Oxford, Architectural Drawings at All Souls College, Oxford: Wren and Hawksmoor, 401 (AS IV.67)

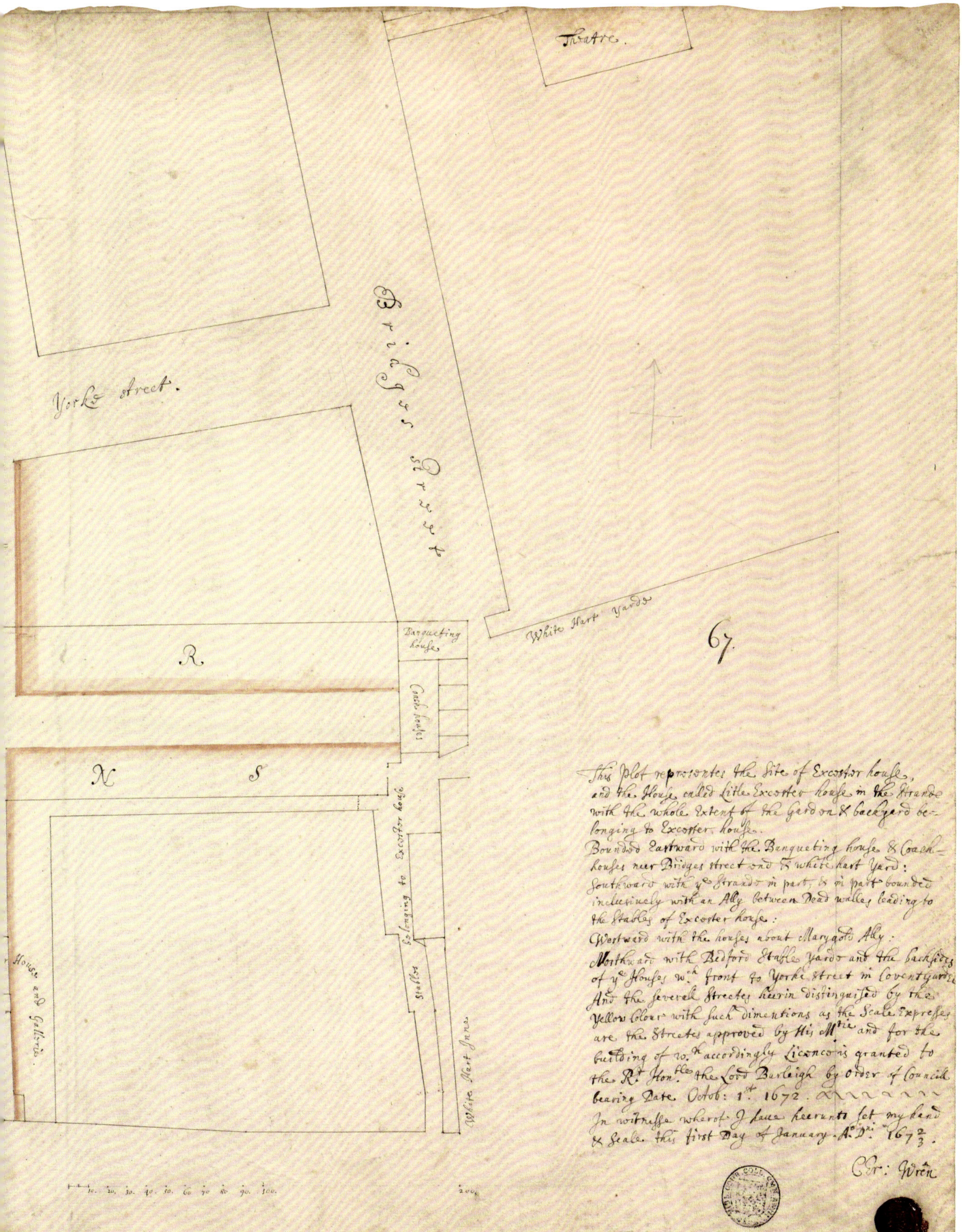
Theatre.
Bridges Street
Yorke street.
White Hart Yarde
67
Banqueting house
Coach houses
R
N
S
Belonging to Excester house
Stables
White Hart Inne
Houses and Gallerie
10. 20. 30. 40. 50. 60 70 80 90. 100.
200.
This plot representes the site of Excester house, and the House called Litle Excester house in the Strande with the whole Extent of the Garden & backyard be-longing to Excester house.
Bounded Eastward with the Banqueting house & Coach-houses neer Bridges street and ye white hart Yard:
Southward with ye Strande in part, & in part bounded inclusively with an Ally between Dead walles leading to the Stables of Excester house:
Westward with the houses about Marygold Ally:
Northward with Bedford Stable yarde and the backsides of ye Houses wch front to Yorke Street in Covent garden
And the severall Streetes heerin distinguished by the Yellow Colour with such dimentions as the Scale expresses are the Streetes approved by His Matie and for the building of wch accordingly Licence is granted to the Rt Honble the Lord Burleigh by Order of Councill bearing Date Octob: 1st 1672.
In witnesse wherof I have heerunto set my hand & Seale this first Day of January Ao Dni 1672/3.
Chr: Wren

begun the process for its development by obtaining a licence to build in October 1672 and, at the beginning of 1673, Christopher Wren approved the scheme shown in Figure 26.[24]

It seems no progress was made until the Earl let two leases to Barbon, one for Great Exeter House and the other for Little Exeter House, with a combined ground rent of £500 per annum. Barbon was to demolish and rebuild 'several new dwelling houses [...] to be formed into streets by way of improvement', but the Earl covenanted that he would issue new leases to the builders, at ground rents to be determined by Barbon, but only after the houses should be 'tiled, leaded, or otherwise covered in'. This avoided the problem of builders failing to finish their work, and essentially Barbon was being employed as a middleman, but the Earl retained supervision by requiring all the leases to go through the hands of his agent Francis Child (later knighted) 'whom he solely instructed in the said matter, and not the said Dr Barbon'.[25]

Barbon did not build the houses himself, although one lease is in the name of his agent John Bland, but engaged with eighteen builders or investors, one of whom was his sister-in-law Rebecca Hayes and another three were also builders on the Essex House site. Barbon's lease was finally completed in June 1676 and he promptly set about mortgaging it, approaching another scrivener, Thomas Browne, who 'after much importuning' lent increasing sums which reached £7,000 by August 1679.

Meanwhile Barbon was negotiating with the prospective builders, at least seventeen in total, who had refused to accept what were effectively subleases from him on the basis they did not want to 'adventure vast and great sums of money' solely on 'leases derived out of the original leases which might become void and voidable by his default'.[26] They opted for agreements with him whereby he covenanted to implement the Earl's offer of leases directly to them, as in fact was used for Barbon's development at Devonshire Square, near Bishopsgate. For their part the agreement committed them to complete the building by August 1677 and to a series of requirements for the houses including that the fronts should be continuous and uniform and generally meeting the standard of a second-rate house as in the Act for Rebuilding the City. (This last requirement was probably imposed by the Privy Council licence.) The builders also had to pay so much per foot for the building of a drain and to pave the front with black and white tiles as for Crane Court.

Although Browne may have lent the first sums to Barbon, he soon brought in other investors, including first the merchants Peter Vanderput and James Host; later the loan was transferred to another merchant, John Hunyades, who had approached Browne with £7,000 asking for recommendations for its investment.[27] The builders asked Barbon for their leases in 1677 but he refused on the grounds the houses were not yet finished. There followed a series of arguments about the making of the leases and Browne subsequently maintained that Barbon had failed to pay any interest or ground rents and himself took action to get the money from the tenants, ejecting those who failed to pay. Law cases rumbled on and even after Barbon's death twenty years later John Bland was complaining that he had not had his lease. His complaint was even greater because the original agreements with the builders provided for John Bland to prepare their leases and be paid for so doing. Francis Child had taken John Bland's drafts but kept the payment himself. John Bland had lost over £40 as a result.

In fact, Barbon did not build exactly according to the approved plan, and his main interest may well have been in an addition, the building of the Exeter Exchange, which was the seventeenth-century equivalent of a shopping mall. It was built following the success of the nearby New Exchange, but Barbon may well have had in mind Thomas Gresham's great success in the last century with the Royal Exchange. The Exeter Exchange was also a success; a French traveller described it shortly after its construction as 'in the style of a palace, adorned with many columns, large doorways and distinguished by decorations and statues',[28] while in 1693 another described it 'on the uppermost floors there are ongoing auctions of excellent paintings and below numerous beautiful shops with all sorts of fashionable things for the convenience of the ladies'.[29] There were forty-eight shops on the ground floor, but it went into decline at the start of the eighteenth century and later was famous for its menagerie. Figures 27 and 28 show it shortly before being demolished in 1829.

Barbon's second development at this time was in St James's Square. Although the early sales of lots in this square were to aristocrats, from 1673–75 the Earl of St Albans went on to sell them to a number of builders including Richard Frith, who bought three, and Barbon, who bought one in April 1675.[30] In this case the freehold was included, at least when the house was completed, which Barbon achieved in 1677; he sold the house to the Earl of Kent for £6,400 by the end of the year. Robert Hooke had inspected the house on behalf of a prospective buyer but had not recommended its purchase, and it appears that Barbon had used William Combes, a gentleman and servant of the Earl, to introduce him to the Earl, for which Barbon promised a payment of £200.[31] He then tried to avoid payment but was taken to the Court of Common Pleas, which Barbon countered with a case in Chancery. It is not known how this was resolved.

These three developments show Barbon operating on a much larger scale than previously, even for the four adjacent Mincing Lane houses, but they did not stop him taking advantage of other opportunities as they came up. Trevor House on fashionable Cannon Row, Westminster, came up for sale in 1675 following the death of its owner, Sir James Trevor, a couple of years earlier. Although described as a 'mansion', it was not in the same league as Essex or Exeter Houses, and Barbon snapped it up, knocked it down and built a modern house in its place as well as using the garden which went down to the Thames to build a house, warehouse and wharf. He had sold out by October 1678 for just over £1,000.[32] His partner for this project was John Rowley, with whom he would do a number of future deals.

Fig. 27. Exeter Exchange, *c.* 1805, watercolour by Charles Tomkins.

© Trustees of the British Museum, 1880,1113.2857

Fig. 28. Exeter Exchange, 1829, steel engraving by Thomas Barber after Thomas Hosmer Shepherd.

© Trustees of the British Museum, 1880,0911.754

Between the four developments, he had to raise over £20,000, a very large sum for someone with relatively little large-scale track record and only small capital of his own. Moreover, most of the debt was outstanding at the same time when he would have had other demands from the remaining elements of his rebuilding in the City and for his work building chambers for the Middle Temple. Chapter XII and XIII will give a full analysis of Barbon's methods, both for building and finance, drawing together on the totality of his developments. What is clear is that he had moved to a much more aggressive approach, using the full panoply of litigation and delay inherent in the legal progress in a way that he had not done earlier. The extent to which he invented these methods may be arguable, but he used them on a scale and to an extent that was new. This might well have suggested that potential partners would have been wary of doing business with him, but although a number certainly suffered the effects of not being paid to the timetable they had expected, or even at all, it is noticeable that many of those who lent him money or built houses with his leases, did so time and time again.

The Politics of Housing: Barbon Enters the Fray

Barbon's first political engagements followed naturally from his development of Essex House and its grounds into the streets of Essex Street, Little Essex Street and Devereux Court.[33] This development was not aimed at the nobility but for a range of other uses, not all of them attractive to some other City dwellers. The layout linked the better houses in the street directly to the Strand (albeit through a gap not as wide as first intended) and to the Temple, leaving the commercial premises accessed by Milford Lane; there is an interesting contrast with York House which kept the old architecturally handsome Watergate to serve the new development focused on the river rather than the Strand. As a result, one writer claimed that Barbon had turned a bishop's lodging into 'houses and tenements for taverns, alehouses, cookshoppes and vaulting schools, and the garden adjoining the river onto wharves for brewers and woodmongers'.[34] Strype, however, gave a very different picture, describing Essex Street as 'a broad clean and handsome street [...] it consisteth of two rows of good built houses, well inhabited by gentry', and Devereux Court 'a large place with good houses, and by reason of its vicinity to the Temple hath a good resort, consisting of public houses and noted coffee houses'.[35] As we have seen, one of these was the famous Grecian Coffee House.

It is quite likely that both opinions were justified, reflecting differing views of the way London should develop. As we have seen, these arguments had been raging since the reign of Queen Elizabeth and, stimulated by the changes to London after the Fire, they continued to do so in the 1670s and afterwards. There were a number of underlying reasons. Some regretted the loss of green fields and the amenity which they had provided; others worried about those coming to live in or near London and the crime and disease they might encourage. The move to the west, with loss of controls by the City government or the guilds, was seen to threaten the economy of the City itself, with the profitable retail trade moving to areas where there were fewer constraints and regulations. City magnates also realized that it would reduce the number of people qualified to take on the range of official posts in the City, which were both time-consuming and required considerable personal expense.

Attempts to control the number of new houses in London, or at least tax them, had not gone away. While a Bill introduced into the House of Lords at the end of 1675 was at last reported out in March 1677, the Committee claiming to have found 'difficulties in their proceedings', the Commons reopened the debate in February 1678, although principally with a concern to raise funds. For the first time, Barbon entered the political arena and demonstrated his skills as a controversialist. He produced three pamphlets in 1678, as far as we know the first of his published writing, although published anonymously, as were most publications by merchants.[36] The first two were written specifically to influence the debates in Parliament in 1678 and were designed to refute the arguments of those who opposed new building or wanted to tax such houses. They were widely circulated to MPs and set out some of the counter-arguments.

The first pamphlet was concerned to refute some of the more extreme assessments of 20,000 or 30,000 new houses.[37] Barbon claimed to have added up all the returns from the churchwardens over the years and so showed that there were no more than 7,500 houses built between 1620 to 1656, those on which Cromwell had levied a fine, and no more than 10,000 from 1656 to 1677. His figures demonstrated that the higher claims for the total were quite impossible, particularly assertions that there had been 3,500 new houses in the parish of St Martin's compared with his suggestion of 1,750. He demonstrated that he was familiar with the methods of political economy used by William Petty and John Graunt in their studies of London population by using the numbers of births and deaths to confirm that his numbers were the right order of magnitude.

He went on to calculate the value of the houses built since 1656 and estimated that they were roughly equal in value to those built between 1620 and 1656, and so the tax on post-1656 houses would not raise any more than in Cromwell's time which, he claimed, only raised £20,000 after four years rather than the £70,000 supposedly due. By depressing future building, the Crown would lose customs revenue on 'the timber, boards, wainscot, and iron being not less that £10,000 pa'. Moreover, the tax would be unfair to so many people: those who had already paid some tax, the builders, and the owners of the great houses who gave up rent on them to allow development. Norman Brett James has analysed the figures in detail and finds inconsistencies with other records but is inclined nevertheless to endorse the figures for the totals.[38]

Barbon produced another pamphlet at the same time more closely targeted on the issue of taxing new houses, an issue that was being discussed yet again as a means of raising money for the Crown.[39] It presented a very detailed argument with many references to specific legislation, individual court cases, and scattered with Latin tags, but its main points were as before: the tax was unfair, had been difficult to collect, and would cause significant economic problems as well as acting as a deterrent to building. He even claimed that the imposition of the tax, with the difficulty of deciding on whom it should fall once the house had been occupied for up to twenty years, 'would breed perpetual dissention between landlord and tenant, father and son, where any settlement of marriages have been made'.

What part Barbon's intervention played is impossible to say, but the House of Lords Bill sank without trace while the Commons struggled with efforts to discover the facts about building in London. At one point the Speaker was ordered 'to issue out his warrants to the Ministers, Churchwardens, and Collectors for the Poor, of the several parishes without the City of London' to assist the Committee 'to draw up a list of all such houses erected within their respective parishes [...] since the year 1656'. Barbon's own computations may well have been the best that the Committee had.[40] Andrew Marvell commented that 'The Bill of the new buildings makes no progress. The surveys not being yet finished'.[41] There were still, however, worries about the tax being imposed and in May 1678, when the Bill was still in its Committee stage, Richard Frith had to give a bond of indemnity against any such tax laid on the house as a reason of the impending bill to his prospective purchaser for a house in St James's Square.[42] In the end the Bill was voted out, the last straw being a bid by the City itself to be exempt from the tax, and a final attempt on June 25 that year, a resolution to raise £200,000 by taxing houses built since 1656 within ten miles of London, was defeated by 117 votes to 88.[43] By then the City had already relented and taken many steps to attract craftsmen and traders back within the walls.

Barbon's first two pamphlets that year were principally concerned to counter the most extreme charges about the scale of new building and to ensure that the proposed tax was defeated. The third was very different and took head on the two main arguments that had caused this tax issue to return to Parliament so often. These went wider than straight nimbyism, and reflected the concerns highlighted earlier, the first that London drained money from the rest of the country, and the second that new building in the suburbs provided unregulated, and so unfair, competition for the City itself and so damaged its trade. The pamphlet, which ran to over twenty pages, was entitled *A Discourse showing the great advantages that New Buildings and the Enlargement of Towns and Cities do bring to a Nation*. It also contained Barbon's first attempt at a new economic theory, which he would develop further later. This argued that competitive consumption, driven by fashion rather than need — emulation in his words — was an important driver of growth and economic wellbeing.

Barbon argued that new building provides a wide range of employment, both in construction and in the various crafts needed to decorate a house. The concentration of people in a city creates sufficient demand for a wide range of skills that cannot be provided economically in the country. Moreover, he argued that city dwellers spend a higher proportion of their income on items other than food, which are more labour intensive than agriculture:

> Now five pounds spent in clothes is of more advantage to the nation than twenty pounds spent in eating and drinking. In the country the air is sharp and provokes hunger and the great end of all men's labour there is to satisfy that craving appetite. And the pleasures of a country life are good eating and drinking, but in the city the air is thicker and less quantity of meat sufficeth and not being so violently pressed by that appetite their minds are more at leisure to gratify ambition which is expressed by clothing and furnishing of their houses and in the use of several other things that are invented for the pomp and ease of life. Now that he who spends five hundred pounds per annum if he lives in the country he spends four in eating and drinking and but one in clothes whereas if he live in the city he spends one half of his revenue in clothes and other necessaries for his house. Now for every five pounds that is spent in clothing and furnishing a house there is above ten persons to one that gets by the expense of the same money in meat and drink.[44]

For Barbon, new building and the enlarging of towns increased the strength of a nation. Large cities were easier to defend and 'were the glory and reputation of a nation'.[45] They encouraged strangers and travellers to visit and spend their money. He commented: 'How great a profit does arise from this curious humour of seeing of rarities is best known to the inhabitants of Italy.' Cities were also easier to govern than more dispersed populations and their economy provided more tax revenue to the Crown, all of which was enhanced by being larger.

He claimed that it was ridiculous to suppose that builders would build houses that were not needed because they had to make their return from rents, and if the houses could not be let, they would not build them. While it was true that some rents within the City had fallen since the Fire, they were still three times what they had been a century before. This was due to the large number of houses built in the suburbs and gives examples of the effect. New building in Spitalfields had raised the rents of houses in Bishopsgate Without by 50 per cent, while the rents in the Strand had more than doubled on account of the building in nearby Covent Garden, Piccadilly and St James's. More people brought more trade, which increased rents, while the number of people could not be increased without further building. He also argued strongly that 'the builders, traders, and inhabitants of the new houses bring more trade to the City than the new traders in the suburbs take away'[46] and that this was reinforced by the fact that many of the new traders were actually the former apprentices of the City merchants who would have taken some of their business anyway.

He rejected the argument that any fall in rents in the country was due to the migration of people to London, but rather that the increase in productivity by the various agricultural improvements that had been adopted, coupled with the drop in population from the Plague and emigration 'to new plantations and to improve Ireland', resulted in a fall in prices. He advocated two remedies, one an Act of Parliament to reduce interest rates (always of interest to a property speculator!) and the second a general Act of naturalization to invite foreigners to live in England and so increase demand.

Barbon used his understanding of the approaches used in political economy which we saw in the previous two pamphlets. By comparing relative numbers of burials he showed that by 1677 the population of the City was within a few per cent of its pre-Fire and 1650 total, while the population of the whole of the Bills of Mortality area had just about doubled in the same period. He also demonstrated that the population of the City itself remained constant for forty years until 1650 when the replacement of some large buildings by tenements allowed the population to grow.

Not all his arguments were sound. His assertion that non-food purchases are more labour intensive than agriculture, although possibly correct, is based solely on the fact that he could produce a larger number of trades involved. Equally, his assertion that no builder would build if he could not let the property took no account of the cyclical nature of the property market, as observable in the seventeenth century as now. It glossed over the large number of empty houses in the City during the early 1670s, when there was manifestly building in the suburbs, although he might well have argued that there were in practice two separate markets and the City itself was largely rebuilt by 1677. It is interesting how modern his views are. They demonstrated some appreciation of the laws of supply and demand, his recognition of tourism as a revenue generator, a willingness to contemplate immigration, and perhaps an anticipation of the hierarchy of needs developed by Maslow in the twentieth century.[47]

Two of Barbon's arguments about population are contentious. Graunt had shown that there were very many more deaths than births annually in London,[48] and this pattern continued for the rest of the century.[49] He argued that what would otherwise have caused a steady drop in London's population was compensated by a migration from the country to London of some 6,000 people a year'. He went on to show that the growth in population in the rest of the country (where births outnumbered deaths) would have been sufficient to provide this as well as allowing an increase in the overall population. Graunt attributed the lower birth rate to the unhealthy state of London and the presence of many apprentices or other young people who were not able to marry, those who came to London leaving their wives at home, or indeed seamen who were away, so leaving their wives without children. Barbon, on the other hand, attributed the relatively smaller number of baptisms to the fact that Dissenters did not register births but did so for deaths. (He would have known this from his own experience; his father did not register Nicholas's birth at the parish church, presumably baptizing the child himself.) However, in the time that Graunt was studying, that is up to 1662, the Puritan clergy were still ensconced in the City parish churches and it was only some of the separatists or those opposed to the baptism of children who did not register baptisms with the parish. Barbon's argument would have more force after 1662 when Puritan clergy were ejected from their parishes, but even so it was unlikely to explain the difference in number.

Barbon was also concerned to avoid the charge that the growth of London depopulated the country, and produced some surprising arguments to suggest that the population increased faster in a city than the country:

> A sedentary life, good food, and warm clothing are the greatest friends to propagation and there are advantages to city life. Men that live in cities use not their bodies to so much labour as country employments require. And then the employments of the brain are better paid [...] and by being better paid they are better fed [...] better clothed and warmer housed. By this means their bodies are not so much exposed to the

> inconveniences of weather for too much heat or cold do either too much exhaust or chill the spirit. And that is the reason that all creatures that live wild do propagate in the spring or fall when the air is the most temperate and creatures that are kept tame, as pigeons and rabbits, do propagate oftener than wild because they are better fed, less in motion, and not so much exposed to the inconveniences of weather.

This ran completely counter to Graunt's conclusion that fertility was lower in the City, for which he gave a yet further reason, very different from Barbon: 'the minds of men in the London are more thoughtful, and full of business, than in the country, where their work is corporal labour and exercises, all which promote breeding whereas anxieties of the mind hinder it.'[50]

Barbon then produced perhaps his most startling statement, surely tongue in cheek, that the lack of building in London in the earlier part of the century meant that lack of housing compelled people to emigrate to New England, Virginia, and Barbados: 'How great an advantage so great a number of people which are in all these plantations would have been to the nation and what little profit they now yield is apparent to every man that considers.' While accepting that 'some are of the opinion but that [the migrations] were occasioned by the laws against dissenters from the Church of England', he backs up his view by pointing out that Cromwell's restriction on building in 1657 immediately preceded the plantation of Jamaica, even though 'there was then liberty of conscience'.[51]

By the middle of 1678 the argument about a tax on new building in and around London, whether to raise funds for the Crown or to restrict building, had been won.[52] What was still controversial, and remained so until the eighteenth century, was Barbon's argument about the merits of luxury expenditure and 'emulation'.[53] This was set out as follows:

> increasing of the inhabitants of a city increaseth the emulation of the people, and emulation increaseth industry and industry riches. There are two great causes of labour and industry, necessity of food and emulation. The necessity of hunger makes men industrious but when hunger is satisfied industry is at an end till a new provocation of hunger makes them work again and those people that have no other design but to satisfy that necessity continue always miserably poor [...] As the Proverb saith, when the belly is full the bones will be at rest. But emulation provokes a continued industry, and will not [...] be ever satisfied. The cobbler is always endeavouring to live as well as the shoemaker, and the shoemaker as well as any in the parish. So every neighbour and every artist is endeavouring to outvie each other, and all men by a perpetual industry are struggling to mend their former condition and thus the people grow rich which is the great advantage of a nation. And this benefit ariseth solely from cities, for in a country solitude there is little emulation for there if a man be fed and clothed he is a prince to himself for there is no body by him that is better fed and clothed.[54]

It may well have been that Barbon had been stimulated to promote the benefits of emulation by the swing of opinion against France, which had started in 1674 and led to a prohibition on French imports, many of which were considered luxurious, such as wine, linen, and brandy.[55] Barbon himself enjoyed the good things of life and made a point of flaunting his consumption at business meetings, as recalled by Roger North: 'Then he would make his entry, as fine and as richly dressed as a lord of the bedchamber on a birthday. And I must own I have often seen him so dressed.'[56]

Barbon was not merely promoting his desire for luxury. While a few months previously John Houghton had argued that wealth and display helped to prevent national decline, Barbon's approach was much more directed to demonstrating the economic merits of luxury consumption.[57] Emulation stimulated economic growth and could continue indefinitely. High taxes on luxuries, usually imported, were often promoted not just as a way of improving the balance of trade but, and probably thought more importantly, to act as a constraint on high living and what Locke called 'vices tending to prodigality'.[58]

CHAPTER V

EXPANSION: ST MARTIN'S LANE/SOHO, THE TEMPLE, NEWPORT GROUND AND WESTMINSTER

By 1677 Barbon had bought, developed and sold the Essex House site, had bought and largely developed Exeter House, and had a track record of rebuilding sites in the City that had been destroyed by the Great Fire. His *Discourse* of 1678 had set out his stall about the advantages to London and the nation of new building in and around the City and he was naturally already very actively engaged in this. By the mid-1670s the development for housing of land west of St Martin's Lane was well established. We have already seen Barbon build a house on St James's Square, and he was keen to do more and on a larger scale — he later explained to Roger North that 'it was not worth his while to deal little; that a bricklayer could do'.[1] For the rest of his life, with very few exceptions, he was to concentrate on larger sites.

These sites became available on a haphazard basis, often as the aristocratic owner found himself able to dispose of them, delays sometimes stemming from the issues involved in confirming unambiguous ownership or from a previous use being discontinued. Barbon bought them on an opportunistic basis as they came up, purchasing the freehold when it was available, but otherwise being content with a long lease, usually of up to sixty years. Some were greenfield sites while others required more or less demolition and reconstruction.

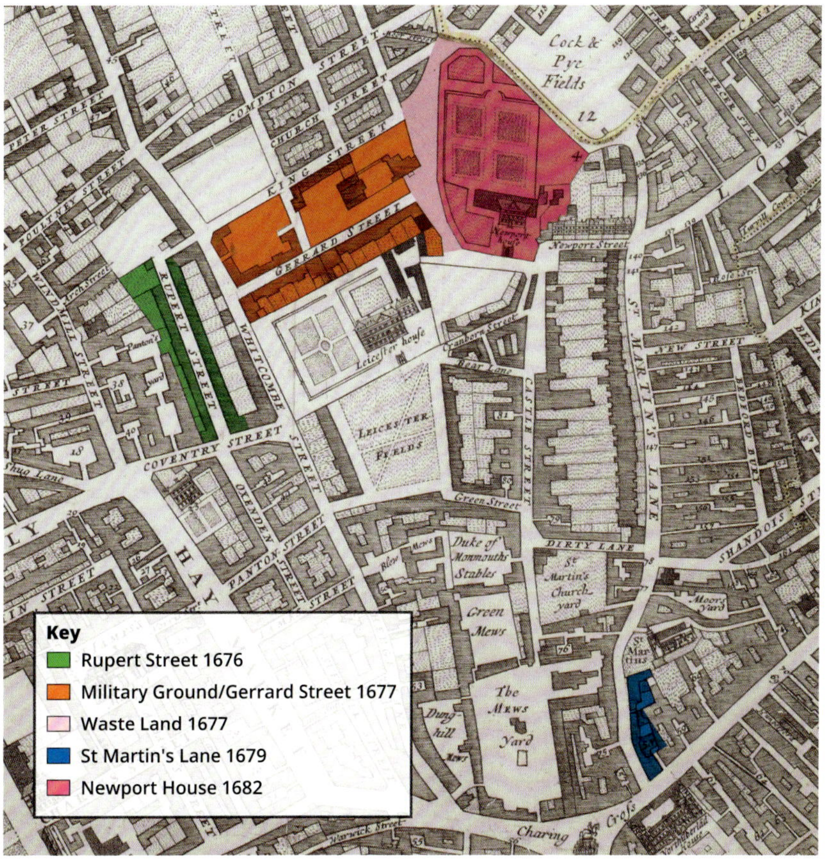

Fig. 29. Barbon's purchases near St Martin's Lane in 1676–79 and 1682, detail from Morgan's *London &c. Actually Survey'd*, 1682.

By permission of the British Library, Maps Crace Port. 2.58

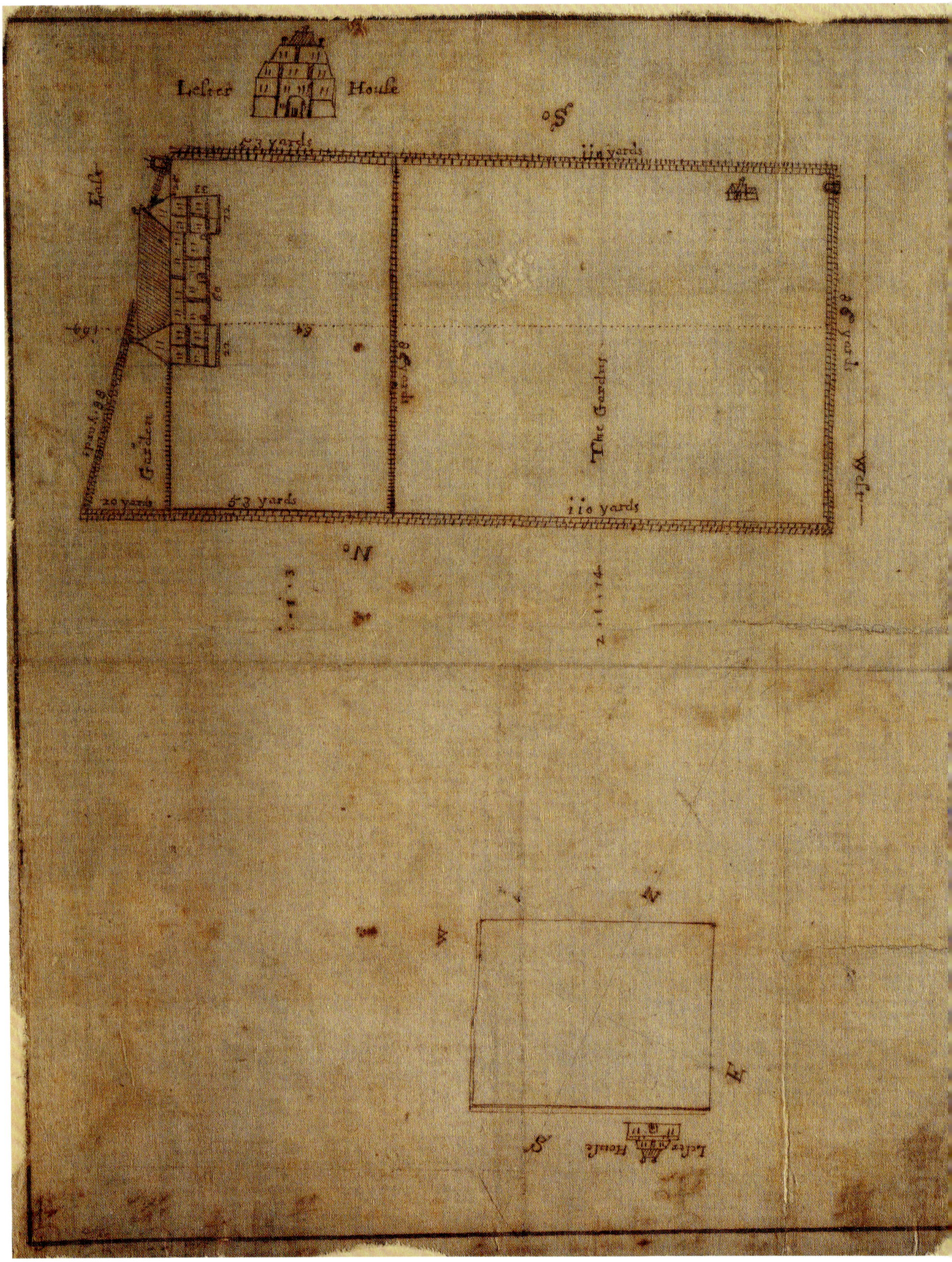
53 yards
110 yards
The Garden
Garden
20 yards
53 yards
110 yards
88 yards
N
S
W
E

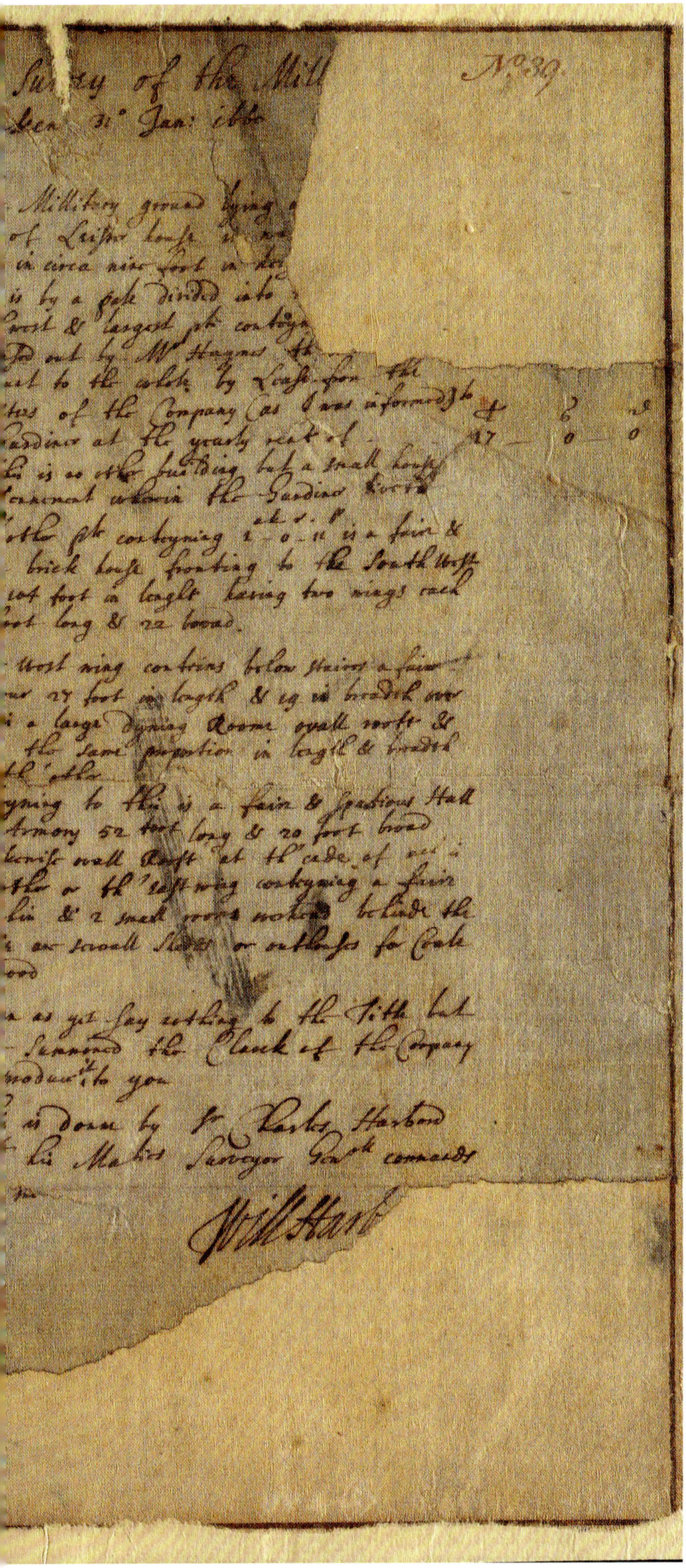

Between 1676 and 1679 he purchased four sites in the St Martin's Lane area, shown in Figure 29, based on the Morgan map of 1682. It also shows a fifth site, the nearby Newport House which he was to purchase in 1682. This represented a very large amount of potential development, not least because he had also taken advantage of two opportunities in the City, purchasing a site for two houses at College Hill near Thames Street as well as Old Devonshire House near Bishopsgate, the large house of the Cavendish family.

This large amount of development may have been the reason for Barbon failing to complete the College Hill houses, the last of his City developments, for more than ten years. At the Great Fire the site was owned by Sir Henry and Elizabeth Caesar; after their deaths their son, Sir Charles Caesar, negotiated the sale with the Skinners' Company and James Fairclough, a doctor who had several sites set out by the City Surveyors in other parts of the City. The Skinners' Company wished to add part of the ground to their hall and garden, entered from Dowgate Hill to the east. In 1674 the ground was sold by Caesar to Fairclough who immediately sold to the Skinners and by 1676 the Company had sold the unwanted parts to Sir John Moore for £1,000. The minutes of the Skinners' Court of Assistants show that Moore had been interested since at least May 1674 and that in 1675 he had been successful in persuading the Company not to insist on his leaving 20 feet of open ground between its garden wall and his proposed new buildings.

Barbon then approached Moore, asking to build on the land, 'expecting to make a considerable improvement thereby'. By 1678 a complicated deal had emerged whereby Barbon gained access to the site as part of a package also involving Crane Court and his house in St James's Square. Further complications followed as Barbon failed to make his contributions, always 'earnestly importuning' for extra time to

Fig. 30. Plan of the Military Ground, 1661.

pay. Although Barbon had promised to build quickly, Moore was still complaining to Chancery at the end of 1686 that the houses were unfinished.[2]

We also know of at least two other sites which he attempted to buy in this period but failed. One was Soho Fields for which he was outbid by Richard Frith, which led to the development around what is now Frith and Greek Streets, and another where his proposal for developing the Royal Mews at the bottom of St Martin's Lane was turned down by the Treasury. Given his general lack of capital, there was no possibility that he could proceed quickly with all these developments, even with the profits of up to £8,000 from the Essex Street development. It is not surprising that all these purchases were made jointly with one or more partners.

Rupert Street was probably the first purchase, as Henry Jermyn, the Earl of St Albans, sold the property very soon after being granted the freehold by Charles II in 1676. Building seems to have proceeded quickly and Morgan's map of 1682 shows the street as completed. In this case the original purchase had been made by Barbon, John Rowley, a timber merchant, and a third partner, the lawyer John Duckett with Barbon's former lawyer, Thomas Fountaine, again being involved, this time as their trustee.[3] A single street was constructed with no attempt made to provide connections with nearby development. An attempt in 1677 by Barbon to sell the leases of the houses closest to Piccadilly fell through because of outstanding mortgages and doubts about title, but shortly afterwards he sold the freehold of some of the houses for £3,600.[4] Strype described it as 'a pretty handsome, well-built street', but nothing now remains from the seventeenth century.[5]

His next purchase, in July 1677, was a 51-year lease of the Military Ground which includes all the land round Gerrard Street shown in Figure 29 which he bought from Lord Gerard, later the Earl of Macclesfield, together with some adjacent waste land. John Rowley was again his partner. This liaison would have difficulties since Rowley later went bankrupt and Barbon found himself temporarily in debtors' prison from having guaranteed some bonds for him.[6] Having been a military training ground, the site was largely clear except for the surrounding walls and an old armoury which may have been incorporated into the new houses (Fig. 30).

Barbon knocked down the walls with frontages to the west and to the north onto King Street but left the one on the south which formed the boundary with Leicester House. The new road, Gerrard Street, ran down the middle parallel to that boundary but he also needed to provide some decent access to his new street which would otherwise have been confined to the notoriously narrow Whitcomb Street.[7] He put in a new road, Macclesfield Street — named after Lord Gerard's new title, connected directly north with Dean Street and hence to the main Tyburn Road to Oxford.[8] His approach to maximizing the return on the site is demonstrated by his selling its grass for £3![9] Gerrard Street was then laid out with houses on the south side of the street, universally three storeys high with garrets, although of different widths, and with gardens running down to Leicester House.[10] Figure 31 shows one of these in the nineteenth century, No. 43 — next door to where John Dryden lived. The houses fronting onto the north of the street were, with two exceptions, smaller and less attractive.

Although Barbon had acquired the lease in July 1677, building was to take some considerable time, not being complete until at least eight years later. While he appears to have started at least some of the houses himself, including both the large Gerard House taken by the Earl of Macclesfield and what would be the house of the Earl, later Duke of Devonshire, he began letting leases to builders from 1678, often as part payment for work they had already done for him. In this way he was able to maintain some degree of consistency of style and this extended to the interiors which were wainscoted and painted.[11] Three houses were significantly larger than the rest, Gerard House facing the end of Macclesfield Street, shown in Figure 32 after conversion to shops, No. 9, Gerrard Street, the home of Lady Wiseman, and the house of the Earl of Devonshire at the east end of the street. Gerard House had a splendid staircase, built to the requirements of the first occupier (Fig. 33).

As well as these members of the aristocracy, there were several senior officials and politicians and by any standards it was a successful development. Strype described it in 1720 as 'a very good Street, well built, and inhabited by Gentry, and some Noblemen'.[12] Nevertheless, as was usual in the London of the time, the residents were mixed; the smaller houses were taken by tavern owners and tradespeople, including suppliers to the royal households. A row of these houses in a small road called Hayes Court, later Newport Place, east of the Earl of Devonshire's house, was named after either Barbon's wife or his sister-in-law, Rebecca Hayes, who had also taken building leases in the Essex Street development and

Fig. 31. No. 43 Gerrard Street, 1858, watercolour by John Wykeham Archer.

© Trustees of the British Museum, 1874,0314.30

Fig. 32. Gerard House, 1887, watercolour by J. Appleton.

Image © London Metropolitan Archives (City of London), no. 19642

Fig. 33. Staircase of Gerard House, 1884, watercolour by John Crowther.

Image © London Metropolitan Archives (City of London), no.29272

Fig. 34. Hayes Court from King Street, 1880, watercolour by J. P. Emslie.

Image © London Metropolitan Archives (City of London), no. 307639

would later build eighteen houses in Newport Ground. These are shown in a watercolour from 1880; while the shop fronts had been added later, the upper storeys appear seventeenth century.

Figure 35 shows the houses in and around Gerrard Street. The wide, central, part of what is now Newport Place (marked in red) was left open by Barbon, possibly because he intended, when he obtained possession of the Newport House site on the east, to lay out a square with the Earl of Devonshire's house on its north side. The open space is called 'Bearbone Square' on Rocque's map of 1746.

In 1673 the brewer, Joseph Girle, had leased Soho Fields from Henry Jermyn, the Earl of St Albans, and by 1676 he had obtained Letters Patent granting him full development rights. Barbon tried to buy these rights but lost out to Richard Frith in April 1677; however, he soon saw an opportunity to gain

Fig. 35. Gerrard Street development, marked on F. H. W. Sheppard, *Survey of London*, vol, 33: *St Anne Soho* (London, 1966), fig. 86, based on the Ordnance Survey, 1869–74, and a plan of 1660/1 (The National Archives, MPE 1/1083).

http://www.british-history.ac.uk/survey-london/vols33-4

some benefit from Frith's development. Before the development rights had been granted, Girle had already sublet some small sites for agricultural use. These were not owned by Frith, but he nevertheless proceeded to dig trenches across the land without permission, as of course Barbon did from time to time in other places. Barbon was already well acquainted with the site from his negotiations and when he saw Frith marking out and trenching the site in 1677, he bought the subleases himself, acting through the agency of one of the sublessees whose land he had already agreed to purchase as part of the attempt to buy the whole site. Even though the sublessees were smart enough to recognize that they were in a buyers' market, and Barbon's agent complained that he was not getting paid enough, Barbon was able to ensure that Frith had 'to alter all the streets and mark them to be placed on another part of the field'.[13] Figure 36 shows the relationship between Frith's land in Soho Fields (blue) and Barbon's (red). The street that would have had to be most changed as a result was Dean Street, but its present course is uninterrupted, suggesting that Barbon eventually agreed to be bought off.[14] Frith sold the head lease in the early 1680s and the purchaser leased the potentially blocking piece of land to Barbon who developed it over the next few years.[15]

Barbon's final development in this area was on the eastern side of St Martin's Lane, south of the church. Here he demolished the old Swan Inn in 1679, rebuilt it and the other dwellings and did a number of deals with the parish, selling ground to widen the road and provide more space for the graveyard. As well as his receiving £350 for this, the parish granted his 'lady' (who had lived in the parish before her marriage) a piece of silver plate worth £20.[16] The buildings, one inn and fifteen other houses, became a package that he used to underpin his fire insurance company. The ground rents were high, £100 for the Swan Inn and over £90 for the six houses in Hunt's Court, described by Strype as 'a pretty handsome square Court, with five or six good built and inhabited houses, having a good air from a garden on the east side, and hath a

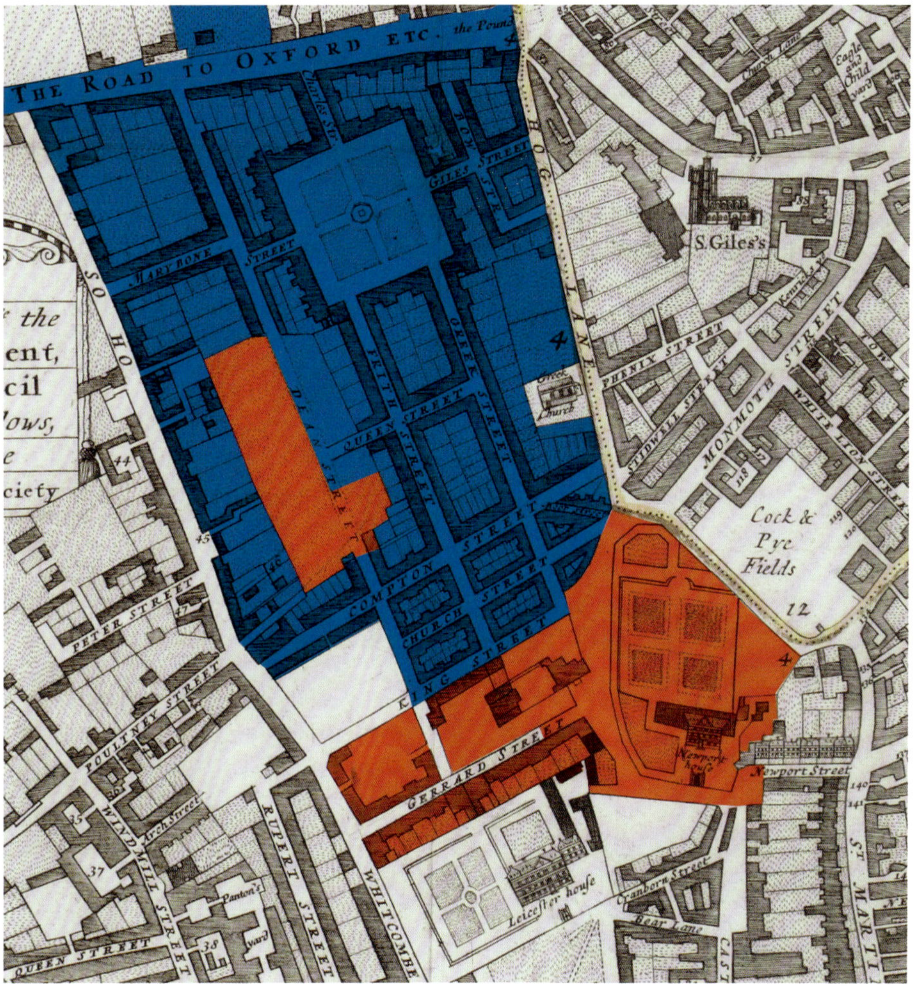

Fig. 36. Barbon's (red) and Frith's (blue) lands in Soho Fields, detail from Morgan's *London &c. Actually Survey'd*, 1682.

By permission of the British Library, Maps Crace Port. 2.58

free stone pavement, with a door at the entrance, to shut up a nights for the security of its inhabitants'.[17] Figure 37 shows St Martin's Lane in 1825, including Hunt's Court. Altogether the St Martin's Lane site generated almost £350 p.a. in ground rents and Barbon received around £7,000 for their leases in 1683.

Fig. 37. St Martin's Lane, 1825, drawing by George Scharf.

Middle Temple

At the beginning of 1679 another opportunity arose for which Barbon was well placed to take advantage. A very bad fire in the Middle Temple destroyed many of the buildings — despite beer from a nearby brewery being used to try to put the fire out. Figure 38, using the Ogilby map of 1676, shows the extent of the fire.[18] The map reflects the position before Barbon rebuilt the west side of Essex Court and it is instructive to note that his new building there was not burnt down, probably because it had been built in a more substantial manner than the Temple's older, probably timber-framed, buildings which were described as 'better burnt than left, being for the most part such ragged deformed stuff'.[19] This was the first time that Roger North, then a junior barrister in the Middle Temple, came across Barbon and they became well acquainted. He took a close interest in the rebuilding and ended up very supportive of Barbon, although fully aware of the potential problems in employing him, describing them in some detail.[20]

The fire occurred at a time when there was much argument between the Benchers of the Inn, who controlled decision-making, and the rank-and-file barristers. Neither side trusted the other to look after anything but their own interests. A major argument was whether the rebuilding should take place on the same foundations as before or whether the opportunity should be taken to redesign the courts and provide additional accommodation. In the event the latter course was chosen, but this meant that the new chambers were not always in the same position or the same size as the former, raising all kinds of questions about allocation. There was the further question of how to finance the Benchers' chambers, historically occupied for free.

The first solution to the financing issues was to raise funds by selling the gardens and waste land, and the then Treasurer of the Middle Temple, William Ettrick, did a deal with someone described as his cousin and kinsman.[21] This was John Fitch, a member of a family responsible for many state and military construction projects and, like Ettrick, with Dorset connections.[22] Unfortunately, Fitch started work without sorting out who would pay for it and, when he started digging up the gardens and cutting down trees, there was uproar and he was forced to abandon the project. It was at this stage that

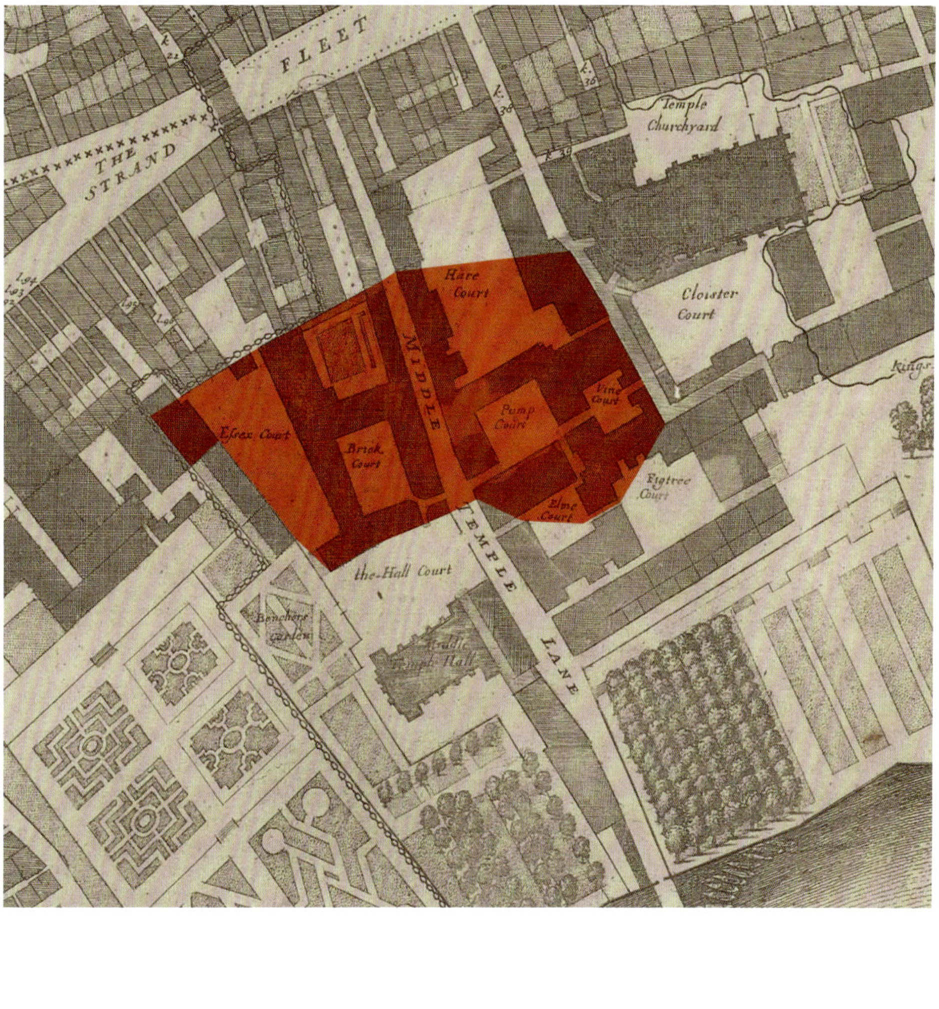

Fig. 38. Extent of 1679 fire in Middle Temple, detail from Ogilby and Morgan's *Large and Accurate Map of London*, 1676.

By permission of the British Library, Maps Crace Port. 2.61

Barbon came into the picture. He was already well known to the Middle Temple from his, previous activities, including building New and Garden Courts and rebuilding Nos 2–3 Essex Court. In addition he understood the Temple's desire to increase the amount of accommodation available and had a plan to achieve that. Crane Court was nearby and so he was a neighbour, and his extensive use of the law in his dealings naturally ensured he knew many of the individual lawyers.

North makes clear that Barbon was particularly suited to this job, commenting:

> He had dealt before with the Society [...] He knew our way of disposing our rooms, what conveniences we had need of, and being a very good contriver could apply to serve not only our occasions but our fancies; and likewise knew the state of our interests, and the value of them, and what profit was to be made by dealing with us. And in general he knew the best way of access to the business and how to make his profit out of it.

The new arrangement of the buildings is shown in a plan drawn up in 1732 (Fig. 39) to formalize the division of the Temple site between the Middle and Inner Temples.[23] This shows the changes that were made in 1679. Brick Court was opened up to Middle Temple Lane with a new building separating Essex and Brick Courts and another new building on the north of Essex and Brick Courts.

The problem was how to satisfy all the members who wished to maintain if not improve their accommodation while making sure to cover the financial interests of the Benchers, who did not expect to have to contribute. Knowing of the recent controversies, Barbon applied himself directly to the members — North commenting that this was the right way 'in a mob age' — and first put up a 'straw man' involving an independent assessment of the value of each set of chambers with those with higher value chambers being given priority in allocation. This was easily dismissed, since no one was prepared to accept independent assessment, and Barbon then proposed that everyone should have a chamber in the new building as near as possible to where their old one had been, paying more if it was bigger than his old one, and correspondingly less if smaller. After some uncertainty, North himself accepted this approach and decided to 'drive it through' against the opposition which 'met at taverns, and several

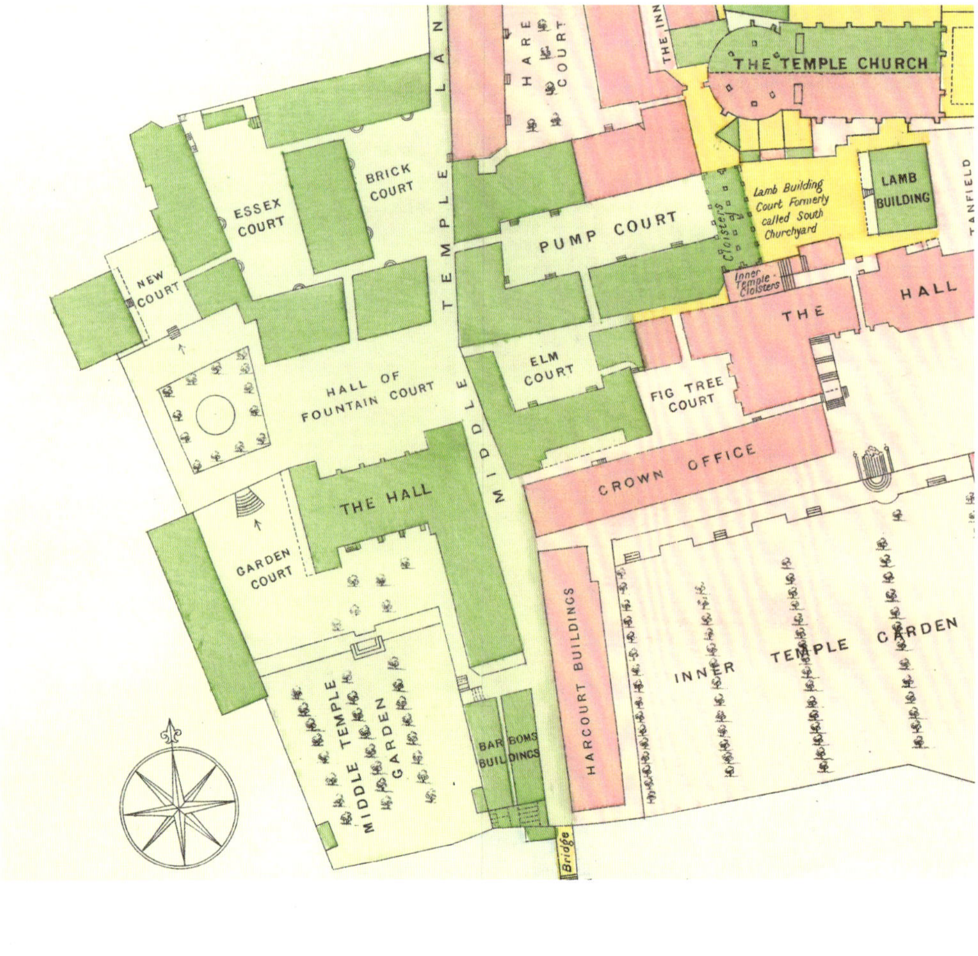

Fig. 39. Plan of Middle Temple in 1732 from Charles Worsley, *Master Worsley's Book on the History and Constitution of the Honourable Society of the Middle Temple* (1732), ed. A. R. Ingpen (London, 1910), p. 274. Image used by kind permission of The Honourable Society of the Middle Temple

times sallied down upon the buildings, and threw down what they could, and we were never safe till the walls were out of reach, and then they acquiesced'.

North himself had started with a ground-floor set of chambers on the south side of Essex Court on the west side next to the Benchers' garden. This building is now No. 1 Essex Court (Fig. 40) and was rebuilt by Barbon with two sets of chambers per floor; the accounts include five assigned to individual members while three became Bencher's chambers. After the rebuild North was able to move to the second floor on the same staircase which he regarded as his good fortune and retained it until 1717.[24] A slightly later addition was made when what had been an old banqueting hall on the north-east side of the fountain was rebuilt with approval being given in 1683. This provided one extra room to the four chambers at the west end of Essex Court, and a sundial at the top of the south elevation of No. 1 Fountain Court carries the date 1685, presumably to mark the completion of the extra building.[25] We do not know whether Barbon was involved in this addition which would have been around the time he had signed off the rebuilding project in early 1684.[26]

The biggest changes were for Brick Court. Figure 38 shows that the pre-fire buildings had run the length of what was then a smaller Essex Court than now, and along the side of Middle Temple Lane. They were replaced by an entirely new building (Nos 2 and 3 Brick Court) in the middle of the two Courts, as well as new buildings along the north and south side of the Courts (Nos 1 and 4 Brick Court; see Fig. 39).

None of those buildings remain now. No. 3 Brick Court, the more northerly of the two in the middle, had been burnt down in 1704 and rebuilt, but at the request of its residents was made two feet higher than previously.[27] Together with No. 2, it survived until destroyed by bombs in the Second World War, and Figure 41 shows Nos 2 and 3 Brick Court with No. 4 at the end, as they were in 1882. As can be seen, the more northerly of the two is slightly higher than the other and we can assume that Nos 2 and 4 are the buildings Barbon erected, with of course any later modifications. No. 4 Brick Court, with No. 5 Essex Court, was rebuilt in 1883 and No. 1 Brick Court was demolished and rebuilt in 1908 (see the plan at Fig. 49).[28]

The rebuilding of Pump Court was more complicated and Barbon did not rebuild all the burnt chambers there. This was probably because No. 6 Pump Court on the north side was essentially one building with No. 1 Hare Court of the Inner Temple and it made sense for them to be rebuilt as one. Although at first it seemed likely that Barbon would act as contractor for the Inner Temple as well, the Inner Temple soon rejected this, sticking to its normal method of expecting residents of chambers to finance any rebuilding.[29] Accordingly, the tenants of the chambers on the north side of Pump Court petitioned to be allowed to repair their chambers themselves rather than have them rebuilt by Barbon.[30] The financing may have been easier for them because the set included no Bench chambers and permission to use their own builders was granted, provided they paid Barbon an agreed amount of compensation. Given the north facade in Pump Court is largely the same as the others, it would appear that the Middle Temple made the same stipulation as for Nos 2–3 Essex Court, that it should be 'built alike with brick and adorned with stone like Dr Barbon's building'.[31]

Fig. 40. No. 1 Essex Court, Middle Temple, 2022.
Photograph by Sheila O'Connell. Image used by kind permission of The Honourable Society of the Middle Temple

The account book for the chambers built by Barbon after the Fire is still in the Middle Temple's possession and records the payments received by Barbon as compensation for not building on the north side of Pump Court and confirming that he did build the remainder, that is Nos 1–5.[32] The south side was bombed in the Second World War and rebuilt in 1952, but the west side, corresponding to Nos 4 and 5, still remains (see Fig. 42). No. 6 was set higher than the others in the Court because of the need to maintain levels with Hare Court on the north side of the building.

One of the attractions of Barbon for the Middle Temple was his ability to use the rebuilding to increase the number of chambers. Examples included his redesigning of Brick and Essex Courts and his combining Pump and Vine Courts. The cloisters at the east end of this rebuilt Court provided another opportunity. The original cloisters were of one floor only and Barbon, with an eye for making the most of a site, had proposed replacing them with a solid building to provide more sets of chambers; the Inner Temple wanted to retain the cloisters in their old state. At first the two could not agree and this may have been the cause of the Inner Temple changing its mind on using Barbon. Both Inns then embarked separately and competitively on reconstruction work, while the Inner Temple proceeded to legal action against its fellow lawyers.[33] The Inner Temple account books record the payment of £3 'to the laborers for three severall tymes throwing in the earth upon the Middle Temple digging their foundacon in the Cloysters'.[34] Meanwhile Barbon had included in his contract a clause 'indemnifying him from all charge damage which may be sustained by any opposition from the Inner Temple'.[35]

Barbon's first sketch for the rebuilding of the cloisters (Fig. 43) included proposals for land in both Middle and Inner Temples,[36] and although his proposal does take in extra ground over the original cloisters, they would have been narrower than he would suggest later or what was eventually built.

There is also a plan (Fig. 44) showing how Barbon intended to organize the structural timbers in his first proposal for maintaining the cloisters, although it is not clear exactly how this is related to the pillars in the cloisters themselves.[37] It was in any case overtaken by the wider cloisters proposed by Wren.

The story is usually that resolution came after mediation by the Lord Chancellor and the adoption of a fresh plan prepared by Sir Christopher Wren with the elegant compromise of retaining the cloisters but increasing their width with a larger building above. Mediation was indeed provided by the Lord Chancellor, but this was after Wren had produced very significant criticism of Barbon's second proposals.

Fig. 41. Nos 2, 3 and 4 Brick Court, Middle Temple, 1882, watercolour by John Crowther.

Image © London Metropolitan Archives (City of London), no.17991

Fig. 42. Nos 4–5 Pump Court, Middle Temple, 2022.

Photograph by Sheila O'Connell. Image used by kind permission of The Honourable Society of the Middle Temple

Wren wrote that Barbon's proposed pillars were too small as well as too far apart 'either for beauty or necessary strength', the floors too wide for stability, and the chimneys a fire hazard. His conclusion was 'I cannot but judge it too weak and insufficient'.[38] Whatever the souce of Barbon's proposals, this criticism is strong evidence that Barbon was not actually a builder, let alone an architect. As later chapters will make clear, there is no evidence that he had the requisite knowledge.

We can compare the two proposals from the sketches still in the Middle Temple Archive (Figs 45 and 46). Barbon's does not show the pillars in the middle which, although included in his proposal, as they were in the earlier one, did not have the walls of the higher floors placed directly above them. It is instructive that Barbon provided for three shops, again to improve the commercial return.

Barbon retained responsibility for building the Cloisters and the accounts book shows that he allocated a number of chambers in those staircases while the builder, John Foltrop, had to be given another £250 by the Middle Temple for the additional work contained in the new design. In view of Wren's criticisms of Barbon's proposals it is ironic that the Benchers were supposed to be worried about the stability of his own design and asked for greater support. The story goes that he provided extra columns but contrived that they stopped an inch before the ceiling so gave no more support. Wren's cloisters were destroyed by bombing in the Second World War so this story can no longer be authenticated.[39]

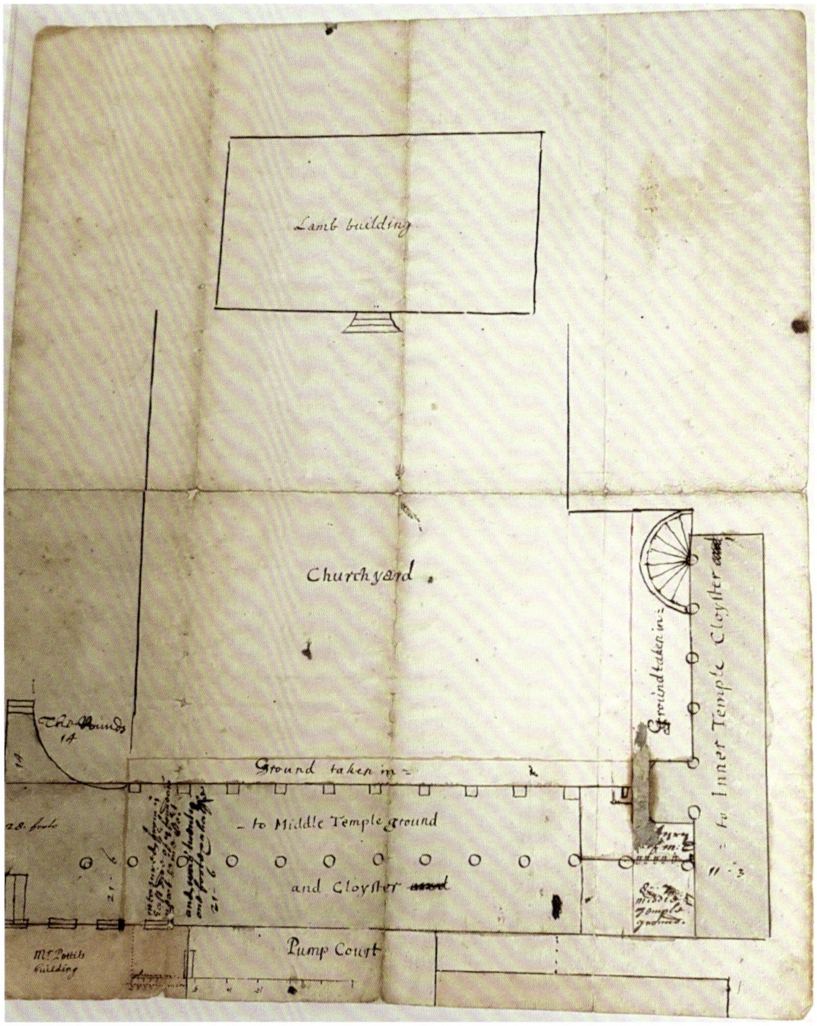

Fig. 43. Barbon's first proposals for the cloisters.
Image used by kind permission of The Honourable Society of the Middle Temple; Middle Temple Archive, MT.6/RBW/17

We do not have a picture of Wren's cloisters as they were originally built by Barbon; one, Figure 48, taken in 1929, shows substantial differences to Wren's elevation, and the result seems less consciously architectural than his design. It has eight arches rather than seven, the eaves cornice has been replaced by a parapet, the north-east tower has gone, and each floor has a string course rather than, as in Wren's design, only at first- and third-floor level.

The only one of these changes that was due to Barbon, or possibly to his builder Foltrop, was the addition of the third string course which may have been introduced as a practical builder's solution to providing a good anchorage for beams. The other sets of chambers that Barbon built in the Middle Temple all have this third string and its reintroduction would have ensured the continuity of the line round Nos 1–5 Pump Court. The other changes all took place in the nineteenth century. The eaves cornice was replaced by the parapet walls, as they were on many other of his chambers, while the tower at the north-east of the cloisters in Wren's elevation was taken down as a result of Robert Smirke's restoration of the Temple Church in 1825, which placed the staircase on the north side of the cloisters, rather than projecting east, and so introduced the eighth arch.[40]

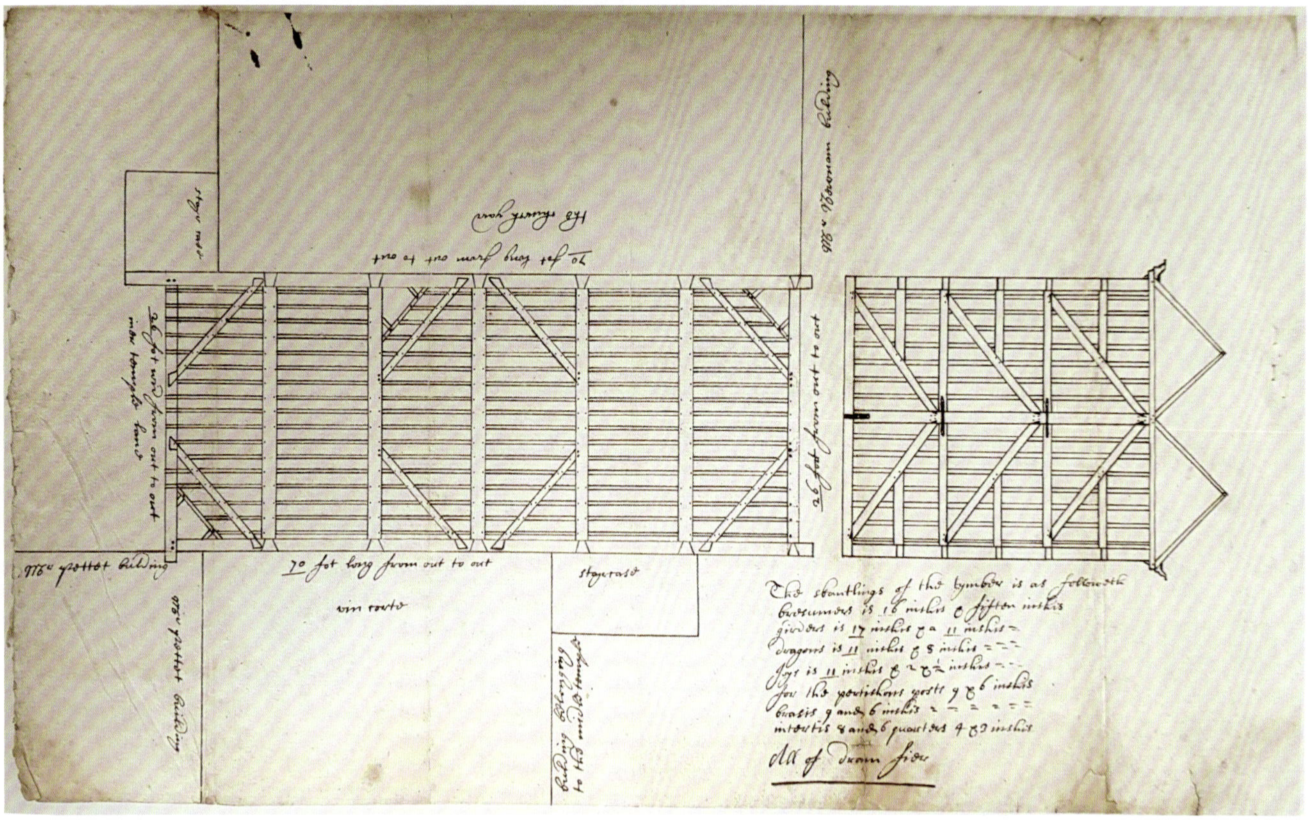

Fig. 44. Barbon's proposals for structural timbers in a cloisters building.
Image used by kind permission of The Honourable Society of the Middle Temple; Middle Temple Archive, MT.6/RBW/17

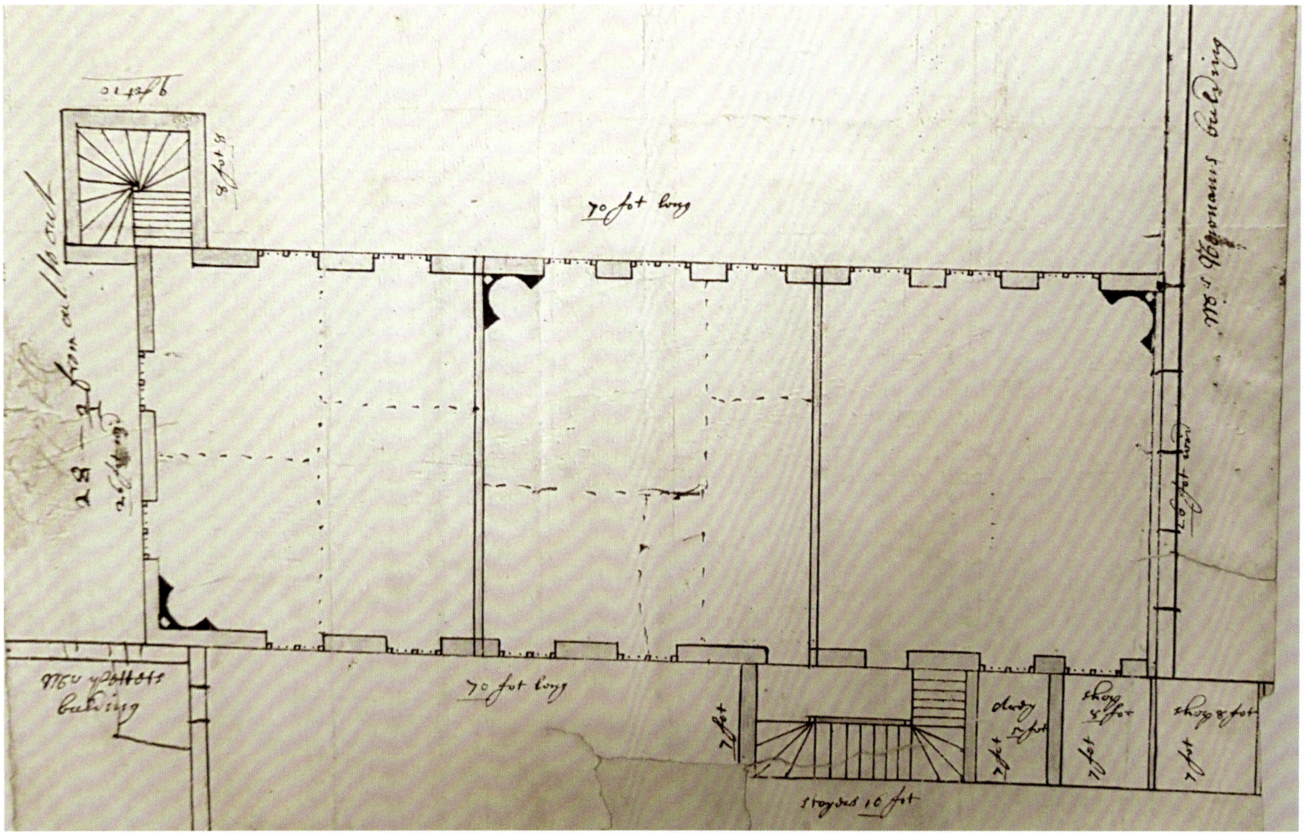

Fig. 45. Barbon's proposals for Middle Temple building.
Image used by kind permission of The Honourable Society of the Middle Temple; Middle Temple Archive, MT.6/RBW 18, 5–7

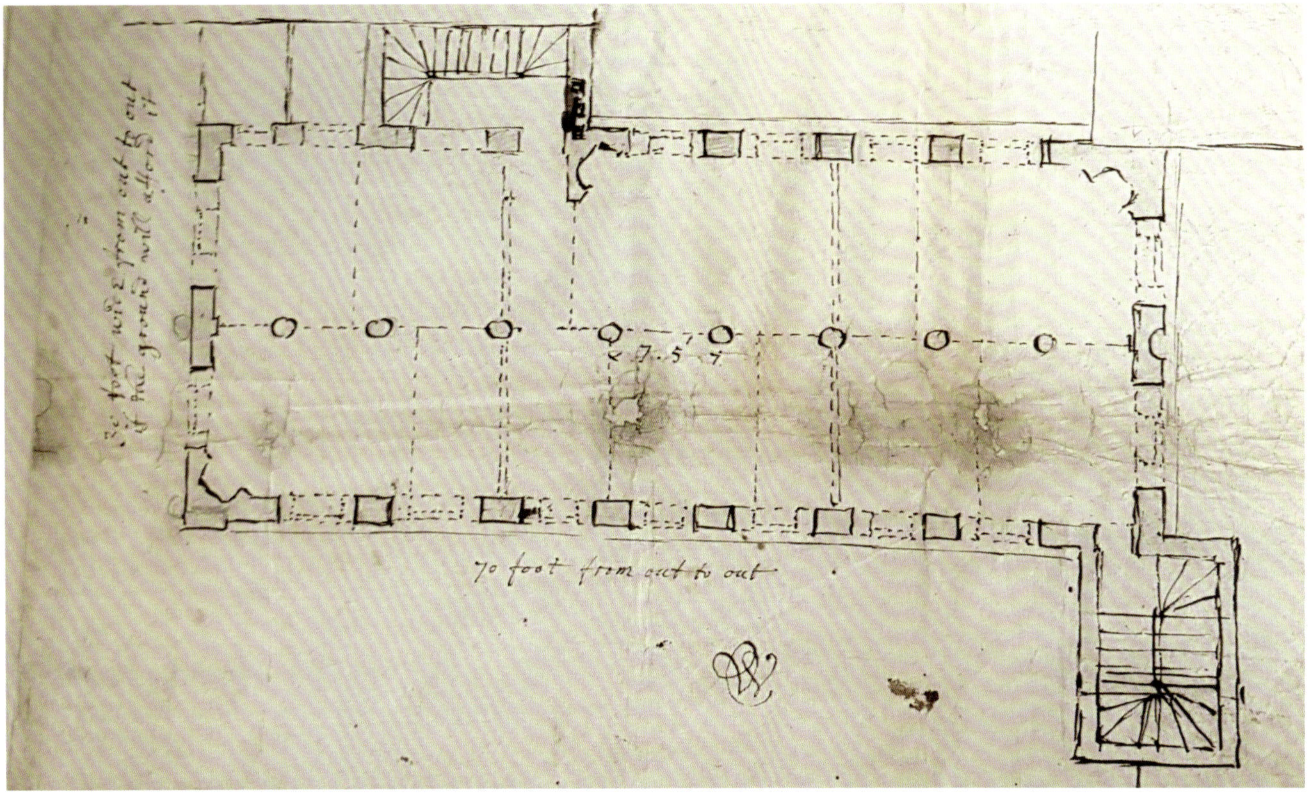

Fig. 46. Wren's proposals for Middle Temple cloisters.
Image used by kind permission of The Honourable Society of the Middle Temple; Middle Temple Archive, MT.6/RBW 18, 2

Fig. 47. Wren's sketch of facade of Middle Temple cloisters.
Image used by kind permission of The Honourable Society of the Middle Temple; Middle Temple Archive, MT.6/RBW 18, 2

Fig. 48. Middle Temple Cloisters, from *An Inventory of the Historical Monuments in London*, vol. 4, *The City* (London: RCHME, 1929).

The cloisters were not the only cause of difficulties with building Barbon's chambers which, as North describes it, did not proceed without incident. Not only were there those who tried to prevent the agreed plans, but there were continued arguments between the members over who was entitled to have their chambers built first and quarrels about the destination of deliveries of bricks. In some cases, the bricks were substandard and only usable for inside walls rather than on the outside facing, although it was not clear whether this was the fault of the brick suppliers or of Barbon trying to build on the cheap.[41] North attributed these problems to Barbon continually being short of cash but concluded that in the end the building was 'happily finished'. It was during North's time as Middle Temple Treasurer in 1684 that Barbon was eventually given a gratuity of one hundred guineas.[42] He would continue to build in the Middle Temple for at least the rest of that decade. Many of his buildings still survive, even if often altered through the centuries, but as for almost all his work, there is nothing stylistic that can be used to identify them as by Barbon rather than by any other seventeenth-century contractor. Figure 49 shows the extent of Barbon's buildings

Fig. 49. Barbon's buildings in Middle Temple. Based on https://assets.templemusic.org/media/514/original/e780fccd4543479b4043.jpg

Image used by kind permission of The Honourable Society of the Middle Temple in the Middle Temple and what happened to them. It includes both buildings within the original boundary of the Middle Temple and those outside but acquired more recently in Devereux Court and Essex Street.

Near Original	New Court	1676
	32, 34 Essex Street	1676 some refronting
	35 Essex Street	1676 some refronting
	2–3 Essex Court	1677
	1 Essex Court	1680
	4 (north), 5 Pump Court	1680
Rebuilt	1, 2 Garden Court (later 3–4)	1676 rebuilt 1883
	Devereux Chambers	1676 stuccoed etc 1790
	33 Essex Street	1676 rebuilt 1881
	24–27 Essex Street (now Blackstone House)	1676 rebuilt 1953 and later
	5 Essex Court	1680 rebuilt 1882
	4 Brick Court	1680 rebuilt 1882
	1 Brick Court	1680 rebuilt 1908
Bombed	9 Devereux Court	1676 rebuilt 1952
	1–4 Pump Court	1680 rebuilt 1952
	Cloisters	1682 rebuilt 1952
	3–4 Garden Court (later 3-6 Plowden Buildings now Ashley building)	1688 rebuilt 1958

Newport Ground

George Porter, a descendant of the Earl of Newport, had tried for some time to sell Newport House east of Gerrard Street but was only able to do so when he came of age in 1681. Being so close to Barbon's other developments it is not surprising that he bought it, paying £9,500 for the five-acre freehold of house and garden. This was promptly mortgaged to some of his usual financial partners, Roger Jackson, Sir James Ward and two trustees on behalf of Thomas Price, who in turn borrowed from Felix Calvert.[43] By 1684 the site was providing security for over £30,000 of borrowing, all but £8,000 down to Barbon himself. While there was no doubt at least a degree of using the same security more than once, such a large difference can only be explained by the mortgage of the ground rents based on putative future income. The whole financial operation was then put at risk by the bankruptcy of the major creditor, the goldsmith Thomas Price who was indebted to Charles II 'in a great sume of money', resulting in his interest in Newport Ground being seized by the Crown for satisfaction of the debt. There followed five years of legal wrangling in the Court of Exchequer where all the different mortgagees had to prove their entitlement, resulting in Barbon being ordered to sell. He finally did so in 1690, receiving £22,600, all of which went to his mortgagors.[44]

The small matter of these legal battles did nothing to stop Barbon from proceeding with the development. He demolished the house, again making the most reuse of the materials, and began issuing building leases in July 1683. When all these leases were issued, they produced £1,000 annual ground rent, providing the basis, with one or two additions, for the price received by Barbon in 1690. The layout is shown in red in Figure 50, although Barbon did not get the licence for the market in the middle of Newport Ground until April 1686.

Grafton Street and Porter Street were two of the first streets completed and had a heavy concentration of Huguenots, many of whom were goldsmiths or active in related trades. This was the reason for the presence of the Huguenot church there, the community having taken over in 1682 the church built by the Greek Orthodox Church. It appears that the Greek Archbishop had first approached Barbon in 1676, who had promptly offered to build one, at his expense, in his Gerrard Street development where Figure 35 shows there was indeed a chapel. However, when the Archbishop told the Bishop of London of this, the Bishop intervened to persuade Richard Frith to provide the land as part of the deal with St Martin's which led to the building of the main parish church of Soho, St Anne's.[45] Frith did the bricklaying himself, albeit with substandard bricks provided by his lessor Joseph Girle.[46]

Litchfield Street, started in 1684 but not completed until 1691, was more fashionable than the other streets on the Newport Ground estate with several titled inhabitants, leading Strype to describe it as 'a place furnished with good buildings and well inhabited'.[47] There is now very little remaining from the seventeenth century but a watercolour from 1883 shows Porter Street to the left and Litchfield Street to the right (Fig. 51).

While Newport Court had been occupied by Huguenots shortly after its construction, it degenerated later and became known as Butchers Row. Figures 52 and 53 show this as in 1881 and 1886 respectively. Those on the north side (on left in Fig. 52) were demolished in the 1880s while the south survived (Fig. 53). The only houses remaining from Barbon's time (still with the ground floor as shop fronts) are Nos 21–24a, the run of four three-storey houses in Figure 53 with the nine windows irregularly spaced.

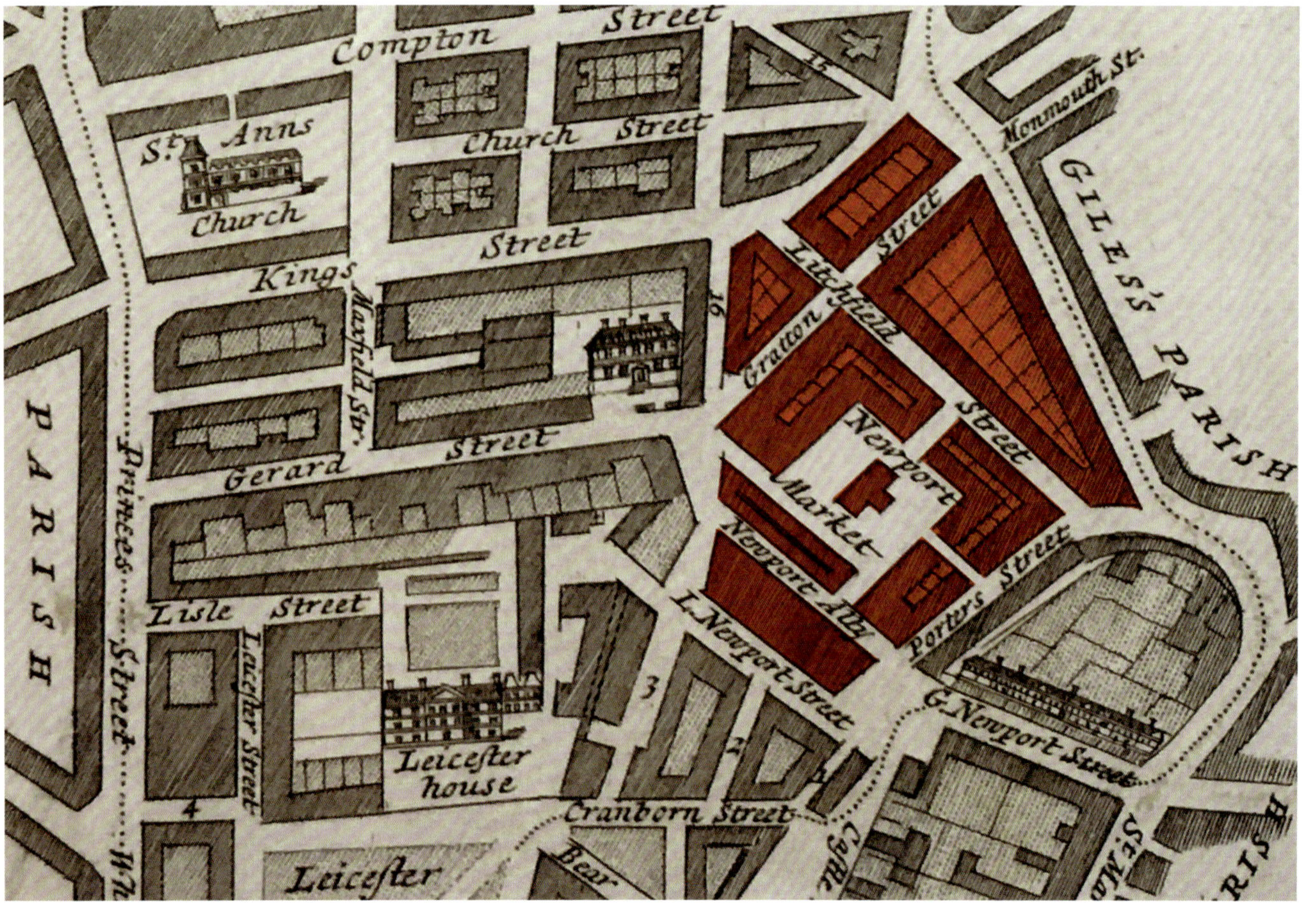

Fig. 50. Newport Ground, detail from Richard Blome's Map of St Anne's Parish, *c.* 1700. Grafton Street has been misspelt as 'Gratton' Street.

By permission of the British Library, Maps Crace Port. 12.36

Fig. 51. Porter Street and Litchfield Street, 1883, watercolour by J. P. Emslie.

Image © London Metropolitan Archives (City of London), no. 307637

Fig. 52. Newport Court looking east, 1881, watercolour by J. P. Emslie.

Image © London Metropolitan Archives (City of London), no. 307653

Fig. 53. Newport Court looking west, 1886, watercolour by J. P. Emslie.

Image © London Metropolitan Archives (City of London), no. 307656

By August 1686 Barbon had mortgaged the market rights and leases on pieces of ground used for the market to some merchants for £2,000. The market became a great success, generating an annual gross profit of £250, albeit with maintenance costs to pay; Defoe described it as one of London's principal meat markets.[48] The value of the market and its rights led to great legal complications and it was finally bought by Sir Nathaniel Curzon in 1692 for £2,149 10s., the sum then owing on the mortgages. Barbon did, however, retain the equity of redemption (the right of the original mortgagor, even if in default, to pay off all outstanding principal with interest and costs and reclaim the property) which was one of the assets he bequeathed in his will. Curzon later purchased this from the executors for £2,000.

St Margaret's Westminster

Barbon continued to be active in the parish of St Margaret's Westminster and his various sites are shown in Figure 55. We saw his first foray in 1675 when he redeveloped the site of Trevor House and sold it on quickly (see p. 43). His next, in 1682, saw a much more significant development as he purchased a large number of existing leases and buildings including at least two taverns, demolished them and created two new streets, Charles Street and Duke Street, financed by the goldsmith Thomas Price and with the involvement of his long-standing lawyer Thomas Fountaine.[49] Some of it he repackaged and sold very quickly to Sir John Shorter, a future Lord Mayor. The rest provided some difficulty since he had purchased leases from several owners, knocked down the houses and built new ones, but not with the same boundaries. This made difficult the establishment of unambiguous ownership of any of the land and buildings, but this did not deter Barbon. As he said, 'he did not know the title to all the estate, they being a late purchaser of the premises, leaving this to counsel', but was able to put together a package worth about £600 in annual rent. He first agreed a sale to Edward Buckley, a brewer and Fire Office associate, for £11,000 in 1682, but in the event the deal was for £8,900, perhaps because Buckley was (rightly) concerned about the validity of Barbon's title.

Three years later one of the freeholders (who had previously refused Barbon's offer for the freehold) arrived in London, discovered that the original houses on his and others' land had been demolished, but could not tell whether the new houses were wholly or partially on his land or not.[50] The solution was to sell the freehold to Barbon and Thomas Price, the goldsmith financing the deal. A deal was done but Barbon took no steps to pass on the effects to Buckley who had in the meantime been happily receiving the ground rents. Litigation followed two years later when Barbon had failed to pay for the freehold.

Charles Street, running down to St James's Park was an attractive street and it was not difficult to find tenants. Strype described it as 'a fine large street with good houses well inhabited'.[51] A plan attached to one of the Close Rolls recording the sale is shown in Figure 54.

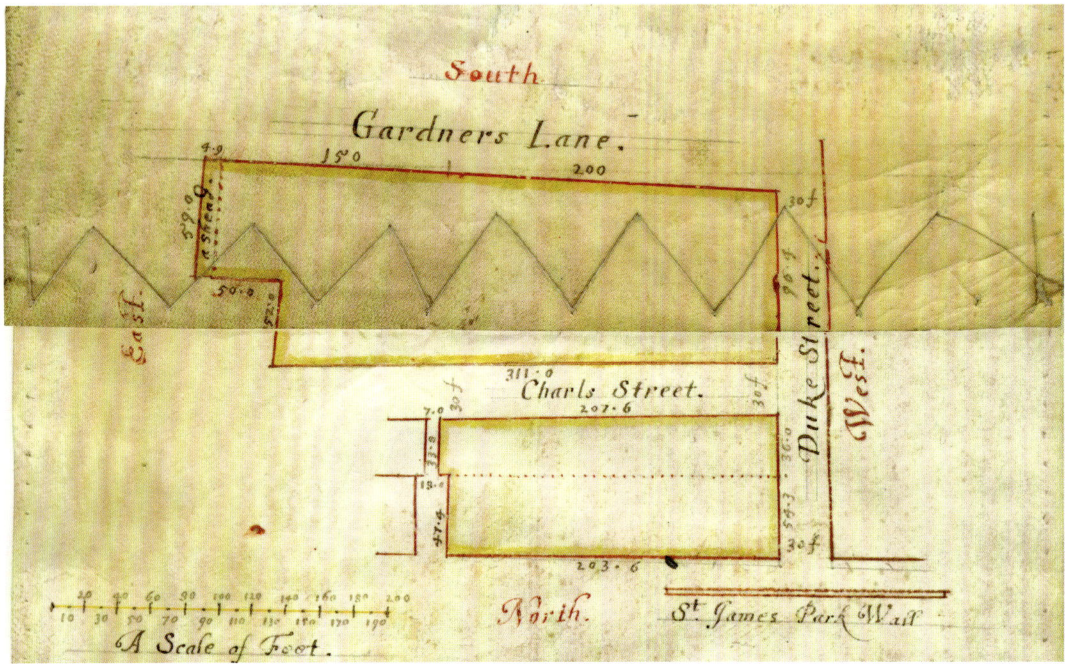

Fig. 54. Plan of Barbon's Charles Street site.
© The National Archives, C 54/4576

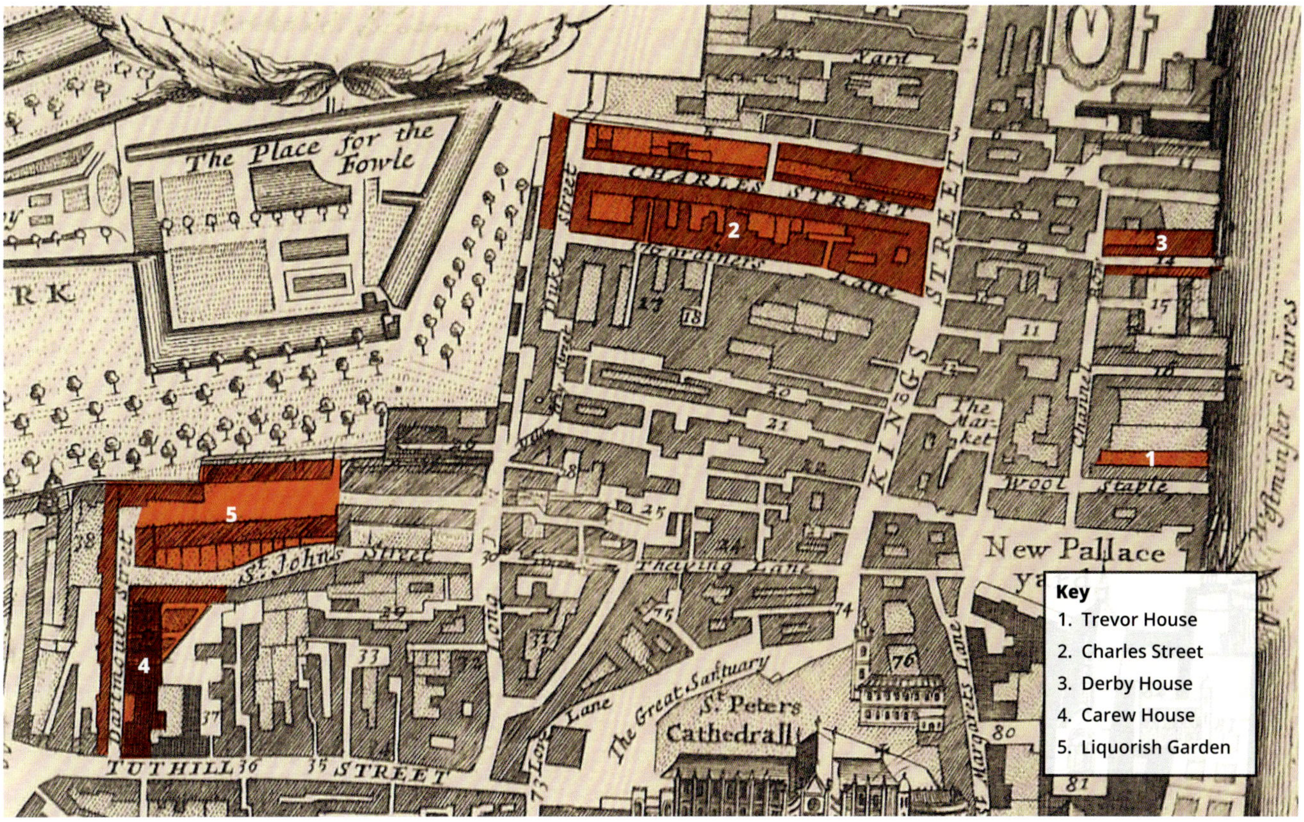

Fig. 55. Barbon's building in Westminster, detail from Richard Blome's map of the Parish of St Margaret, Westminster, *c.* 1700.
By permission of the British Library, Maps Crace Port. 11.7.(1.)

Duke Street had the advantage on its west side of overlooking the Park to which the houses often had a private entrance. Barbon created a building lease for one of these in 1683, letting it to the timber merchant John Banks, but another five ran into difficulties on top of the ambiguity about title.[52] One of Barbon's financiers was the goldsmith Michael Scrimshire, and Barbon was indeed his largest debtor, owing over £10,000.[53] As a result, he had assigned Scrimshire a number of his assets, including the leases on the ground on the west side of Duke Street. Unfortunately, Scrimshire went bankrupt in April 1683, and the trustees of the bankruptcy naturally laid claim to those leases. This further doubt about whether Barbon had good title must have reinforced the difficulty for him in raising the substantial funds to build the new houses that were needed to allow him to realize any profits from the site. In any case, most, if not all, of the profits would have gone to the bankruptcy trustees, hardly giving him an incentive to proceed. Neither was Price in any position to take things forward as he too became bankrupt at the end of 1685.[54] The houses remained barely started with complaints that Barbon had left building rubbish on the other side of the wall in St James's Park.[55] It was not until 1695 that the trustees borrowed £4,500 to pay the builder John Foltrop to finish the five houses. They were then let very profitably, with one being tenanted by the widow of Judge Jeffreys, albeit only for a short time.[56]

A further opportunity came up with the sale of Derby House. A grand house, taken by government in the Civil War and giving its name to the Derby House Committee, it had been used by the Admiralty for some time. Samuel Pepys wrote many letters from there after he became Secretary in 1673 and his name appears in the rate book for the house. The Earl of Derby believed that the Commissioners of the Navy had been interested in buying the house from him and told his agent to try them out at £3,000, but to be prepared to accept £2,500.[57] Nothing came of that and Barbon acquired it in 1683 for the lower value, possibly using the funds from the sale of the Charles Street site.

The purchase involved some complicated financial transactions and several of Barbon's regular financiers such as John Adams, Roger Jackson, Sir James Ward and Arnold Browne. The house was demolished and Browne and Barbon granted several building leases for what became Derby Court.

Some of these houses were substantial since they were later insured against fire for £2,000 each, ironically with the competitor to Barbon's fire insurance company.[58] When they burnt down in 1697, the complicated leases set up by Barbon resulted in a long battle over who was entitled to the insurance payments and who had the obligation under the leases to rebuild.[59]

These were not the only houses that Barbon had in the parish of St Margaret Westminster. By 1683 he had agreed to develop Carew House, the home of Lord Dartmouth on the north side of Tothill Street. By October 1683 he had knocked Carew House down and began to lay out what became Dartmouth Street.[60] It is not clear how quickly this was developed, but there are records of building leases being granted by Barbon and Lord Dartmouth on the west side of the street in 1688.[61] Barbon went on to purchase the gardens just north of Carew House which were called Liquorish Garden (No. 5 in Fig. 55) which had been leased to Lord Dartmouth and provided the land for what became Queen Street. It is not clear how much of a part Barbon played in the further development of Queen Street, although the records of the Westminster Sewer Commissioners show that he had been involved in moving, cleaning or replacing the sewers in Liquorish Garden from 1686, or more accurately that he was ordered to do so, but did not, incurring fines as a result.[62] Nevertheless, towards the end of 1688 Barbon did grant a building lease, jointly with Lord Dartmouth, to Richard Frith for a house at the top end of the street, next to St James's Park on what would become Queen Street.[63] This house was built, and still exists as Nos 36–38 Old Queen Street, but the lease gave rise to subsequent litigation with Barbon shortly before Frith died in 1695, raising the usual questions about how many of the previous lease holders still had rights to the income.[64]

As the next chapters will show, the years after 1683 were busy times for Barbon with many other developments. The fact that he sold out from both Charles Street and Derby House as quickly as he did suggests that his involvement stemmed from no more than having seen an opportunity to make a quick profit and taking it. This was indeed how he had started after the Fire. But it is possible that by then his interests may have been moving away from solely quick profits to developments that would leave a real mark on London, such as creating another market or shopping area, perhaps a residential square, or even underpinning his projects such as fire insurance, covered in the next chapter. Alternatively, it may have been no more than needing the funds to support larger and potentially more profitable operations elsewhere.

Against this background, his approach to Carew House looks odd. Dartmouth Street was in a good area and, when finally built, would be described by Strype as 'a very handsome open Street, graced with good Buildings, fit for the Reception of Gentry'.[65] But why did this development not proceed as others had done?

We do not know the answer and it may have been no more than lack of resources, whether financial or organizational. An alternative may be linked to his proposal of a couple of years earlier for rebuilding the Royal Mews for which he would have needed a site near St James's Park, discussed in greater detail in Chapter XIII. Lord Dartmouth was a favourite of both Charles II and James II and had been Master of the Horse for the Duke of York in 1673, becoming Master of the King's Horse when the Duke became King in 1685. Dartmouth himself, possibly stimulated by Barbon, may have realized the potential of Carew House for redevelopment as the new Royal Mews, particularly when augmented by Liquorish Garden. A collection of papers associated with Lord Dartmouth does contain an outline design for a

Fig. 56. *The Upright* [elevation] *of the Kings Mewse.*

© The National Archives, WORK 30/6465/1

new Royal Mews (Fig. 56) but it is not dated.[66] As a result, we do not know whether this reflected a commission from Dartmouth himself, from a previous Master of the Horse, or even from Barbon.

Nevertheless, although William III only stripped Dartmouth of his various positions in January 1689, it may have been clear for some time that no one would favour a site owned by Dartmouth for the development. This would account for the site having been kept on hold since 1683 and only developed from the end of 1688, with Barbon playing little part in it.

Commentary

By the end of the 1670s Barbon was already operating on a grand scale. Apart from these three large projects, Gerrard Street/Military Ground, Newport Ground and St Martin's Lane, he was still finalizing work on Essex and Exeter Houses, on Mincing Lane and other smaller sites in the City. On top of this, he had purchased Old Devonshire House near Bishopsgate, knocked the house down, and was beginning to lay it out as what would become Devonshire Square. While this went slowly, he did grant a lease to the Quakers who had built their Meeting House there in 1678.[67] He sold the Square, still largely undeveloped, in 1682 for £7,200 to raise money for another purchase. By then the plan for the Square was already decided and was attached to the deeds. It is shown in Figure 57, and the completed Square as it was in 1725 in Figure 58. A little later he gave up the lease of the Military Ground/Gerrard Street area to John Jeffreys who, if not directly related to Judge Jeffreys, had close familial connections, in lieu of repayment of £5,000 he had borrowed with it as security.

Barbon was one of the few to have multiple large sites on the go at the same time. Indeed, over his lifetime there was no one who attempted — or secured the completion of — so many. Evidence for this comes from the records of the Westminster Sewer Commission, created to oversee the building, cleansing, repair and maintenance of the public sewers within their area. This included giving permission to attach new houses to those sewers and to levy charges for so doing or for their maintenance. Between 1681 and 1720, 80 per cent of those asking for permission to attach dwellings were shopkeepers, widows or gentlemen of quality, for whom building a house was a once in a lifetime business venture, not a new career.[68] Even including those with two or three projects, the average number of houses built was no more than five. Four developers stand out: Barbon himself, Richard Frith, the scrivener Huntley Bigg, and Thomas Ingram, an ironmonger about whom there is no more information. This group had five projects each with an overall average of forty houses per project, building a third of all houses recorded as joining the Westminster sewers.

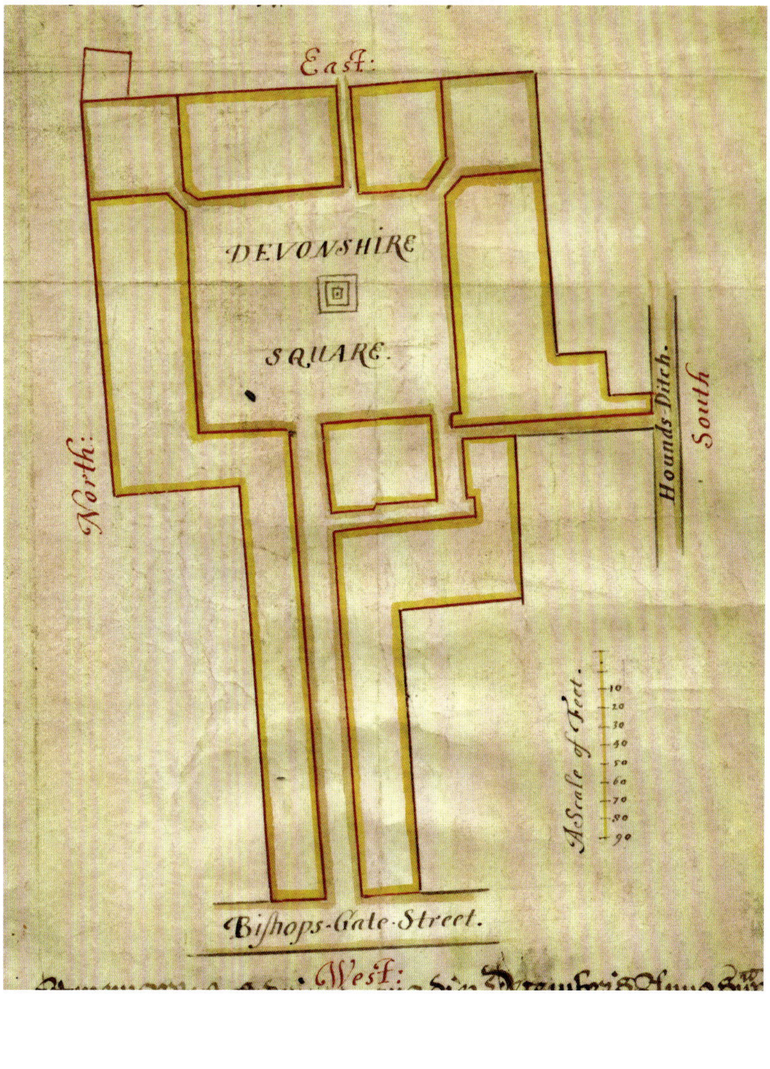

Fig. 57. Barbon's plan for Devonshire Square.
© The National Archives, C 54/4576

Fig. 58. Devonshire Square, etching by Sutton Nicholls, 1725.
© Trustees of the British Museum, 1800,1113.3931

It should not be thought that Barbon's houses were mean or even badly built, although inevitably there would be complaints from time to time, including that they were unfinished. The quotes that have already been given from Strype, although writing twenty or thirty years after Barbon's houses were built, still describe them as 'well built'. Strype may not be entirely reliable in these descriptions since he also described Downing Street, notorious for being built cheaply and on unsuitable boggy surroundings, and some modest timber houses in Southwark, in the same way.[69] However, the houses were still attractive enough to be taken by aristocracy and senior officials almost forty years later in the 1720s, and the streets were still viewed as 'handsome'. While most developments in the seventeenth century were mixed, the much-repeated description of Barbon as a slum landlord is entirely based on the single claim by a cleric annoyed with the commercial development of Essex House, a former bishop's house.[70] It is one of the many commonly used pejorative descriptions of Barbon that turns out to be largely incorrect.

It is not always easy to disentangle the financial details of Barbon's transactions. Much depended on the amount and timing of interest he paid but, given his lack of capital, his cash flow was always under severe pressure. Chapter XIII will deal in detail with how he dealt with this problem, but an important element was, of course, always to delay for as long as possible paying any money that he owed. He would also mortgage any purchase as soon as possible in order to provide funds for laying out the site and any demolishing, making the maximum reuse of materials. His next step was to get as much value quickly from the building leases. As we saw for Essex House, he would divide the site up by frontage on the road and calculate what would be the ground rent after building. He would then develop some of the sites himself, lease others to builders, while a third category would be 'leased' to his nominees to allow him to claim that all were under development. He could then raise money by selling new leases at the capitalized value of those ground rents (i.e., the total ground rent paid over twenty years). Roger North saw Barbon as the inventor of this process.[71] Despite innumerable legal actions against him and his continued flirting with bankruptcy, the evidence from his continued business activities shows that he remained able to raise funds and that very often the same people were prepared to lend him money over and over again.

CHAPTER VI

FIRE INSURANCE

One of Nicholas Barbon's many claims to fame is that he was the first to develop the provision of fire insurance. While there is some truth in this, at least as far as England is concerned, it is by no means the whole story. But it does provide a good example of his ability to use advertisement and publicity, aggressive pamphletting and a variety of legal actions to further his cause and deal with competitors. Fire insurance obviously had great relevance to his property activity: he used his portfolio, with that of others, to provide security for the insurance, and he argued that the fact of being insured would increase the value of a property, an obvious attraction to a major property owner such as himself. His involvement with fire insurance is intimately connected with his own property development, a point missed or glossed over by most historians of insurance.

Insurance was not a new idea in the latter part of the seventeenth century and was well developed on the marine side. While some merchants managed their risk by having a wide portfolio of shares as small as 1/64 of a cargo, others underwrote the whole ship and paid insurance. One merchant paid 2.5 per cent for trade with Constantinople and 1.5 per cent for trade with Scandinavia, reflecting the different risks of the journeys.[1] There had been talk of fire insurance since the 1630s but it had always raised substantial practical questions.[2] It was required for longer periods of time rather than a single voyage and the risk needed to be spread over many properties with a good geographical dispersion. While premiums might be small, they had to be sufficient to build up a reserve in good years to meet high losses when they arose. All this pointed to a permanent organization, with a fund and staff to administer it, rather than the arrangements for marine insurance where the risks were taken on an ad hoc basis by groups of underwriters.

The first attempt to provide such insurance was a plan laid before the Privy Council in 1635 for insurance at one shilling per cent per annum, but this came to nothing. The next proposal was a petition by William Riley and Edward Mabb to King Charles I for a patent to run for forty-one years, to cover London, Westminster, Southwark and their suburbs, costing 12d. for every house of £20 annual rent and pro rata for larger or smaller rentals.[3] They offered to deposit £5,000 as security with the interest being rolled up until it reached £10,000. The King approved this application in October 1638, accepting officials' reservation that 'no man be pressed to come forward in to subscribe, but every man left to his voluntary choice'. The Attorney General was asked to prepare the necessary legislation, but nothing was heard of it. This may have been because of the outbreak of the Civil War shortly afterwards, but it assumed the provision of fire engines in each ward and a nightly watch for fires and it was not clear who would pay for these.

Nothing more was done about fire insurance until just after the Restoration when a scheme was proposed by 'several persons of quality and eminent citizens of London'. The King referred the scheme to the Common Council of the City which rejected it because it was thought 'impossible for private persons to manage and unreasonable that they (and not the City) should reap the profits of such an undertaking'.[4] Sir William Petty made clear in 1662 that while there was some fire insurance in other countries, he was unaware of any in England.[5]

The Great Fire of London, starting on 2 September 1666, focused minds on the need to do more to prevent fires and encouraged further thinking about insurance. In some ways, it was lucky for the development of insurance that there had been none in place before the Great Fire. It destroyed 13,200 houses, eighty-seven churches as well as St Paul's Cathedral, forty-four company halls and many public buildings.[6] The damage was estimated at over £10,000,000, an enormous sum that would have been far beyond the capacity of any insurance arrangements but the future possibilities were indicated by the inclusion of an insurance office in Wren's plan for rebuilding the City of London, although this probably related to the office that kept the records of marine insurance.

Ideas for fire insurance continued to emerge. A merchant, Benjamin Delaune, whose cousin and family had died when their house burnt down in 1662, put forward proposals in 1669 which were taken up by others in a petition to the Common Council, referred to a committee, but never made progress. Nevertheless, they had some wider distribution since the postscript to a pamphlet published in 1672 hoped that it would be 'an encouragement to the publication of certain papers on the insurance of houses and Goods from fire, at the rate of one pound per cent per annum, which hath for several months been seriously debated with many judicious persons within this City'.[7]

Meanwhile, a more detailed scheme was being worked up by another merchant, Augustin Newbold. His first proposal, sent to the Common Council, was in 1674; it was modified in 1675 and 1678 and a final version, following agreement in principle, published on 1 January 1680.[8] There were minor modifications between these various proposals with the last one assuming a third of the 12,000 new brick houses, with average value of £250, would insure at a premium of 5 per cent per annum, generating a fund of £50,000. Newbold changed his mind about who should operate this fund, proposing at first the City itself and then a joint stock company, but as part of the approval process the Lord Mayor decreed that it should be managed by the City. Further committee work was still required to finalize the details, but a notice was published in a newspaper in early April to announce that full details would be published shortly.[9]

While admitting that his proposal had been 'some years lying by', Newbold's paper also claimed that previous attempts to provide fire insurance had proved fruitless. This was soon to change as a new proposal emerged very soon after the fact of the City scheme became public. This was Barbon's own proposal.[10] He went about the process carefully, publishing first a pamphlet with a series of propositions setting out the advantages of fire insurance and an outline of how he proposed to handle it.

He started by arguing that fire insurance would enhance the freehold value of houses from fourteen or fifteen years' purchase of ground rents to eighteen or twenty with the result that leases would be worth more, but he recognized that the insurance had to be supported by a good quality and permanent fund or security and that the premium for insuring had to be low enough to encourage people to insure. The amount of security necessary was determined by only two recent fires having had losses greater than £40,000, the Great Fire of London in 1666 and a fire in Southwark in 1676 where 400 houses were burnt. It was reasonable to suppose that not everyone would insure and that those who did would be dispersed about the city, so that probably only 10 per cent or so of houses destroyed by a large fire would be insured. He concluded that a fund of £1,500 or £2,000 annually in ground rents, worth £30,000 or £40,000 respectively over twenty years, would be sufficient security to insure 10,000 houses. The rate would be 6d. in the pound annual rent for brick houses (with ground rent subtracted) with twice the rate for timber houses. Insurance would be for periods of between seven and thirty-one years, with discounts for the longer periods.

The pamphlet went on to identify the insurers as Samuel Vincent, Nicholas Barbon and others, and the ground rents proposed as security as £1,050 in Essex Buildings in the Strand, £347 per annum in St Martin's Lane and £700 in Devonshire Buildings near Bishopsgate, of which £400 was already built and the remainder building. He included a draft of the proposed insurance policy together with an invitation to discuss at the fund's office and a further discount offered for early subscriptions. He promised to settle £1,500 of the ground rents in any case and the full £2,000 if the scheme met with approval. A further advertisement followed shortly clarifying that houses pulled down or blown up to stop a fire spreading were also covered and modifying the arrangements when houses were only damaged.[11] The opening of his office 'at the backside of the Royal Exchange' in Threadneedle Street was announced on 7 May 1680.[12] This was followed by notices of two meetings, one of subscribers and another with interested parties to appoint Trustees and a group of lawyers to satisfy themselves of the details of the contracts.[13]

The fact that Barbon issued clarification so soon suggests that there was already considerable discussion about his proposals. This must have included some real doubts about its efficacy because towards the end of 1680 he issued another pamphlet allowing the proposals to be 'more fully and largely discoursed of'.[14] This analysed all the fires in and around London between 1666 and 1680, thirty-five in all with 750 houses destroyed, the largest in Southwark where 400 houses were burnt. Current subscriptions to his insurance confirmed that the policies were on houses distributed round London, even 'on the other side of the water' in Southwark, and in any case he did not expect to insure more than 10 per cent of any large fire. Thus a security of £40,000, enough to pay for the rebuilding of 200 houses at an average of £200, each quite apart from the insurance premiums, was sufficient in practice to cover a fire of 2,000 houses. He noted in passing that it would be expected that there would be fewer fires in the future since a higher proportion of the houses were made of brick rather than timber and his fund would be providing a trained and experienced fire-fighting force. He went on to demonstrate that the fund would still be sufficient if every house were insured, provided that a further £20,000 of capitalized ground rents were provided for every further ten thousand insured.

Preparatory work continued for some time. Trustees were chosen at the June meeting, as was a group of lawyers to examine the proposals for the trust deed and various contracts. The trustees were carefully chosen from those with extensive financial operations and prominent positions in the City. Sir Joseph Sheldon, the former Lord Mayor, died less than three weeks after appointment; the other trustees included two current or future sheriffs of London, no fewer than four lawyers, one of whom, Sir George Treby, was Recorder of London and later Lord Chief Justice, while Sir Michael Heneage and George Bradbury both ended their careers with senior positions in the Exchequer Court. Others were substantial merchants heavily engaged in supplying both Army and Navy, and in tax farming of the Excise. They knew, and did considerable business with, each other. The lawyers on the contract committee were no less distinguished, including Sir Francis Pemberton, the current Lord Chief Justice, Sir Francis Winnington and Sir William Jones who had been solicitor general and attorney general respectively until the year before, and William Williams, a recent Speaker to the House of Commons. The results of their cogitations were given effect in a deed of 29 July 1681.[15]

The results were announced in September 1681, when the trustees were also confirmed.[16] There had been much debate on the value of the security needed to underpin the insurance: most had been prepared to accept the proposal of £40,000 worth of capitalized ground rents insuring 10,000 houses and an additional £10,000 for every 10,000 houses partly on the grounds that they would be dispersed and so unlikely to have large numbers destroyed in one fire, but some potential participants remained uncertain. Accordingly, the insurers had agreed to double the security so that £40,000 would be used to cover the first 5,000 houses and £10,000 security required for each further 5,000 houses. Concern had also been expressed about using the ground rents of the Devonshire Buildings since they were still incomplete, and the partners agreed not to settle these rents yet but to use the ground rents of Essex Buildings and the houses in St Martin's Lane (£1,400 per annum in total worth £28,000) to cover the insurance of 3,000 houses. Further property would be used to cover any expansion to 5,000 houses. The lawyers had also proposed that the insurers should not have the option of rebuilding houses that had been destroyed but should return cash, 'necessary to avoid those disputes which might arise about the dimensions, form and substantialness of building'. Finally, the same additional year's discount was offered to those who subscribed to the original proposals to those who now took up insurance before November 1, 1681. The oldest surviving policy, number 111, is dated 5 October 1681.[17]

These proposals appear to have been successful. The individual insurance policies were numbered sequentially, as required by the trust deed, and we know from policies whose documents still survive that over six hundred were issued by the beginning of 1682 and over 1,600 by the end of that year. However, they were not alone. Barbon's progress had finally stimulated the City to action. The Committee concerned had reviewed Newbold's proposals in June and agreed them in principle in October, four weeks after Barbon's announcement that all was settled. Narcissus Luttrell noted this and realized the implications for Barbon's project, writing, 'if this is carried on it will be a great injury to Dr Barbone, who first invented it, and hath set up an office for it and is likely to get vastly by it'.[18] The Court endorsed Newbold's proposals in November, they were published, and subscriptions opened on 16 November. Barbon immediately began to lobby against the City offering insurance with his first pamphlet appearing at about the same time as the Committee gave Newbold's proposals approval in principle.

Before we come to this exchange of four or five pamphlets, it is worth considering why Barbon structured his fire insurance in the way he did, since he had clearly anticipated some of the arguments that might be raised against him. He adopted a process of careful consultation with a range of interested parties, exposing the detail of the ground rents, having trustees agreed in advance with those consulted, and ensured the legal documents were endorsed by a group of eminent lawyers. Moreover, he made changes as a result of this consultation: he modified the legal documentation, reduced the possibility of arguments after a fire by simplifying the process for reimbursement and, most importantly, agreed to substantial increases in the amount of security required to underwrite the policies. These changes increased his costs and decreased his income.

He made careful choice of both ground rents and partners. He needed about £2,000 per annum in ground rents and it was clearly beneficial to have them in as few sites as possible in order to make the structure more comprehensible and so reduce potential argument about the suitability of the sites, as well as the practical point of reducing the extent of the legal documentation. The sum required was large and his options were necessarily constrained. Essentially Essex Buildings, the development of the Essex House site off the Strand, was the largest element in his portfolio and one which he had sold to Samuel Vincent. The second element was the development in St Martin's Lane where Barbon had built and sold part to Samuel Tookie and Benjamin Bartlett. These two with Vincent were his first partners in the fire insurance business. There were fourteen shares altogether; Vincent held ten and a half shares, Tookie one and a half, with Barbon and Bartlett one each. Each share consisted of a number of leases with the associated ground rents.

The other substantial element of his portfolio was Devonshire Buildings, where he had estimated the ground rents at an annual £700, bringing the total up to the necessary £2,000. He had acquired the property in 1675 and by 1679 had demolished Old Devonshire House and laid out Devonshire Street, Devonshire Square, Cavendish Court and a passage into Houndsditch, but the difficulty was that most of it was still to be developed. This was picked up in the comments on the scheme, forcing him to withdraw it or at least hold for later. He eventually sold the site in 1682 to Francis Dashwood for £7,200, probably to raise the funds for the purchase of the land he did eventually use as the remaining security for the insurance.

All those involved in fire insurance argued that it raised the value of insured property and that will of course have been attractive to Barbon. But there were other financial incentives. While the fire insurance trust deeds gave the trustees the right to apply the ground rents to pay any fire losses that could not be covered by premiums, the owners of the land continued to receive those ground rents in the meanwhile. On the assumption that the insurance was indeed profitable, any profits or dividends provided an increased return on the capital employed on the sites and so increased their value. Ground rents were traditionally viewed as a relatively safe investment since a leaseholder who defaulted was at risk of losing the entire lease. Increasing their effective return by using them to secure insurance could therefore attract those who normally saw the return on ground rents as too low compared with other more commercial investments or, on the other hand, stimulating the cautious who were attracted by the assumed security of ground rents but were prepared to go for a somewhat better return. All this had the potential for increasing the attractiveness, and hence the price, of Barbon's ground rents compared to those not used to secure insurance. In addition, there was, at least to start with, the prospect of a very positive cash flow, admittedly with unknown future liabilities, but certainly of interest to a man like Barbon who was always short of cash.

Barbon realized that his reputation was viewed, at least, as mixed. He needed to find partners with good contacts as well as substantial financial resources, although, as we shall see, many of them were not always successful. His first three partners, as well as having already collaborated with him on development, met this test. Samuel Vincent, with whom he had cooperated on Essex House itself, had extensive financial interests including the victualling of the Navy, while Benjamin Bartlett and Samuel Tookie were both goldsmiths whose trade often provided a banking function.

The next step was to try to dissuade the City itself from competing with him. His first attempt came in a pamphlet in which he argued that the only possible reasons for the City offering the same insurance as his proposals would be that they offered better security, or that the City would benefit from the profits.[19] He argued that there was no better security than ground rents and the City could not better that, so the estimates of profitability made by Newbold were completely wrong. Using the premium that he had received 'by the computation of several hundred houses already insured', he argued that Newbold had grossly overestimated the likely income and, by considering how many houses had burnt in the City over the last fifteen years, he showed that Newbold had significantly underestimated the probable losses. He argued that it would weaken the City's credit for other aspects of its work if large amounts of its assets were used to give security for fire insurance and that in any case it would be much harder for people to deal with the City than with private individuals because its political processes would always cause delay. He ended with a flourish by announcing that everyone who had insured with his insurance office would have the right until 1 January 1682 to surrender their policies with a refund, less a payment for the period insured, and move to the City scheme if that should prove to have better security or easier terms.

There was certainly some force in Barbon's arguments. He had direct and recent experience of what premiums had been paid, which reflected the value of houses insured as well as the effect of discounts for longer periods. Equally, he had done his homework on the number of houses that had been burnt since the Great Fire (ninety-seven in total in the City) and his calculations benefited from his scheme, including many houses outside the City walls; these were on average cheaper to rebuild than those in Newbold's scheme which were confined to inside the City. Nevertheless, he admitted that 'whether the premium (as it is now settled) is well adjusted is not in the power of man to determine because the design is new and nothing but experience can do it'. His arguments about the delays in dealing with the City no doubt reflected the experience of many but, as we will see, were firmly rejected by the proponents of Newbold's scheme. Underlying the exchange were the perennial arguments about whether the benefits of a proposal should accrue to the public purse or be better and more efficiently managed in the private sector. As an afterthought, he produced a subsequent letter with another argument that, when deciding whether to blow up a house to prevent fire from spreading, magistrates might be influenced to choose ones not insured by the City in order to protect its funds or even to encourage insurance.[20] A monopoly insurance, certainly if effectively compulsory, run by the City would amount to a tax.

Barbon's pamphlet did not discourage the City. The Court of Common Council endorsed the proposals of its Committee and published them with a table of premiums and opening subscriptions.[21] These undercut those of Barbon and offered insurance in perpetuity for a single payment, while setting in hand the settlement of £100,000 worth of lands and ground rents as security. Barbon immediately returned to the charge with a new pamphlet *Observations on the Proposals of the City, to insure Houses in case of Fire*.[22] While admitting that the City had considered proposals for fire insurance as long ago as 1670, he dismissed them as so impractical that the City had been forced to put them aside and would have been unable to proceed if they had not copied his proposals. He claimed that the 'Gentlemen of the Insurance Office' (his organization) had even offered to refer their scheme to the Council to judge which proposal was indeed the original, and if it was proved that the City proposal was the earlier or that it added anything new, they would withdraw. This offer was not taken up. He then complained that the City has deliberately put its prices just below his own, 'probably valued as a contrivance to draw customers' and announced his own at a still lower price, now a one-off payment of £2 5s. 10d. for thirty-one years' insurance for a brick house worth £100 or a rate of 5d. per pound rent. He committed to setting his price below that of the City in all circumstances, although he did not propose to put it lower still unless the City was to do so, pointing out that this did not reduce the value of his underlying security, although it made it less likely that the City would make money.

Barbon also pointed out that the City's offer to insure against fire in perpetuity, 'another stratagem to bring in customers', was illogical and dangerous because the security could not survive for the same period and one would never know whether it was sufficient. He returned to the argument that it would be difficult to litigate with the City: the administration's hands were full with other responsibilities which must be weakened if some land was used as security for other matters. In case anyone felt disadvantaged by having paid a higher premium than now on offer, he invited all those who had insured with his Office to claim back the overpayment compared with the new rates or agree an extension of the insurance period. Finally, he confirmed that the ground rents of Devonshire Buildings would be settled in the next legal term and another parcel of ground rents in Westminster had been provided which would bring the total to an annual £4,000. Chambers at the Inns of Court and Chancery would also be insured.

None of this dissuaded the City, which authorized the go ahead of Newbold's scheme on 15 December 1681. The Lord Mayor himself insured several houses and encouraged others on the Court of Common Council to do likewise. Note was taken of 'two small pamphlets lately printed tending to the disarrangement and disability of the City to undertake the said design' and the Court invited its insurance committee to vindicate the City's 'reputation and credit' as it saw fit. Shortly afterwards, the Court noted,

> divers citizens of this City are trustees for some private persons who have undertaken to insure houses from fire. Inasmuch as such undertaking will be greatly prejudicial to this design of the City, this Court is of the opinion that the said citizens ought to decline and revoke their said trusts, and this Court does desire the said citizens to decline and withdraw their said trusts.[23]

Following this up, pamphlets appeared early the next year written by friends of the City proposal. Both were written by 'Mr L. R.' in the form of letters to his honoured friend 'Mr M. T.', a member of the City's Committee on fire insurance.[24] The first one answered Barbon's first pamphlet[25] and associated letter and the second his second one.[26] Both were hard-hitting about Barbon and his partners and clearly used them to settle some old scores, not least his habit of delaying paying his bills for as long as possible.

L. R. first dismissed Barbon's claim to be the first into the field, pointing out that the City had been thinking about fire insurance since at least 1670 and commenting, 'I do not think it strange that he who refuses to pay what he is indebted to others would refuse to acknowledge what he owes to you'. L. R. returned to this in his *Second Letter*, rehearsing at length the whole history of the City's interest in fire insurance and arguing that any profits from the exercise should go to the City rather than to 'a few foreigners and private men' or 'foreigners or outlying deer'.[27] However small the profit,

> I am sure that it is too much for one that hath made it his business to run up a multiple of houses in the adjacent parts as if he were resolved to drain the City of its inhabitants and trade. I think he may have done almost as much prejudice to the City by building houses as the Papists by firing them.

He pooh-poohed the idea that private individuals could provide better security than the City, not least because he described Barbon as

> a person whose chamber door daily suffers an assault and battery from a whole posse of bricklayers, carpenters, masons etc., and who if one may judge by the several actions of debt that every term are brought against him, is in fair way to retire for refuge into one of his own chambers that he has built in the Temple

and one of his partners

> though he may be thought to be shot up into some considerable height from a low and ordinary condition (as rushes do from mud) yet is every day liable to be called up to an account for maladministration of a public office; and if he should be in arrears to his Majesty, even those lands or ground rents which he offers as a security would be seized in the behalf of his Majesty.

This was probably a reference to Vincent, whom Roger North described: 'I knew one bred a servant, and by accident grew rich. His character was industrious and servile, and from a walking surveyor of the excise was taken into a revenue farm, and so by others' brains got his estate.'[28] In his *Second Letter*, L. R. added the charge that one of the partners was liable to a statute of bankruptcy three years previously.

L. R. dismissed the argument that the City would be slow in paying or would use the money for other things, pointing out that the security would be in trust and therefore out of the City's control (a point he did not seem to realize also applied to the trust set up by Barbon's scheme) and that other schemes managed by the City, such as the revenues for maintaining London Bridge or money entrusted to them by Parliament for building churches, had worked well. He claimed that hospitals managed by the City were well run while those by private persons were 'usually made lodges for their porters or stables for their foundered grooms'. In a final insult to Barbon, he argued that the City arrangements 'shall pay the losses of those whose houses are burnt down sooner than the enquirer shall the wages of those that built his up'.

The *Second Letter* answered Barbon's *Observations on the Proposals* in vituperative terms. The City's security was larger and the trust would protect the insured in the unlikely event that the City lost its Charter, the legal document that granted the City its powers. A conveyance was even at that moment being drawn up with the identified ground rents, and the costings had been worked out 'under the hands of the two most exquisite arithmeticians'. In any case,

> who would trust people who are very forward to take money upon almost any terms as sponges suck up water, but the many suits that are every term between them and their creditors who are at so much trouble and charge to recover their own plainly show 'tis very hard to wring and squeeze it out again.

And the point was rammed home later in the letter:

> I think that it would be very honourable and just if the *Observator* would pay those debts which he hath fairly contracted and have been applied to his proper benefit [...] For then multitudes of poor men and their families would be relieved, who not being paid for their work which he set them about, have their mouths full (not of bread) but of complaints and have little else to drink besides their own tears.

In the end, Barbon's arguments did have an effect, and on 13 November 1682 the City decided that 'the encumbrance to the entire estate [...] far from bringing a prospect of benefit to the Chamber had proved prejudicial thereunto', resolving to drop the insurance project and instructing the Chamberlain to repay money which had been advanced and then to cancel the policies. Even so, policies continued to be agreed until at least May 1683 (1,670 in total) and the City did not finally close the business until an application was made to the King's Bench for a writ of mandamus which was granted since the City failed to make its case for having the powers to run insurance.[29] In fact, the Crown had already started its case to remove the Charter from the City as part of Charles II's desire to control its personnel and government; it was finally removed in 1683 and, with it, control of its own governance.[30] One of the writers of the time charged the Corporation with 'inability to repay monies secured by their bonds' and hence 'how could they be expected that the insured have better justice when a great loss by fire happens than those persons who have held the City's bonds have had'.[31] Only ten years later the City virtually went bankrupt, having drawn on, and failed to repay, the moneys of the Orphans' Fund, resulting in almost half of its property having to be used as security for its repayments to the Fund.[32] Writing sometime later, Strype said that the City project did not take, 'perhaps because the credit of the City at this time was low'.[33]

Barbon's insurance office had sold over 1,600 policies by the end of 1682 with up to £10,000 of premiums. The fact of insurance was talked about in the press with Charles Molloy including a reference to it in his 1682 edition of *De Jure Maritimo et Navali*.[34] Figure 59 shows an example of one of the early policies, signed by Barbon and Tookie. The seal bears the sign of a phoenix arising from its ashes, although not quite the same design as later appeared on their literature.

Both Roger Morrice and Narcissus Luttrell commented that several buildings that were destroyed in the Wapping Fire in November 1682 were insured by Barbon, including those of Sir William Warren who went on to be a trustee.[35] This fire, which started in Cinnamon Lane, Wapping, took place only six days after the City's decision to quit fire insurance, and burnt many hundreds of houses. It is hardly surprising that Barbon took the opportunity to advertise his Office's preparedness to pay the losses for Wapping immediately rather than after the contracted delay of two months, albeit with a discount for interest lost.[36] This demonstrated both that his was the only insurance available for the future and that he was able to meet his obligations without difficulty. It was, perhaps, a piece of luck that this very large fire happened not long after the start of his activities and so not many of the Wapping houses had been insured.

More than £1,000 more in ground rents was required before expanding the business to 10,000 houses as planned, and Barbon concluded that as the prospect of his building on the Devonshire Buildings site was slight he had to look for other security. New partners were needed and Vincent, with 75 per cent of the fourteen original shares, was keen to reduce his exposure to the insurance company and diversify out of Essex Buildings. The first new partner was easily found, John Parsons, a brewer who was already one of Vincent's partners in the contract for victualling the Navy. They were described as

> men esteemed to be of such solid fortunes, and bound to his Majesty, my lords of the admiralty, and we the officers of his navy, have great assurance given us that his Majesty's service shall no more be liable to any disappointment upon the score of victualling.[37]

Parsons had insured ten of his houses as early as November 1681and became interested in participating in the business, according to a later lawsuit, because 'the said undertaking being then likely to be a prosperous and advantageous business'.[38] Parsons joined with Barbon in the next purchase from the Crown of three sites: Little Tower Hill within the Tower Liberties, the Old Artillery Ground near Bishopsgate Street, and Well Close. The Artillery Ground cost £5,700 and Well Close and Little Tower Hill together £3,200, with Barbon probably meeting his costs from the proceeds of disposing of his Devonshire House site. He failed to pay for the three sites on time but, although he had bought them through nominees George Bradbury and Edward Noell, the Secretary to the Treasury knew to write

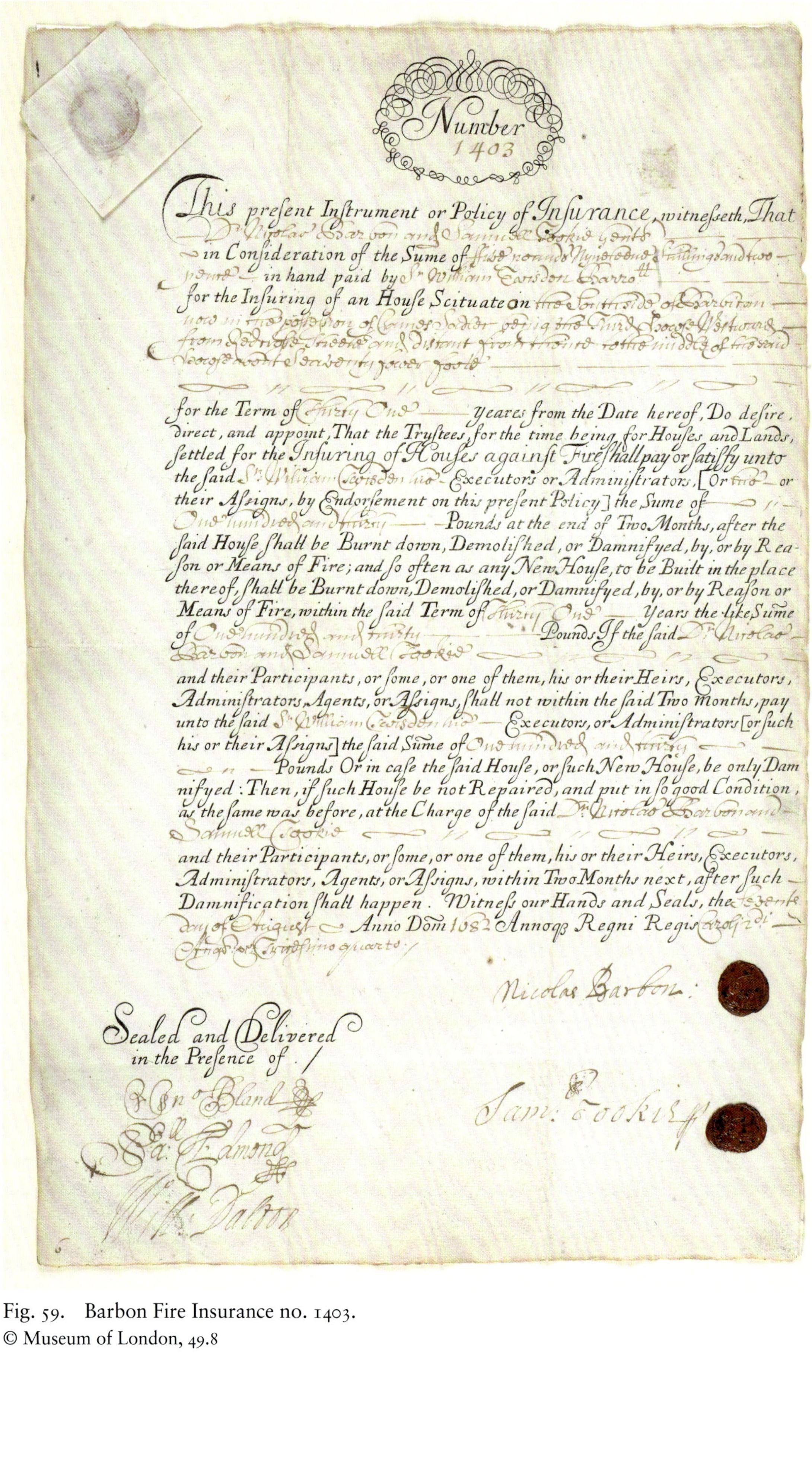

Number
1403

This present Instrument or Policy of Insurance, witnesseth, That Dr Nicolas Barbon and Samuell Tookie gents in Consideration of the Sume of in hand paid by Sr William for the Insuring of an House Scituate on for the Term of Thirty One Yeares from the Date hereof, Do desire, direct, and appoint, That the Trustees, for the time being, for Houses and Lands, settled for the Insuring of Houses against Fire shall pay or satisfy unto the said Sr William Executors or Administrators, [Or or their Assigns, by Endorsement on this present Policy] the Sume of One hundred and thirty Pounds at the end of Two Months, after the said House shall be Burnt down, Demolished, or Damnifyed, by, or by Reason or Means of Fire; and so often as any New House, to be Built in the place thereof, shall be Burnt down, Demolished, or Damnifyed, by, or by Reason or Means of Fire, within the said Term of Thirty One Years the like Sume of One hundred and thirty Pounds If the said Dr Nicolas Barbon and Samuell Tookie and their Participants, or some, or one of them, his or their Heirs, Executors, Administrators, Agents, or Assigns, shall not within the said Two Months, pay unto the said Sr William Executors, or Administrators [or such his or their Assigns] the said Sume of One hundred and thirty Pounds Or in case the said House, or such New House, be only Damnifyed: Then, if such House be not Repaired, and put in so good Condition, as the same was before, at the Charge of the said Dr Nicolas Barbon and Samuell Tookie and their Participants, or some, or one of them, his or their Heirs, Executors, Administrators, Agents, or Assigns, within Two Months next, after such Damnification shall happen. Witness our Hands and Seals, the day of August Anno Dom 1682 Annoqꝫ Regni Regis

Nicolas Barbon

Sealed and Delivered in the Presence of /

Jno Bland

Wil Dalton

Sam: Tookie

Fig. 59. Barbon Fire Insurance no. 1403.

directly to Barbon, threatening to sell elsewhere if he did not pay up. Only then did Barbon pay the money. Building leases were granted quickly for the Old Artillery Ground and Tower Hill and by November 1682 the neighbouring Navy Victualling Office complained that Barbon was encroaching on their land.[39] The two sites were claimed to generate just over £400 per annum of ground rents, a claim that was not unreasonable even if the development would take a little time. This left £705 per annum still needed to meet their commitment for insuring 10,000 houses.

Meanwhile, Parsons confirmed his interest by buying Benjamin Bartlett's share in the insurance office in July 1683, becoming the fourth of Barbon's existing business partners who joined. Barbon, Vincent, Tookie and he were clear about the need to introduce new partners — and new capital — into the project and saw great attraction at being able to sell some of their leases with associated ground rents, whether to reduce their borrowings or to raise money for other investments. It was relatively easy to sell leases whose income depended on ground rents that had already been developed such as Essex Buildings, St Martin's Lane and even Little Tower Hill and the Artillery Ground. Barbon, Vincent and Tookie were able to sell leases with over £10,000 worth of ground rents from Essex Buildings and St Martin's Lane, redistribute the proceeds among themselves, and bring in five new partners. Edward Noel and Sebastian Lyford took on the shares based on Essex Buildings while Samuel Newton and Thomas Price bought the major part of the St Martin's Lane development. Bernard Turner purchased a small part of the St Martin's Lane leases and almost two-thirds of the Artillery Ground. Barbon kept Little Tower Hill for himself.

Well Close was an essential part of the package required to underwrite the insurance of 10,000 houses but its development was beyond the capacity of Barbon and Parsons to finance alone; additional investors were needed to make it credible. Barbon intended his new development of Well Close to appeal to the well-to-do members of the East End's maritime community, but it was arguably unattractive and Defoe later recalled that it was 'so remote from houses that it used to be a very dangerous place to go over after it was dark'.[40]

Nevertheless, Barbon and Parsons were not deterred. They created leases on a range of sites in Well Close sufficient to make sure the desired value of ground rents could be achieved. These leases were let to either William Prideaux, one of Barbon's servants, or to Joseph Hartwell who was Parsons' servant.[41] The leases all had the same date of 1 October 1683 and comprised over a third of the total from Well Close by value; while half of these leases remained in the possession of Barbon and Parsons, they had still managed to raise £10,000 from sites that had virtually no building on them and so with the ground rents at risk. Such was the attraction of having a part of the insurance company that this did not deter a further three investors from purchasing the leases, Felix Calvert, John Wilson and John Hinde, although later Calvert would complain that he had been 'prevailed on' to buy his share.[42]

A new trust deed was produced with new share structure, reflecting the changed ownership of the leases, and several new trustees to replace some who had died or were no longer active. The resulting twenty-one shares were divided with Vincent having six shares, Barbon three, Parsons and Turner two each and the remaining eight partners a single share each. The deed was signed at the end of December 1683.[43] Well Close was declared as producing £816 per annum in ground rents, more than enough to carry the total over £2,500. There can have been little building completed on Well Close at the time of the trust deed and the lack of building there would be a source of continuing complaint for many years. The lack of secure ground rents caused two problems: first, it undermined the supposed security of the whole exercise, a point that would be commented on in future pamphlets, and second, perhaps more pressing from the point of view of the new investors, it put at risk the stated annual income from ground rents. The ground rents allocated to the trust and the ownership of the various shares are identified in the deed and a number of subsequent legal cases.[44]

All the new partners had close business relationships with each other and the existing partners. Vincent, Parsons and Calvert were all members of a group of London financiers who controlled the lucrative tax farm of the excise. Turner, Lyford and Newton also provided securities and obtained sub-farming contracts. Calvert was appointed a Commissioner of the Excise when the contractors were superseded by a Board in 1684 and Edward Noel, a lawyer who often acted for Barbon, was the Registrar and Secretary until he too was appointed Commissioner in 1702. Hinde was involved in the farm of the Hearth Tax from 1674 to 1679 and Vincent also shared in the farm of Law Duty from 1672 to 1675. Five of them were goldsmith/bankers and were listed as keeping running cashes in the *Little*

Directory of 1677. Tookie was in partnership with Turner who was a leading creditor of the Crown, as were Thomas Price and John Hinde, both of whom later went bankrupt, although in Hinde's case that was as much due to his involvement with building speculation.

The trustees were in the same mould. Some were merchants with close ties to the Navy, such as Sir William Warren, a timber merchant and ship builder; Peter Rich and Nathaniel Hawes supplied gunpowder and cheese respectively to the armed forces; Sir Richard Haddock and Anthony Sturt were Commissioners for Victualling the Navy, from which Sturt and John Parsons were dismissed for adulterating supplies; while Samuel Dashwood and Rowland Ingram had substantial merchant activities. There were also three prominent lawyers, Michael Heneage, William Thompson and George Bradbury, the last of whom often acted for Barbon. The trustees also did business together and with the partners. Dashwood was Calvert's partner in farming the excise. They were also connected by marriage: Anthony Sturt's son married Parsons' daughter, Elizabeth, while one of Warren's sons had Ingram as godfather and another married Ingram's niece. Many of the trustees owned large numbers of buildings such as warehouses and saw fire insurance as an integral part of protecting their business.

These partners were all heavily involved with the Crown's financial affairs, whether as suppliers of victualling to the Navy or in running tax farms or both. Both activities involved substantial sums of money, potentially good returns but with corresponding risks; fire insurance offered an opportunity to diversify their activities. As Parsons would point out in one of the later law cases involving these shares, the new partners did not themselves have large developments which could provide the necessary security in ground rents.[45] This may well have been because ground rents alone provided too low a rate of return for these adventurous investors. However, they did have access to ready funds to buy them. This provided a great opportunity for Vincent to realize some of the value from Essex Buildings and for Barbon and Parsons to sell half the Well Close site at a full price long before it would be developed. Although Hinde was the only one of the partners who was himself involved in substantial development, it seems implausible that the new investors did not realize that it would be necessary to build houses on the Well Close in order to secure the ground rents. The trust deed included an explicit covenant to build, binding Barbon, Parsons, Calvert, Turner, Wilson and Hinde 'that before Michaelmas next they will build, finish and make habitable their shares property to the respective values of their shares in the schedules'. It would require considerable further investment in buildings before the ground rents would be worth what they were sold for, although even ten years later the trustees were still arguing that at the time of the leases the premises 'were begun and in a great probability to be finished, completed and made habitable and to be of good value'.[46] Despite the covenant, there may well have been different expectations of who would secure the necessary building and who would finance it, producing a series of lawsuits over the next fifteen years. In 1683 those were problems of the future.

Barbon was left as the sole supplier of fire insurance, which began to call itself the Fire Office. Business was doing well and some time that year a second office was established over the Rainbow Coffee House near the Temple, Fleet Street. The first office, described as 'on the backside of the Royal Exchange', had appeared in the rate book as 'Dr Barbon's office' in 1681 but by 1684 and later it was in the name of Mr Tookey (probably Samuel Tookie), moving to Cornhill in 1686.[47] This change may well have reflected changes in Barbon's financial involvement. In early 1684 he had mortgaged all three of his shares, in both cases to another shareholder. The two shares based on the ground rents in the Artillery Ground and Well Close were mortgaged to Felix Calvert and the share based on Little Tower Hill was mortgaged to Thomas Price. These raised £6,000, more than he would ever have been able to raise on that security without the insurance connection. He failed to repay the mortgage and 6 per cent interest and both Calvert and Price became owners of the ground rents.[48] One of the investors in St Martin's Lane, Samuel Newton, sold his share at the same time to Price who shortly resold it and the Little Tower Hill share. Barbon's only remaining financial link was his continued right to the equity of redemption. Apart from Barbon and Newton, only two others disposed of their shares quickly, both in 1685, John Hinde, who himself was facing bankruptcy, and Samuel Vincent, who sold one of his six shares to Henry Jermyn, Lord Dover.

The Fire Office was not left alone in the field for long. Towards the end of 1683 a new proposal for fire insurance emerged, from an organization called the Friendly Society promoted by William Hale and Henry Spelman.[49] This was a mutual insurance with a small refundable deposit and an annual fee together with a commitment to pay up to a certain amount if any of the insured houses were burnt.

Once enough people had subscribed, the organizers would settle £16,000 worth of land on trustees as security and add to this £4,000 personal security, although these securities dealt only with the problem of the members not paying their share rather than securing the insurance as a whole.

The Fire Office was curiously silent in response to this emergence of a competitor and only responded after the Friendly Society had published a revised version in October the next year, together with a brief statement of the details of the arrangements.[50] These increased the refundable deposit from 15s. to £1 on a £300 house, but otherwise left the charges unchanged. The Society had already obtained enough subscribers to go ahead and settle the promised £16,000 on trustees; like Barbon, it had obtained the advice of several distinguished lawyers, including Sir Francis Pemberton who had already advised Barbon. Again, like Barbon, the Society had appointed illustrious trustees, including Sir Christopher Wren, a Lord Mayor, and another six knights of the realm all of whom had already subscribed, and firefighters would be provided.

It is difficult to determine which of the two approaches represented the better value. It cost £3 2s. 6d. to insure a £300 brick house for eight years with the Fire Office, compared with a basic £1 12s. plus the contribution for burnt houses with the Friendly Society and a further £1 refundable deposit. The Society, using Barbon's own figures, pointed out that only 'near 100' houses had burnt in the City in fifteen years since the Great Fire which, with an average cost of £300, meant a loss of £2,000 a year; this was calculated as requiring an annual payment of 2s. on a £300 house, giving an estimated full cost of £2 8s. The undertakers would make a profit of 4s. for each £300 house insured, less the costs of the operation, including running any fire service, but 6 per cent interest on the repayable deposit of £1 gave them a further 1s 2½d. Over a longer period, the benefit went the other way. It cost £6 17s. 6d. to insure a £300 brick house with the Fire Office for thirty-one years, but with the Friendly Society it cost 4s. a year or £6 4s. plus any contribution to other insured houses that might burn down in that period, which would surely happen over that period.

Despite having sold his shares, Barbon entered the fray in early 1685, publishing *A letter to a Gentleman in the Country*[51] arguing that the Friendly Society provided less security, was more expensive and would have less experience in fighting fires since his 'industrious men [...] like old disciplined soldiers, that do greater things, than ten times that number of raw and inexperienced men'. This provoked a quick response from Henry Spelman, although the exchange was markedly less vituperative than the earlier correspondence with the City with no personal abuse.[52] Each argued that their security was better and their cost less, but the arguments they produced tended to be based on extreme cases chosen for their purpose, although Spelman did point out that the Fire Office's additional ground rents in the Well Close area were unlikely to provide as much security as claimed.

The relative value for money was crucially dependent on the number of houses burnt each year and, for the Friendly Society, how many members there were to pay for any damage. It is not entirely clear whether the Friendly Society was prepared to insure throughout London and the suburbs. While it certainly was doing so by the mid-1690s, all the examples in its first literature are taken on evidence from the City only. Barbon's *A letter to a Gentleman in the Country* reveals that in the first three years of operation the Fire Office had insured 4,000 houses at an average premium of £4 10s., corresponding to a period of twelve years with a £300 house, although he reported a mixture of eight-, twelve- and twenty-one-year policies. He said that the Fire Office had paid about £7,000 for losses, corresponding to about eight houses a year burnt in London and the suburbs. This seems a high rate given that this covered some 120,000 houses, of which he was only insuring some 3 per cent, and his previous statistics suggested about fifty-four houses were burnt every year. It suggests potential problems with the economics since, as Barbon himself made clear, he had paid out about 39 per cent of the premiums during only 25 per cent of the period insured.

The problem appears even worse for the Friendly Society. Although there are no general records, the *London Gazette* contains two announcements calling for its members to contribute for losses.[53] The first one described a loss of £965 and required a contribution of 5s. 1d. per £100 insured, and the second whose fire was just under a year later required a contribution of 2s. 2¼d. per £100 insured. This shows that about 1,265 houses were insured by the Society in June 1685 and 1950 in June 1686, many fewer than the Fire Office. The level of contributions is significantly higher than had been suggested earlier by the Society, bringing the cost for a £300 house after only three years to £2 13s. 9¾d. These increased costs stemmed from a higher number of losses as well as fewer members to pay; an average cost for fires over the next five years equal to that originally predicted would make insuring with the Society marginally more expensive than with the Fire Office.

There was undoubtedly an expectation at the time that the incidence of fires would decline, given that more houses were built of brick and the greater controls on fireproofing. Added to this was the commonly held view, inscribed on the Monument itself in 1681 following the Popish Plot and repeated by Barbon in one of his early pamphlets, that papists had been responsible for the Great Fire of London — and other more recent ones. It was presumed that the papists were now being controlled. In fact, as has been shown recently, the frequency of large fires increased in London after the Great Fire, partly because the fireproofing controls were often ignored, but more importantly because the growth of trade in London resulted in the increased storage of flammable commodities such as sugar, tobacco, pitch and tar.[54] The very large fire in Wapping in 1682, which may have damaged over 1,000 buildings, was but one example. The future did not resemble the past and Barbon's argument that 'what never was, never may be, and is not reasonable to expect' was flawed.[55] Whatever the case, fire insurance was by now well established in the people's consciousness and a description of the stalls on the River Thames during the great freeze of early 1684 included one for insurance.[56] A print of how the river looked at that time (Fig. 60) includes that stall, which had already adopted a phoenix as its sign, a forerunner of its future change of name. One of the Frost Ballads may have referred to this:

In roast beef and brandy much money is spent
In booths made of blankets that pay no ground rent
With old fashioned chimneys the rooms are secured
And the houses from danger of fire ensured.[57]

By 1685 both insurance companies were in action and by the end of the year the Fire Office had had a net cash inflow, after losses, of over £10,000. Small wonder that they had paid themselves good dividends, up to £250 per share according to Edward Noel's evidence to a later legal dispute.[58] As might be expected the Fire Office had the more customers, reflecting its somewhat longer history: by the beginning of 1687 it had some 5,650 houses insured while the Friendly Society had 3,400.[59] However, despite having less financial involvement, Barbon continued to look for ways to reduce the competition to his project and his next tactic was to apply for a patent for fire insurance, aiming to exclude the Friendly Society altogether. After some preliminary legal skirmishing, a petition was submitted to the Privy Council in April 1687.[60] This claimed that the Fire Office had invented fire insurance and

Fig. 60. Insurance booth on the ice, detail from *A Wonderful Fair or a Fair of Wonders [...] on the River of Thames, in the time of the terrible frost, December 1684*.
By permission of the British Library, Maps K.Top.27.38.2

had already paid out £20,000 (perhaps uncomfortably close to the £25,000 or so that it had taken in premiums) but its rival the Friendly Society had caused 'great discouragement and damage'. Roger Morrice reported that although the Fire Office had done very well to start with, 'it has become an expensive office'.[61] As a result, he claimed that 'Merchants have in private agreed upon, and made such private contracts for insurance as has used to be made in that public office', but reported that the contracts appeared to have been ruled invalid 'to the great grief of the merchants'. Considerable delay followed, caused in part by the ill health of Spelman's partner William Hale, who died early the next year. The case was finally heard on Friday 16 December. Morrice reported that

> all seemed to agree that Mr Spillman's security was upon a far greater fund if not upon a better, Spillman's fund reaching to the securing of above a double number to what Dr Barebones does, and Spillman's propositions being more easy to the people, so that it was the general sense of the Board that both should have patents, it being a general good [...] It was said that would be a prejudice to Dr Barebone who was the first inventor. It was answered that was but a personal consideration and the public advantage was that which should govern the Board.[62]

Morrice claimed that George Jeffreys, the Lord Chancellor, was 'very zealous for Dr Barebone' but was the only one who spoke in his favour. The outcome was that the Board found that 'it appeared to the Board that the way of insuring the houses by the Friendly Society is of more benefit and satisfaction to the public than by the Fire Office' and awarded a patent to the Friendly Society, but required them to present a written proposal 'whereby the said Vincent and partners may be preserved from ruin'.

Naturally, the Fire Office challenged this and at the same time two other petitions were launched, one by Edward Hildeyard claiming that he too had proposed a mutual fire insurance, and one from two gunners, Thomas Silver and Thomas Dodge, on behalf of themselves and others claiming that they were the only persons 'engaged in blowing up of houses and otherwise extinguishing fires' and asking for an allowance of £150 a year towards 'their charge, hazard and pains, for such service'. The case was finally settled on January 20 1688 when the Board found that the Fire Office had indeed been first and that it had been found 'to be of good public use for the quieting the minds of our subjects, owners and inhabitants of houses, and hath much raised the value of such houses in purchases and securities'.

However, by a Judgement of Solomon the Fire Office was granted a patent for one year but thereafter only every other three months, alternating with the Friendly Office. For good measure, it was ruled that Edward Hildeyard, Sir Thomas Fitch and Charles Whitaker should be entitled to one quarter of the Friendly Society's undertaking, taken from the portion owned by Spelman. Powers were also reserved in the patent to order the insurers to pay allowances to gunners who assisted in extinguishing fires and these were duly exercised so that each insurer had to pay £60 a year to be distributed by the Master-General of the Ordnance 'according to the respective services, merits, hazards and accidents of the persons employed therein'.[63] Although the Fire Office's patent was promulgated, it is not clear the extent to which either patent was ever in force, but a Friendly Society notice in the *London Gazette* calling for contributions to meet a loss, also included the sentence, 'In February next, by permission and order of His Majesty, the Friendly Society may proceed in insuring houses as formerly.'[64] This would have represented the twelve months delay required by the original decision. It appears that, after that, both companies continued to issue policies. The two insurers later found themselves taken to task for not paying the sum owned to the gunners and eventually petitioned to surrender their patent and not to pay the gunners since they had used their own servants for the purpose.[65]

There is equally little evidence about the profitability of either scheme. The Friendly Society was crucially dependent on its members paying the contributions as and when demanded, although the required deposit will have given some security against non-payment. If these were received, the undertakers would have made a profit of 4s. a year for every £300 house insured, less the administrative costs. Figures for the Fire Office suggest that the outgoings were less than, but very close to, the premiums, but this may conceal the considerable returns that could have been had for investing the premiums before they were applied to the costs. We have already seen that substantial dividends were paid at an early stage of operation and there is evidence that dividends were paid later since Samuel Tookie maintained in one litigation that there was an unclaimed dividend of some thirty-four guineas in 1697.[66] Defoe, however, while declining to evaluate the two schemes, opined that the Friendly Society 'brings most money to the contriver'.[67]

Another way of evaluating the profitability of the Fire Office might be to look at the sale of the shares and identify any premium over the value of the ground rents which could be attributed to the value of the insurance business. This is, however, very difficult because many of the transfers began as mortgages with the security called in when not repaid, as was the case for Barbon. Many of the original partners either held their shares for many years or passed them on by sale or legacy within their families, although Samuel Vincent did dispose of all his shares by the middle of 1688, perhaps as part of clarifying his estate since he died not long after, leaving Tookie, who may have been related by marriage, as one of his executors. What is very striking are the people who bought Vincent's shares. Very few of them were cautious investors seeking a marginally higher return than ground rents. After sometimes passing through the hands of middlemen, most of the shares ended up with people who were, like Vincent and many of the original partners, large-scale investors and farmers of the excise. They were often connected through marriage or business ties, particularly in the brewing industry which provided no fewer than six partners: John Parsons, Felix Calvert and his son William, John Perry, Edward Buckley and Felix Feast. Perry was Buckley's brother-in-law with whom he farmed the excise, and the son-in-law of one of the original trustees of the insurance, Rowland Ingram. Feast was a partner and cousin of the Calvert family, buying what were Barbon's shares from him, and was executor of Tookie's will, effecting the sale of Tookie's share close to or even after his death. Two other partners, Sir John Johnson and George Hudson, were goldsmiths, and Richard Alie was related by marriage to one of the trustees. All of them were sophisticated and experienced investors. A few fractions of shares were also purchased by people who already owned the lease of one of the properties. Narcissus Luttrell was one of these who ended up with one-ninth of a share.[68]

Not everyone was impressed by the shares. John Hinde had sold his share to be held in trust for Sir William Stapleton, the Governor of the Leeward Islands who died in 1686 leaving his financial affairs in such a state that they had to be sorted out by Act of Parliament; his widow held the share in trust for their son.[69] When Dame Anne had asked her husband why on earth he had become involved 'of a thing of that nature', he explained that he had done it as a favour; she was convinced that her husband had been deceived by someone unloading doubtful debt on him, a view that was reinforced not only by profits of £126 on the share which she had received being reclaimed, but levies being made for losses.

The lack of building on Well Close was a continuing sore. There were countless lawsuits between the parties: the trustees put pressure on the partners to complete the building; the partners continued to find difficulties or claimed it was no longer their responsibility; a range of others who had lent funds to the participants attempted to get their money back. The original owners were Parsons and Barbon, and it was their estimates of the future ground rents that were used to establish how much security the site could provide. However, delivering the rents did require the buildings to be built and neither Parsons nor Barbon had the funds, nor did they choose to allocate much of the share price they received to doing so. The two men of straw (William Prideaux and Joseph Hartwell) who were ostensibly the tenants paid the ground rents for a short time but soon stopped, leading some of the partners to start legal proceedings.[70] The December 1683 trust deed setting up the insurance contained a clause whereby all six people with shares related to Well Close, that is Parsons, Barbon, Turner, Calvert, Wilson and Hinde, covenanted together to complete the building by Michaelmas 1684. Very little happened. In April 1684 Barbon raised £5,000 on the security of the buildings that he intended to build on his share, but although he spent a little money, most of it went elsewhere. Two years later he had not paid the interest on the £5,000 and he was arrested in an action of debt. This prompted Barbon to pay the interest and make elaborate arrangements for the eventual repayment of the principal, partly in cash and partly in property.[71] The result of this was that it was never clear which of the various tenants or subtenants had the responsibility of satisfying the covenant to build or, if they had, whether they had the access to land to allow them to do so. Similar problems occurred with the shares that had belonged to Hinde and Wilson. Calvert was in the same position, claiming that Barbon had promised him that he would not have to complete the building. It is arguable that it was still Barbon's responsibility after he had mortgaged his shares to Calvert, but by 1686 Calvert had taken ownership and taken out any of Barbon's remaining rights, confirmed by a further payment in 1691 by the then owner, his son William. Building was only completed after Calvert had assigned his shares to his cousin Felix Feast.[72]

Meanwhile, the trustees had a problem because, as Spelman had pointed out in his counter to Barbon's attack on the Friendly Society, the ground rents of Well Close were not sufficient to justify the security claimed for them and thus failed to underpin the insurance scheme. The natural approach might have been to sue Parsons and Barbon, but Parsons, from 1685, and Barbon, from 1690, were MPs and the trustees felt that any action 'would have been much hindered and obstructed by privilege of parliament'. They decided to sue those partners who owned the Well Close sites, and often, much to their disgust, the intermediate tenants as well.[73] The trustees did have one success in that some of Parson's houses which the Fire Office had insured burnt down and he naturally claimed for the loss, estimated at £1,510. The payment was withheld on the grounds that he was in default on his covenant to build on Well Close. This refusal was maintained even when Parsons assigned his insurance to one of his servants who applied for the loss as though independent.[74]

By the early 1690s Barbon had essentially given up all involvement in the Fire Office although his name continued to be associated with it. The two companies continued to compete and in 1693 the Fire Office started to offer the alternative of mutual insurance[75] although, as the Friendly Society would point out later, it did not settle any ground rents to underpin this. There is only patchy information about the relative growth of the two insurance schemes. Several commentators gave estimates of the number of policies, some data comes from the firms themselves, and the sequential numbering of policies with dates is another indicator. The final source is the calls for contributions from the Friendly Society which were occasionally published in the *London Gazette* and give an estimate of the policies in force at the time of the fire. There is no evidence that the Fire Office ever went above the 10,000 of their original limit, but the Friendly Society did claim up to 18,000 policies, although this was challenged on the basis that this was the total number ever issued rather than the number operative at the time. This may have been true for the Fire Office as well, although at least some individual policies were renewed.

Despite the end of his connections with the Fire Office, Barbon did not give up on insurance. In 1693 he applied for patent for 'a mill or engine for raising, without horses, water out of the Thames or other rivers within the flux or reflux of the sea'; this was granted and the patent issued formally in December that year.[76] The next month he transferred the patent to trustees, including at least four other MPs and a senior judge, with a view to making a business of it. Two of the MPs were the country party leaders Robert Harley and Thomas Foley who were also great supporters of Barbon's land bank (see Chapter X). The deed stated that Barbon had found a method for laying pipes near to houses to have water always ready in case of fire, and proposed to set up an office for insurance of houses and goods against fires and to annex this to the waterworks undertaking.[77] This would have been the first attempt to insure goods and was some fourteen years before the first scheme put into operation which became the Sun Fire Office. It was duly advertised with much elan, restating his claim that insurance increased the security of houses and therefore made them almost as valuable as land.[78] He includes some interesting statistics, pointing out than in the previous more than ten years some £30,000 had been paid in compensation for fire, while £100,000 of losses had been uninsured. Both insurance companies made their accounts public so Barbon will have had access to their results and, if correct, these statistics would suggest that almost 25 per cent of burnt dwellings in London and the suburbs were insured and that the annual number of houses burnt had decreased from about fifty-four in the period 1666–82 to thirty-six in 1681–94. Neither of these seems likely and we must suppose that for one reason or another the two sets of data are not directly comparable.

Barbon attributed the severe losses to lack of easy access to water, a problem he had solved since

> He that first invented the insuring of houses from fire has been trying several experiments for the more easy raising of Thames water and has at last invented such an engine as will raise the Thames water in any quantity to any height without the charge of horses.

He explained that the stock, shares, and rent of the waterworks and insurance were 'settled after the manner of the lands in the Fire Office' and were at least one third cheaper than the Friendly Society which could be afforded by the improved access to water to extinguish the fires. Nothing appears to have come of this venture. Barbon had still not forgotten insurance by 1695 and his Land Bank settlement included a provision that the trustees could use £10,000 worth of the land assets as insurance for the bank's bills that might otherwise be unpaid.[79]

William Hale had died in 1688, leaving his share of the Friendly Society to his son, also William, and Barbon's chief competitor, Henry Spelman, died in 1697. His nephew and heir, William Spelman, died the next year, and a monument in Henry's local church of Wickmere in Norfolk (Fig. 61) recalls his invention and foundation of the London Society for repairing damage from fire. Despite Spelman's

Fig. 61. Henry Spelman Memorial, Wickmere Church. © Sarah Cocke (https://www.flickr.com/photos/21804434@N02/34134544703/in/photostream/)

leading part in the creation of the Friendly Society, the emblem chosen to mark the houses that they insured was based on the crest of William Hale's arms showing a snake entwined round five golden arrows with black heads and silver feathers (Fig. 62).

By 1698, Barbon's reputation was at a low ebb and the Fire Office would hardly have been pleased to see his two attempts to start rival fire insurances. When a new deed was created in early 1698 to settle the leases on new trustees, given that all but two of the original ones had died, the recitals claimed that the insurance had been started by Vincent, Bartlett, Parsons and Tookie with no mention of Barbon's role, even though they did refer later to what had happened to his shares.[80] The distancing from Barbon was completed when an advertisement was placed later in the year which, while admitting that Barbon had been one of the originators of the Fire Office, made clear that

> that the fund [...] settled as above doth not belong to any of the new offices, nor are any of the Gentlemen of the Fire Office, first settled, any ways concerned with the said Dr Barbon, or any of the new offices for insuring houses from fire.[81]

Barbon was already sufficiently ill to have written his last will and he died two weeks later. Nevertheless, his name continued to be connected with the Fire Office and a few years later, when the Fire Office petitioned for protection from impressment for the twenty-one watermen who provided its firefighting service, it referred to itself as 'commonly called Barbon's insurance'.[82] The petition also revealed that the watermen wore the badge of a phoenix, perhaps the source of the Office's name change a few years later (Fig. 63).

Figure 64 shows the growth of the two companies, but the numbers relate to the total number of policies issued rather than the number operative at any time. Many of the early Fire Office policies were for the maximum thirty-one years, but it soon reduced this to a maximum of seven years, although we know that many were renewed.

While the Fire Office issued policy no. 9457 in April 1697, it only issued sixteen more policies over the next four months, and it seems likely that it was largely confining itself to renewal of existing policies. In 1705 the Fire Office renamed itself Phoenix, but it appears that it did not expand over the original 10,000 houses. Meanwhile it sought to combat any suggestion that the Friendly Society was more successful, by pointing out that the Society's claims to have 16,000 policies in 1704 were overstated since 11,800 of them were already expired.[83] This is certainly consistent with information from the *London Gazette* in 1694, where the required contribution for a burnt house from Friendly Society members suggested around 4,000 houses insured, and with a similar demand for contributions in 1704 cited by the Fire Office.[84]

By 1710 other fire insurance companies had started operation. These included another mutual, not backed up by any ground rents, started in 1696 as the Amicable but soon changing its name to the Hand

Fig. 62. Friendly Society Symbol.
By permission of the British Library, 816.m.10.(108.)

Fig. 63. Phoenix insurance sign.
By permission of the British Library, 816.m.10.(100.)

in Hand, which outlasted both the Phoenix and the Friendly Society. What became the Sun Insurance was begun by Charles Povey in 1706. In the light of this increased competition, it is hardly surprising that there was still skirmishing between the two original companies. The Phoenix spread information that the Friendly Society was late in paying its bills, causing the Society to sponsor advertisements by those who had received their money on time and to point out that one of the Phoenix's principal proprietors had insured £8,000 worth of houses with them, and that another now deceased had done likewise.[85] In fact, the original prospectus of the Amicable insurance lists John Parsons as one of its founder members and it is known that he had transferred all his fire insurance to that company by 1713, having sold one, if not both, of his shares in the Phoenix in 1712.[86] This may have been as a response to the withholding of his insurance claims by the Fire Office because of his failure to build in Well Close, although by 1694 he had built his own London house there.

The Fire Office had paid over £40,000 of claims by 1705 and in that year it was still a going concern.[87] But in 1712 policies taken out at the start of its operation for the maximum of thirty-one years, as for example the insurance of the Apothecaries' Hall for £2,000, would have expired and the last known

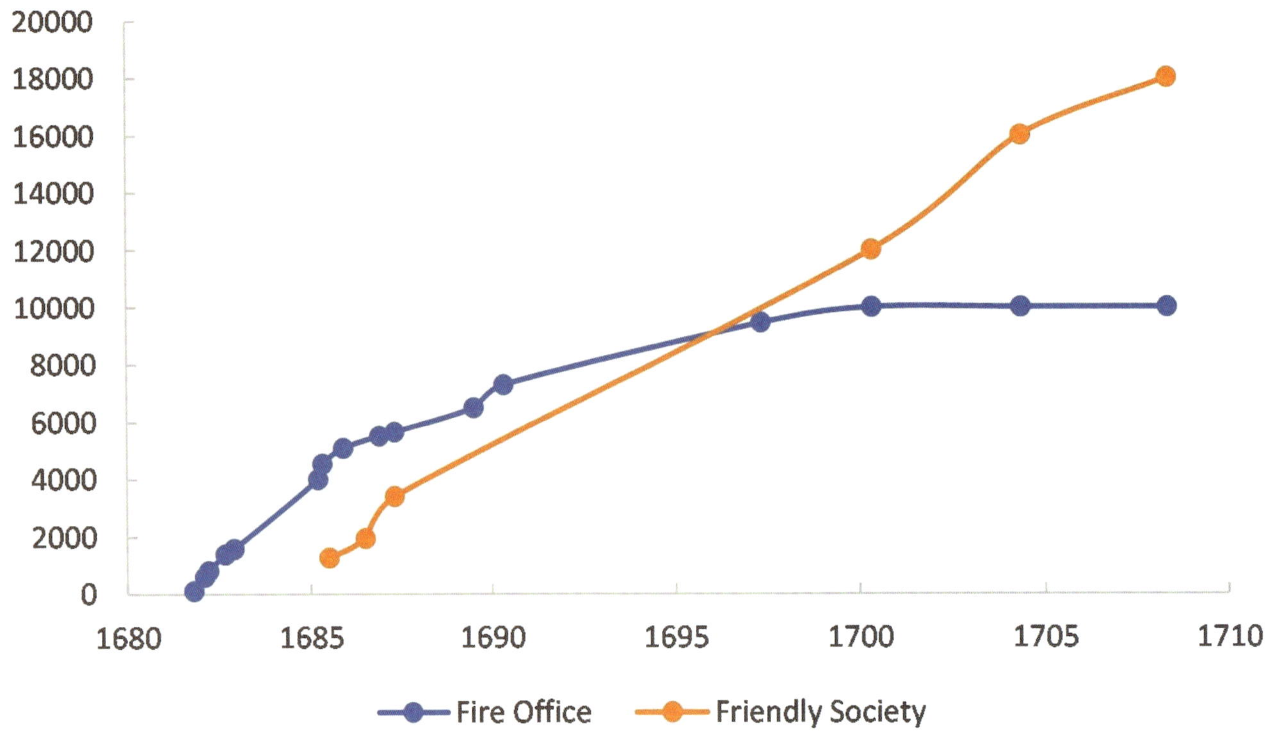

Fig. 64. Total number of policies issued.
Drawn by Timothy Walker

renewal would have expired in 1716.[88] This would be consistent with an advertisement placed by the Friendly Society in 1718 claiming that the Phoenix had discontinued insurance three or four years previously.[89] We also know from the sale of some of the ground rents by Felix Feast, still the owner of two shares in 1720, that by then new insurance had been discontinued with no more than 250 houses still insured and those only until April 1722.[90] All previous claims had been 'punctually paid and satisfied' but Feast gave the purchaser of his shares a warranty against future claims. We can assume therefore that the Phoenix was itself wound up in 1722; it is unconnected with the later Phoenix Insurance Company, founded in 1782. The future of the Friendly Society is less clear. In 1720 it advertised that it was creating offices round the country to insure houses outside London, but there is no information about whether it merged with another fire insurance company or was itself wound up.[91]

Conclusions

Fire and other kinds of insurance were to develop in the eighteenth century, and there is no doubt that at the time and subsequently Nicholas Barbon is identified as the first provider of fire insurance, an identification that he did all that he could to strengthen and continue. Whether he invented fire insurance is less clear, and as ever he was very good at taking someone else's proposals and making them work. He enjoyed promoting new practical ideas. Fire insurance also played to a number of his interests. Everyone at the time accepted that it increased the value of ground rents and buildings by improving the security of the investment. When the Fire Office started, it was a means for Barbon to create value without having to build on the sites used as security. He could never have obtained such a high price for those sites with few buildings. Even though he mortgaged the Well Close sites for only three-quarters of what he had claimed they were worth, and failed to pay back the mortgage, essentially he was able to raise substantially more than they would have been worth without the connection to insurance. Thirdly, by supporting further building around the outskirts of the City, he was able to promote his vision of a growing London as a positive factor in the development of the country's economy. Finally, it introduced him to a new set of investors, the tax farmers, victuallers to the armed forces and brewers who were beginning to look for new types of investment as the state began to take more control of tax collection.

It is instructive to consider how he promoted his ideas for insurance. He clearly did research on the number of fires there had been and used this as the basis of his calculations and arguments about how much security was needed. He did this more than once since similar calculations were done for the start of the original scheme and for that related to his water engine patent. This was very much in the tradition of 'political arithmetic' following William Petty (whom he had clearly read). He also entered into arguments, publishing pamphlets and advertisements so that no one could doubt his involvement. His skills as a controversialist were put to good effect and he encouraged his printers to use graphic design to promote his ideas.[92] He saw how to use insurance as a means to borrow more money than he would otherwise have been able and to forge alliances with potential investors with substantial funds.

CHAPTER VII

MORE BUILDING

We now put the fire insurance aside and return to Barbon's building activity. So far we have attempted to tell the story in a chronological record of when he started development on sites, but this does not give a full picture of his activity, particularly because that development often lasted for many years. His early days when he rebuilt houses that had been burned down in the Fire of London or when he had been able to develop a site moderately quickly, as for Exeter House, were long gone. By early in 1683 he had large numbers of sites under development, all requiring funds and all under some pressure. The lists below set out the ongoing commitments.

LARGELY SOLD
Miscellaneous sites following Fire
Essex Street
Middle Temple
Rupert Street
St Martins' Lane
Mincing Lane
Trevor House
Old Devonshire House
Military Ground

RETAINED	
Exeter House and Exchange	bought in 1676
Newport House	bought in 1682
Gerrard Street	completed 1685
Litchfield Street	started 1684, completed in 1691
Newport Market	started in 1686 sold in 1690
College Hill	bought 1678 completed and sold 1687/8
Charles Street	leases sold in 1682, freehold in 1685
Duke Street	one lease sold in 1683, others assigned to Scrimshire
Derby House	started in 1683
Dean Street	started 1683 completed 1691
Carew House	started 1683
Artillery Ground	bought 1681, completed 1682
Little Tower Hill	bought 1681, completed 1682
Well Close Square	bought 1681, largely completed 1698

The last three of the retained sites were part of the backing for Barbon's fire insurance and were briefly described in the previous chapter. Barbon and his partner Parsons had been forced to find alternative ground rents quickly to secure his fire insurance company when it became clear that he could not use the Old Devonshire House site near Bishopsgate for that purpose. It is not surprising therefore that when Barbon was one of the few people approached by the Treasury to buy three sites just east of the City, he saw them as the solution to his problem. Figure 65 shows their location.

The first two sites, purchased early in 1682, were close to existing development and Barbon and his partners had no difficulty in letting building leases. We know little about Little Tower Hill, the east part of which was redeveloped when the Royal Mint moved there early in the nineteenth century. It is clear, however, that Barbon proceeded quickly with the site because his builders were alleged to be encroaching on the nearby Ordnance Office and Robert Hooke's advice was sought in May 1682 on how to prevent it.[1] There were no problems in including this site in the fire insurance portfolio and it was clearly profitable for Barbon in its own right, let alone with the added advantage of the link to fire insurance.

Figure 67 shows the layout of the second site, the Artillery Ground, as it was in 1680. Although located conveniently for the silk merchants of Spitalfields, its layout at the time precluded a good carriage road to the highway of Bishopsgate Street and this, perhaps, was the reason that few larger houses were built there.

The Treasury was very much aware of the potential of the site and consulted Sir Christopher Wren about its possible value. It went on the market at a minimum price of £4,000 and Barbon and Parsons ended up paying £5,700 for it. Barbon's main interest, of course, was in getting houses built quickly to justify the ground rents needed to provide security for the fire insurance contracts. At least seventeen different builders were involved in the Artillery Ground, including John Foltrop who often worked with Barbon; the houses were almost invariably relatively small with frontages of only sixteen feet.[2] The result was that the value of the ground rents when developed was only just over £283 giving a capital value (i.e., twenty years ground rent) of £5,670, slightly less than Barbon had paid for it. Assuming that its development potential would have been clear to Barbon, this can only be explained by his urgent need to have ground rents to provide security for his fire insurance. Very little of substance remains of these houses, but Figure 66 shows some houses in Steward and Fort Streets, Spitalfields, long since demolished, as they were in 1914.

As can be seen from Figure 65, the third of these sites, Well Close, was much less well situated, being further away from the City and in a relatively unattractive location. A detail of the Morgan map (Fig. 68) shows that the open space was overlooked by buildings from across the roads that are now Cable Street, Ensign Street and the Highway. These would have been cheap houses and commercial premises,

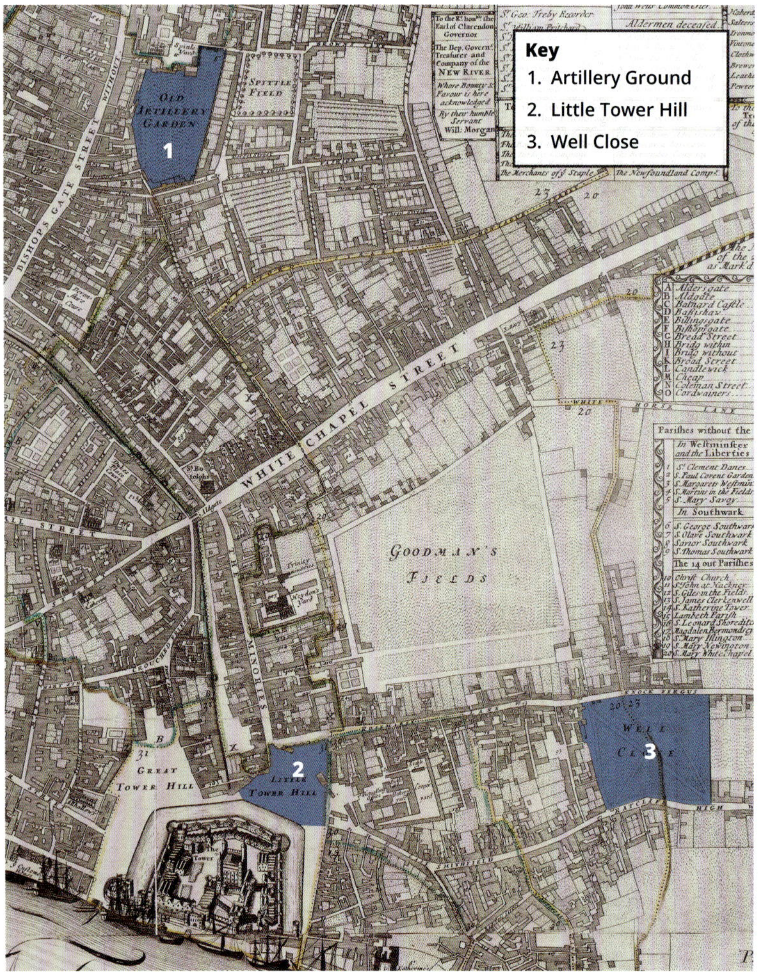

Fig. 65. Barbon's development sites east of the City, detail from Morgan's *London &c. Actually Survey'd*, 1682.
By permission of the British Library, Maps Crace Port. 2.58

hardly the kind of environment to attract those who wanted superior houses, backing up Defoe's comments quoted in the last chapter about it being a dangerous place at night.[3]

John Rocque's map of 1746 (Fig. 69) shows how Barbon got round this problem, possibly working with the surveyor Isaac Rowe who appears as a sublessee and who, like Barbon, had Northamptonshire connections. Well Close Square itself is insulated from the main roads while the diagonal alleys running from the corners of the square to the corners of the Close as a whole reflect the original paths shown in Morgan's map. This was an innovative arrangement that Barbon would use again in Red Lion Square.

Fig. 66. Houses at the junction of Steward and Fort Streets, 1914, watercolour by E. A. Phipson.

Image © London Metropolitan Archives (City of London), SC/PZ/ST/01/089

Despite this, as we saw in Chapter VI, the development in Well Close took a long time and provoked substantial litigation. However, Barbon's interest was in issuing building leases and starting building rather than in finishing it. Builders were reluctant to take on the leases and Barbon created more and more layers of leases to obscure what was actually happening, or rather not happening. His frequent builder, John Foltrop, took seven building leases from Barbon as well as two more on his own account; William Prideaux, one of Barbon's servants, took seventeen leases while Joseph Hartwell, a servant of his codeveloper John Parsons, took a further five. None of these resulted in quick building. These houses were larger than those in the Artillery Ground with frontages starting at a minimum of twenty feet, usually with three bays, examples are shown in Figures 70 and 71, and. were in the end taken up by a number of marine captains as had been Barbon's intention; Sir John Parsons himself built a large five-bay house in the square and lived there for some years. His house subsequently became the Court House, retaining a splendid staircase that may be due to Barbon. The church, usually known as Danish, but strictly Danish and Norwegian, was built there and Nos 20–21 Well Close Square became the Danish consulate for a short time in the eighteenth century. Figure 70 shows the church in 1696 with the buildings of Well Close Square in the background, while Figure 71 shows some of the buildings in 1961.

At the end of 1683, Barbon was engaged in developing Newport House with the market once it received its licence in 1686; he was well advanced with his building in Westminster, and was making progress in the three sites near the Tower, albeit slowly with Well Close Square. His fire insurance operations were well in hand and he was well known as a successful 'projector', even though everyone also knew that, like other such projectors, his cash flow was always under pressure and payment only came slowly. Barbon was not, however, one to rest on his laurels. He had already played a prominent part in London development, both by redeveloping large houses that no longer suited their owner's purposes, and by building on greenfield sites where they became available. London was still expanding, and he continued to keep his eye out for new possibilities.

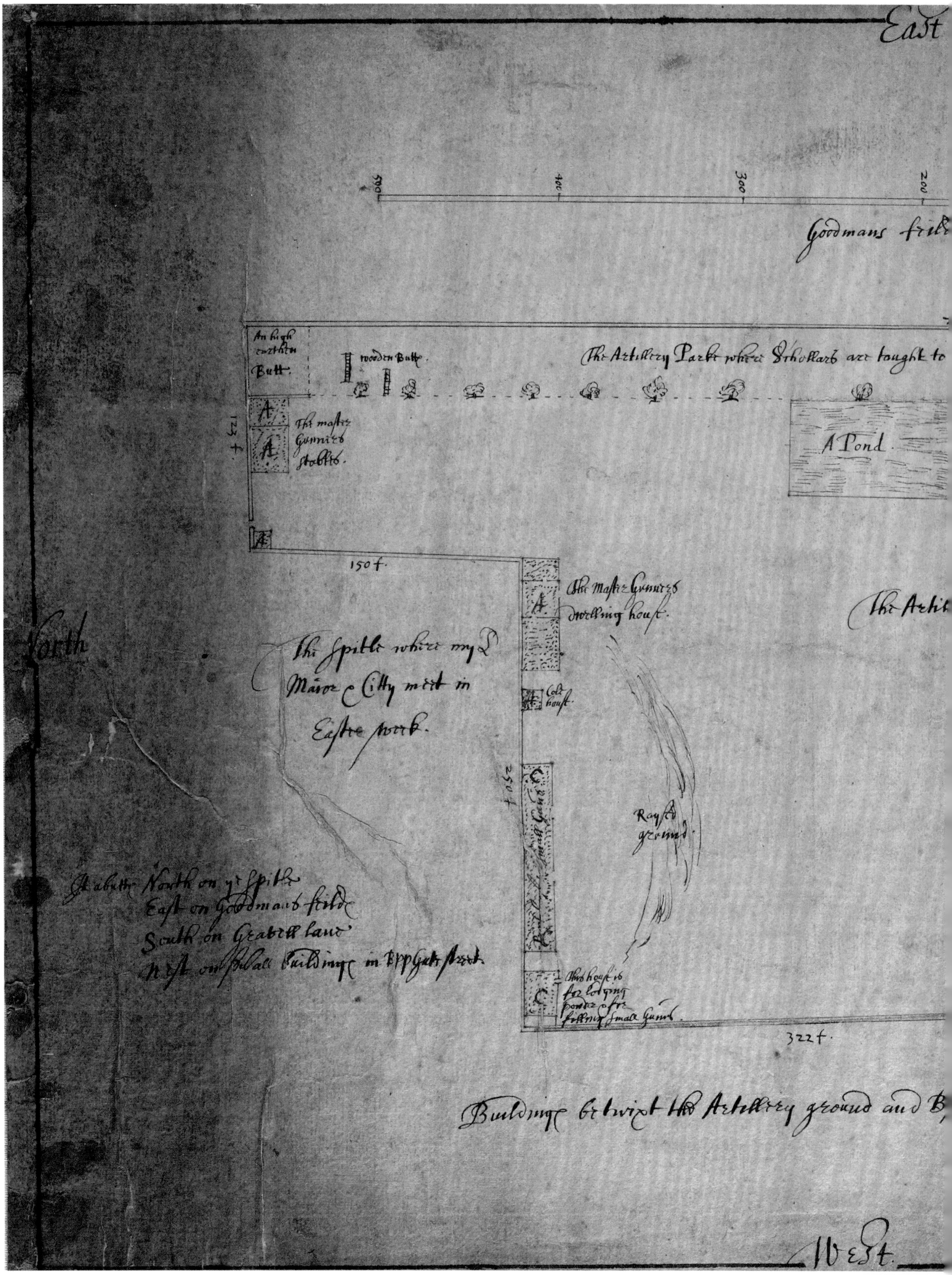
East
Goodmans
wooden Butts
A Pond
150 f.
North
322 f.
West

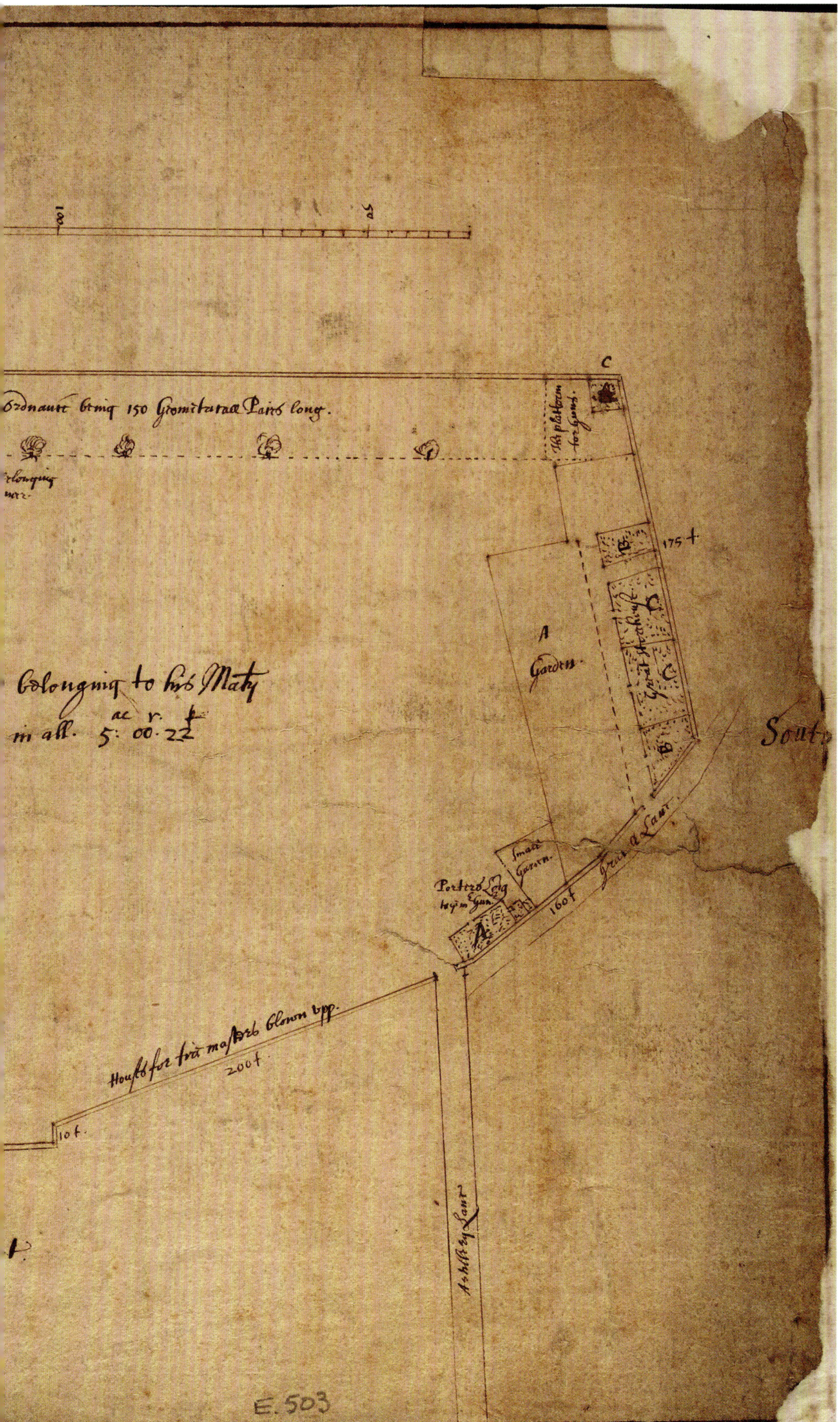

Fig. 67. Map of the Artillery Ground, 1680.
© The National Archives, MPE 1/503

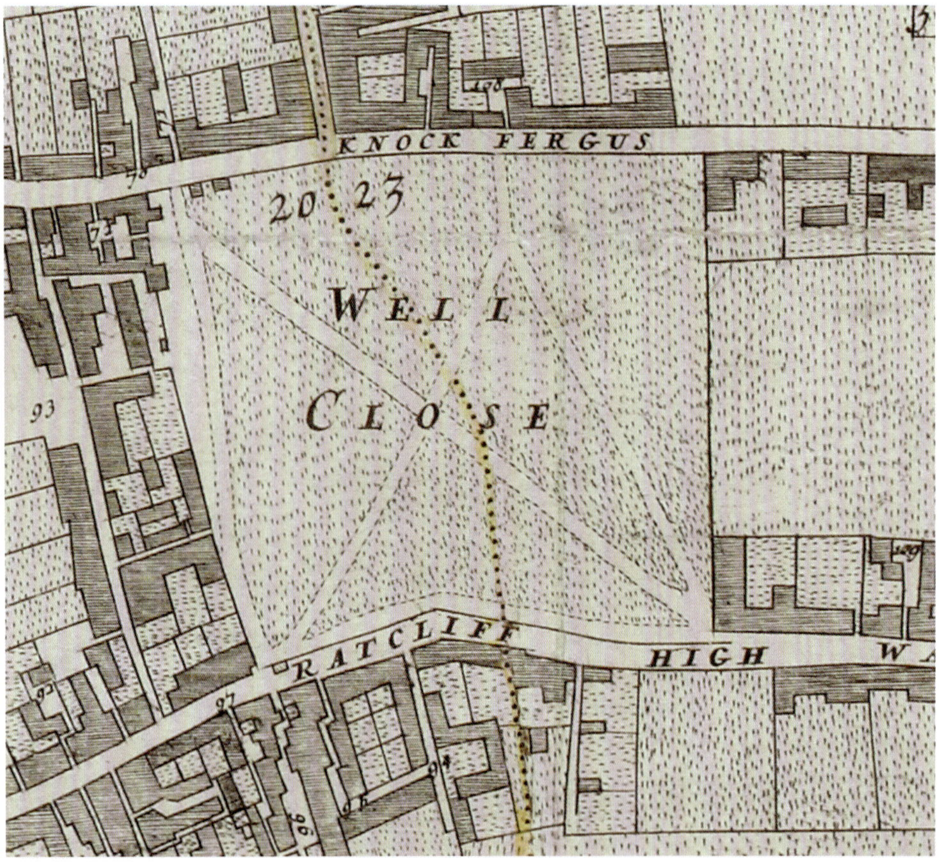

Fig. 68. Well Close, 1682, detail from Morgan's *London &c. Actually Survey'd*, 1682.
By permission of the British Library, Maps Crace Port. 2.58

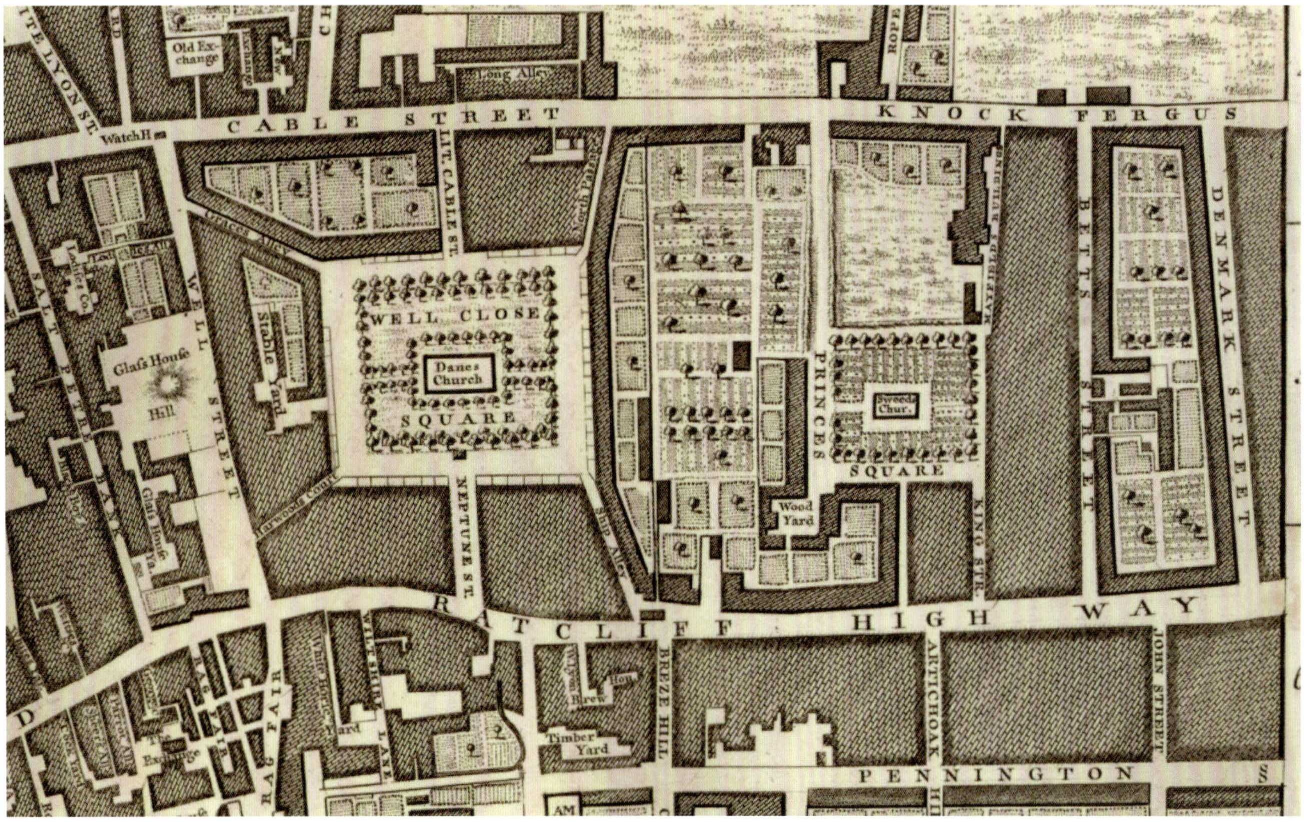

Fig. 69. Well Close Square, 1746, detail from Rocque's *Plan of the Cities of London and Westminster, and Borough of Southwark*, 1746.
© Trustees of the British Museum, A,14.2-25

Fig. 70. Danish Church and Well Close Square, engraving by Jan Kip, 1696.
© Trustees of the British Museum, Ee,8.99

Fig. 71. Well Close Square, south side, photograph, 1961.
Image © London Metropolitan Archives (City of London), no. 121582

Red Lion Fields

One such opportunity appeared early in 1683 as Red Lion Fields became available. It was a site of over eleven acres just north of High Holborn, taking its name from the Red Lion Inn and handily placed for the lawyers in Gray's Inn as shown in Figure 72. Its development is a very good example of the difficulties faced in establishing title to property subject to many layers of leases, the scope for delaying payments as a result, and the potential problems in translating this into houses on the ground when powerful local interests were opposed. The clash between the various interests became a *cause célèbre* and was reported in a number of contemporary diaries and letters. It was discussed by the Privy Council which instructed the Attorney General to take action; injunctions were sought. The Lord Chancellor himself became a mediator in the disputes, and there are records relating to at least thirteen related legal cases over the next ten years. It is worth setting out the story at some length since many writers have used these events to confirm their view of Barbon as an unscrupulous property developer.

We start with the legal issues. The site's owner, Sir Richard Fisher, granted a lease of the property in March 1683 to the speculator, Thomas Neale, who the next day himself assigned the lease to the goldsmith, John Hinde. Both of these were well known to Barbon and had indeed worked with him before, whether by lending money or joining in development. Barbon had clearly persuaded his interlocuters that, as he put in in a later legal document, 'by his skill and knowledge in building he could make a greater improvement than could be made by either Sir Richard Fisher or John Hinde'.[4] Accordingly Hinde negotiated a further deal in January 1684 with Fisher and Barbon that allowed him to purchase the freehold from Fisher and then sell it to Barbon or, if he failed to purchase the freehold, to sell Barbon the lease that he had acquired the previous year.[5]

Hinde failed to buy the freehold, but in July 1684 entered into another agreement with a Samuel Browne to sell the lease to Browne with Barbon undertaking to pay if Browne did not. Hinde linked this deal to the additional sale of a field in the nearby Lamb's Conduit Fields used for making bricks. These deals ran parallel to Barbon borrowing £500 from Browne to start work on the site secured on his agreement with Hinde. However, Hinde failed to implement these agreements too.[6] Indeed, his own financial affairs were already under some considerable pressure and a few months later he borrowed £12,000 secured on the Red Lion Fields lease from an Edward Seymour, who it turns out was a trustee for another of Hinde's creditors. By February 1685 the lease was transferred to Seymour.[7]

Fig. 72. Red Lion Fields, 1682, detail from Morgan's *London &c. Actually Survey'd*, 1682.

By permission of the British Library, Maps Crace Port. 2.58

Hinde had not paid any of the ground rents owing to Fisher, nor had Hinde or anyone else paid a capital sum for lease or freehold. Fisher therefore believed himself entitled to take back the leases, and in May 1685 he agreed to transfer the various leases and freeholds to trustees acting for Barbon with some complicated arrangements allowing Fisher to be paid out of the future ground rents rather than with a capital sum. The next problem occurred in September when Hinde was made bankrupt because of his debts to the Crown and committed to the Fleet prison, where he would die soon after. By November 1685 a Commission in Bankruptcy had been issued and the Commissioners, whose job it was to try to sort matters out, applied to the Courts to use Hinde's leases on Red Lion Fields to repay his creditors, naturally rejecting Fisher's claims to have taken back the lease.[8] As a result the lease and the right to the ground rents thereof were severally claimed by Fisher, Barbon, Barbon's trustees, Seymour and various of Hinde's creditors as well as the Commissioners of Bankruptcy. These complications and the interactions between the various leases, and indeed a number of other side deals, would continue to cause problems and litigation continued at least until the mid-1690s.

Not everyone was happy about the development, in particular the members of Gray's Inn who wanted to retain the green space near their Inn. They had already crossed swords with Hinde over his brickmaking, beginning litigation to prevent this, and as early as February 1683 had taken legal advice on how they might stop the building in Red Lion Fields.[9] At the same time, Barbon, thinking to use the tactics which had been successful with the Middle Temple for the development of Essex House, offered to build them a new chapel at his expense, worth £8,000, if they would sell him the waste land that the Inn had next to Gray's Inn Lane and confirm their acceptance of his building on Red Lion Fields. The Inn declined this offer.[10]

It might be thought that these various arguments would have effectively prevented any building on the site, but Barbon was not to be deterred. All those involved saw Barbon as the eventual developer and he began work starting not long after March 1684, the date when the original deal with Hinde and Fisher, if implemented, would have passed the site to him. He did not have an easy ride.

One has to assume that the Inn's initial legal consideration did not identify any means to stop Barbon building. They began by trying persuasion. Once Barbon's workmen had started laying out the site and digging trenches, the Benchers of the Inn sent deputies with fifty or sixty supporters in their gowns. John Verney's letter to his father Ralph Verney reported,

> When the workmen saw them coming, they were going to run away, but on second thoughts stayed. When the deputies came, they forbad all the workmen, who very willingly obeyed, saying they would rather want work than offend them.[11]

Unsurprisingly, Barbon was having nothing of this and sent the workmen back. This time Nicholas Luttrell takes up the story and his diary reports that on 10 June,

> Dr Barebone, the great builder, having some time since bought the Red Lyon Fields near Gray's Inn Walks to build on, and having for that purpose employed several workmen to go on with the same, the Gentlemen of Gray's Inn took notice of it, and thinking it an injury to them, went with a considerable body of a hundred persons: upon which the workmen assaulted the gentlemen and threw bricks at them again; so a sharp engagement ensued, but the gentlemen routed them at the last and brought away one or two of the workmen to Gray's Inn; in this skirmish one or two of the gentlemen and servants of the house were hurt, and several of the workmen.[12]

Barbon was not prepared to be deprived of his business. By the next day (11 June) he had recruited support, possibly soldiers in workmen's clothes, and according to a complaint to the Privy Council,

> marched about the fields in the head of two hundred men shouting and hollowing within the hearing of Gray's Inn and waving their hats as by way of challenge to the gentlemen of the Society to come out and encounter them, the said Barebone himself exhorting them that they should not be discouraged for he would back them with a thousand the next morning.[13]

The lawyers and their supporters could not resist and the next day they attacked Barbon's team again. This time we have the report of Roger Morrice, who makes clear in his diary for 12 June that not only did Barbon's workmen defeat the lawyers, but the Courts sided firmly with him, requiring the gentlemen's offence to be published with all severity and ordering that

> the sheriff should come with his Posse Comitatus and go into Gray's Inn with a sufficient force, and take with him such Bricklayers as had broken heads etc and apprehend and commit such Gentlemen as the said Bricklayers should charge to have been in the quarrel and riot.[14]

A request to appeal was refused and the Lord Chief Justice, George Jeffreys, was reported by John Verney as telling 'the Benchers that if they cannot govern their house, he will send someone to do it for them'.[15] This did not stop Gray's Inn from trying other legal approaches. They were too late to use the common law because the long vacation was beginning, and so the next week they approached the Chancery Court seeking an injunction to prevent him doing any more building, claiming Barbon was blocking up well-used and old paths and intended to erect many small houses 'to the prejudice of the Society and persons of quality that resort there and to the walks for their health and recreation, and they will lose their wholesome air'.[16] Barbon merely pointed out that any paths were only recent, and that he would build

> fair large houses for persons of estate and value before which this defendant intends to leave a very open square unbuilt with pleasant walks therein in which the gentlemen of the said society or any the persons of quality that visit them may walk and take the air if they please.

He added that there remained six or seven acres between the Inn and the proposed square which could not be seen from it, and would in any case be much more pleasant than the present cow houses and dunghills.[17]

The next tactic was to procure towards the end of July a complaint from the Middlesex Justices of the Peace making most of the same points, including problems with his rubbish tips, as well as alleging that Barbon was blocking the road, the Kings Way, by his deliveries of brick, lime and sand.[18] Although the Privy Council asked the Attorney General to consider what legal means might be used to stop Barbon from encroaching or abusing the road, its use for normal deliveries could not be prevented. It also asked the Attorney General to prosecute Barbon and the rest of the rioters, but given the previous Court decisions reported by Roger Morrice, this would only have rebounded on Gray's Inn itself. Indeed, Barbon struck back at attempts to use injunctions to stop him building by instituting large numbers of legal actions against Edward Guise, the Justice of the Peace who was issuing them, to the extent that Guise returned to the Privy Council asking that his costs in defending these should be met by the public purse.[19]

Gray's Inn's actions ended up causing problems for the Inn. The Lord Chief Justice's involvement resulted in him being given the role of mediator between the Inn and a number of builders active in the locality, not just Barbon. The mediation with Barbon dragged on until at least the middle of 1685, by which time the building was well past being prevented. To add insult to injury, the Inn had to offer 'a treat for the Lord Chief Justice' in the Gray's Inn chambers of his arch enemy Sir William Williams.[20] Mediation with Barbon and other builders continued for some time in connection with Lamb's Conduit Fields and it was not until 1688 that Jeffreys, by now Lord Chancellor, visited the Gravel Hill Fields just north of Gray's Inn where his mediation allowed John Skipwith to build two rows of fifteen houses but with palisades to hide them from Gray's Inn Road.[21]

Opposition to new building on the edges of cities is not unusual, and it is not always unfounded, not least because of the inconveniences to residents of being near a building site. But while there is no doubt that Barbon fought his corner vigorously, literally as well as figuratively, it is difficult to put the blame for any fighting or rioting anywhere other than on the shoulders of Gray's Inn who, having failed with the unprovoked use of force, then attempted to use their legal skills to stop him, and failed again. As Barbon commented in one of the early legal actions, he believed the opposition came 'principally from the private interest or design of some gentlemen of the Inn who have houses near the field in Holborn or Bloomsbury, backing on to the field'.[22] Barbon was no saint, but the story of Red Lion Square demonstrates that many of his opponents were furthering their own interest as much as he was, and were entirely prepared to take action against him that was either illegal or an abuse of the law. It is their descriptions of him in lawsuits that have lived on, but much of the descriptions of him as immoral and unscrupulous are built on what his opponents claimed in attempts to build their legal case.

The way was now open for Barbon to proceed with the building, and four months before he finalized a detailed lease with Richard Fisher covering the development, he had already issued building agreements, one of which, dated 13 January 1685, still exists. It will be discussed at greater length in Chapter VIII. As well as committing him to procuring a lease for the builder, it confirms that, as he had told the Chancery Court earlier, he was indeed concerned that the houses should be well built. His final lease with Fisher would require that the houses should be uniform and at least as good as the houses in the nearby Brook Street, and this had been anticipated by the building agreement specifying relevant construction details.

Barbon had to work hard to find sufficient builders to meet the requirement in the lease from Fisher that the buildings were completed by Michaelmas Day 1688, and a number of his usual contacts appeared. These included William Edge who had been involved in the Essex House development, the plasterer Alexander Cutting who had also taken a lease in Grafton Street and would be one of the witnesses to Barbon's will, and the lawyer William Milman who claimed that he had been encouraged to build by Barbon to

> preserve the project of building the said ground from being ruined and lost which then for want of undertakers to build began to decline and was in great danger (as some other places taken by the said Nicholas Barbon had been) of being wholly neglected.[23]

It is impossible to work out how much profit Barbon made from this development. Fisher had driven a very hard bargain, requiring indemnity from any payments resulting from Hinde's bankruptcy, payment of all the back rents and ground rents owing, and a transfer of £515 per annum of ground rents relating to completed houses to be chosen by Fisher. There was also an option for Barbon to purchase the freeholds of these houses for a further £11,330. Barbon had tried hard in his various actions to get some recompense for not having had 'quiet possession' due to the arguments with Gray's Inn, even though he 'did at last with great pains and charges overcome the difficulties [...] although he was by the said troubles forced to break his design and model'.[24] The final layout is shown in Figure 73.

The map shows how the Square was created in the middle of Red Lion Fields and retained the diagonal paths noticeable on the earlier map in the same way as in Well Close Square. The Square was protected from the traffic and noise of the main roads which would have had smaller houses on them. The building is shown in more detail in Figure 74, which is taken from a record of an estate owned by Sir Jeremy Sambrooke comprising houses bought from Fisher and Barbon. This plan represents the

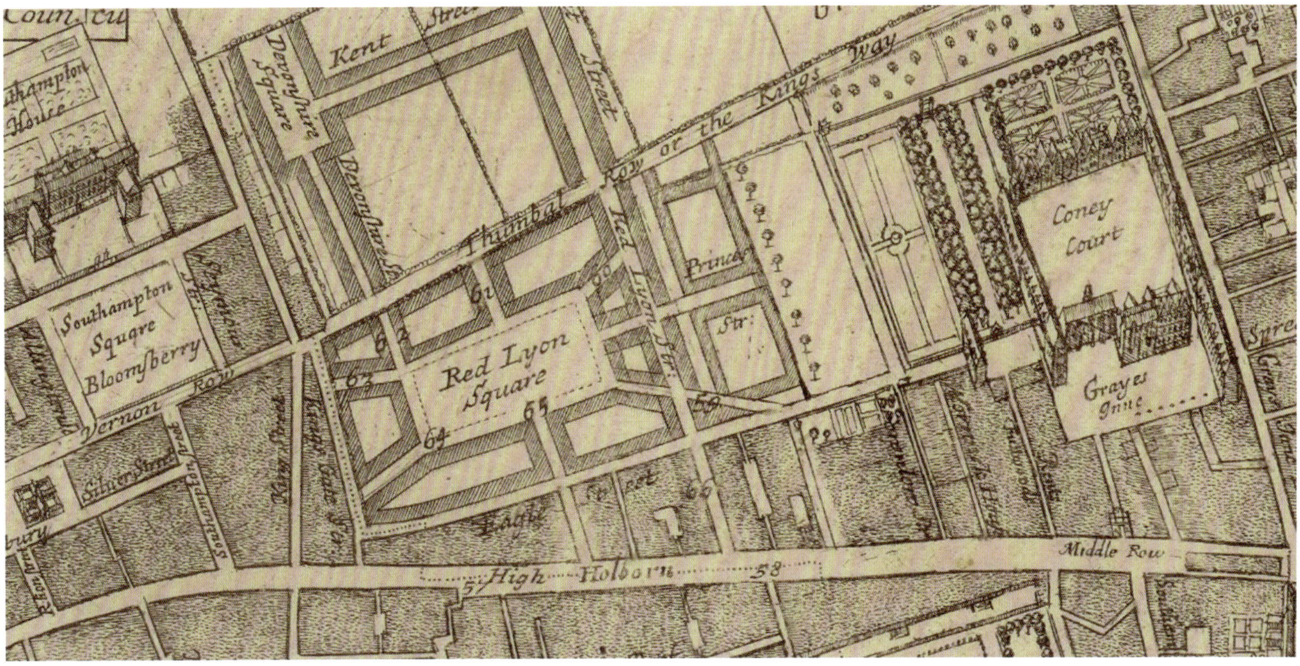

Fig. 73. Red Lion Square, 1700, detail from Morden and Lea's *Actuall Survey of London, Westminster & Southwark*, 1700.
Key: 63 – Orange Street; 64 – Fisher Street
Private Collection

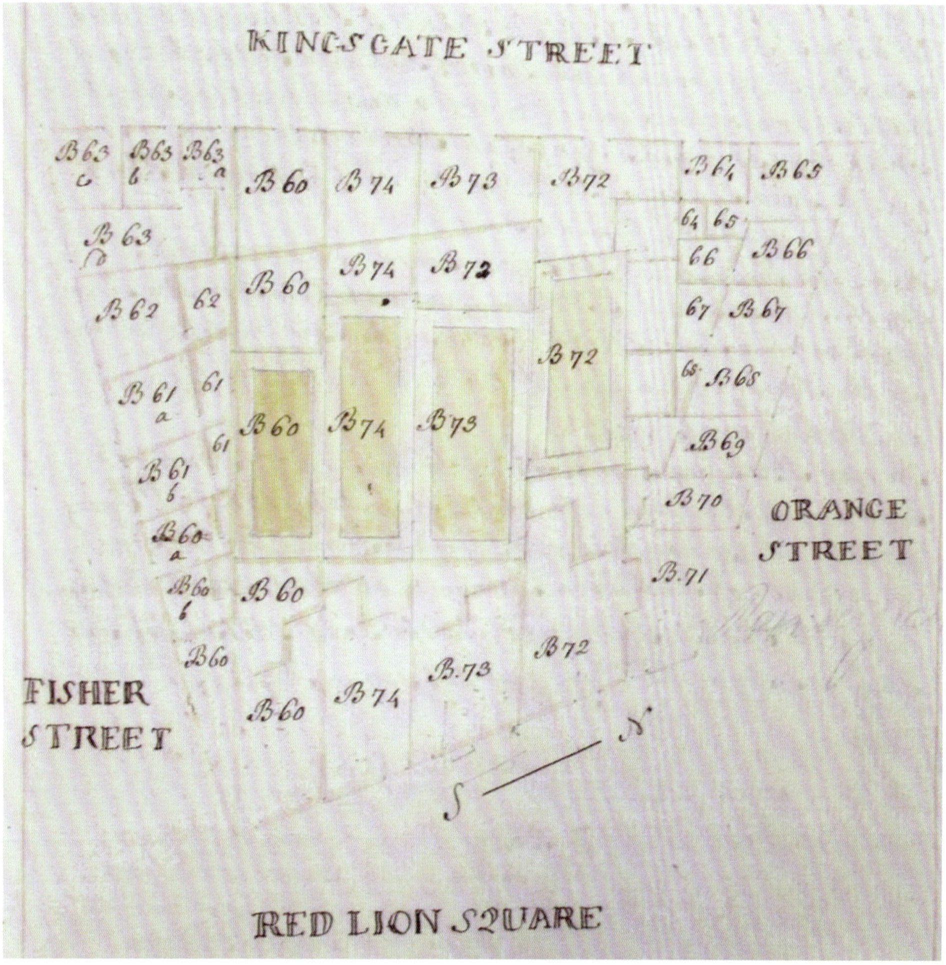

Fig. 74. Detailed plan of the west side of the Red Lion Square development. © Camden Local Studies and Archives Centre, A01595

block comprising the west side of Red Lion Square and Fisher, Orange, Kingsgate Streets with the green colour in the middle confirming the Morden and Lea Map which shows the sites had some garden.

The house numbered B73 on the plan which had a 33-foot frontage onto the west side of the Square, was lived in by John Shorter, whose father had bought houses in Charles Street from Barbon a few years earlier. The four sites running from Red Lion Square to Kingsgate Street were all in the same ownership and comprised the large houses fronting on to the Square with a stable and coach-house at the other end of each plot. This is an early example of the form which became typical from the 1720s onwards in the West End when mews began to develop with a stable and coach-house at the end of each plot. The form can be traced back to Covent Garden and Lincoln's Inn Fields, but many seventeenth-century plans created more communal stable yards in the back lands and in many cases there was no direct access between a house and a stable; in Great Ormond Street, for instance, there were two stable yards south of the street, perhaps to preserve the open views north from the larger houses on the north side of the street.

Whatever the financial results, Red Lion Square became a popular place to live, with many MPs and lawyers, including members of Gray's Inn. Strype, writing some time before 1720, says,

> it hath graceful buildings on all sides, which are inhabited by gentry or Persons of Repute; the houses have palisado pails and a freestone pavement between them. The middle of the Square is enclosed from the street or passage to the houses by a handsome high palisade pail, with rows of trees, gravel walks and grass plots within, all neatly kept for the inhabitants to walk in.[25]

Figure 75 shows the square in 1725 with the hills of Highgate and Hampstead behind.

Few of the original houses survive; Nos 14 to 17 were built around 1686 but given a new facade in the nineteenth century; having been converted internally to modern offices, they were marketed in 2020 as 'The Barbon Buildings'.[26]

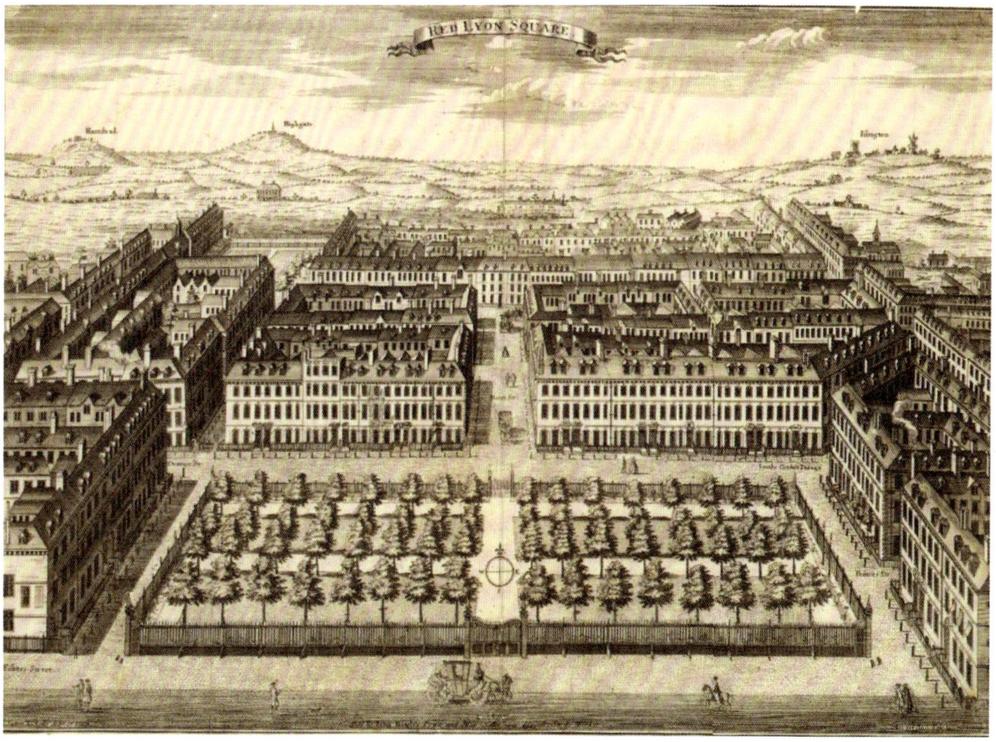

Fig. 75. Red Lion Square, etching by Sutton Nicholls, *c.* 1725. © Trustees of the British Museum, 1880,1113.4397

An Apology for the Builder

The arguments over Red Lion Square may have exacerbated worries about the scale of development in London, and the accession of James II in February 1685, coupled with a new Parliament with a Tory majority possibly less inclined to support the growth of the City, allowed the subject to be raised again. Less than a month after the new Parliament assembled and the same day as a petition of Barbon's concerning the regulation of Hackney Carriages was referred to the committee examining a bill on the subject, another Commons committee *resolved* that 'a Tax be laid upon new Buildings erected upon new Foundations'. The next day, 18 June 1685, the whole House approved this, although restricting it to 'Buildings within the Limits of the Bills of Mortality, except any such built within the Compass of the late general Fires in the City of *London,* and Borough of *Southwark*'; this meant the suburbs. Committees were then set up to prepare the necessary legislation and to consider how much money such a tax would raise. Barbon's fellow developer, John Parsons, was one of the MPs deputed to consider the likely sum raised by the proposed tax, but he was not the only committee member with a similar interest in development. As with previous committees on this subject, neither of them ever reported back, in this case because they never had the chance. The session ended in early July and James prorogued Parliament soon after its new session in November 1685. It never met again.

There was no reason at the time that Barbon could have predicted that the proposal would be so easily kicked into the long grass, and he felt the need to set out the arguments for the new Parliament and indeed the new King. He repackaged his *Discourse showing the great advantages that new Buildings and the enlargement of Towns and Cities do bring to a Nation* of 1678 and published a new pamphlet entitled *An Apology for the Builder, or A discourse shewing the cause and effects of the increase of Building.* As was usual for such pamphlets, it was published anonymously and clearly designed for MPs and others interested in influencing the policy towards builders, rather than for the consumption of the general public. It is usually dismissed as mere special pleading, but that rather misses the point. It was not designed as an academic work on economics, but as a means to influence the House of Commons not to introduce a tax on new building in and around London.

While the two pamphlets are about the same length and contain many of the same facts and arguments, there are differences between them. The *Apology for the Builder* starts with an extended history, running to almost half the length of the piece, designed to demonstrate the historical growth in population, in biblical and classical times as well as in England. By then a number of writers apart from Graunt[27] had used the Bills of Mortality to demonstrate the increase in London's population and Barbon cites two of them: the former Lord Chief Justice Hales's *Primitive Origination of Mankind* had been published posthumously in 1677, possibly too late for reference in Barbon's previous pamphlets, and Sir William Petty's *Of the Growth of the City of London and of the Measures, Periods, Causes and Consequences thereof* which was published in 1682 or 1683 and updated previous work to include the results of the most recent Bills of Mortality.

Barbon goes on to argue that population growth necessarily brings a demand for increased numbers of houses but uses Morgan's map of 1682 to show that the average rate of building was under three hundred houses a year. There is less numerical argumentation overall than in the *Discourse*, but the *Apology* is still very similar, although occasionally basing the figures on slightly different years; the only obvious updating of the numbers comes by using the most recent Bills of Mortality to confirm the continued growth in London's population. He repeats the argument from the *Discourse* that building in the suburbs increases the rents of property closer to the centre, even showing that rents in the Strand have gone up 20 per cent even since his last pamphlet. He also includes more recent examples since his last pamphlet, including ones of relevance to his own building in Leicester Fields and off the Ratcliffe Highway, the latter possibly to promote his Well Close Square development.[28]

The chief difference between the two pamphlets is his concentration on the role of the capital, rather than just any city. He argues that a 'Nation cannot increase without the Metropolis be enlarged and how dangerous a consequence it may be to obstruct its growth',[29] and that a growing capital is the clearest symptom of the health of a country. For him,

> the Metropolis is the heart of a nation, through which the trade and commodities of it circulate, like the blood through the heart, which by its motion giveth life and growth to the rest of the body, and if that declines, or be obstructed in its growth, the whole body falls into consumption.[30]

Here was the doctor using a medical analogy to his advantage. He went on in similar vein,

> if those Gentlemen that fancy the City to be the Head of the nation, would but fancy it like the heart, they would never be afraid of it growing too big. For I have never read of such a disease, that the Heart was too big for the Body.[31]

He took the opportunity to make points that would attract the new King. Growing cities meant increased customs duties and other taxes on imports such as tonnage and poundage, all of which the new Parliament had just granted James for life. Recognizing James's reputation as a successful soldier and admiral, he pointed out that if London had been allowed to grow to its full potential, it would have had

> Such a vast number of ships; being situate on an island and navigable river; filled with innumerable inhabitants, of such natural courage as the English are; and to be so easily transported on a sudden with all things necessary for war, it would long before this time have been a terror to all Europe; and now would have had the opportunity, under the government of such a martial prince as now reigns, to be made the metropolis of the world; to have caused England's monarch to be acknowledged Lord of all the navigable cities and seaports towns in the world; to have made an universal monarchy over the seas, an empire no less glorious, and of much more profit, than of the land, and of larger extent, than either Caesar's or Alexander's.[32]

This is boosterism taken to its ultimate conclusion, but no doubt he had in mind that James II had been Duke of York and Lord High Admiral when the Navy captured New Amsterdam and renamed it New York in his honour. It is, perhaps, also a little unfair to dismiss too quickly his vision for an expanded London as the centre of a world empire based on sea power. After all, that did indeed come to fruition, even if not until the nineteenth century.

Apart from this, the overall flavour of the *Apology* is of a quick production to counter the decision of the House of Commons to support taxing new building in London. Barbon barely mentioned his support of 'emulation' as a driver for growth in the economy and generally the arguments are more condensed. He was quite content to do no more than repeat his arguments with minimal updating of the figures and references. The extended historical introduction coupled with the references to Petty and Hales may have been designed to emphasize that this was not just a builder supporting his own business, but someone who thought about the whole economy, an issue to which he would return at length in his next publication five years later, *The Discourse of Trade*.

Developing Red Lion Square, writing *Apology for the Builder* and maintaining his other projects did not absorb all Barbon's energy. He still had some work to do in the City, and in 1687 finally completed his building in College Hill, on the east side at the north end. This allowed him, together with his financier Sir John Moore, to sell the 'two new brick capital messuages' to yet another of Barbon's regular financiers, Sir Thomas Cooke. Moore got £1,750 and Barbon £1,450; in 1697 Cooke sold the property to the merchant Sir John Lethieullier.[33]

The northern house of the two, which became Turners' Hall in 1736, was demolished and only the southern house still survives as No. 22A College Hill, somewhat altered but a recognizably late seventeenth-century house. What are extraordinary are the two seventeenth-century gateways on College Hill which also still survive; recent photographs are shown below in Figure 76.

Barbon only very rarely provided decoration for his houses, it being an unnecessary cost, not least because it could be added by the eventual tenant to his particular taste. However, these two gateways are of unusual width and form, and naturally raise the question of why the grandeur. We know that the two gateways did not exist at the time Barbon and Moore bought the site since the Ogilby and Morgan map of 1676 (Fig. 77) shows only one entrance to what appears to be a courtyard. By the time of Rocque's map of 1746 (Fig. 78) there were two gateways, with the two houses built by Barbon, one of which had by then become the hall of the Turners' Company.

Many have seen Wren's hand in the gateways. They were drawn in 1842 by the architect Charles Robert Cockerell (Fig. 79) in preparation for his tribute to Sir Christopher Wren though there is no evidence that Wren was in any way associated with them. Later, in 1897, the antiquary and London topographer Philip Norman wrote that the 'two fine gateways, with sculptured pediments, which might have been designed by Wren' may have been the entrances to the stables of Buckingham House

Fig. 76. College Hill gateways.
Photographs by Timothy Walker

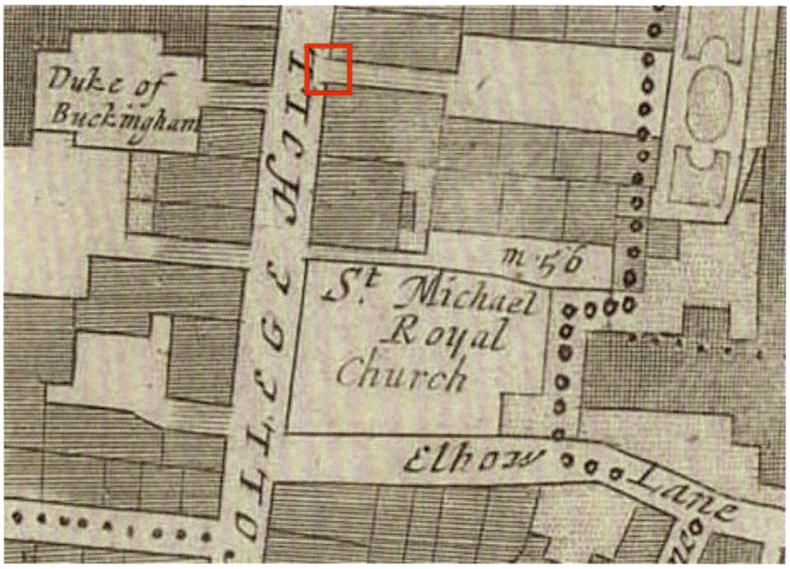

Fig. 77. College Hill, 1676, detail from Ogilby and Morgan's *Large and Accurate Map of London*, 1676. An entrance is shown on the east side of College Hill leading to a courtyard north of the church of St Michael Royal.

By permission of the British Library, Maps Crace Port. 2.61

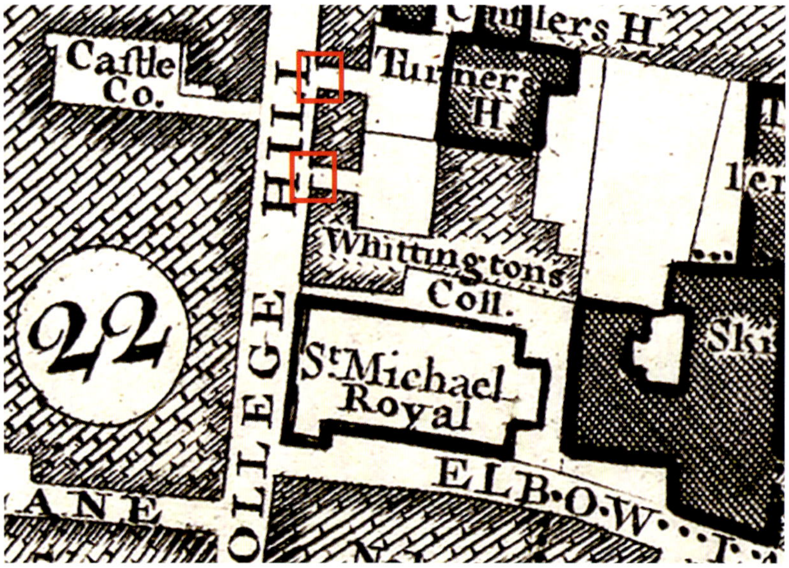

Fig. 78. College Hill, 1746, detail from Rocque's *Plan of the Cities of London and Westminster, and Borough of Southwark*, 1746. Two entrances are shown on the east side of College Hill leading to houses north of the church of St Michael Royal.

which stood on the opposite side of College Hill; this was the house where Sir John Lethieullier lived in succession to the Duke of Buckingham. That Lethieullier owned properties on both sides of College Hill may explain the mistaken reference in Edward Hatton's *New View* in 1708 that Buckingham House was on the east side of College Hill. The Duke's house on the west side is shown in Ogilby and Morgan's map and his presence in the City (following his sale of York House, Strand) is satirized in verse:

> From Dam me, whatever we don't Understand,
> From Purchasing at Dowgate, and Selling i/th Strand,
> Calling Streets by our Name, when we have Sold the Land
>   Libera Nos.
> From Borrowing our own House to Treat Scholars Ill,
> And then be Unchancellord against our Will,
> Nought left of a Colledge but our own Colledge-hill
>   Libera nos.[34]

An association with the Duke of Buckingham would perhaps explain the unusual elaboration of the gateways, and the courtyard shown in the Ogilby and Morgan map could have been stables. However, there is a clear route in the freehold title of the property from a pre-Great Fire owner through to Lethieullier, in which there is no mention of the Duke of Buckingham. A fanciful explanation might be

Fig. 79. College Hill gateways, drawing by C. R. Cockerell, 1842.

that the gateway shown in Ogilby and Morgan was the entrance to the Duke's short-lived stables with an elaborate gateway, copied shortly afterwards by Barbon when he built the two houses on the site, but the more likely explanation is that the two gateways are Barbon's.

Even before he had completed the work covered in this chapter, Barbon made a purchase of a very different kind: the country house Osterley Park, costing him £9,500 in March 1684.[35] This had been through a large number of owners since being enlarged and developed by the merchant and financier, Sir Thomas Gresham. It was the only building outside London that Barbon bought — apart from those needed to secure his position as an MP in a rotten borough — and it appears that he bought it entirely for his own purposes, and not to turn a profit. He may well have found attractive the idea of living in a house so strongly connected to Gresham, inventor of Gresham's law of money and the developer of the Royal Exchange, on which Barbon had based his own Exeter Exchange. He promptly mortgaged it, together with Exeter Exchange, for £12,000, and then began to make alterations. These will be covered in Chapter XIV, but suffice it to say now that while he failed to pay the interest, he contrived to remain in occupation of the building until his death in 1698 by using his parliamentary privilege to avoid repossession.

Shortly after this, Barbon began his last project in the Middle Temple, it having been agreed in June 1687 that he should build 'a substantial ornamental brick building with four chambers on a floor' twenty feet south of the existing garden building. Barbon undertook to prepare a model, ready within a week.[36] He employed John Foltrop as builder, agreeing that Foltrop would have the disposal of at least some of the chambers; the building was to be finished by April 1688. They jointly borrowed £500 from William Milman at 6 per cent, but in fact Milman paid only £480, so raising the interest rate above the legal rate. In a dispute between Barbon and Foltrop in 1689 Foltrop presented an account which showed that he had received £1,840 for chambers but had spent more than £2,266, some of it repairing storm damage already suffered by that date.[37] A book in the Middle Temple Archive shows that Foltrop and Barbon were disposing of chambers there until 1693.[38]

These chambers were at the southern end of the west side of Middle Temple Lane, by Temple Stairs. In the deed of partition between the Inner and Middle Temples in 1732 they were described as Barbon's Buildings; they later became No. 1 Garden Court and eventually Nos 3–6 Plowden Buildings. They were bombed and the site is now the Middle Temple Library. In *Master Worsley's Book* the buildings were described as two parallel ranges, and this form can be seen in views of the Middle Temple from the river (Fig. 80).[39] The buildings were recorded by the Royal Commission on Historical Monuments as providing four sets of chambers on each floor, the Middle Temple requirement of 1687, and having an eight-window front; this does not match Emslie's 1880 drawing of the garden front which shows nine windows (Fig. 81).[40] No plan of this building has been found. The date and the clearly distinct building with parallel ranges and four sets of chambers per floor suggest that a drawing of chambers in the Bodleian Library could be an unexecuted scheme for this site (Fig. 82). The drawing is for a larger building than that eventually built; the two ranges are linked by bridges and separated by three large lightwells taking up a significant amount of the floor plan. It would not be surprising if this scheme was set aside.

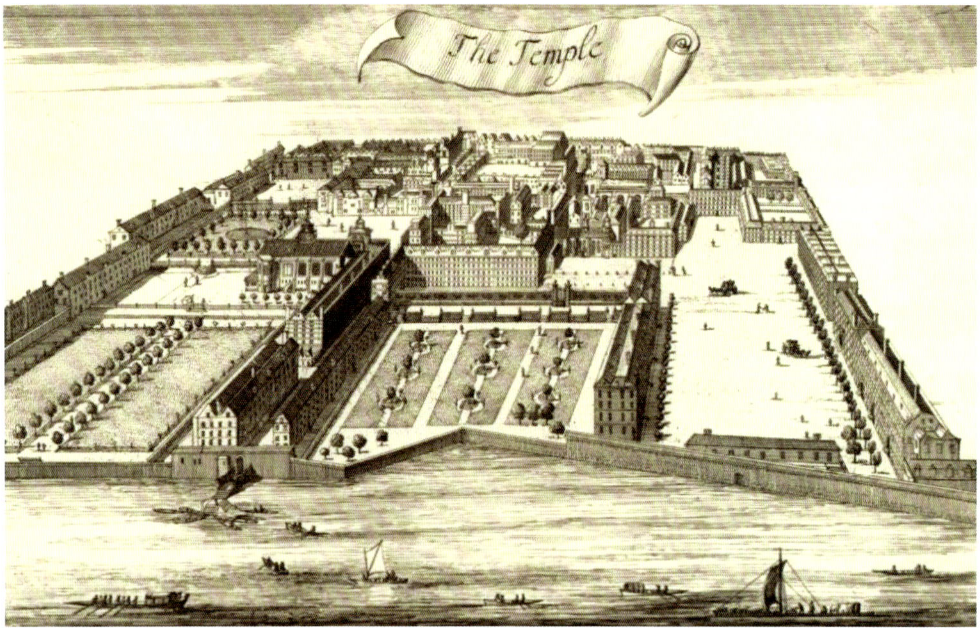

Fig. 80. Middle Temple from the river, etching from Stow's *Survey of the Cities of London and Westminster*, 1720.
© Trustees of the British Museum, 1880,1113.1466

Fig. 81. Nos 3–6 Plowden Buildings, Middle Temple Lane, drawing by J. P. Emslie, 1880.
Image © London Metropolitan Archives (City of London), no. 6439

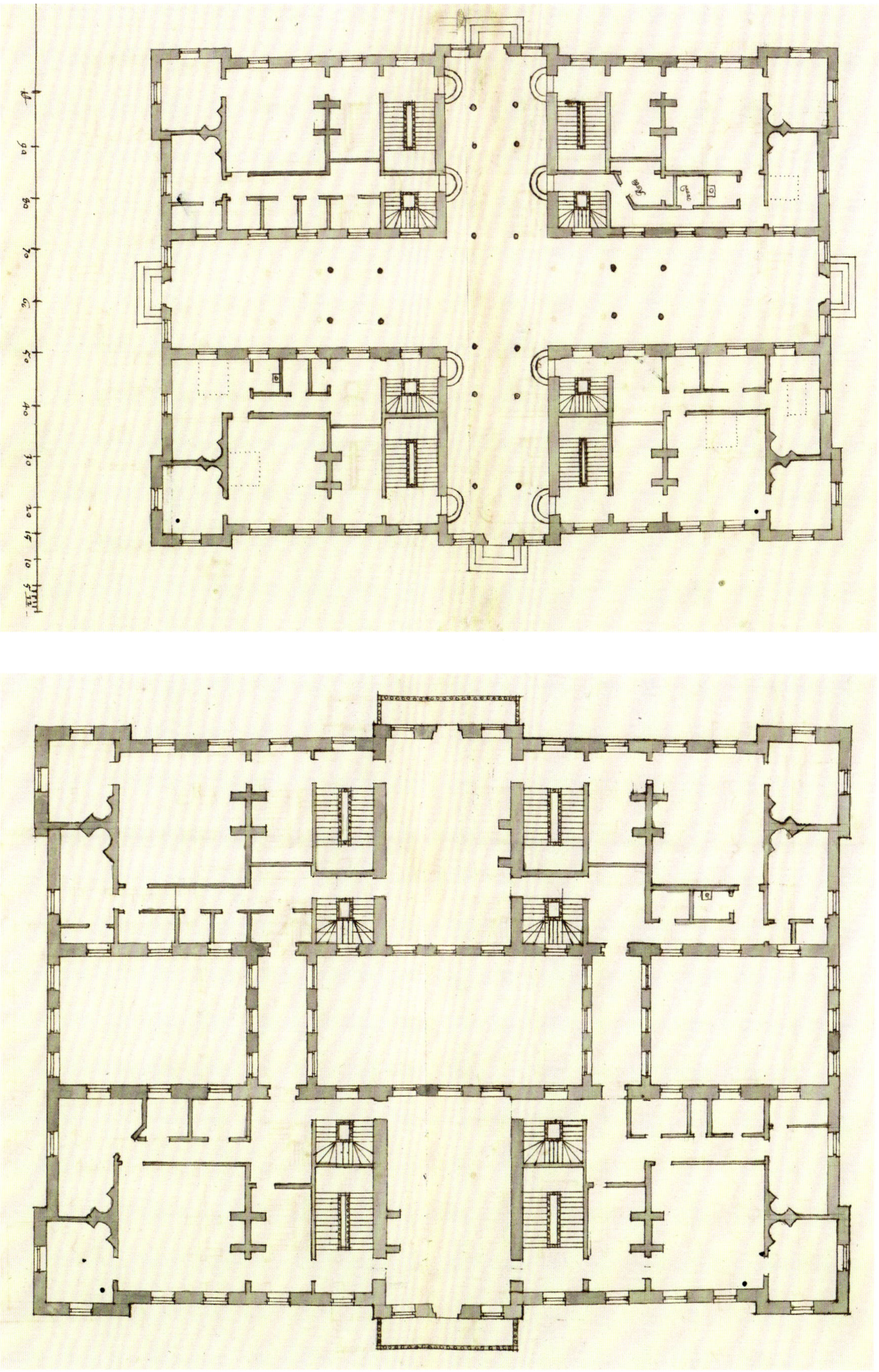

Fig. 82. Floor plans for an unexecuted scheme.

CHAPTER VIII

PARLIAMENT AND *A DISCOURSE OF TRADE*

Many of Barbon's business associates were Members of Parliament and it is hardly surprising that he too thought about becoming an MP as his father had done before him. Quite apart from the social status, contacts and inside information that the position would bring, it gave immunity from any civil action, of crucial importance to him. We know from a court case brought by Barbon in 1681 that he had told the defendant, Sir Thomas Draper, that he 'was likely to be a member of parliament and did intend to pay no rent to this defendant'.[1] In the event he did not become an MP until March 1690 when he was elected for the borough of Bramber in Sussex.

Bramber was ideal for Barbon. Four miles from the sea, north of Shoreham in Sussex, it was described by Defoe thus:

> Bramber (a little ruin of a castle excepted) hardly deserves the name of a town, having not above 15 or 16 families in it, and of them not many above asking you alms as you ride by; the chiefest house in the town is a tavern, and here as I have been told, the vintner or alehouse keeper, boasted that upon an election, just then over, he had made £300 of one pipe of canary.[2]

The right of election in Bramber was confined to about thirty people, although this could vary depending on the extent to which the tenements were divided. Barbon had bought a number of properties there and a further number were owned by John Jeffreys, the son of Judge Jeffreys, but then still a minor. Neither had a controlling interest and the borough was open to corruption.[3] In 1690 Barbon ran there with another doctor, the eminent physician John Radcliffe, and although they were challenged by the defeated candidate, Judge Jeffreys' son-in-law, William Stringer, their election was upheld. Barbon's various connections with Judge Jeffreys may have been the reason that he was appointed in November to the bill committee charged to effect the forfeiture of Jeffreys' estate which was eventually withdrawn.[4]

One might wonder what Barbon's politics were, but that is to misunderstand the polity of the late seventeenth century. By the 1690s, the Tories came to represent and support the Anglican Church, the landed gentry and the maintenance of a relatively strong monarchy. The Whigs, on the other hand, were more tolerant of, or were themselves, dissenters and supported mercantile and industrial interests; they were also generally supportive of Parliament's supremacy over the Crown. But these generalizations hid a wide variety of changing opinions. Many became Members in order to further their own interests, financial or otherwise; party politics was only just beginning. Voting patterns were variable and MPs could be influenced by the offer of lucrative appointments for themselves or family, thus becoming 'placemen'. An alternative way of classifying political opinions was the distinction between 'court' and 'country'. Court MPs were generally supportive of spending plans put forward by the government necessary for the war against France and so wanted effective taxes implemented quickly; country MPs, however, were more interested in making peace and were distrustful of the government's financial proposals, wanting to exercise close parliamentary controls on military expenditure with few long-term commitments. This would give greater power over spending to the many landed gentry MPs who felt that they bore the major burden of taxation while London-based merchants and financiers gained the benefits.[5] The court and country distinction did not map directly onto Whig/Tory, particularly from 1694 when the Whig 'Junto' took control, offending some fellow Whigs who increasingly joined the country group.

With Barbon's financial, urban and dissenting background, he might have been expected to be both Whig and court, and this was indeed so to begin with. Soon after Barbon became an MP in 1690, he was classed as a Whig by the Tory Lord Carmarthen (later Duke of Leeds) although later that year Carmarthen saw him as a potential supporter. He was classified as a court supporter in 1691 when he supported the Ministry's proposals for the size of the army, and again in 1693 but his support over the army estimates then was qualified. Although he did not share his father's Nonconformism, he acted in 1692 as a teller for a defeated clause that would have provided Quakers with an alternative to swearing an oath of fidelity to the Crown in relation to certain transactions in Ireland.[6] He also joined the court members in opposing the 1692 'Placemen Bill' which would have prevented office holders from being MPs and, early the next year, in opposing the clause in the Triennial Bill that would have required annual sessions of Parliament.[7]

Being an MP played to Barbon's sense of his own importance, but his chief interest was in building up support for his various projects and protecting himself from lawsuits. The first occasion was no more than two months after his election, when the trustees of his fire insurance company recognized that they could not sue him together with John Parsons (also an MP) to complete their buildings at Well Close (see Chapter VI) because they 'would have been much hindered and obstructed by privilege of parliament'.[8] He used parliamentary privilege again in May 1693 when inhabitants of Chancery Lane and Ficket Field in Lincoln's Inn objected that his building there was obstructing their light and right of way. He refused to answer the indictment for nuisance and made clear that he would continue with his building.[9] In 1695 he also prevented the City of London from trying to remove his licence for Brookfield Market, east of Hyde Park, a profitable operation in competition with Smithfield.[10] The stream of law cases involving him which had been so common from the mid-1670s came to an end, although at least one case was revived after his death when he could no longer 'insist on his privileges'.[11] When a list of 'placemen' was produced in 1693, Barbon's name was included not because he held any position but because 'his privileges are worth to him £1,000 p.a.'.[12] This was widely recognized, as in the satirical poem,

In new foundations has the ruins laid
Of many artists whom he never paid,
Stuffed the Kings-Bench, the Fleet, Mint, and White-Friars
With broken building knights, Alsatia squires,
(To avoid which fate himself was forced to tamper
For a dear bargain with the men of Bramber).[13]

He was not particularly active in Parliament itself during his first eighteen months there but was appointed to bill committees dealing with London issues such as paving streets in Westminster or recovering small debts there, and he brought a petition in support of occupants of his development in Soho Square who wanted to limit the funds raised to complete St Anne's church. He failed to amend the bill in the Commons, but it was eventually blocked in the Lords.[14] He also served on the committee for bills allowing surgeons to administer medicines internally and exempting apothecaries from sitting on parish committees. Medicine was not the only area where his special expertise was recognized, and in early 1692 he was appointed to the committee to view the ceiling and roof of the House following a warning report from Sir Christopher Wren. Barbon, the only committee member with any real knowledge of building, reported 'that they do find the Walls and Timber so much decayed, that they are of Opinion, the Building is in a dangerous Condition, and not capable of further Repair'. A humble address was presented to the King requesting 'that a convenient Place may be provided for the Commons of Parliament to sit in; the Building where they now sit being in a ruinous and dangerous Condition'. Wren joined the committee and further work was undertaken which removed the fourteenth-century clerestory and constructed a new roof at a lower level. Galleries were also constructed which were supported at the lobby end by two iron pillars, manufactured by the blacksmith, Jean Tijou, a structural innovation that would not be repeated for fifty years. The Commons returned from their temporary quarters in the Court of Requests in November 1692, but while they were well pleased with the changes, more work had been done than in the original estimate of £2,540 and the cost rose to £4,598.[15]

There were three controversial areas where Barbon did become involved, whether by writing pamphlets or promoting projects. The first was dealt with by his pamphlet, *A Discourse of Trade*; the latter two, the creation of a bank and arguments about what to do about the country's coinage, will be dealt with in later chapters. The politics of these three controversies must be seen against a background of the war against France. While the position of many MPs was often determined by whether or not the war effort was advanced, Barbon's position seems to have been driven principally by his own independent thinking.

A Discourse of Trade

Trade had always been a subject of argument but became a major political issue after the Glorious Revolution. All kinds of lobby groups wanted either protective tariffs for their industry, greater freedom to export, or lower tariffs on imports. Some were concerned about the outflow of bullion from England. The Stuarts had favoured relations with France and there had been substantial trade between the two countries, although purchases of wine and fashionable items resulted in a positive balance in favour of France, particularly as France had banned imports of English manufactured goods. William III's desire for war with France reversed this. French imports were banned as from August 1690 and the ban was extended for a further three years in 1692 as Parliament took a larger part in the regulation of economic affairs generally.

We do not know the exact date of publication of *A Discourse of Trade*: original copies of the pamphlet carry the date '1690', suggesting that it appeared after 25 March — the date the new year officially started. Since Barbon was elected MP some three weeks earlier on 3 March, it seems likely that the pamphlet was at least published, if not written, after his election and could even have been published at late as the following March. In any case he will have been well aware of the large variety of protectionist proposals produced after the Revolution and his preface to *A Discourse* makes clear his dissatisfaction with them. As he points out:

> The merchant, and other traders who should understand the true nature of trade, do either not understand it, or else, lest it might hinder their private gain, will not discover it [...] And how fair and convincing soever their premises may appear for the enlarging and advancement of trade, the conclusions of their arguments, which are for limiting and confining of it to a number, persons and places, are directly opposite to the enlarging of it.[16]

Barbon is clear that trade should be considered as a whole, rather than in connection with a single product or country, and that it needs to be put into what we would call the overall macroeconomic context. His *Discourse of Trade* accordingly goes wider than just trade including material on the role of money and interest rates, as well as commenting on such things as the nature of value and credit. He also drew on the arguments that he had introduced in 1678 in his *Discourse showing the great advantages that New Buildings and the Enlargement of Towns and Cities do bring to a Nation* and in 1685 in *An Apology for the Builder*. He was to develop his ideas still further, or at least express them even more trenchantly, in his later work on the recoinage, *A Discourse concerning coining the new money lighter*, and it is convenient to include the non-monetary aspects of that work here.[17]

His *Discourse showing the great advantages that New Buildings ... do bring to a Nation* had set out his vision of increased demand and a growing economy with improvement possible for everyone. It was consumers, stimulated by fashion and similar desires, that created growth in the economy and consequent improvement.[18] He now expanded on that, saying, 'It is not necessity that causes consumption, nature may be satisfied with little; but it is the wants of the mind, fashion, and desire of novelties and things scarce, that causeth trade.'[19]

Contrary to those who believed that land was the only source of wealth and so a limiting factor on its growth, Barbon saw no limit on economic growth with man able to increase the stock of wealth by his labour and ingenuity. Contrasting the finance of a nation with that of a domestic household, he claimed 'the stock of a nation is infinite and can never be consumed'.[20] While we might not now agree with his claim that 'the riches of the country [are] perpetual, and never to be consumed [...] and the minerals of the earth are inexhaustible', this has to be understood in terms of the seventeenth-century concept of 'plenitude', the idea that nature had an immeasurable abundance.[21] Easier for us to accept is his characterization of the 'wants of the mind' as infinite, confirming the scope for economic growth.

Having established his commitment to the idea of economic growth, he then based much of his approach on the working of the market. 'Things have no value in themselves; it is opinion and fashion brings them into use and gives them a value'; value was to be given by the price at any time, there being no fixed price for anything. He saw that to be as true for necessities such as food as for wants of the mind, although he pointed out that the latter

> have only an imaginary or artificial value, which depends only on opinion, and change their values according to the humour or fancy of the persons who use them and are, like rich apparel that lose their value because they are out of fashion.[22]

His summing up could hardly be a clearer statement of the laws of supply and demand: 'Plenty makes things cheap and scarcity dear' and 'the market is the best judge of value; for by the concourse of buyers and sellers, the quantity of wares, and the occasion for them are best known: things are just worth so much as they can be sold for'.[23]

He was equally clear on money which 'is an imaginary value made by a law, for the conveniency of exchange'.[24] What made a coin worth its face value was the stamp of government on it, not any intrinsic value of the metal that made it up; as he said, 'The value of gold and silver is uncertain, and varies.' In other words, they are commodities like everything else; indeed, there is no need for money to be made of just gold or silver, although they have the advantage of being relatively scarce, and so harder to counterfeit. He would revert to this subject six years later in the controversy over recoinage.

He also touched on the topic which would form his last great project, that of creating a bank. He began by pointing out that just as value is created by the market rather than by any intrinsic factors, so 'credit is a value raised by opinion, it buys goods as money does; and in all trading cities there's more wares sold on credit than for present money'.[25] This led on naturally to the need for a public bank in London as in Venice and Amsterdam. Neither in *A Discourse*, nor when he raised the subject in Parliament in early 1693,[26] did he make any suggestion that it should be based on land, a point that will be picked up in the next chapter on land banks.

Having laid out his basic approach, Barbon then went on to consider the use and benefit of trade and those things that promote or diminish it. Trade, he said, 'is to make and provide things necessary; or useful for the support, defence, ease, pleasure, and pomp of life'.[27] By so doing, manufacturing would not only provide desired goods but employment as well and so raise the rent of the land that produced the raw materials, an important part of his argument that trade and industry are beneficial to landowners. He also argued that trade brings peace as well as facilitating the defence of the realm by enabling the purchase of those goods necessary for war that can only be obtained from overseas, a point that he stressed had been missed by previous writers on government such as Livy and Machiavelli. Moreover, trade is good for government since increased employment increases its revenue through customs and excise taxes.

For Barbon, the chief causes that promote trade are 'Industry in the poor and liberality in the rich' while 'prodigality is a vice that is prejudicial to the man but not to trade'. He spelled this out further:

> A conspiracy of the rich men to be covetous and not spend would be as dangerous to a trading state as a foreign war; for though they themselves get nothing by their covetousness, nor grow the richer, yet they would make the nation poor and the government great losers in the customs and excise that arise from expense.[28]

Naturally, he was opposed to sumptuary laws and two areas of spending were singled out as being particularly important:

> the promoting of new fashions ought to be encouraged because it provides a livelihood for a great part of mankind [...] building is the chiefest promoter of trade; it employs a greater number of trades and people than feeding and clothing.[29]

This led him on to the advantages of large cities and a restatement of the role of emulation, first proposed by him more than twenty years earlier:

> There is another advantage to trade, by enlarging of cities; the two beneficial expenses of clothing and lodging are increased; man being naturally ambitious, the living together occasion emulation, which is seen as out-vying one another in apparel, equipage, and furniture of the house; where if man lived solitary alone his chiefest expense would be food.[30]

As he set out in the preface to the *Discourse*, he believed protectionism was one of the main problems for trade, particularly outright prohibitions which would have the added effect of stimulating the country with banned goods to impose corresponding bans on English exports. This was particularly true when imports of commodities were banned since that lost the possibility of English labour being used to process them or use them for manufacturing. Prohibitions would also prevent England from benefiting from the income for providing freight transport. He was against the creation of trading monopolies such as those enjoyed by the East India Company and the Merchant Adventurers which reserved the rights to trade with certain countries. These were removed in 1689 and he voted against their reinstatement in 1693.[31] Similarly, his interest was reflected in his appointment to the committee to consider what became the 1694 Act which allowed for the first time exports of iron and copper from England.[32]

Much of Barbon's argument was concerned with imports which either reflected a comparative advantage of other countries (for example, French wine) or goods that were essentially fashion items. In neither case did he see imports as a direct threat to English goods since they were distinct, with the differences in, say, French hats and Flanders lace being what made them attractive, just as other countries desired English cloth, hats or gloves. Indeed, he saw exports principally as being the means for disposing of any English excess production. He did allow that 'if the bringing in of foreign goods should hinder the making and consuming of the native, which will very seldom happen', it would be acceptable to impose what he later called 'well regulated and proportioned duties'.[33] Such duties would result in the imported goods being preserved 'for the use of the gentry who may esteem them because they are dear [...] [and] the revenue of the Crown will be increased'.[34] Later, in his work on the recoinage, he was to go much further and wrote 'the freer the trade is, the better the nation will thrive'.[35]

Underlying all these arguments was his position on whether a positive balance of trade was to be sought after and the desirability of preventing an outflow of bullion, which some regarded as the only form of wealth. Barbon ably dismissed both these arguments, spending some long time, arguably too long, demonstrating that it was impossible to define or measure the balance of trade and rejecting the view that bullion was the only form of wealth since 'one sort of commodity is as good as another, be it of the same value'.[36]

But perhaps his strongest, and most long-standing, criticism for an adverse effect on trade was of the high statutory maximum rate of interest in England, 6 per cent as compared to only 3 per cent in the Netherlands, which he saw as giving the Dutch a considerable advantage. Reducing interest rates would of course have been of great help to him in his business, and it is interesting that his analysis did indeed approach the subject from the point of view of the borrower rather than the lender. Whereas Locke saw interest as the price of the hire of money, Barbon saw it as a payment for the services of the investment goods which loan monies made possible,[37] making clear that 'the merchant expects by dealing to get more than interest by his goods because of bad debts and other hazards which he runs'.[38]

> Interest is the rent of stock and is the same as the rent of lands. The first is the rent of wrought or artificial stock, the latter of the unwrought stock. Interest is commonly reckoned for money because the money borrowed at interest is to be repaid in money, but this is a mistake; for the interest is paid for stock; for the money borrowed is laid out to buy goods or pay for them before bought; No man takes up money at interest to lay it by him and lose the interest of it.[39]

He blithely stated that landowners would not suffer from a loss of rent because lower interest rates would increase the value of their land.

He is also attributed with the authorship of a pamphlet in 1694: *An Answer to a paper entituled Reasons against Reducing Interest Rates to four per cent.*[40] Lowering interest rates was a policy close to his heart and the pamphlet is reminiscent of his style. It contained what is almost a direct quote from *A Discourse of Trade* on interest being the rent of wrought stock and certainly reflected his views. Shortly before he died in 1698, he introduced a bill into Parliament that would have lowered the rate of interest, but it did not proceed.

Commentary

There was no pressing need for Barbon to issue a pamphlet on trade issues, but it was entirely in character for him to want to mark his entry into Parliament with a flourish and to display his capacity to comment on matters of national interest. This may well have been why a second edition of his *Apology for the builder* had appeared in 1689.[41] As we have seen, *A Discourse of Trade* allowed him to reaffirm and extend the argument of his previous writings and also provided the basis for his intervention in the controversy over recoinage six years later. Many economists and economic historians have analysed Barbon's writing, usually to comment on how closely he approaches modern economics or may be seen to have anticipated Adam Smith. This is what one writer has called 'processionalism'.[42] Equally, others have tried to place him in some category of mercantilism, but the problems with this (usually of definition) are demonstrated by the fact that others call him anti-mercantilist. Essentially, they use different definitions, and in any case it is not clear that it is a particularly useful classification. Barbon was neither a bullionist nor concerned about the balance of trade and was generally in favour of free trade, while conceding that tariffs (but not prohibitions) might be useful on some occasions. He viewed the market as the best judge of value and was happy to accept the disruption to the old order of things that came with reliance on the market. Nevertheless, he also saw a role for government (or at least Parliament) in influencing the economy, including reducing interest rates, and was in favour of promoting employment, often using levels of employment as criteria to judge the benefits of particular forms of trade.

There is little point in analysing Barbon in terms of modern economics. While it is certainly possible to see pointers to later economists, there are often inconsistencies or contradictions as well as pieces that run counter to modern thinking. His desire for the rich to spend and avoid insufficiency of demand has echoes of Keynes's *General Theory*; his recognition of trade as 'an affair of state' was picked up by Hume; his support of free trade and countries concentrating on products where they have advantage anticipates Smith and Ricardo, although he is not opposed to tariffs, particularly to raise income for the Crown. His theories of money, value and interest have modern elements but, as will be shown later, history has seen his views on recoinage and revaluation through the filter of whether devaluations are thought immoral or merely a practical response to circumstances.

A better approach is to consider how he reflected his own times and to compare him with contemporary writers.[43] He is often criticized for his economic writing being special pleading on behalf of his own interests, but it would have been more surprising if it was not. Certainly, all other writers on economic matters of his time did exactly the same, even John Locke, who identified the national interest as that of the landed classes. Most other writers on economic matters of the time were either merchants themselves or employees of the East India Company, the first of whom was Thomas Mun who became a director of the Company after a successful career as a merchant. His first efforts were devoted to defending the Company from charges that they exported too much bullion from England by claiming that very many of their imports were then re-exported and so in aggregate produced a payments surplus.[44] Mun went on to write about trade more generally, continuing to argue that the nation's overall balance of trade needed to be positive, but this was not published in his lifetime and only appeared in 1664.[45]

We know that Barbon had read this work because Mun was explicitly criticized for his 'mistake' in advocating frugality as well as sumptuary laws to restrict the use of foreign fashions and other luxuries.[46] Many other writers, such as Charles Davenant, then seeking a post in the Company, took the same position as Mun on the balance of trade, while the most prominent was Sir Josiah Child, another pillar of the East India Company. Child had also defended the Company against changes of exporting bullion but still saw a positive balance of payments as the only way of increasing the nation's supply of bullion and hence its wealth. He was ostensibly in favour of free trade — except where it affected the Company adversely — but in reality this was overridden by his view of the balance of payments. The clearest statement of Child's view came in the 1690 reissue of his 1668 book as *A Discourse about Trade*: '[I]t's our interest by example and other means (not distasteful) above all kinds of commodities to prevent, as much as may be, the importation of foreign manufactures.'[47] He made impassioned pleas for a reduction of the rate of interest and it is his pamphlet that provoked John Locke to respond, also setting out his view of money.

Evidence that at least some contemporaries read Barbon comes from a pamphlet entitled *Reasons for the abatement of interest to four in the hundred and the objections against it fairly stated and briefly answered*, by someone with the initials E. H.[48] He too favoured a law reducing interest rates and quoted explicitly from Barbon's *Discourse of Trade* and from Josiah Child's *Discourse*. His final summing up, 'No law can be greater advantage to the nation than an Act to reduce interest rates to four per cent. It will produce the most general good with the least private disadvantage', was identical to the conclusion in Barbon's 1694 pamphlet.

A very different approach was taken by Sir Dudley North, manifestly a Tory politically, whose *Discourses on Trade* were published posthumously in 1692.[49] These were the most radical, recommending free trade with no priority being given to bullion or the balance of trade. For North, tariffs were for raising revenue and should be applied to those goods that could best bear them without regard for the country they came from or for competing English goods. Indeed, he had taken this position when acting for King James II, proposing tariffs on goods imported by both the East India Company and his own Levant Company. He was also opposed to legislation to reduce interest rates.

Much of Dudley North's *Discourses* had been put together a few years earlier and it was his brother, Roger, who edited them for publication and added a preface of his own. There are striking parallels with Barbon: North defined interest as 'rent for stock' and used the term 'stockowner' in parallel to that of landowner; he pointed out that 'gold and silver are in no sort different from other commodities';[50] he echoed Barbon on emulation, saying, 'The main spur to trade, or rather to industry and ingenuity, is the exorbitant appetites of man' giving the following as an example:

> The meaner sort seeing their fellows become rich, and great, are spurred up to imitate their industry. A tradesman sees his neighbour keep a coach, presently all his endeavour is at work to do the like, and many times is beggared by it; however the extraordinary application he made to support his vanity was beneficial to the public, though not enough to answer his false measures to himself.

Not surprisingly, he opposed sumptuary laws and went further, writing, 'Laws to hamper trade, whether foreign or domestic, relating to money or other merchandises, are not ingredients to make people rich.'[51] In his preface, Roger North went much further than his brother in favour of laissez-faire, writing, 'All favour to one trade or interest against another is an abuse.'[52]

Dudley North's *Discourses* appear to have little circulation at the time and may even have been withdrawn.[53] Although Barbon published up to a year earlier, North's work had been written sometime before, probably as a basis for speeches in Parliament. While it seems unlikely that Barbon had influenced Dudley North, it is interesting to speculate whether Roger North could have been influenced by Barbon, or indeed vice versa. Roger North's writings refer to conversations with him on building in London, and Barbon continued to do work at the Middle Temple into the 1690s. They had a relationship that went beyond that of a simple client/builder and it is entirely likely that they would have discussed the beneficial effects of building on employment, as well as current political matters such as trade.[54]

Barbon was indeed one of the few writing at the time who genuinely supported free trade. His views were not unqualified, in that he accepted the possibility of protective tariffs in what he described as unlikely circumstances partly because he saw 'all foreign wares, especially the dearer sort are used chiefly for ornaments, and as badges of riches because they are foreign and rare; and not from any extraordinary quality of goodness in the make of them'.[55] It is for this reason that he approved tariffs as a means of raising revenue, particularly from the better off, but he was also opposed to other restrictions, including tariffs on selective countries and monopolies for trading companies. He did, however, give an implicit approval to the Navigation Acts, which required the use of English ships and crews, since on many occasions he described one of the advantages of trade as the income that arose from the carriage of goods. Here it is worth noting that Adam Smith also endorsed the Navigation Acts, despite their constraint of trade, because of the improvements they brought to the country's security.[56]

Although, like that of merchants, Barbon's business was affected by the general state of the economy, his interests as a property speculator, large borrower and provider of insurance were radically different. As well as growth in the economy, he wanted interest rates to come down, and finance to be more available and in increasingly sophisticated ways. This would also help his principal preoccupation of making London flourish. *A Discourse of Trade* repeats almost word for word the panegyric in *An Apology for the Builder* that by being a sea power based on expanding trade England would increase 'not only to preserve its Antient Sovereignty over the Narrow Seas, but to extend its Dominion over all the Great Ocean'.[57]

Most writers have assumed that Barbon was a Tory, largely because of his involvement in the land bank. The next chapter will show that what Barbon wanted was to be part of a bank: he had no great concern that it should be financed by land and only adopted that approach opportunistically to achieve his end, ditching the land element temporarily in the final version, albeit possibly inadvertently. He also recognized that his vision of a growing economy, support of improvement and a flourishing London at the centre of a worldwide trade network needed to be sold to those still wedded to the concept of land as the source of wealth. That is why, just as he had done in the *Apology for the Builder* five years previously, he emphasized the point that this vision led to increased wealth for those who owned land.

As we saw at the beginning of this chapter, Barbon was viewed at the start of his parliamentary career as supporting the court and Whig interests. Over the next few years in Parliament, he became increasingly aligned with the country interests and the Tories, but this was to further his financial and commercial interests rather than as a change of his views. We have already seen the involvement of the Tory MP John Parsons in the original fire insurance project. Barbon also developed Ficket Field near Lincoln's Inn in partnership with Sir Thomas Cooke, the Tory MP and governor of the East India Company who had helped him finance the purchase of Essex House twenty years earlier. He also chose no fewer than four Tory MPs to be trustees of the new fire insurance company he launched in 1694, based on his patent for obtaining water from the Thames (see Chapter VI).[58] It made no progress, but appointing one of the leaders of the country party (Robert Harley) and the brother (Thomas) of another (Paul Foley) can have done him no harm. These relationships were to form the basis of his project to create the bank that he had argued for and whose story is dealt with in Chapter X.

CHAPTER IX

NEMESIS IN HOLBORN

Barbon's entry into Parliament did not mean that his building activity diminished, rather that the focus changed. Apart from the purchase from the Crown of the land to the east of the City, added to the settlement of the Fire Office in 1683 and remaining largely unbuilt, most of Barbon's developments until this time had been brought to a state at which they could be sold on with secured ground rents. What remained was a large tract of land in the parish of St Andrew Holborn which he had assembled over a long period in the 1680s. With the enormous development of London in the twenty years after the Great Fire, Barbon may have believed that it would be possible successfully to build on these acquisitions. However, the later Holborn developments proved his undoing and much of what he attempted north of Theobalds Road was left incomplete at his death.

Part of this may have been due to the external financial circumstances. The 1690s were times of shortage of credit, principally caused by William III's wars with France; Barbon's awareness of the bigger financial picture is seen in his scheme for a land bank and his contribution to the debate on the coinage in these years which are covered elsewhere. But his problem in Holborn was simply that he had over-reached himself, owing money on too many mortgages on property on the fringes of the built-up area at a time when he could not find builders. Only occasionally does the bigger picture come into the many legal cases surrounding these developments when one mortgagee lamented that he could not find anyone to take a Barbon mortgage off his hands 'by reason of the badness of the times'.[1] It is probably significant that his contemporaneous development of New Square in Lincoln's Inn, with a much more secure future customer base, was concluded successfully.

Barbon had arrived in Holborn early in 1684, coming in on the back of the agreement for Sir Richard Fisher's estate in Red Lion Fields, first made in 1683 with Thomas Neale (see Chapter VII). In the next few years he built up an estate which, with Red Lion Fields, gave him freehold or leasehold title to about fifty acres north of the backs of buildings in High Holborn. Figure 83 shows the sources of the various pieces of land which made up his estate. Barbon adopted different approaches in acquiring these sites, depending on their ownership. He persuaded Sir Richard Fisher, who was seeking to maximize the value of his inheritance, that he was the person capable of achieving the best return while the purchases from Bonny and the Howkins were largely financial transactions. More interesting was his approach to the three charities involved, Rugby School, Bedford Corporation and St Clement Danes. In each case he was able to demonstrate, probably to less sophisticated trustees, how their income from the land could be increased considerably by leasing to him rather than the existing lessees. For Rugby he showed how a division of the site between its three joint owners would unlock its potential and delivered this in Chancery. On top of that he offered two of them an immediate cash sum which, unusually for him, he paid upfront and on time.

By the Restoration there had been extensive development south of the route from Holborn to St Giles. Holborn itself was built up on its northern side but the land behind remained mostly open apart from the enclave of Gray's Inn. This land had been crossed in the Middle Ages by the water supplies to Greyfriars, subsequently taken over by Christ's Hospital, and to the conduit in St Sepulchre's parish rebuilt by William Lamb in 1577. From the early seventeenth century the land was crossed by the road to Theobalds in Hertfordshire opened up by James I after his acquisition of that house from the Earl of Salisbury, and by the water mains of the New River Company. In the Civil War the 'lines of communication', the defences of London built by Parliament, had crossed the northern limits of the area. All these earlier topographical features had some influence on how Barbon was able to proceed.

Following the creation of Lincoln's Inn Fields to the south of Holborn, the seemingly inexorable growth of London development may have appeared inevitable. After the Restoration, further to the west, the Earl of Southampton began his development of a 'little town', in front of his house in

Bloomsbury, becoming the centrepiece of what after 1667 became the Bedford Estate in St Giles in the Fields. Building leases were granted by the Earl in Bloomsbury Square in the 1660s; this was the first formal layout of streets north of the road from Holborn to St Giles (Fig. 84).

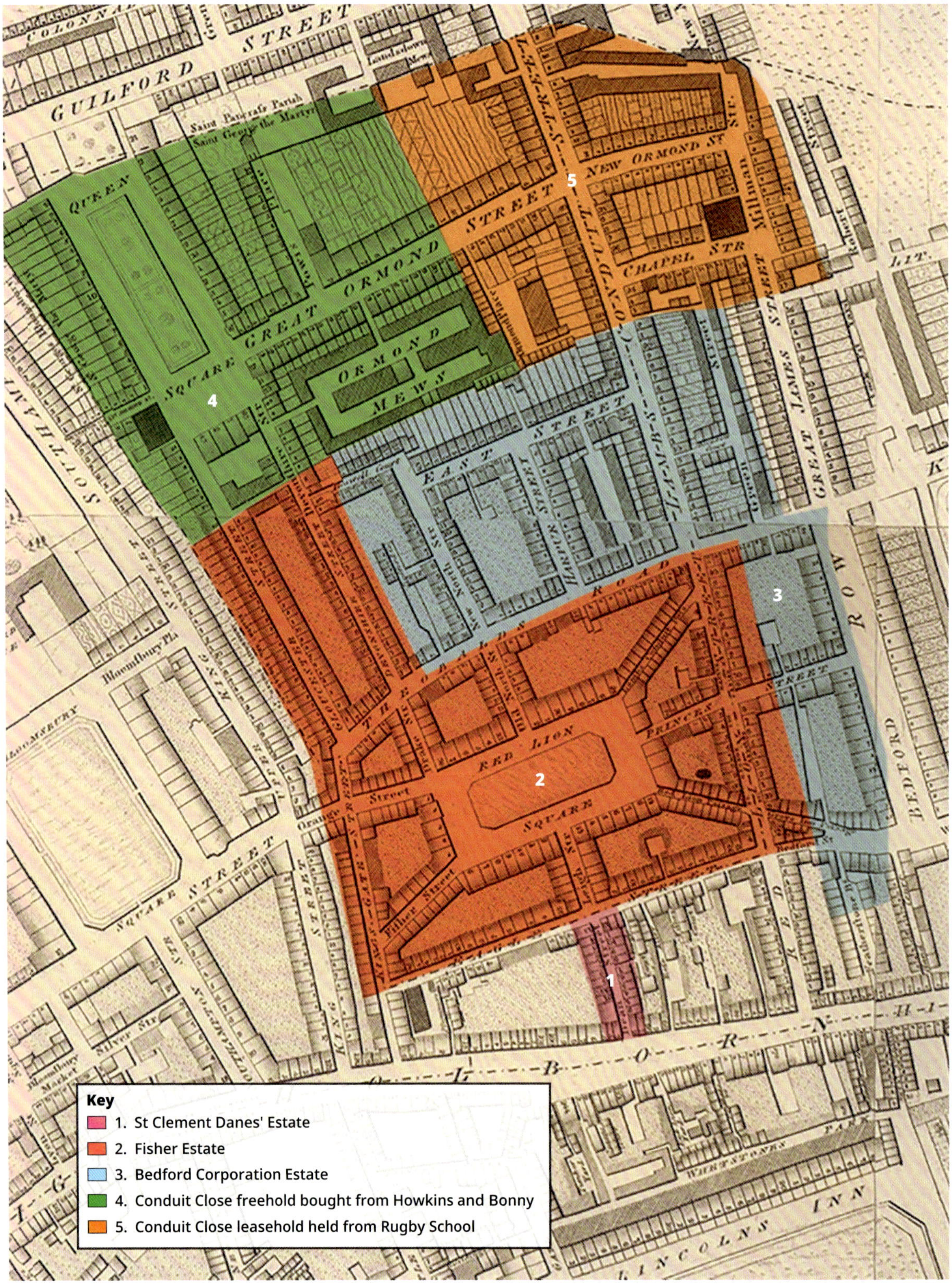

Fig. 83. The sources of the various pieces of land which made up Barbon's estate north of High Holborn, detail from Horwood's *Plan of the Cities of London and Westminster*, *c.* 1792–99. Private collection

Fig. 84. The area north of High Holborn developed by Barbon, detail from Morgan's *London &c. Actually Survey'd*, 1682. Theobalds Road is marked 'The Kings Way'.
By permission of the British Library, Maps Crace Port. 2.58

The Bedford Corporation Estate

Sir Thomas Fisher's land, in fields called Red Lion Field and Little Conduit Shot, had only been brought into a consolidated block of which he could make the lease to John Hinde after an exchange of eight intermixed holdings with the Corporation of Bedford decreed in Chancery in 1654. Figure 85 is a sketch plan of 1650 in Bedford Corporation's archives showing the arrangement of these plots.[2]

This exchange made Theobalds Road an important boundary; the road had more or less divided the two fields into equal northern and southern halves, and the decree gave Fisher most of the land to the south and Bedford Corporation most of that to the north; it also gave Fisher a small plot at the western end of the northern half, where there was a bowling green which he wished to have, shown on Richard Daynes's plan of 1643 (Fig. 87). In return Bedford Corporation gained a plot at the eastern end of the southern half on which the western side of Bedford Row was built. The ground of Theobalds Road was included in the allocation to the Corporation.[3]

How early the land to the east of King Street had been thought suitable for building is not clear. In 1668 William Thompson, gentleman, and the proprietor of the Three Cups Inn in Holborn, took a 41-year lease from Bedford Corporation of all their property at £99 p.a.[4] This term was long enough for building, the same as used by the Earl of Southampton for Bloomsbury Square, but the value for Thompson may have been in uses other than building. In a dispute which dragged out between 1682 and 1684, when the New River Company complained that Thompson had broken their pipes along Theobalds Road, he answered that the road was not a common highway but one only open to the King and his servants and those that paid him for opening the gates which lay at Kings Gate by Red Lion Field in Holborn and a gate in Gray's Inn Lane by the backside of Gray's Inn Walks.[5] Thompson also let an old building to Thomas Birch, citizen and Merchant Taylor, who used the space for drying clothes; in 1679 Thompson agreed with Birch for the rebuilding of his premises in brick and taking the profits made from charges for using Theobalds Road.[6] Thompson also recouped some of the rent due

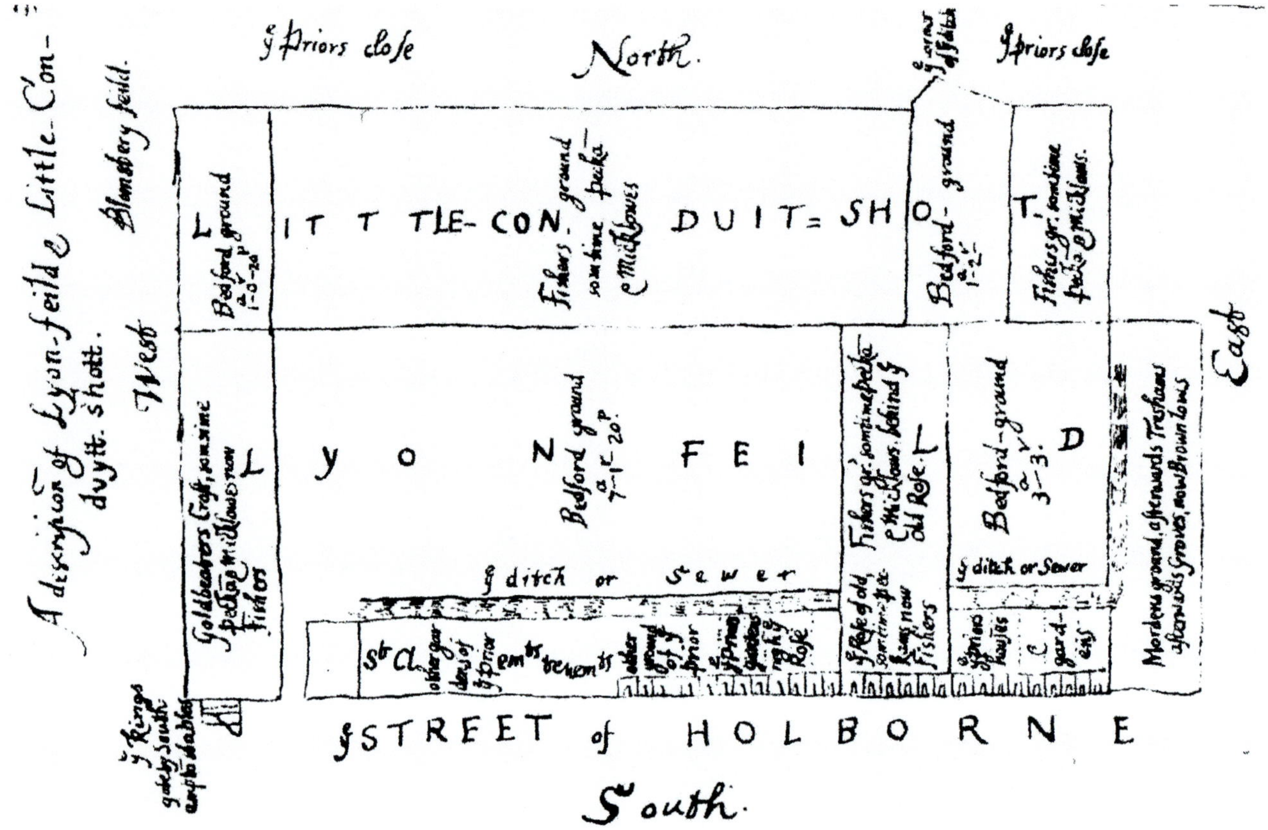

Fig. 85. Plan of land north of Holborn, 1650, redrawn by Alan Cirket from a plan now in Bedfordshire Archives (BorBH2/7).

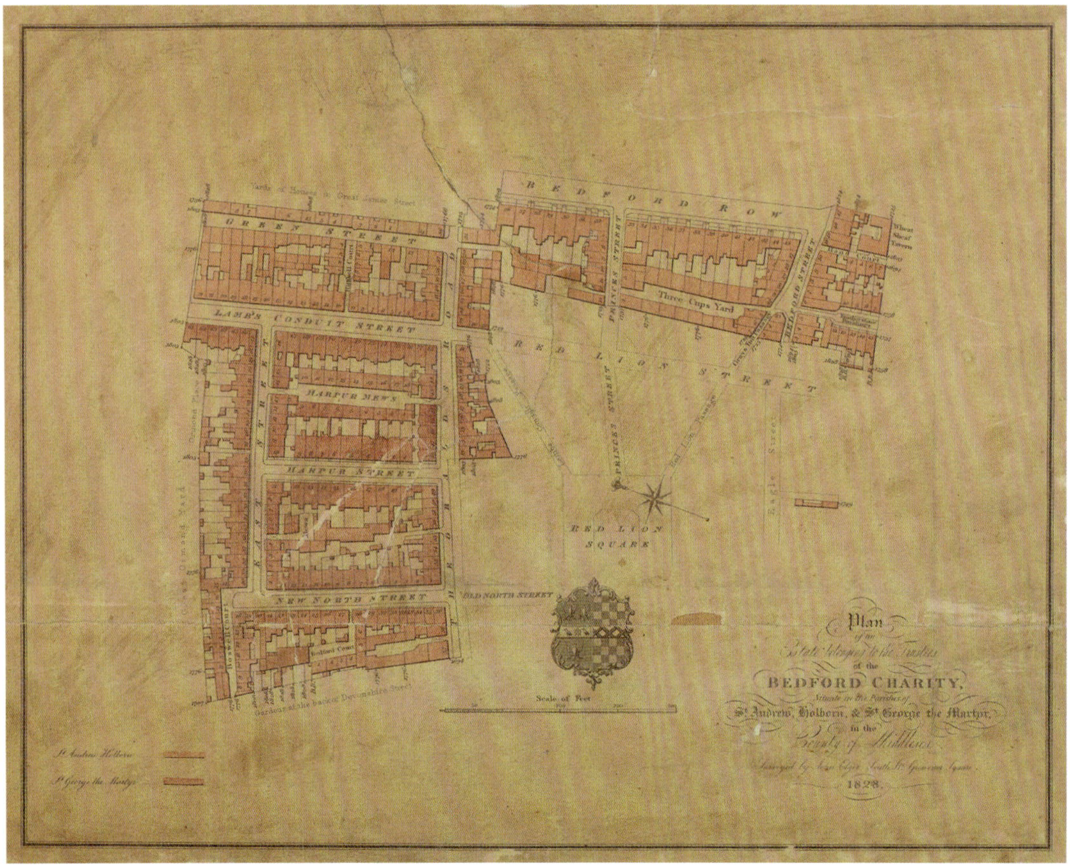

Fig. 86. Plan of Bedford Corporation Property, 1828.

Fig. 87. Plan of Conduit Close by Richard Daynes, 1643.

to the Corporation by making two long subleases in 1672 and 1673 to John Coleman, a victualler from St Giles in the Fields, at rents totalling £24 p.a. On this ground, next to the path north from the Three Cups Inn in Holborn to Lamb's Conduit, Coleman built 'a substantial and large music house' with gravel walks, fruit trees and arbours suitable for 'an entertaining house'. The music house is one of the scatter of buildings in the fields shown in Morgan's 1682 map (Fig. 84).[7]

At the same time as Barbon was planning the development of the Fisher property to form Red Lion Square he was also looking at the Bedford Corporation property to the north and east, across Theobalds Road and facing Gray's Inn, then in lease to Thompson. Between the Fisher property and the Inn there were two plots, one allocated to the Corporation in the exchange of 1654 and immediately adjacent to the Fisher land, the other further east, named in the 1654 plan as Brownlow's ground; this latter plot, later called Jockey Field on which the east side of Bedford Row was eventually built, was never in Barbon's hands.

The year 1684 was a difficult time for Bedford Corporation. Like sixty-nine other boroughs, its Charter had been cancelled by Charles II and a new one would cost at least £100, which could only be paid for by an unpopular 'Town Tax' raised locally. The Mayor of Bedford, Paul Cobb, came to London to try to sort it all out. Barbon must have realized that Bedford Corporation needed money quickly and he neatly provided the solution by offering a fine, or fee, in this case £250 in immediate cash, for a reversionary lease of the Corporation property to begin at the expiry of Thompson's lease in 1709, at an increased rent of £150 p.a. This was agreed in December 1684. Cobb had great fun in spending the money and his account to the Corporation included details of what he had spent on entertaining, including a dinner for Barbon and eighteen bottles of wine for seven judges. The account showed that almost £29 of the original sum 'remains in Mr Cobb's hands' and it took five years and the threat of legal action for the Corporation to get it back.[8]

Before Barbon could build he needed to acquire the remainder of Thompson's term, eventually secured in February 1687, reputedly at a cost of £4,920. Much of the information about the state of the property before his acquisition comes from his efforts to dispossess Thompson's tenants: Barbon claimed, for instance, that the music house was by then too costly to repair and he had sold the materials for £40; others claimed that he had dug trenches across ground of which they were rightly in possession through their under-leases from Thompson.[9]

Inevitably Barbon's acquisitions were immediately mortgaged. His reversionary lease from the Corporation was already mortgaged to George Dodson of Barnard's Inn before he had the assignment from Thompson. Then, in February 1687, with that assignment secured, Barbon raised £6,000 on the property from Richard Webb of the Inner Temple and Richard Chiswell, citizen and Stationer, each providing £3,000. Chiswell was later to publish Barbon's writings on the recoinage. Of this £6,000, after buying Thompson's lease and settling the mortgage to Dodson, Barbon received only £321 6s. 6d. himself. The day immediately after this mortgage Barbon mortgaged his equity of redemption to secure a further £8,000 from the financier Richard Kent and £5,500 from George White, a merchant, but he still claimed an equitable interest in Bedford Corporation property in his will in 1698. A later Chancery suit shows that the £3,000 provided by Webb was in fact the money of Matthew Blucke of Hunsdon in Hertfordshire who used Thomas Ellerker and John Williams, scriveners, as his agents; when Blucke tried to recover his money he was told that his security depended on improvement of the property by building.[10] Barbon quickly set about finding builders for this ground but neglected to pay the Corporation the rent due; the minutes of the Corporation show frequent attempts to use the law either to recover their money or eject Barbon from the site. Barbon's next ruse, in 1692, was to offer two farms, whereabouts not revealed, worth £164, in exchange for the freehold. This was refused.[11] Meanwhile, although the first building lease traced dates from December 1688, most of the leases for houses north of Theobalds Road were eventually made by Webb and Chiswell and the estate was not fully developed until the second decade of the eighteenth century (Fig. 86).[12] Nevertheless, while the historian of the Harpur Trust was scathing about Barbon's behaviour he recognized that it was from Barbon's development that the Trust found itself with an annual income of £2,274 when the site reverted to its ownership at the end of the lease in 1760.[13]

The St Clement Danes Estate

In 1552 the parish of St Clement Danes had bought property on the north side of Holborn, then at the north-west corner of London. The property was described in 1544 as twelve messuages with a close and waste land to the west, apparently including a slaughterhouse; the income from this investment was to benefit twelve poor persons of the parish. In later years the frontages were numbered from Nos 77 to 110 High Holborn.[14] With Red Lion Square in building to the north, Barbon began to look at this property as well. In February 1687 he reached an agreement with the parish trustees for a lease for fifty-six years from Lady Day 1687 at £24 p.a., a payment of £1,000 for the benefit of the poor of St Clement Danes, and a covenant to build according to a 'platform' annexed to the agreement. As the Holborn frontage was already built up Barbon had to deal with existing tenants and did not take the whole of the parish property. His principal purpose was to create a direct access to his Holborn developments, not only Red Lion Square and Sir Richard Fisher's estate, but also the holdings he was building up on the Bedford Corporation property and Conduit Close further north. These could be reached only from the King's private road, Theobalds Road, and Gray's Inn Lane, though there were footpaths across the fields. On the land he took from St Clement Danes, Barbon went in for demolition, creating the opening of Dane (or Dean) Street directly into the square. Morden's map (Fig. 92) shows two streets leading north off Holborn to Barbon's land, one the southern end of Red Lion Street on the direct line to Lamb's Conduit, the other Dane Street leading directly into the south side of Red Lion Square. Barbon was certainly responsible for Dane Street but who made the other opening is not known. The southern end of Dane (Dean) Street, south of Eagle Street, which Barbon created, has subsequently been blocked.[15]

Unusually, Barbon paid his £1,000 promptly; it is accounted for in the parish accounts for the year beginning in April 1687. These accounts also record payments at various inns in respect of meetings with Barbon or views of the site, including a payment of £12 at the Five Bells at the sealing of the lease. In fact, Barbon took two leases, backdated to February 1687, which represent the east and west sides of Dane Street where he built houses. The following December Barbon mortgaged these to Richard Ingram, an ironmonger of St Mary-le-Strand; the amount he raised on this mortgage is not stated. After laying out his street to lead directly into Red Lion Square, Barbon and his mortgagee made two leases in February 1688 to John Prince, a bricklayer from St Margaret Westminster.[16] The ground was described as on the east side of a street to be called Dean Street (*sic*). Prince immediately began to build, or at least make subleases, including some to William Gillingham and William Keene, both bricklayers from Westminster, but by the autumn of 1688 no houses were finished and some remained roofless. In September 1688 Ingram assigned them to a trustee on behalf of George, Marquis of Halifax, for £945. As elsewhere, building had started but the completion of the development was left to the mortgagee and by early 1690 the new mortgagee was told that £1,000 would be needed to finish them. Halifax stepped in somewhat earlier than either Curzon or Milman would do in Conduit Close, and while Barbon is recorded as paying the parish its rent in the year beginning April 1690, by the following year the rent was paid on Halifax's behalf and he completed the houses. A series of six undated and uncaptioned plans in the archive of the St Clement Danes Holborn Estate Charity represent what was built.[17]

Conduit Close

Most of Conduit Close was the northern part of Barbon's holding. His acquisition of the property was complex and his development in the end largely unstarted, let alone complete, by the time of his death in 1698. On the 1650 sketch plan of the property to the south (Fig. 85) it is described as Prior's Close, reflecting its origins as property from which Greyfriars in Newgate Street in the City had in the medieval period drawn its water.[18] In the plan drawn by Richard Daynes in 1643 (Fig. 87) it was divided into two parts, Chimney Conduit Field to the west and Lamb's Conduit Field to the east; this plan shows two conduits, Chimney Conduit (sometimes also known as Devil's Conduit) at the north-west corner and Lamb's Conduit near the middle of the northern boundary.

Chimney Conduit, at the head of the Greyfriars system and formed by damming a tributary of the Fleet, is shown in a plan of 1664/5 of the Manor of Bloomsbury;[19] the route crossing the fields is shown in a 1676 plan by William Leybourn (Fig. 88). On this route there was an additional conduit, the White Conduit, just to the east of what is now Lamb's Conduit Street. Christ's Hospital which had inherited

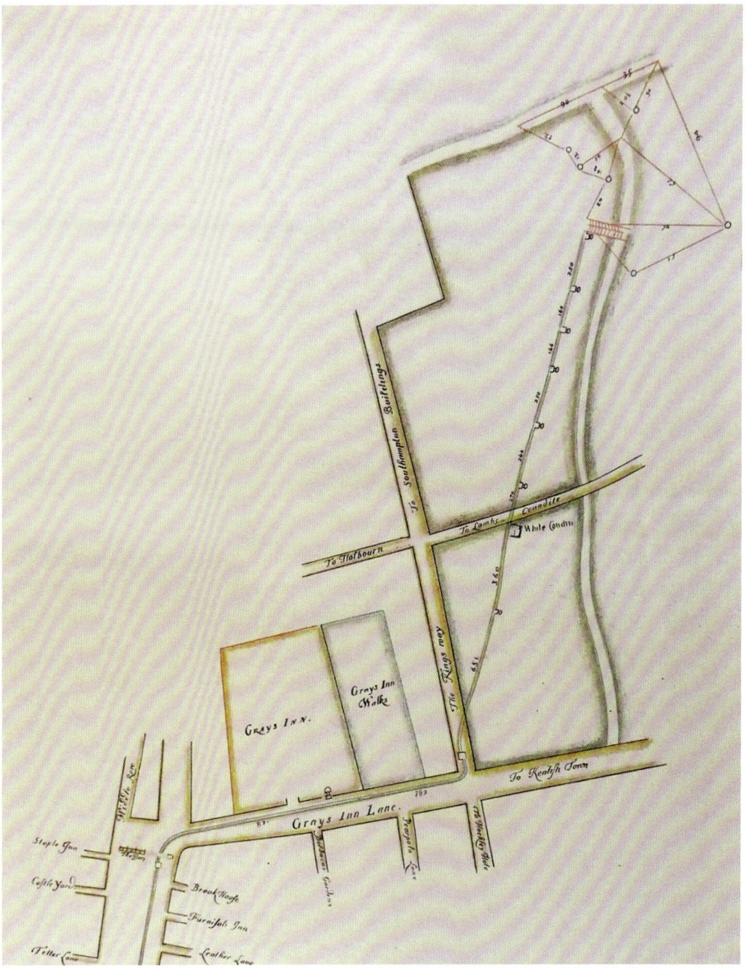

Fig. 88. Part of William Leybourn's plan of Christ's Hospital water supply, 1676.
From Philip Norman, 'On the White Conduit ...', *Archaeologia*, 61/2 (1909), pp. 347–56, pl. 46

the Greyfriars site in the City claimed the right to the water supply, but not the ground in Holborn. Lamb's Conduit was a separate system, provided at first in 1498 to supply water to a public conduit at the corner of Cow Lane, Cock Lane and Snow Hill in Smithfield and rebuilt in 1577 by William Lamb.[20]

In 1560 Conduit Close had been bought by Lawrence Sherriff, citizen and Grocer, by whose will, in 1567, one third of the Close was given to trustees for the maintenance of Rugby School which he had founded, the other two thirds to members of his family.[21] No division of the property was made; in the century following Sherriff's death the School had great difficulty in collecting its share of the rent. It seems likely that Daynes's plan of 1643 was made in connection with one of the lawsuits arising from these disputes. It was alleged that in part the property had been damaged by the construction of the Civil War defences of London across the site and the Daynes plan shows the 'lines of communication' where they crossed Conduit Close, before linking to the important fort at Southampton (later Bedford) House just to the west. In 1676 there was a reference to the military ground in or near Southampton Buildings close to the Chimney Conduit and some time after 1678 an agreement to build a small house on ground commonly called the artillery ground.[22] In 1683 Narcissus Luttrell noted a proposal to build 'a large four square house with three galleries round' for bullfighting in Red Lion Fields, in the artillery ground there.[23]

Exactly when Barbon first negotiated for Conduit Close is not clear. In May 1686, after he had been granted his reversionary lease of the Bedford Corporation land but before he had possession of that ground by acquiring the remaining years of Thompson's lease, Barbon agreed with the trustees of Rugby School for a lease of their one third share of Conduit Close, a lease formally executed on 20 October 1686. The lease was for fifty years from Christmas 1686 at a rent of £50 p.a. and an undertaking to lay out £1,000 on building. The lease followed a decree of 10 October 1686 in a Chancery suit in which Barbon and the School trustees joined forces against the other owners. At the time Conduit Close remained undivided and a key provision in the lease was Barbon's agreement to secure a physical partition of the ground among the owners. At the same time Barbon provided a bond for the performance of his covenants.[24]

To secure the partition Barbon joined again with the School trustees in the following month in a further Chancery suit against the other owners; a court order was made, but no commission for formally setting out the boundaries of the parts was issued until October 1687 and the commissioners' certificate only came in November 1688. The formal document partitioning Conduit Close was eventually made in April 1689. This deed put the property in the hands of trustees (who included Barbon's long-standing partner Samuel Vincent) to secure a common recovery through which possession would be vested in the individual owners as ordered in Chancery. By this time Barbon had taken an interest in a further half of Conduit Close. For the one sixth of the Close which he did not acquire he paid the owners to which it was allocated, Charles and Mary Newman, a sum of £300 for equity of partition.[25] The earliest known version of this plan is that attached to a lease of 1702 to Sir William Milman, Barbon's principal mortgagee of the one third allotted to Rugby School, when he took a further lease from the School trustees to lengthen Barbon's term; just as Barbon had taken a further lease from Bedford Corporation to lengthen Thompson's term. What this plan shows is that Barbon arranged the ground so that he could take the western half of Conduit Close freehold (though by then already mortgaged); the next block was his Rugby School leasehold and the easternmost one sixth was never his (Fig. 89).[26]

Lawrence Sherriff had died childless and after his death the ownership of the two thirds not bequeathed to Rugby School became divided, initially among the descendants of his sister, Bridget Howkins. In November 1686, when Barbon and the School trustees started the Chancery suit to force the partition of the ground, the other owners were William and John Howkins who also owned one third, and Charles and Mary Newman and Thomas and Mary Bonny who shared the other third. In their replies to Barbon's proposal to divide Conduit Close the respondents pointed out that until this time the ground had been enjoyed in common because of the water supply to Christ's Hospital and other places in the City and that Barbon's proposals would prejudice these supplies. Certainly, Christ's Hospital was concerned that Barbon's buildings would affect their supply and in 1690 proposed to re-route their conduit, negotiating with Barbon who agreed to pay half the estimated cost of £320; alternatively, he offered them £200 or a house worth £250 to remove the conduit completely from his ground, but nothing came of either option.[27] Shortly after, in 1692, Barbon and Bonny made agreements with the New River Company for the Company to lay pipes across their property.[28]

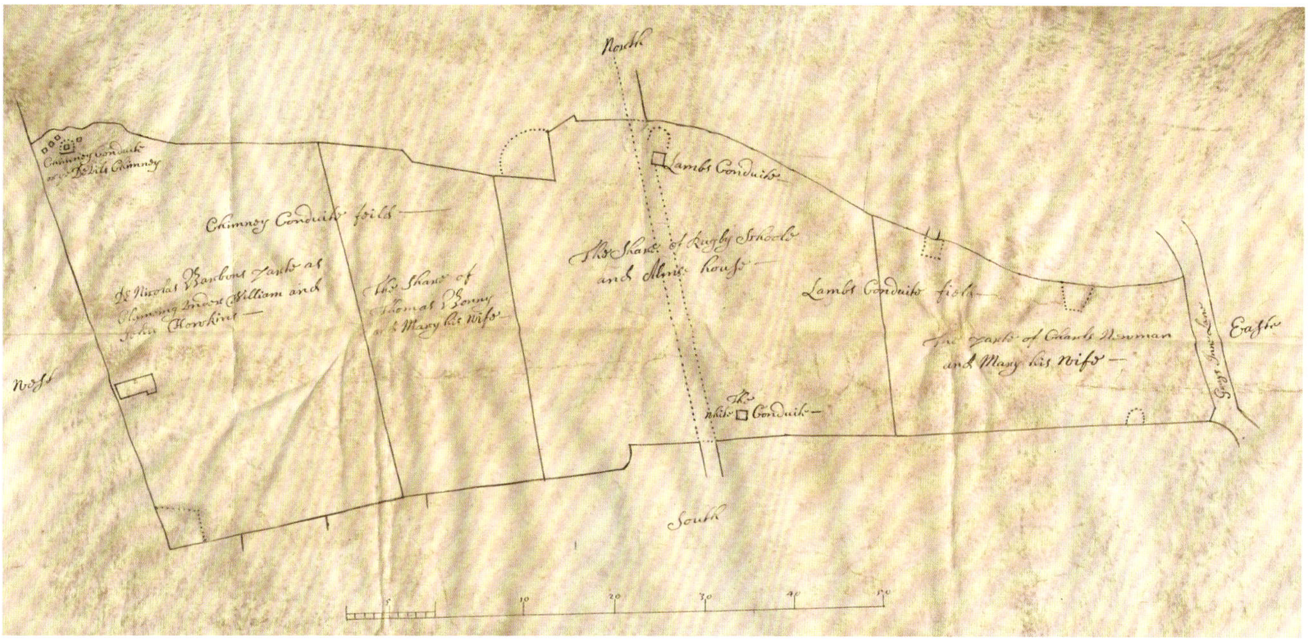

Fig. 89. Plan of Conduit Close attached to 1702 lease to Sir William Milman.

Thomas Bonny was the important man on the ground. In his reply to Barbon's suit he said that he had held Conduit Close from the various owners for several years. Notwithstanding the claim that the Close was kept united to maintain the water supplies, it is clear from this suit that some parts were subject to under-leases.[29] What Thomas Bonny used Conduit Close for before 1688 is not clear. In a Chancery suit of 1691, he is described as 'gentleman' but in a later suit of 1694 he is described as 'cowkeeper'. In this latter case he refers to considerable losses which he had lately suffered.[30] It is difficult not to believe that these losses were incurred because Bonny had got himself involved in Barbon's affairs. In August 1688, between the time that Barbon and the School trustees first tried to partition Conduit Close in 1686 and the formal partition in 1689, Bonny had agreed with Barbon to sell his freehold one sixth of the ground, apparently for £750, and in return Barbon agreed to lease back to Bonny a portion of the ground on the east side of what became Lamb's Conduit Street. Building on this ground was the ultimate intention but first it could be dug over for brick earth. A draft agreement provided for Barbon to have half the brick earth and two stools for brickmaking, Bonny to have one stool (a stool was the amount of ground which could be used for brickmaking by one team of six people). In the event the agreement provided for one stool each and Barbon quickly sold his right to make bricks to William Chipps, a coffeeman; Bonny and Chipps began to make bricks but their efforts were thwarted by Barbon not fulfilling his part of the agreement by which he should have made the lease to Bonny. In the end Bonny (by then described again as a 'gentleman' and now of Westminster rather than St Andrew Holborn) got a lease of ground in 1701 from Sir William Milman (Fig. 90). A deed attached to this lease notes Bonny's agreement with Barbon, but that by then Barbon was dead and nothing was built. Even then nothing was done until most of the ground on the east side of Lamb's Conduit Street was eventually built under leases granted by Milman's heirs in 1719–20.[31]

Bonny's one-sixth share of Conduit Close, laid out in 1686 and shown in the 1702 plan (Fig. 89), lay immediately to the west of the Rugby School land. The easternmost one sixth of Conduit Close, allotted to Charles and Mary Newman, forms no part of the Barbon story; there is a record of their sale of the property in 1705.[32] The one third of Conduit Close which was owned by William and John Howkins, shown in the 1702 plan as the western part, was also in Barbon's hands before the formal partition of April 1689 as he was able to mortgage it in January of that year. As might be expected, Barbon lost no time in raising money on the properties which came into his hands. In Conduit Close the principal mortgagees were eventually Sir William Milman for the leasehold third which Barbon held from Rugby School, and Sir Nathaniel Curzon of Kedleston for most of the freehold half which Barbon bought from Thomas Bonny and the Howkins. Both Milman and Curzon eventually took over

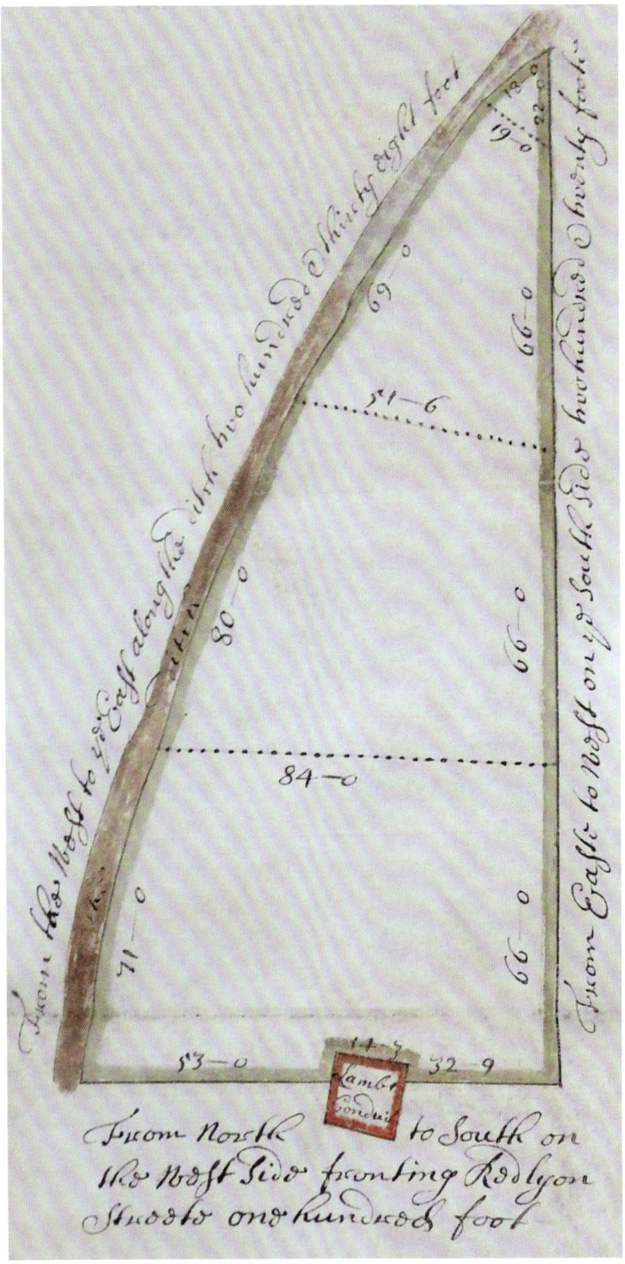

Fig. 90. Ground east of Lamb's Conduit let to Thomas Bonny in 1701.

the development that had been begun by Barbon and was left in chaos at his death in 1698, but this involved their sorting out the financial mess. In his will Barbon still claimed an equity of redemption in both the freehold and leasehold parts, but in a suit brought by Milman after Barbon's death his executor John Asgill admitted that the equitable interest had little or no value.[33]

A January 1689 mortgage showed that Barbon raised £12,000 on the security of the freehold half of Conduit Close, to be formally allocated to him in April 1689, along with his holdings in Brookfield, east of Hyde Park, and the Newport estate, near St Martin's Lane. This money was borrowed from Richard Kent who at the same time borrowed the money from Curzon. Some sites on the north side of what became Great Ormond Street appear to have been sold outright. After Kent's death, by the end of 1695, the debt due to Curzon for the original mortgage, the buying out of some earlier charges on the property and unpaid interest amounted to over £18,000. Barbon claimed that he had prepared a scheme for development with a street plan by which the extent of the street frontages could be calculated; by this plan Conduit Close would be worth £2,000 p.a. and upwards and therefore adequate security. After Kent's death Curzon tried to get possession of the property, it being clear that Barbon's scheme had come to nothing, but Barbon obstructed this by claiming his privilege of parliament; by July 1699, after Barbon's death, the debt due to Curzon was £23,344.[34]

The way Barbon's debts rose in the 1690s can be seen in a series of documents which followed the mortgage he raised from Sir William Milman on the security of the Rugby School lease. Milman seems first to have become involved with this ground in October 1689 when he took over a mortgage of a plot of land, eventually the north side of Great Ormond Street and the west side of Lamb's Conduit Street, on which Barbon planned to build eighteen houses. Milman was an Inner Temple lawyer who had already dealt with Barbon over property in Red Lion Square where he had two houses on leases made in April 1687. He appears also to have lent money secured on buildings in Veysey's ground in Soho (a bowling green) and on the new buildings built by John Foltrop in the Middle Temple. Milman's own dealings, beyond those with Barbon, were extensive and complex, with other properties in the City, Covent Garden, St James's, Chelsea, Teddington and Yorkshire. In August 1687 Barbon had agreed to supply Milman with 100,000 bricks at 11s. per 1,000 and to do plasterer's work worth £50 in Red Lion Fields. What had perhaps at first been a give-and-take arrangement between two property developers soon became a largely one-way operation. In October 1689 Barbon's debt to Milman was stated at £2,072 for which his lease from Rugby School was security; Barbon's equity of redemption excepted one plot with a 26-foot frontage on to what would become Great Ormond Street, perhaps intended by Milman as a house for himself and shown in a later survey of the Rugby estate as Lady Milman's house.[35]

The mortgage of 4 October 1689 is endorsed with five receipts between 4 and 18 October for sums totalling £410; this may reflect the difficulty of providing large sums in cash at one time. The balance of the £2,072 was accounted for by Barbon's debts which Milman took over. Despite a small payment by Barbon early in 1690 and a much larger one in 1694 by Vincent's widow, the annual interest meant that the debt rose inexorably and by February 1698, shortly before Barbon's death, the debt was £2,844.[36] In March 1700 Milman reached an agreement with Barbon's executors, John Asgill and Rebecca Hayes, on the basis that Barbon had not improved the ground as intended, 'but had let it lie ruinous and unbuilt which still continues so'. To save the legal costs of a decree of foreclosure Milman bought out the executors' interests, paying token sums of £3 to Asgill and 10 guineas to Hayes.[37]

The Progress of Building in the 1690s

From the mid-1680s Barbon had a clear and ambitious vision for his Holborn property. A new street leading north to Lamb's Conduit, now Red Lion Street and Lamb's Conduit Street, would form a north–south axis, crossed by the east–west route of Theobalds Road. South of this was the new Red Lion Square with its walks and garden. To the north there would be a further east–west route from Lamb's Conduit to another new square; these became Great Ormond Street and Queen Square. The references to 'platforms' and 'models' in the lawsuits of the late 1680s show that this street plan was established at the start even if many of the streets were not lined with houses until well after Barbon's death.

Barbon hoped to provide the area with a church. In February 1694 a petition from inhabitants near Red Lion Square was presented to the House of Commons saying that the parish of St Andrew Holborn was much enlarged by new buildings so that there were too many souls for the care of one minister and the church was not big enough. Despite Bedford Corporation seeking to prevent a potential loss of land by asking the two Bedford MPs to lobby against this proposal, the Commons gave leave for a bill to be introduced for making a new parish which Barbon was instructed to prepare. A bill was presented in February 1696 and a second reading ordered, but thereafter nothing more is heard of the proposal before Barbon died in 1698.[38] In the end a chapel was provided by subscription to service the area, built by the bricklayer Arthur Tooley in 1705 under a lease from Sir Nathaniel Curzon; this was then adopted in 1713 by the Commissioners for Fifty New Churches as St George the Martyr, Queen Square.[39]

Barbon also hoped that this Holborn development would have social prestige from the Earl of Devonshire building a house there. In 1678 Barbon had bought Old Devonshire House in Bishopsgate and built Devonshire Square on the site, the 3rd Earl of Devonshire had occupied Newport House in Soho, bought by Barbon in 1682, and in 1689 the 4th Earl occupied a house built by Barbon on the Military Ground in Soho. The 3rd Earl had lent Barbon money secured on Exeter Exchange and Osterley. So there was an established connection between Barbon and the Cavendish family.[40] In 1688 the 4th Earl's son (later 2nd Duke of Devonshire) had married Rachel Russell, daughter of the executed Lord William Russell, whose family base was at Southampton, later Bedford, House, on the north side of Bloomsbury Square. The closeness of the families is shown by the Devonshire tenure of Montagu House in Great Russell Street when it was burnt down in 1685. In the collection of William Talman, architect for Chatsworth, is a drawing of a house proposed for the Earl of Devonshire in Lamb's Conduit Fields (Fig. 91). In January 1689 Barbon sold ground to Richard Kent, part of his purchase from William and John Howkins described as lying on the north side of a 'new intended street to be called Cavendish Street' and bounded on the west by premises agreed to be sold to the Earl of Devonshire.

Cavendish Street was what became Great Ormond Street. John Strype's edition of Stow's *Survey* refers to this proposed house as intended for one of the sons of the Duke of Devonshire. Barbon's hope that the two great Whig families would have houses close to each other came to nothing and eventually the Devonshires made their permanent base in Piccadilly on the site of Berkeley House, bought in 1698.[41] The evidence of the 1689 sale to Richard Kent points to a proposed Devonshire House on the north side of Great Ormond Street, but it should be noticed that the north end of Devonshire (later Queen) Square was left open, almost as if a house facing the square, as Southampton/Bedford House did in Bloomsbury Square, was intended to take the site; Morden's map of 1700 shows the area sketchily laid out (Fig. 92).

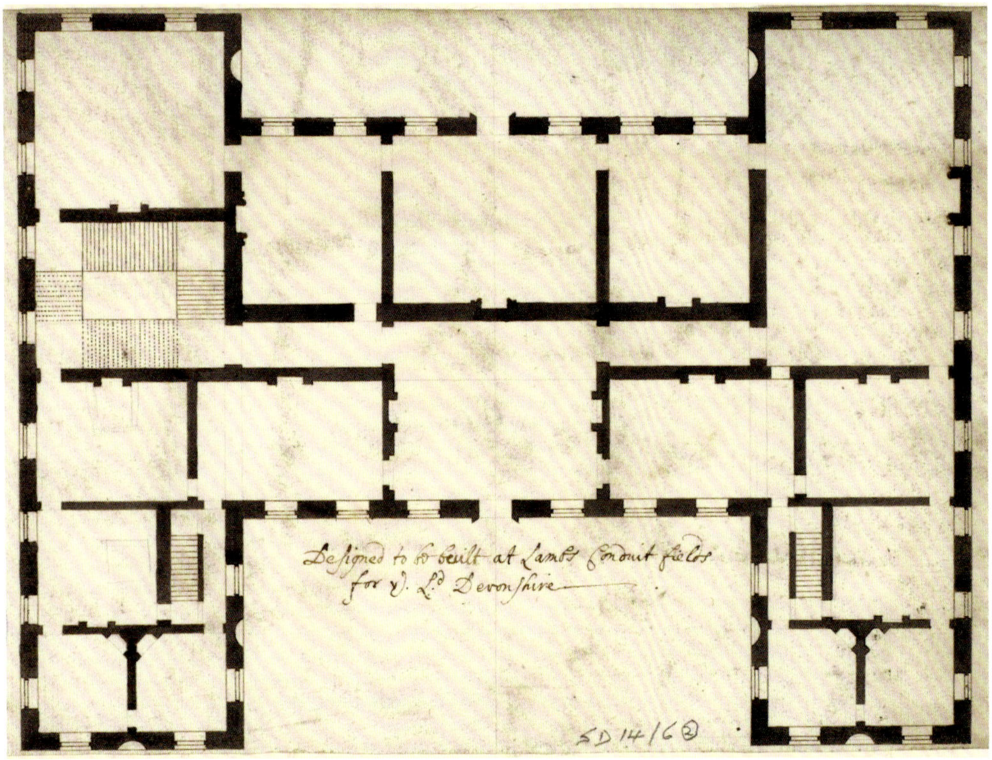

Fig. 91. William Talman's design for a house in Lamb's Conduit Fields.

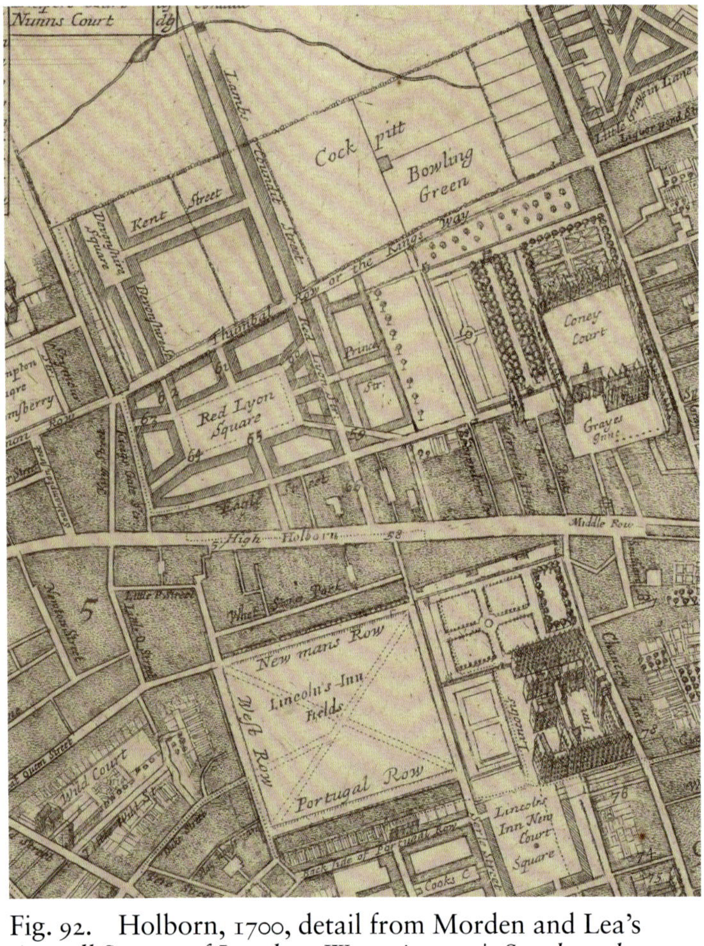

Fig. 92. Holborn, 1700, detail from Morden and Lea's *Actuall Survey of London, Westminster & Southwark*, 1700. Private Collection

The rough outline of the area shown on Morden's map reflected the embryonic state of Barbon's development north of Theobalds Road at this time. Red Lion Square is recognizably complete, but the road north to Lamb's Conduit, Devonshire (Queen) Square and the route linking the two, which became Great Ormond Street, are imprecise. Devonshire Square is approached from Theobalds Road by a single street, not the two eventually built. It has already been shown that Red Lion Square was completed successfully; Barbon had sold his interest in the Fisher property before his death. The printed form of building agreement for a house in the square (Fig. 104) is framed in general terms and must have been drawn up in view of the great developments in Holborn which Barbon planned. It was surely used elsewhere.

South of Theobalds Road, besides Red Lion Square, Barbon built the west side of Bedford Row and the side streets leading towards the square; builders included the bricklayer and architectural writer Venterus Mandey.[42] The houses in Bedford Row, then only the west side facing the open space of Gray's Inn walks, were substantial and valuable, as shown in a dispute over the commission on the sale of the house occupied by Sir James Butler. This had been built by William Chamberlain, a joiner, and was held on a ground rent of £5 p.a. but worth £76 p.a. at the rack rent paid by the actual occupier of the house. The lease was sold by Chamberlain in 1695 or 1696 for £880 to James Smith, a Ludgate Hill draper, who paid 5 guineas each to John Tasker, a surveyor, and to Richard Johnson, a painter, for finding the investment; Tasker was also paid £5 by Chamberlain. After the sale William Palmer, a broker, claimed that Chamberlain had entrusted him with the sale at a commission of the usual rate of 20s. per £100, that Smith had bought it for £1,000 and that Chamberlain owed him his commission; Chamberlain's blunt reply was that the purchase was made through Tasker and Johnson and that as far as his agreement with Palmer was concerned it was 'no purchase, no pay'.[43] There are six surviving Barbon houses in Bedford Row of which No. 36 contains a lead cistern dated 1691 (Figs 93–94).

While by the early 1690s Barbon had more or less completed development south of Theobalds Road, the pattern to the north was very different. There is evidence of a few leases or sales on isolated sites, enough to show that at least some building had begun. Close to the corner where Theobalds Road turned south to go to Kings Gate, next to where the Bedford Estate in Bloomsbury was already built, Barbon and his mortgagees sold four houses to Roger Hudson, a goldsmith, with much ground extending northwards along Devonshire Street, described as thirty feet wide and leading to a new intended square (Devonshire, later Queen, Square).[44] This was part of the plot allocated to Sir Thomas Fisher in the 1654 partition between him and Bedford Corporation which Fisher had kept because he wanted the bowling green. Another part had been sold in March 1692 by Sir Richard Fisher and Barbon to William Chipps, the coffeeman-turned-brickmaker. This was eventually bought from Chipps' heirs and mortgagees in 1695, with five other houses south of Theobalds Road, by Thomas Tayler of Clapham. It was then described as 'formerly a bowling garden' and had seventeen houses, sixteen of them in Devonshire Street, the other fronting a passage leading to Bloomsbury.[45] But while some of the ground taken by Hudson may have been built before Barbon's death in 1698, much was not. In August 1706 Hudson agreed with John Banks and William Hawkins for the building of forty-one houses in (Old) Gloucester Street, the houses to be completed within eighteen months in the same way as another house already in building. Banks, a timber merchant as well as carpenter/developer, had built one of Barbon's houses in Duke Street, St Margaret Westminster, in 1683 (see pp. 68–69). In fact, the houses in Gloucester Street were built by the local carpenter Simeon Betts or his sub-tenants.[46] Both Devonshire Street (now Boswell Street) and (Old) Gloucester Street crossed the boundary between what had been Fisher's ground and Conduit Close, the northern ends nearest Queen Square being on the ground which came to Sir Nathaniel Curzon. Houses in Curzon's part of Gloucester Street were eventually

Fig. 93. Lead cistern at 36 Bedford Row, photograph, 1959.
Image © London Metropolitan Archives (City of London), no. 69466

Fig. 94. Nos 42–43 Bedford Row (after refronting in 1965), 2021.
Photograph by Timothy Walker

built by Robert Keeley, carpenter, under a lease of May 1707; a Chancery lawsuit of 1711 shows that William Hawkins was agent for Sir Nathaniel Curzon and he appears as lessee of several sites on Curzon's ground.[47]

One of the houses bought by Hudson had been let to Ralph Swaine, a carpenter who built elsewhere on the ground north of Theobalds Road. In 1690 he had taken a lease of ground in a passage (now Cosmo Place) leading from the west side of Devonshire Square to the Bedford Estate; here he covenanted to finish a house of three storeys plus cellars and garrets, so it was incomplete in 1690; it was re-let in 1703 to Thomas Peacock by Sir Nathaniel Curzon. In a Chancery case of 1709, when Richard Kent's nephew tried to exercise his equity of redemption on what by then was a successful development brought about by Curzon, Curzon provided a schedule of 114 leases made on his estate. In addition to the premises re-let to Peacock there were only eight which had been made in Barbon's lifetime, four in 1690 and four in 1693, another one of these also let to Swaine. The schedule shows how the names changed in the early years; three of the 1693 leases refer to a new square, leases made in March 1701 refer to Devonshire Square while by 1703 the leases refer to Queen Square; one of the leases in 1701 was for a site at the corner of Devonshire Square and Kent Street and four other leases were for premises in Kent Street, earlier Cavendish Street, but by 1703 Ormond Street was in use.[48]

These aborted developments were matched at the eastern end of Conduit Close, on the Rugby Estate. In 1697 William Milman, Barbon's mortgagee, said that in 1689 he had agreed with Barbon to make leases of houses begun to be built. Three, on the north side of Great Ormond Street, the first, third and fourth houses east from Barbon's freehold ground, let to Arnold Browne of Mile End Green in trust for George White, merchant, were let in December 1689; another three were let in February 1690 to Robert Cock, a gentleman who endorsed on the leases his agreement to finish and tile the buildings by Midsummer 1692; and three more were let in August 1692 to Arthur Tooley, the bricklayer, and Ralph Swaine, the carpenter. At the same time, in August 1690, Barbon let corner ground on the west side of Lamb's Conduit Street and south side of Great Ormond Street to Thomas Norman, a carpenter. Norman claimed to have spent £800 in building two houses on the site, one by 1696 never let and the other called the Musick House let at £24 p.a.; by 1696 Norman was in the Fleet Prison, sued for debt by his mortgagee. As elsewhere most of these leases were made in hope rather than recognition of completed houses. In 1697 Milman said that Barbon had not kept his word about building and the loss of time meant that the fifty-year term from Christmas 1686 had now become too short for building 'in those out parts of the town where the ground in question lies'. Milman sought leases for seventy or eighty years, more than the sixty-one years which was usual in most Barbon developments; remoteness from the centre was one reason for making building leases longer.[49]

Further west along Great Ormond Street, on Barbon's freehold, mortgaged to Kent and Curzon, building also started quickly. In January 1689 Barbon sold a 78-foot frontage on the north side of the intended Cavendish Street (Great Ormond Street) to Richard Kent with two houses then in building. In June 1690, not long before his death, Kent borrowed £1,000 from Catherine Dunch on the security of these two houses; this was the site immediately east of that intended for the Earl of Devonshire and was itself bounded on the east by ground to be sold to John Foltrop. It may be that these were the houses referred to in the Chancery suit where Foltrop is said to have agreed to build in Duke Street Westminster as substantially as he built in Lamb's Conduit Fields. In December 1694, however, when Dunch went to Chancery to try to recover her debt, the two houses were still unfinished.[50] It would seem that Kent bought with his own money a block of ground on the north side of Great Ormond Street to continue what Barbon had started: one of the leases made by Curzon in 1701 was a plot on the north side of the street bounded on the east by a house built by Kent. Here was the only great house in Lamb's Conduit Fields, Powis House. In 1705 Lord Powis sold his house in Lincoln's Inn Fields, and took a lease from Sir Nathaniel Curzon of a site in Lamb's Conduit Fields which may have been intended to extend the site of the house built by Kent. In January 1713 a deed for the house next door says that it was bounded on the west by the great house, formerly of Richard Kent, now of Lord Powis. This deed dates from two weeks before the house burnt to the ground, allegedly from the carelessness of one of the servants of the French ambassador who was the tenant; the replacement house was illustrated in *Vitruvius Britannicus* in 1715.[51] All this suggests that Lord Powis did not build new when he moved to Great Ormond Street in 1705, but bought a large house built by Kent on the site first proposed for the Earl of

Devonshire's house. Kent was an important financier in his own right, associated with Sir Stephen Fox, a banker with Charles Duncombe and receiver-general of the Customs.[52]

Despite the evidence showing that many houses were incomplete or not started, these early references to the larger houses on the north side of Great Ormond Street suggest that at least some houses were built before Barbon's death which survived to be recorded in drawings or photographs. These include Nos 44 and 49, the latter the house occupied by Dr Richard Mead from 1720 to 1754 which in 1851 became the hospital for sick children. Mead's house was perhaps that built by John Foltrop noted above (Figs 95 and 96). The former No. 40 Great Ormond Street also seems likely to be a house dating from Barbon's lifetime, six windows wide and with a projecting Corinthian doorcase (Figs 97 and 98).

The chaotic state of development north of Theobalds Road is recorded in John Strype's edition of Stow's *Survey* in 1720. His description of this area was dramatic:

> This is like the ruins of Troy; some of the houses carried up to the covering, others about a story, and others only the foundations laid, and this they have been for some years, with no likelihood of finishing.

Strype's *Survey* had been in preparation for some years and other evidence suggests that this description is more accurate for 1700 than for 1720.[53] By the time Defoe came to describe this part of London in 1724 Barbon's vision had been largely accomplished:

> We go on still west, and beginning at Gray's Inn, and going on to those formerly called Red Lyon Fields and Lambs Conduit Fields, we see there a prodigious pile of buildings; it begins at Gray's Inn wall towards Red Lyon Street from whence, in a strait line, 'tis built quite to Lamb's Conduit Fields, north, including a great range of buildings yet unfinish'd, reaching to Bedford Row and the Cockpit, east, and including Red Lyon Square, Ormond Street, and the great new square at the west end of it, and all the streets between that square and King's Gate in Holborn, where it goes out; this pile of buildings is very great, the houses so magnificent and large, that abundance of persons of quality, and some of the nobility are found among them, particularly in Ormond Street, is the D – of Powis's house, built at the expence of France, on account of the former house being burnt, while the Duc D'Aumont, the French Ambassador Extraordinary lived in it; it is now a very noble structure, tho' not large, built of free-stone, and in the most exact manner, according to the rules of architecture, and is said to be, next the Banquetting-House, the most regular building in this part of England.[54]

Even then there were still unfinished parts of the development which Barbon had started more than thirty years before.

Fig. 95. No. 44 Great Ormond Street, the Hospital for Sick Children: Private Nurses House.
© Wellcome Collection

Fig. 96. No. 49 Great Ormond Street, 1882, watercolour by J. P. Emslie.
Wellcome Collection. Attribution 4.0 International (CC BY 4.0)

Fig. 97. No. 40 Great Ormond Street, photograph by Henry Dixon for the Society for Photographing the Relics of Old London, 1883.

Image © London Metropolitan Archives (City of London), no. 25351

Fig. 98. No. 40 Great Ormond Street doorcase, watercolour by John Wykeham Archer, 1860.

© Trustees of the British Museum, 1874,0314.410

Lincoln's Inn

While the 1690s saw Barbon in difficulties, there was one development which he did complete successfully, the building of New Square at Lincoln's Inn. As elsewhere, this was a development started by someone else. New Square was built on Ficket or Little Lincoln's Inn Field, one of the three, with Cup Field and Purse Field, that made up Lincoln's Inn Fields. Cup Field and Purse Field were developed into Lincoln's Inn Fields by William Newton under licence from the Crown in 1638; in 1641 the Earl of Carnwath got licence to build in Ficket Field, with condition to leave part open as a square like Covent Garden. But whatever Carnwath might have planned for Ficket Field came to nothing; despite its obvious attraction to builders it remained largely open at the time of Morgan's map in 1682 where it can be seen (labelled 'Little Lincolns Inn Fields') south east of Lincoln's Inn Fields.[55]

By 1679 Sir John Berkenhead, Master of Requests, owned two thirds of the field freehold and a further sixth on lease from trustees of the school in Calne, Wiltshire, established by John Bentley, with Sir William Hooker the owner of the other sixth. After Berkenhead's death in 1679 his property was bought by Robert Clerke and Henry Serle, both Lincoln's Inn lawyers, and Serle also negotiated for Hooker's share. In May 1680 Clerke and Serle were asked to show their proposals to Lincoln's Inn; they staked out the ground for building and treated with Barbon and Richard Frith. Serle appears to have been less willing than Clerke to bring in others and refused offers, intending to undertake the scheme himself. Lincoln's Inn at first opposed the building, pulling out the stakes set out in 1680, but in November 1681 the Benchers asked Serle to produce a draught of his intended buildings. In July 1682 the Inn reached agreement with Serle who offered most of the new building to his fellow lawyers. This agreement provided for three ranges, 'at all times hereafter to be called by the name of Serle Court' (eventually Serle's name was superseded by its modern name; in 1699, when Barbon's executors sold off his equity of redemption, the sale described the property as 'Serle's Court or Lincoln's Inn New Square'[56]), all chambers of three storeys above cellars to face into the court; Serle should also provide a boghouse and a house for the gardener; west of the ground allocated for the new square Serle would be free to build as he wished. Shortly after, in August 1682 Barbon agreed to buy Clerke's share with money borrowed from Michael Scrimshire, his financier also in St Margaret Westminster. In November 1682 Clerke went to Chancery to try to establish his rights, a suit which Serle claimed had been started by Barbon and Scrimshire in Clerke's name. There followed through the 1680s a maze of legal battles, complicated by Scrimshire's bankruptcy and allegations by Barbon that Serle had burnt the deeds which showed Clerke's title. Matters ended in the House of Lords and the conflict only concluded with Serle's death in 1690. During these years the Inn had regularly extended the three-year limit within which Serle had been expected to build.[57]

Serle died intestate, his heir an infant nephew. A private Act of Parliament settled his property on trustees to dispose of as best they could. The Act stated that Serle had built a great pile of building on Ficket Field which had been raised to a great height but left uncovered, so that further building was needed to make his scheme profitable; an addendum to the Act specifically stated that the Act did not invalidate the agreement between Serle and Lincoln's Inn made in July 1682. Serle had probably made less progress than the Act implies, although when some of the lawyers and other local inhabitants maintained opposition to his proposals and persuaded the Attorney General to take up their case in 1685 Serle claimed that he had started to build. In 1686 he was fined by the Westminster Commissioners of Sewers for breaking their sewers. But there is no record of Serle disposing of anything he had built.[58]

Barbon's only part in Serle's proceedings during the 1680s was his efforts to frustrate them, but the speed with which he acted with the trustees appointed under Serle's estate Act suggest that he was waiting for an opportunity. The settlement of Serle's estate was in November 1690; by January 1691 Barbon and the Act's trustees were in discussion with Lincoln's Inn and in February Barbon agreed to continue under the terms of Serle's agreement of 1682. A proposal to build a new office for the Six Chancery Clerks (Barbon must have been one of their best customers) was dropped when it was opposed by the Inn. Barbon's financiers were now Sir Thomas Cooke, Nicholas Cary and William Atwill, to whom the formal conveyance of Serle's estate was made on 11 March 1691. The price was £23,500, paid in part by the settlement of several of Serle's mortgages, the largest, for £8,000, to the Earl of Bedford. Later that year Cooke settled any outstanding interest that Sir William Hooker might have retained in Ficket Field.[59]

Through 1691 and 1692 the completion of what Serle had started proceeded rapidly; Barbon discussed with Lincoln's Inn landscaping, boundary walls, the boghouse and the gardener's cottage. In March 1692 he may have revived the idea of a new office for the Six Clerks in what was described as 'the newly built square'. By 1693 agreements for the disposal of chambers were being made. An agreement for chambers on the south side of the square by the gateway from Bell Yard was made in April 1693, and a lease for second-floor chambers on the south side on the third staircase west from the Bell Yard gate was made to Benjamin Mildmay in February 1694. In August 1693 Cooke agreed to sell to Henry Penton of Lincoln's Inn a set of first-floor chambers on the west side of New Square; the agreement says that the square was then finishing. The sale to Penton resulting from this agreement was made by Cooke, Cary, Atwill and Barbon in March 1694 and included a covenant by the vendors not to build in the square except what might be allowed for the Six Clerks' Office. In April 1694 Lincoln's Inn ordered that a book be compiled to include the articles with Serle and subsequent dealings, and that this should record the admissions to the chambers in New Square. There are datestones of 1691, 1693 and 1694 on parts of New Square. But even through 1693, local opposition still continued with Barbon and Cooke facing action in law and equity from local residents, by this time Barbon and Cooke were using their claim of parliamentary privilege to continue with his building. At the same time other parts of Ficket Field to the west, not included in Serle's 1682 agreement with Lincoln's Inn, were also being developed, with leases made to building craftsmen including Ralph Swaine, the carpenter found elsewhere as a Barbon lessee.[60] A photograph of New Square as it is now is shown in Figure 100.

Barbon retained an interest in New Square to his death; it is mentioned in his will as Lincoln's Inn Square. But from 1693 the Inn dealt with Sir Thomas Cooke rather than Barbon over issues relating to the completion of the work and Barbon's interest may have been a personal one; he appears to have been

Fig. 99. New Square, Lincoln's Inn, etching by Sutton Nicholls, *c.* 1725.

Fig. 100. New Square, Lincoln's Inn.
Photograph by David Williams, Latitude Stock, Alamy Stock Photo

living there. In June 1692 the Inn ordered that he be admitted to the chambers he then inhabited; these may be identified in a mortgage to Jacob Tonson in 1726 as 'rooms on the south side of Staircase Eight on the west side of Serle's Court, formerly occupied by Nicholas Barbon'. In 1693 Barbon sold the western part of Ficket Field, said then to be almost wholly covered with building, to Cooke, Cary and Atwill, for £18,500, in part satisfaction of a larger sum he owed them. In 1697 Cooke sold his interest (with no mention of Barbon) to Edward Sayer and John Harris, probably trustees for Atwill, and two goldsmiths, Adrian Courtenay and William Hamond. It was to them that Barbon's executors Rebecca Hayes and John Asgill released their equity of redemption in April 1699.[61] Asgill had also lodged briefly in a chamber in New Square; in 1696 Lincoln's Inn ordered that chamber to be padlocked because he was not a member of the Inn, and after he broke the padlock they went to the Lord Chief Justice for a warrant to keep him out.[62]

Brookfield

Among the properties in which Barbon still claimed an interest at his death were Great and Little Brookfield, with 'the beast market and sheep market and fair thereunto belonging kept on the said ground and other ground adjoining and belonging me'. Brookfield, in the parish of St Martin in the Fields, was then at the western edge of the built-up area of London in what is now Mayfair,[63] and was mortgaged to Sir Nathaniel Curzon, so linking this proposed development with Curzon's interests in other Barbon developments, in Conduit Close and Newport Market. The right to hold a market there came from a sale by Henry, Lord Dover, in October 1686 to George Bradbury. Dover was the heir of Henry Jermyn, Earl of St Albans, who had developed much of St James's parish; Bradbury was probably Barbon's trustee, for in May 1688 Barbon and Bradbury mortgaged the market to William Millett. On 7 August 1688 the market was further mortgaged, along with the title to the land which Barbon bought from Lord Dover. Dover himself had only formally received this land, formerly part of Queen Henrietta Maria's estate, a month before under patent of 7 July 1688. A further mortgage in December 1688 makes it clear that the money had been lent by Richard Kent and, as the documents relating to Conduit Close show, Kent was borrowing his money from Sir Nathaniel Curzon. It would seem that Barbon's involvement went back at least to the end of 1685 when a deed between Bradbury, Edward Noel, Thomas Price and Bernard Turner, all known Barbon associates, was witnessed by Barbon.[64]

It may be that Barbon was as much interested in the market rights as in the development potential of the land. As seen in Chapter V, Barbon had bought Newport House in 1682 and developed a successful market under letters patent of April 1686. It was probably this proposed market 'in or near Leicester Fields' which Thomas Lord Jermyn, in a petition to the Privy Council in February 1685, had asked to be stopped as a threat to St James's Market.[65] The Newport Market patent was for all goods except live cattle; by 1725 Defoe described it as one of the principal meat markets of London and for this success to be achieved it had to be associated with a live animal market. In addition to St James's Market, active three days a week, the patent of 21 November 1663 had granted to the Earl of St Albans the right to two weekly markets in the Haymarket for the buying and selling of live cattle and sheep where there had been an informal forage market since the sixteenth century. In 1686 Lord Jermyn succeeded with a petition to James II for this market to be moved to Great Brookfield, and in July 1688, when the days of the market were changed by further patent, there was permission to hold an annual fifteen-day fair, beginning 1 May each year — the origin of Mayfair. It was this land and the associated market rights which by the sales of August 1688 were in the hands of Barbon and his mortgagees.[66] The association of the two markets is shown by the promotion of the Brookfield and Newport Markets Bill in Parliament by Sir Nathaniel Curzon in 1701, but it does not appear that his bill succeeded.[67]

Whereas the Curzon family maintained an interest in Newport Market, but not the adjacent land, until 1828, their acquisition of Great and Little Brookfield became the basis for successful estate development in the eighteenth century. The May Fair prospered enough to become a nuisance, with disorderly scenes suppressed in 1708, but revived for long enough in the eighteenth century to give its name to the whole area; however, the Brookfield live cattle and sheep market does not appear ever to have been a success.[68] At least as far as Little Brookfield is concerned Curzon claimed in 1717 that he had never used it except for the herbage, but there is evidence that Barbon did build as well as establish the market on Great Brookfield. In 1688 he was ordered to lose the benefit of a drain made by Lady Berkeley because he had not paid his share of the cost and in 1695 his name appears in the rate books. In 1696 Lord Berkeley tried to buy ground from Barbon to add to his own site but claimed that Barbon's demands were so extortionate that he would have preferred to blow up his house than accept them.[69]

There are two surviving building leases of September 1694 from Barbon and John Bland to John Carpenter, a carpenter from St Margaret Westminster, of two houses on the south side of the market place for live cattle, the seventh and eighth houses west from the intended sheep market. These houses were only two storeys, plus cellars and garrets, but the leases make it clear that they were part of an ambitious architectural composition for each was to be part of an arcaded piazza ten feet wide. In 1701 Curzon made a lease of ground on the north side of the market and in 1704 an existing lease of unknown date was extended; the site was described as a place in Brookfield Market on the north side of 'a place commonly known by the name of Mayfaire'. That the scheme referred to in the 1694 leases was completed in Barbon's lifetime seems doubtful and Curzon, as in Conduit Close, was left to complete an unfinished Barbon development. But when, in April 1740, Edward Shepherd took articles of agreement from the Curzon family to build Shepherd Market, he appears in fact to have worked from a basis established more than fifty years earlier by Barbon.[70] As in so many other cases, Barbon's vision was eventually realized, but not in his lifetime.

CHAPTER X
LAND BANKS

Financial Background

The fortunes of property speculators have always been tied to that of the economy they are working in, and particularly the state of the country's finances. The first half of the 1690s was a difficult time for the English economy and, as shown by his experience in Holborn, Barbon suffered as borrowing money became both more difficult and more expensive at a time when he was in any case overstretched. The problems stemmed from the need for England to finance the war effort, resulting from William having committed England to what became the Nine Years' War with France. This put considerable strain on the public finances with annual spending more than trebling between 1688 and 1694. The Government was continually looking for new sources of revenue, but soon reached the limit of what could be achieved through expanding customs and excise duties and fell back on a large new land tax of up to 20 per cent of landlords' annual rent rolls.[1] Short-term borrowing was also used to bridge the gap between the approval of expenditure and receipt of the taxes, although this could be expensive. Attention naturally turned to means of longer-term borrowing, which would allow the government to save cash by paying only the interest each year without the capital. While this could be cheaper than short-term borrowing, it worried those who felt it weakened parliamentary control of expenditure and of the war itself.

Initially, long-term borrowing as such was resisted and a number of equivalents were explored. Government was open to innovative ideas from whatever sources, but anything requiring legislation still had to be passed by Parliament and active lobbying was essential to secure the necessary support, including satisfying the authorities that it was neither too expensive nor introduced too much risk for them. Success usually meant that the projector got a slice of the income, whether directly or in the form of a paid position running the scheme. The Bank of England was finally created in 1694 after three years of discussion and lobbying. The idea was that the Bank would lend the Treasury £1.2m at 8 per cent, secured on the tonnage (a tax levied on each imported tun (cask) of wine), but would pay the Treasury not in cash but with its own bills. It then undertook to repay these bills on demand in specie, that is cash in the form of coins. The Bank would pay 3 per cent interest on the bills it issued but, provided it raised the full amount of the £1.2m in subscriptions, it would only be necessary for 25 per cent of this total to be paid up front, to be used as needed for repayment of its bills.

The Bank of England scheme had only been agreed by the Treasury after a group of prominent City merchants had indicated that they would support it, giving some comfort to the Treasury that the Bank's bills would be acceptable. Indeed, the full subscription was achieved within twelve days of its opening.[2] It was those with specie who benefited from the high interest rates, that is the City merchants and financiers, while those with land saw themselves taxed heavily to pay for the war and were now in danger of losing control of government expenditure. They wanted more attractive ways of raising cash from their land than either outright sale or mortgage at what seemed to them as high interest.

Consequently, and despite the very considerable difficulties, not least in liquidity, there were continued attempts to construct a bank from assets based on land, an idea supported by Daniel Defoe who argued 'Land was the best bottom for public banks'.[3] Land bank projectors blithely promised the high returns enjoyed by the 'moneymen' available to those with land-based assets. The added attraction, at least in theory, was that such banks being financed by the landed would be controlled by them rather than City merchants. A number of land bank proposals were put before the House of Commons from 1690, usually from Dr Hugh Chamberlain, but they all failed to make any progress.[4]

In early 1695 John Briscoe, who the year before had already written a 114-page attack on other approaches to long-term borrowing, including the Bank of England, produced one more attempt at a land bank.[5] Landowners would settle their estates with commissioners appointed by either the Crown or Parliament who would then issue bills amounting to the anticipated sale value (twenty times their annual rental income). The bills would be made legal tender, loaned to the Crown at an interest of three per cent, a sixth of which would pay the costs, including salaries of the commissioners. This meant the Crown got its loan cheaply, the landowners got 2.5 per cent interest, and Briscoe's proposed loan of £5,000,000 would generate £25,000 to pay costs and give Briscoe himself an income. For good measure, Briscoe also suggested that subscribing landowners should be relieved of future land tax. Unfortunately, despite being made legal tender, there would be no incentive for anyone to take the bills since they did not pay interest and could not be exchanged for specie. Moreover, given the Treasury had taken three years to accept even bills that were convertible into specie on demand, and then only reluctantly, it is hardly surprising that Briscoe's latest proposal, although referred to a Commons committee, made no progress.

Meanwhile, there was another financial problem arising from the state of England's coinage. Silver coins minted before 1663 were extremely worn, irregular in shape, and progressively subject to clipping, whereby small amounts of silver were removed and eventually melted down and sold as bullion. There were increasing demands for the clipped coin to be removed from circulation, together with proposals that they should be valued according to their weight, that is at less than their face value. This naturally resulted in people hoarding the more modern coins which had milled edges and so were difficult to clip. This produced a relative dearth of silver coins in circulation and uncertainty about their future value. These problems were exacerbated by a number of other factors and, as expectation of reform grew, the uncertainty increased still further.

It might be thought that recoinage is a separate issue from the creation of banks, but this is not so when the money supply is entirely, or is at least dominated by, physical coin, whether gold or silver. Banks could only function if subscribers and depositors believed that they would be able to get their money (i.e., coin) back, a calculation that became even more difficult if there was the prospect of milled coin increasing in value and/or clipped coin decreasing.

This chapter will confirm that the failure of Barbon's so-called land bank was indeed because of the interaction of its launch with the recoinage crisis, but not before it had delivered a severe fright to the Bank of England. However, history is written by the winners. The classic study of the Bank of England expresses surprise that a previous historian should have made 'This failure [of the land bank] into an episode in the history of the Bank', while the most recent one describes it as 'one of the most spectacular flops in financial history'.[6] The saga of the land banks was portrayed by the Whig historian, Thomas Macaulay, as a hopeless attempt by Tory landowners to create the impossible, a bank based on land.[7] Many more recent historians have also seen it as an essentially political battle between Whig and Tory, or court and country. The latest analysis, while accepting the battle for control of the bank(s) that lent to the Crown, places much more emphasis on the groups competing to finance those loans — and to profit from them — and on those who sought to profit from the recoinage crisis.[8]

Barbon's Interest in Banks

Barbon was an MP during this period and was fully aware of the arguments about recoinage, and well able to identify the winners and losers from the various options. His role in these arguments will be dealt with in detail in the next chapter, but he saw the variety of ideas put forward for raising money and discussed in the House of Commons and was active in the relevant parliamentary discussions. The only mention of banking in his writings is in his *Discourse of Trade*.[9] He points out that Amsterdam and Venice benefit from having banks because they 'cause a great dispatch in business', while English merchants have been 'forced to carry their cash to goldsmiths [... whose] notes pass in payments from one to another like notes on a bank'. Credit is still in some measure kept up despite 'very vast sums of money lost'.

> Therefore it is much to be wondered at, that since the City of London is the largest, richest and chiefest city in the world for trade; since there is so much ease, dispatch, and safety in a public bank; and since such vast losses has happened for want of it; that the Merchants and Traders of London have not long before this time addressed themselves, to the government, for the establishing of a public bank.

Having dismissed the possibility in England that a despotic prince might seize a bank, not least since the departure of James II, he goes on:

> In England where the government is not despotic; but the people free; and have as great a share in the sovereign legislative power, as the subjects of any state have or ever had; [...] and where the flourish of trade is as much the interest of the King as of the people, there can be no such cause of fear: for what objections can any man make, that his money in the bank may not be as well secured by a law as his property is?

There is no suggestion that a bank needs to, or should, be secured by land, and he sees merchants and traders as the chief beneficiaries. Drawing on the views, already expressed in *Discourse of Trade*, about the status of money and the need to increase its supply, he proposed the creation of a bank based on paper money during a debate in Parliament in January 1693, arguing:

> to raise a million by way of a bank to make a note or paper go for money, which will be of as good value if you establish it by act of parliament. This is practised in Venice and Amsterdam; in Venice £100 in bank is worth £105 and at Amsterdam £102. This will answer the great want there is of money and will do your business as well.

Luttrell recorded, 'but no one spoke to it'.[10] Barbon returned to the charge at the end of 1694 and put forward a proposal based on a perpetual fund at 6 per cent secured on a revised chimney tax, which excluded the smaller houses, and was described as the basis for 'something like a new kind of bank' which would issue its own bills. This was interesting enough to be picked up by many Parliament watchers who reported that the Ministry had appeared interested although it was not clear the tax would provide enough money.[11] It gave rise to the satirical comment about Barbon,

> He weary grown of ruining by retail
> Gravely prescribes destruction by wholesale;
> [...]
> Revive damned chimney money, and impose
> Gabels on children's warming hands and toes.
> If, doctor like, the builder would advise
> Close-stools and urinals should pay excise,
> Unhappy sure must be that nation's fate
> Where quacks and cullies do direct the state.[12]

Barbon was also on the bill committee that considered Briscoe's proposals in 1695 where they were allowed to die. He saw the desire of many MPs to have a land bank to provide some competition to the Bank of England and was very familiar with the arguments that would be necessary to get any proposal through Parliament. He would also have realised, whether because of his own financial acumen or from his relationship with Robert Harley, that the government would soon require a new long-term loan which could provide the basis for a further bank. Unsurprisingly, he decided to develop one, but while he saw no financial necessity for it to be a land bank, he recognized all too well that any proposal needed to be dressed up as one if it was to have any chance of success. His approach was fundamentally different to true believers such as Briscoe and Chamberlain, and indeed his own eventual partner, John Asgill.

Producing a bank became one of his last projects. It involved many of the attributes of his other grand projects, with spirited controversy with others who had the same in mind and vituperative pamphlets on both sides, not least about who had thought of the idea first. In this case, as for insurance, others had proposed the overall approach but had been unable to come up with detailed proposals which worked, financially and politically. It was Barbon's skill to turn these into something practicable and deliverable. So, while Briscoe pondered how best to proceed, Barbon took up the challenge together with John Asgill, a lawyer who previously had been a partner of Briscoe on schemes to establish fisheries in North America and a joint stock company for establishing workhouses. Asgill and Briscoe together had supported Hugh Chamberlain in some of his previous attempts to create a land bank.

The first advertisement for this proposed bank was artfully crafted.[13] It pointed out that the great advantage coming from the creation of the Bank of England was its effect on lowering the interest rates on tallies (short-term government borrowing secured against future taxes), bills of exchange and money on goods.[14] Its disadvantage was that by taking so much of the free cash available, there had been less money available for the 'owners of land and houses' who had therefore had to pay higher interest rates. But despite the Bank reacting to the complaints by announcing that it would lend on land, the fact that its directors were all merchants or traders meant that the Bank did not have the skills to assess either the owner's title to land or his income from it. Mortgages from the landed gentry were notoriously risky, both because there could be issues with proving title, which required both careful study of repetitious deeds, covenants and so on, and the establishment of the real income from that land, much of which depended on the detail of the tenants' leases, themselves often obscured by history. Barbon's bank claimed to deal with this by ensuring that a majority of its directors would be lawyers 'whose study and practice have made them more acquainted with the titles and values of land' (there was no mention of landowner directors!). Moreover, the proposal to lend on the security of land or houses at the low rate of 3.5 per cent would make it easier for landowners to raise money while lowering interest rates generally for land (and hence raising the value of land) as the Bank of England had done for the monied men. The proposed settlement credited Asgill and Barbon with £3,000 and £2,000 of the land bank's stock on which to receive profits; meanwhile they invited subscriptions of land and, more importantly, of £100,000 specie.

This was already a very different proposal from that of Briscoe or other land banks. It was the specie which would underpin lending to landowners whose only benefit was those lower interest rates, in contrast to receiving interest in some of Briscoe's proposals or being exempt from land tax. The bank would issue bills backed by the lands on which they had given a mortgage, and on which they paid 2 per cent and would redeem for specie on demand, but all the profits would go to those who had subscribed the specie, that is the monied men not the landowners. Although the land assets would provide some backing for the bank's bills, this was essentially what we would call a building society rather than a land bank. It is noteworthy, given Barbon's interests, that the bank expressly proposed to lend on houses and not just land.

Barbon and Asgill pressed on, issuing a fuller account of the scheme,[15] again claiming that 'it will be the support of the Nobility and Gentry of England' and reporting through the newspaper *The Post Boy* their progress in gaining subscriptions. Their offices were in Lincoln's Inn and the top floor of the Exeter Exchange (built by Barbon some twenty years earlier) and the bank was sometimes called after these. Not to be outdone, Briscoe produced a new, albeit sketchy, proposal which recognized the need to proceed without legislation.[16] This was very different from his previous proposals since subscribing landowners now had to pay 3.04 per cent (almost 0.5 per cent less than Barbon charged) if they wished to have their land's value in money or bills, in contrast to his former proposal which paid interest to subscribing landowners. Given his subscribers were entirely landowners, they naturally controlled the bank and received the profits, although a good share was reserved for Briscoe himself. His subscription books opened in early June, only two weeks after those of Barbon.

Barbon adopted the same tactics as he had in the arguments about fire insurance, both attacking on specific points and claiming that Briscoe had pinched the ideas.[17] He pointed out that the bills issued by Briscoe's bank would be of no interest to anyone unless backed by specie, but there were no proposals for so doing. Briscoe's original attempt to deal with this had been no more than bluster, saying

> Some who are desirous to keep the freeholders' necks still under the servile yoke of six per cent per annum interest [...] may make trivial objections against these my proposals, and demand where will the money be found to answer these bills of credit? But I do not think myself obliged to acquaint every impertinent querist with the methods I have to propose for raising a fund of money.

Barbon had great fun with this comment, citing Briscoe's previous business failures and pointing out that it did not come well from 'a person who by common report can give no instance of any advantage from any one of all the projects of which he has been the promoter'. He then caused real annoyance by saying that although Briscoe had produced a number of 'impracticable notions' for a land bank and therefore thought of himself as its 'first proposer', it was well known that others had put proposals to Parliament two years earlier and that all 'the seemingly useful parts of Mr Briscoe's proposals [...] are directly taken from the settlement of [Barbon's] Land Bank'. He concluded that Briscoe's proposals were no more than an attempt 'to disturb the settlement of the Land Bank [...] and to prevent the freeholders from joining'.

Briscoe produced a flurry of responses in the next month or so.[18] All three made clear that he would not reveal his method for raising specie until a meeting of the subscribers, not least because he was worried that others would use his ideas. His *Account of the National Land Bank* claimed that Barbon's recent proposals 'had mostly collected them out of [Briscoe's] own writings' and that they were based upon his foundation, except that they charged slightly higher interest rates for mortgages. His reply to Barbon's pamphlet was forthright, commenting that at least he had been prepared to put his name to his pamphlets while Barbon had not, and that none of his subscribers had ever wished that 'the first promoters had been men of clearer reputation'. Nevertheless, he seems to have realized that he had to answer the point about specie backing for his bills and early in August, claiming to be under pressure from those who wished to subscribe money, he announced that he was indeed prepared to accept specie up to a limit of one million pounds.[19]

Meanwhile both banks gave regular reports of increasing subscriptions, and other marketing information. They both accumulated a range of trustees designed to impress. Paul Foley, Speaker of the House of Commons, was a trustee for Briscoe together with sixteen other MPs. His brother Philip Foley was a trustee for Barbon and three other Foleys subscribed. Robert Harley's cousin Thomas and his younger brother Edward were both trustees of Barbon's bank and Edward wrote to his father, 'I trust God will please to give his blessing to it so as that it may prove of service to the whole nation'.[20] By the end of July, Barbon had already received £110,000, of subscriptions not cash, and a meeting had agreed to go for £150,000; his books were finally closed in the middle of August at £350,000, a week after the legal details of the settlement were completed (which even included an insurance scheme against lost bills). Briscoe was going slower, but having almost £100,000 by the end of August, he issued another pamphlet rehearsing the details of his proposal and announcing his first meeting of subscribers on 10 September.[21] The war of words broke out again. Barbon and Asgill produced a pamphlet distinguishing their bank, 'established by a deed of Settlement enrolled in Chancery' from Briscoe's which was only 'proposed to be established'.[22] Briscoe's advertisement in response to the pamphlet described it as 'stuffed equally with falsities and impertinencies' and 'waved the nauseous drudgery of exposing their nonsense'.[23]

The differences between the various banks are illustrated by comparing those who subscribed to them.[24] Half of the subscribers to the Bank of England came from the City of London, another 16 per cent from Westminster, and 18 per cent from the south-east of England. Briscoe's bank was very different, with only 20 per cent from the City and 10 per cent from Westminster and subscriptions from every county. Forty per cent were from the south-east and 30 per cent from elsewhere in the country, a much greater proportion of provincial landed gentry. These proportions are even more marked if one looks only at those who paid or signed up, as revealed in the complaint leading to its winding up.[25] No fewer than 60 per cent of the land subscribers who committed their land were from outside London and the south-east; the specie subscribers were very different — the vast majority of those who paid the first call for specie were London based, including ten who had already subscribed to the Bank of England.

One study of the subscribers to Barbon's bank has suggested that the composition of subscribers was somewhere between the other two.[26] In fact Barbon's subscribers were much closer to the Bank of England's than Briscoe's, sixty-one, or 15 per cent, were in common, far more than for Briscoe's. As promised by Barbon, his bank had a much higher proportion of lawyers and other professions than the others; there were also many London-based merchants, including Nonconformist merchants with bases in the outskirts of London such as Clapham, Surrey.[27] Barbon subscribers included a fair proportion of those who had done business with him and/or were involved in the building industry or development of London and the suburbs. Examples are the lawyers William Milman and John Bland, the financier and developer Robert Breedon, builders John Foltrop and Alexander Cutting, and Barbon's sister-in-law Rebecca Hayes. Barbon had made clear that his bank would lend for mortgages on houses as well as land, and money lent at 3 per cent would have been very attractive to many developers. While we do not have information on the detail of the bank's mortgages, there is one reference in a Chancery case from 1699.[28] This records that six houses near St James's Park were mortgaged for £2,200 'at very easy interest rates' to Barbon's land bank and the money used to pay their builder John Foltrop, himself associated with Barbon and a subscriber to the bank. It seems likely that this was not an isolated case of Barbon or his associates benefiting from the low interest rates and there is a record of another subscriber to the bank, Samuel Lawrence, a Merchant Taylor, benefiting from a cheap mortgage for the purchase of land in Suffolk, dated 2 November 1695.[29]

The minutes of Briscoe's 'National Land Bank' illustrate the problems he had in raising the money.[30] Getting subscriptions was one thing (the latest list gave 1,300 subscribers, although only about 200 actually signed up to deposit land[31]) but turning these into deposits of money was very different. The last date for actually paying the subscription was postponed, first to the end of October and then to the end of November, and even by January 1696 some subscribers had paid neither the first nor second instalment, despite the offer to pay interest from the original due date of 10 October and subsequently increasing both the interest paid on specie from 3 per cent to 4 per cent, and the proportion of the profits going to those providing specie. There were no funds to provide Briscoe with the £3,000 cash promised as recompense for his hard work (and the minimum required subscription for a director) or the annual salary of £1,000, although he did take £250 for his own purposes. It was even a struggle to find the cash to pay the lease on the office, and the directors issued an order in November that no money should be lent on land until subscriptions were actually paid.

While Barbon's bank had done a little better in attracting subscriptions, it too had difficulty in turning these into deposits of specie. Even so, by early January 1696 the bank had already loaned £45,000 on land and claimed that a further £100,000 worth of mortgages were under consideration.[32] Asgill still had hard feelings about the Bank of England: he claimed that it still did not lend on land, thereby raising the effective interest rate for borrowing, yet opposed land banks which were doing so, and at reasonable rates. Moreover, the Bank of England had refused to accept any bills from land banks despite, Asgill argued, their being better secured as limited to three-quarters of the land subscribed, whereas the Bank of England lent up to the full value of securities deposited with it.[33]

There could not be room for both Barbon's and Briscoe's banks and many were waiting to see which of them would win out before putting up real money, i.e., specie. This was exacerbated by the uncertainties related to recoinage, given that the values of both silver and gold coins could well change, and in either direction. Barbon's bank specifically recognized these problems and put further subscriptions on hold.

There was still one more roll of the dice for a land bank which will be described later in this chapter. Before we do so, it is worth considering why neither of the two banks above achieved sustainable success, even though Barbon's struggled on for a few years. This has been written about by many historians, whose explanations often reflect their view of the politics of the time or their interest (or not) in finance and economics. There is no doubt that the political support for land banks came from the 'country' party, many of whom were Tories, but also including many Whig landowners; their failure is best understood in simple financial economics. The so-called land banks would only succeed if they could attract sufficient specie to guarantee repayment of their bills. Barbon's bank was only a land bank in rhetoric, and because it had promised to lend at low rates on land or houses. By the end of the process, Briscoe's bank was wholly dependent on those subscribing specie, who would have taken the majority of the profits.

The success or otherwise of these banks depended on the attitude of those who might deposit specie. Such investors naturally looked for the best interest they could get and with the least hassle. The profits of Barbon's bank came from the difference between borrowing at 2 per cent (i.e., paying that rate on its bills) and lending at 3 per cent. The rate of return could then be geared up by lending far more than was covered by its specie. Barbon's original account of the bank claimed that returns of up to 40 per cent would be available if they were able to secure three million pounds worth of land and lend against it with a specie base of only £100,000. These returns would certainly have been attractive, although some doubt was cast upon them in a pamphlet by one of Briscoe's backers.[34] Barbon's own proposal did recognize that some further backing might be required, and his settlement contained provision for raising a further £100,000 for this purpose. Even then the return could have reached 22.5 per cent. However, the proposals that had been finally approved for the Bank of England included a 25 per cent reserve of specie, so limiting the potential return. On this basis Barbon's bank would only generate 6 per cent compared with the return on Bank of England stock for original investors of 13.33 per cent.[35]

Briscoe's bank started off even worse; his original proposals, 3 per cent paid to specie subscribers and three quarters of the profits going to land subscribers, meant that a requirement for 25 per cent reserve cover resulted in specie only yielding 5.25 per cent. It was only very late in the day that he increased both the direct interest and the proportion of profits going to specie subscribers, generating a potential return to them of 9 per cent — and of course less to the landowners. This brought in some more money, but it was too late and the six largest specie subscribers still withheld their cash. Briscoe's continued changes caused one commentator to write, 'You have been forced to new model your project diverse times [...] and I remember you were as positive in your first draft or scheme as now.'[36]

On the original basis, neither land bank provided an attractive return to the specie investor compared to that available from other sources, whether the Bank of England or available from the government's tallies for future taxes. This inevitable difficulty brought into play the other important factor, the concerns of government officials about being dependent on paper money with insufficient asset backing. The last thing that they wanted was to find the government paid in bits of paper which were not acceptable to others and so of no use in meeting government obligations. This had been a sticking point over the creation of the Bank of England and had only been resolved when sufficient merchants indicated that they would accept its bills. There was no such commitment for the land banks. It might seem surprising that the two proposals were so clearly uncompetitive, but both had more lucrative operations in mind. Both hoped to be chosen for a future government long-term loan on which they would receive 7 to 8 per cent and which then would be geared up by lending more than was covered by it specie as did the Bank of England; in Barbon's case, his closeness to Robert Harley may have led him to believe that he would have a good chance of so doing. This would have given them comparable returns to those of the Bank of England and so, in principle, make it easy to raise the funds. Barbon and Asgill clearly hoped that by getting their bank operational quickly they would be in the best position to benefit.

In early 1696 both banks were struggling to make progress. Many expected a revaluation of silver coin and a return of the price of guineas to normal (i.e., a devaluation) and were managing their holdings accordingly. Barbon had put subscriptions on hold because of the recoinage issues, while subscriptions to Briscoe's had completely dried up and it was already clear that his bank would not run. By May 1696 those few (sixty-two in total) who had actually deposited cash were already looking for ways of winding up the bank, having discovered a loss of over £6,000.[37] Briscoe had refused an earlier offer from Asgill and Barbon to join their banks together and indeed in one pamphlet he claimed:

> The Lincoln's Inn Bank assumes the name Land bank improperly, for Money is their fund, the society monied men, who appoint trustees, Directors etc., wherein their landed men have no vote, not so much as for a doorkeeper.[38]

Finally, in late January, Briscoe accepted the proposal to unite the banks, much to the disgust of Chamberlain, who commented, 'At last Briscoe begins to sneak to Barebones for shelter, finding that his subscribers of both Land and money do not agree.'[39]

Since the banks were different, they could not be combined directly, and a new proposal had to be made. The difficulty, as it had always been, was to find a way of rewarding landowners while still retaining sufficient return for those who were needed to subscribe the specie which Barbon, Asgill and Briscoe all recognized they had 'thitherto attempted in vain',[40] although the proposals maintained the returns to each of them individually.

Meanwhile, within a couple of weeks the Commons had decided to commit the salt tax to fund a perpetual loan of £1.7 million and had refused to allocate this to the Bank of England, '[the Bank of England Directors] being instruments in the debasing and exporting of our currency, raising our guineas and also all commodities, breaking their faith with parliament by trading and giving credit bills beyond their capital sum'.[41] An Exchequer bank was also voted down, and 'to avoid all parties and interests' it was then resolved both that the loan should be supplied by 'a national land bank to be settled by new subscriptions', that is neither of the existing ones, and that no one concerned in the Bank of England could subscribe to the new bank.[42] Creation of a banking competitor was widely seen, and rightly so, as an attack on the Bank of England; its share price dropped substantially and a satirical pamphlet described a trial of the land bank for murdering the Bank.[43] The Bank of England, aghast at the idea of a competitor, counter-attacked fiercely with extensive lobbying.

There was then a short break in the proceedings following the King's announcement of the discovery of a Jacobite plot to assassinate him. The Commons provided him with the powers needed to track down and execute the conspirators and approved a so-called Association, a document declaring that William was the rightful King, which MPs were invited to sign. This embarrassed many Tories who still held to the principle of hereditary rule and preferred to leave the issue open; up to a hundred refused but Barbon signed immediately. Two weeks later a draft of the land bank bill was presented to the Commons and detailed consideration began. Requirements to involve landowners as investors had been dropped; one pamphlet commented, 'we have thrown out all those land clauses that gave us so much trouble'.[44] A supporter of Chamberlain (still a true believer in land banks) described the three promoters as 'cunning sparks that are joined, who have called one another in print impudent k[naves], libellers, stock jobbers'.[45]

This and a subsequent deterioration in the proposed returns to landowners provoked a split between the supporters of Briscoe and those of Asgill and Barbon. A further satirical pamphlet claimed that Briscoe was encouraging his MP supporters to vote against the land bank bill on the grounds that it was no longer a genuine land bank.[46] Such public arguments undoubtedly weakened the position, although the bill passed successfully by the end of April. The eventual land bank corresponded very closely to a money bank of the same kind as the Bank of England, the only concessions being the commitment to lend £500,000 per year on mortgages at the low rate of 3.5 per cent and to allow landowners who subscribed to use their income from land as security for paying the last quarter of their subscription, the first three quarters being subscribed in cash. No doubt the designers felt this last quarter would never be called. It was not a land bank in anything but name and corresponded to Barbon's first proposal in 1693. There could be no greater confirmation of this than the evidence of the first version of the document setting up the new bank, enabling it to receive the proceeds of the taxes that were to secure the Crown's borrowing and providing for Commissioners to receive subscriptions to be collected in the offices of Barbon's bank. The drafting of this had been left to the promoters who had to hurry to get the King to sign it before leaving for Holland very shortly afterwards. It had not been checked by the law officers and the promoters had forgotten to give the Commissioners the power to accept subscriptions in land. A three-week delay ensued to rectify the mistake.[47]

While these debates were going on, action was taken over recoinage. The details of this will be dealt with in Chapter XI, including a discussion of Barbon's pamphlet arguing against John Locke on 'raising the coin':[48] it is sufficient here merely to state the results. The Recoinage Act which was passed early in 1696 demonetized clipped coin in stages with all being stopped by 4 May except for coin used for paying taxes and loans to the Exchequer until 24 June; controversially the Exchequer would also accept counterfeit coins. After that, clipped coins would only be worth their weight in silver. Their use for taxes meant, in practice, that the state absorbed the losses, particularly as the definition of clipped meant that most small denomination silver coins could remain in circulation. The losses would be met by taxation. There was no devaluation of the pound, although the possibility continued to be discussed until the Commons finally ruled out devaluation at the end of October. There were, however, discussions about the level of guineas and after many arguments the price was fixed at 22s., down from 30s.

These changes gave rise to real problems with massive deflation, reduction in the money supply and insufficient money to ensure trade. The Bank of England's credit was hit, as was the government's credit in Flanders where it lacked the money to pay its suppliers. The monied men who held large stocks of the various coins had to work out their best strategy in securing gain or avoiding losses. Briscoe's bank lost over £1,300 by receiving guineas at the old rate of 30s. to find they were then only worth 22s. Ironically, Briscoe had also taken £517 from the bank's accounts in order to buy shares in the Bank of England, hoping to take the profits himself. As we have seen, the shares went down; he passed on the loss of £94 to the bank.[49]

Although neither Barbon's nor Briscoe's bank had been wound up, the new united land bank began to negotiate with the Treasury to work out the details so that it could begin raising subscriptions. The land element was largely irrelevant, what the bank needed was specie. Many potential subscribers were excluded by reason of being shareholders in the Bank of England (this had covered 15 per cent of Barbon's subscribers) and the main protagonists for the bank were goldsmiths who continued to oppose the Bank of England by what means they could, including promoting a run on the Bank. These goldsmiths pressed for substantial concessions in order to make subscription attractive while the Treasury resisted on the basis of cost and a desire to prevent them from securing undue gains from having hoarded coin. There were many ups and downs but the negotiations failed; the bank was not able to get any meaningful level of subscriptions on the terms offered and so never came into existence. The eventual result was that the Bank of England's position became established, although Barbon helped to float another country proposal for a further alternative to it, based on tallies, which was eventually taken up by the Bank itself.[50] The Bank went on to secure its position as a monopoly and to gain extra powers; Barbon's own opposition to this was demonstrated by his acting as teller for the votes against in the committee.

The goldsmith bankers had been hard hit by the creation of the Bank of England which had taken over much of the profitable lending to the Crown which they had done in the past. Their own credit had been weakened as a result. They had welcomed the possibility of another bank through which they could win back this market; most of them were Tories, but their attitude to the land bank was determined by financial return rather than wider political issues. Their dislike of the Bank of England was mutual; Francis Gwyn, the strongly Tory MP, commented, 'The animosity of land bank & Old Bank seems to men almost as high as Jacobite and Williamite.'[51]

The goldsmiths were also, or were assumed to be, the principal hoarders of guineas and silver coin, milled and clipped. They had to balance their potential gains, or losses, from the various proposals for recoinage and devaluation against the possibility of gains from investing in a new bank. While they wanted to benefit from the next long-term loan to the Crown, this could not be at the expense of their position on bullion and coins. This complicated their negotiating position and allowed the Chancellor of the Exchequer, Charles Montagu, who was determined to keep his position as the only person who could deliver the finance that the King needed for his war, to represent their demands as extravagant. He had already used the uncertainty about the land bank to insert clauses into the bill allowing the creation of an Exchequer bank and was able to play upon the disinclination of the Lords Justices, senior figures acting for King William when he was abroad, to agree large handouts to financiers. As opposition politicians, Harley and Foley did not have sufficient command of the financial details or the wherewithal to offer deals to allow them to intervene effectively. The united land bank failed, not because of complications arising from its land element, which was minimal, but because of the risks inherent in subscribing specie at a time of monetary crisis. Only the goldsmiths could have priced this risk because they had the most to lose on their large stocks of coin. Whether or not they set the price too high, the result was that no financial deal could be done in a time of great uncertainty.

Barbon knew many of the goldsmiths well as they had often been a source of funds for him or indeed joined in his speculative developments. He had used his knowledge, position as an MP and political skills to become one of the principal midwives of the 'united' land bank as an alternative to the Bank of England and was widely recognized as such. It had secured its position by Act of Parliament and, even though it was not the land bank that its supporters originally had in mind, it provided the possibility of competition and greater parliamentary control that the country party wanted. But despite his links with the goldsmiths, Barbon could not deliver the financial deals. While he, but not Briscoe, was one of the twenty-one chosen to negotiate on behalf of the bank, with Asgill as their legal adviser, he played little or no part himself in the final denouement. It was left to those 'monied men' to battle Treasury officials orchestrated by Montagu.

Once the united land bank had been approved by Parliament, subscribers to Briscoe's bank recognized that their bank could not operate. It had already stopped lending at the end of 1695 with little outstanding, but had incurred expenditure on staff, purchase of leases and setting up its offices as well as Briscoe's speculations. By June 1696 its losses were estimated at over £6,500 and those subscribers who had paid specie began proceedings to wind up the bank.

While the bank's settlement gave a share of any profits to those who had only subscribed land, it also required them to share in underwriting losses. The specie subscribers had hoped to extract some cash contribution from the land subscribers, but this was unsuccessful. Apparently, the bills and notes had been made in favour of Briscoe as the constant director and, when he or his representatives appeared before the Common Pleas Court, they said that they would not insist on them and would sign a discharge. The case failed as a result. Briscoe had protected the landed element of his bank! He died on 13 February 1697, but while the specie subscribers returned to Chancery three months later to press their demands the result is unknown.[52]

The united land bank was Barbon's last project, but the bank he had formed with Asgill struggled on for a couple of years paying dividends in 1697 and 1698, surviving Barbon's death in that year. Even so, early in January 1699 a notice appeared in the papers:

> Trustees of the late Land-Bank at Exeter Exchange hope suddenly to divide the Remaining effects of the said Bank, and therefore if any person have a just demand of any debt upon the said Bank, they are desired before the first day of February next to go to Mr Chambers at the Meremaid in Milk Street and acquaint him therewith.[53]

CHAPTER XI

MONEY, MONEY, MONEY

The last chapter referred briefly to the recoinage disputes which provided the opportunity for Barbon's last publication, *A Discourse concerning coining the new money lighter in answer to Mr Lock's considerations about raising the value of money* which appeared in April 1696. This concerned the recoinage and the desirability of devaluing the currency. Barbon's opinion is often described as being between William Lowndes, Secretary to the Treasury, who recommended devaluation,[1] and the philosopher John Locke, who was bitterly and ideologically opposed.[2]

Barbon had already set out his views on money in his *Discourse of Trade* where he wrote:

> Money is a Value made by Law [...] is the Measure of Value [...] It is a Change of Pawn for the Value of all other things [...] Money has the same Value, and performs the same uses, if it be made of anything else [than gold or silver].[3]

This view was anathema to Locke, who had already published his contrary concept of money.[4] Barbon's pamphlet developed the approach set out in his *Discourse of Trade* and is significant in the history of economics because of his approach to macroeconomics and to the concept of money, which are arguably more important than his views on devaluation itself. Much of the argument was cast in the thinking of the time and we will not conduct a blow-by-blow analysis of the views of Barbon, Locke, Lowndes and others but rather concentrate on what their interventions reveal about their thinking on money and the economy. We shall also look at why Barbon intervened, and why he chose the time that he did.

Many others as well as Barbon participated in the discussion on recoinage. The Government specifically asked Isaac Newton, Christopher Wren and a few others for their views, and no fewer than 250 contemporary pamphlets and books on the subject have survived reflecting a wide variety of views. It has been a subject of interest and controversy ever since, and books and papers continue to be written about it.[5] Although there is no doubt about which view prevailed, that of Locke, there continues to be argument about why that was the result, who 'won' the intellectual and practical arguments, and who was 'right'. We begin by rehearsing the background.

Monetary Background

Although people wrote IOUs and the Government issued debt which could then be sold on, usually at a discount, money in the seventeenth century largely meant coin. This could be of gold or silver, but the value of the gold coin, the guinea, was left to fluctuate with the market price of gold. There were no substantial silver mines in England so the supply of coin was restricted to that brought to the Mint for coining. This could only come from melting down silver plate or by importing silver bullion or coin from abroad.

Most precious metal coins in circulation were silver, produced by the Royal Mint and containing a fixed weight of silver appropriate to the denomination of the coin. The Mint produced coins for customers who brought their raw silver to it such that a crown coin (5s.) contained $^{30}/_{31}$ troy ounces of silver together with a small amount of alloy to improve its wear. The result was sterling silver, 92.5 per cent fine metal.

Modern coin, minted since 1663, was made in a press, had milled edges and was difficult to clip. Older coin, minted before 1663, had been made by hammering, and was often of irregular size or shape. It was possible to clip away small pieces, melt them down and sell them as bullion while still passing the coin at its full value. Strictly speaking, clipped money was not legal tender in that people were not obliged to accept it, but most did unless the coin was in very bad shape. There were increasing demands for the clipped coin to be removed from circulation, together with proposals that they should be valued according to their weight, that is at less than their face value. As a result, people wanted to get rid of the hammered coin as quickly as possible, while milled coin was hoarded or melted down to sell as bullion to pay for goods bought overseas, producing a relative dearth of silver coins in circulation.

A further complication was the fact that the relative price of gold and silver had changed, reflecting the increase in the gold supply due to discoveries in Portuguese Brazil, and might differ in different countries, offering the possibility of arbitrage.[6] Early in the century, gold had been undervalued in England compared with silver and the price at which government would accept it as payment was raised on several occasions. At this official rate, 21s. 6d., the price ratio between gold and silver in 1688 was 15.58, higher than in many continental markets — for example, the ratio in Amsterdam was 14.93, so silver bought less gold in England than in the Netherlands. When the potential arbitrage profit was greater than the transaction costs (shipping, insurance, etc.) silver bullion would be exported, gold bought in exchange, and that gold used to purchase silver (or commodities) in England. Further opportunities for arbitrage arose from the use of bills of exchange, orders to pay denominated in foreign money and payable in a foreign port, which had their own exchange rate reflecting the balance between supply and demand.[7]

Until the end of the 1680s, the monetary system in England was reasonably stable. Clipping was contained with the average silver coin being about 10 per cent underweight but passing for full value with little problem. This reduction in weight was not much greater than would have been expected from the natural wear for hammered coins minted at least thirty or even more years previously. Figure 101 shows two Charles I silver half-crowns, the bottom one is within 1 per cent of its original weight, while the top one, as well as being heavily worn, has been clipped back to its inner ring and is only 66 per cent of its original weight.

Silver bullion was priced at only 1d. or 2d. above the mint price of 62d., but most of the new coins were hoarded or melted down for export, albeit illegally. Gold continued to be imported and coined into guineas which maintained a roughly constant price of about 21s. 6d.

There were many complaints about the 'shortage of money', particularly in relation to the lack of small coins, a problem that had plagued the English economy for a long time.[8] Some attributed this to the continued export of silver bullion to pay for imports, particularly by the East India Company (who paid slightly over the odds for it[9]), although this may have been offset or more by what was received from their reexports of Indian goods. The increase in supply of gold coins was of little help in this respect since the guinea, worth slightly more than two weeks' wages for a labourer in London, was of little use for everyday purposes.

The picture changed after the Glorious Revolution. The war with France had an adverse effect on trade and also required large remittances to pay for the cost of maintaining troops on the Continent. The exchange rate for coins reflected their relative actual metal content and transaction costs, but the exchange rate for bills of exchange with the Dutch, which also reflected supply and demand, fell by 20 per cent; the price of silver bullion rose by 20 per cent to 75d., making the price of silver set by the Royal Mint uncompetitive. As a result, the amount of silver minted into coins fell to just over 10 per cent of the annual average over the previous thirty years, while clipping increased to such a state that by mid-1695 silver coin used to pay for taxes was only half the weight it should have been. Almost 9.2 million ounces of silver were lost by clipping from English coin between 1689 and 1695, of which 8.4 million were exported.[10] The amount of silver lost by clipping would have been worth almost £2,400,000 at former prices, about 25 per cent of the value of the total silver coin in circulation.[11] Such a massive reduction in the money supply would have caused serious deflation, but as long as people were content to take clipped coins at face value, this prospective reduction of the money supply was avoided.

Meanwhile, by 1695 the price of guineas had risen from 21s. 6d. to 30s., prompting enormous speculation since it became worthwhile to buy gold on the Continent and import it for milling by the Mint as guineas. Amazingly, 721,000 guineas had been produced in the eleven months up to February 1696, including 140,000 for one man.[12] This promoted inflation as merchants looked for ways of spending guineas on goods that could be exported,[13] and inflation was also encouraged by the issue of negotiable bills by the Bank of England.[14] In 1693 the price of raw materials went up by almost 30 per cent, dropping at the end of 1694 but returning to the early 1694 levels by the end of 1695.

While clipped coins had circulated at face value during the early 1690s, this became increasingly difficult during 1695 when the coins had lost half their weight. Domestic trade was adversely affected, and a barter economy began to emerge. Some argued that the problems could be solved by aligning the value of the silver coinage with the higher price of bullion. A silver coin of a certain weight would then be increased in value (hence the expression 'raising the coin'), equivalent to a devaluation of the currency in terms of its silver content. Any discussion of devaluation encouraged still further the hoarding of full-weight coins while the prospect of recoinage, whereby clipped coins would be valued by weight and therefore halved in value, meant an increasing reluctance to accept them. Tax collectors were reluctant to take clipped coin at face value or to accept guineas at their very high valuation in case they might fall.

Fig. 101. Charles I silver half crowns. The upper coin has been clipped back to its inner ring.
Photograph, Lloyd Bennett, *Coins of Britain*, Monmouth, 2019

In the early 1690s there had been no agreement that a recoinage was needed, and many thought it extremely inadvisable when the country was at war. Nevertheless, by the end of 1695 a consensus had developed that recoinage was necessary to restore confidence in the currency; the questions became those of the detailed mechanics and who would pay for the substantial costs involved. The use of the Mint was free to those who brought metal to it, but the state picked up the costs of melting down the hammered coins and then reminting them. The losses from the reduction in value of the clipped coins themselves also had to be borne by someone.

The Problem and Solutions

Some of the arguments arose because there was disagreement on what was the problem, let alone the solution. One school of thought argued that the problem was solely due to the clipping of coins, another that the cause was the export of bullion, particularly by the East India Company or for the war, and yet another that it was all down to the speculators who engaged in arbitrage and were variously described as 'Jews and other foreigners' or 'moneyed men', that is bankers and goldsmiths.

Few could adopt a disinterested approach. Different solutions favoured different interests; a devaluation of the pound in relation to silver increased the value of silver coins ('raising the coin'). This benefited those who had hoarded unclipped coins (usually presumed to be those goldsmiths who acted as bankers). Conversely, it was of no help to those who exported the metal; indeed, it made it more expensive in pounds for them to buy silver in England. Alternatively, demonetarizing clipped coins, valuing them by their weight of silver rather than by their denomination, would immediately devalue them. Since these were the most commonly held by the general public, this was widely thought a significant political risk. If the losses were met by the state, there followed the question of how those losses should be funded.

Many, if not all, of those contributing to the contemporary arguments sought to promote or defend interests of their own. Some wanted to profit from the potential changes; others sought to prevent or limit the opportunities for profiteering. Merchants wanted to avoid devaluation; opponents of the war wanted decisions that would make the war harder to finance; landowners wanted to preserve their real incomes. The Treasury's concern was to be able to raise the necessary funds and limit pressures for reduced or late payment of taxes as well as to minimize the overall cost to the Exchequer.

A number of bills had been introduced into Parliament in a variety of attempts to deal with the problems of clipping, export of bullion and relative unavailability of silver coin. One of these, introduced into the Commons at the end of 1692, was indeed voted to be considered by a Committee of the whole House, the next stage of the process. Among other things, it would have devalued the coin to bring it into line with the fact that silver bullion was going for 64d. an ounce as opposed to the valuation used in coin of 62d.. Both Barbon and Charles Montagu (before he became Chancellor of the Exchequer) voted for the Bill moving to the next stage, but the Committee failed to meet and the Bill was lost by the Prorogation of Parliament in March 1693.[15] Recoinage even appeared in the theatre. A play first performed in January 1696 has one of its leading men forced to tip a servant a guinea because he has no silver money, and the dialogue contains many references to 'reform of the coin'.[16]

The result of the parliamentary discussions eventually produced an Act of Parliament providing for the recoinage in early 1696. It set a date by which clipped coins would cease to be acceptable at face value, phased for different denominations, after which they would be valued only by weight. A longer period was provided when they could be used for payment of taxes. A further Act reduced the rate at which the Treasury would accept guineas to 22s. and allowed payment of a small premium for those who presented silver plate or full-weight hammered coins for minting. The state would bear the cost of minting the new silver coins, as well as the losses on clipped coin used to pay taxes and, controversially, the losses on the roughly million pounds worth of counterfeit coin. Those still holding clipped coins when they were demonetized would bear the corresponding losses, although they might be able to mitigate these by selling them, albeit probably not at full value, to those who could use them to pay taxes. When this was coupled with the severe operational difficulties faced by the Mint in gearing up to the enormous scale of the reminting, a vicious monetary squeeze ensued, with large and continuing shortages of coin.

There remained the possibility of devaluation, which meant that those hoarding full-weight coins continued to do so in anticipation of their being revalued. The argument is usually viewed as one between Lowndes and Locke. Lowndes had produced a lengthy analysis showing that there had been numerous devaluations in the past and recommending that there be a 20 per cent devaluation to align the coinage with the current price of bullion; this meant that the crown coin that was worth 60d. (5s.) would then be worth 75d. (6s. 3d.). He argued that this would remove the incentive to melt coins down, would increase the availability of money reducing the present need for paper credit, 'which is at best hazardous, and may be carried too far', or barter, and would reduce the costs to the state of recompensing the owners of clipped coin.[17] He dismissed the possibility that it would cause prices to rise significantly, although he accepted there would be some long-term effects on the balance of payments. Lowndes was supported by Isaac Newton, who also argued in favour of devaluation.[18]

Arguably, decisions on the coinage were a matter for the Royal Prerogative. However, it was judged prudent to have the final decision on both recoinage and whether or not to devalue made by Parliament, and the process of decision-taking has recently been analysed in great detail.[19] This most recent scholarship has shown that many of the Parliamentary arguments about devaluation were tactical. The chief concern of Montagu, by then Chancellor of the Exchequer and leader of the government party, was to secure his position as the only person who could deliver the funding required by the King for his war. As we saw in the last chapter, for him this meant protecting the Bank of England, as well as ensuring that those financiers able to provide the necessary funds for the war would be recompensed appropriately in one way or another. He had been in favour of devaluation for some time and it was he who required Lowndes to write the report in support. After recoinage had been agreed he then tried to keep guineas high to preserve the possibility of devaluation, but finally changed his approach and delivered the reduction in the price of guineas to 22s. Later in 1696 he at last secured the endorsement of Parliament to no devaluation. There is little evidence that he was swayed by arguments of economic or monetary policy although, within his overall priorities, he was naturally concerned to minimize any unrest that might arise from too little money being available after a recoinage.

Locke versus Lowndes

It has to be admitted that, by modern standards, the level of analysis by proponents as well as opponents of devaluation was limited. Lowndes was not a theoretician but a practical administrator. In any case, his report was written under instruction from Montagu and, apart from the history of devaluations, did little more than rehearse the conclusions of a recent Committee of the House of Commons. Given he had previously opposed devaluation, it is likely that it did not reflect his own views.[20] Little real numerical analysis was carried out and while Lowndes produced figures on the amount and state of the silver in circulation, the role of guineas or paper bills in the money supply were largely ignored. At least one regular listing of prices was published, but no systematic analysis of inflation. Although the price of silver bullion only increased rapidly towards the end of 1695, the price of government purchases had been high for some time and had risen by 20 or 30 per cent compared to 1690 by the middle of 1695; this was of more concern to Lowndes when he wrote his report than the much smaller inflation in prices generally.[21]

Locke had a much more theoretical approach. He was a bullionist, believing that wealth was only in silver — 'it is by having a greater quantity of silver that men thrive and grow rich' — carrying the consequence that balance of payments deficits were bad since the export of silver necessary to pay for them reduced the wealth of the country.[22] He maintained 'it is silver by its quantity, and not denomination, that is the price of things',[23] despite well-established English case law to the opposite effect and the evidence to the contrary from the general acceptance of clipped coins.[24] For Locke it was evident that 'an equal quantity of silver is always of equal value to an equal quantity of silver'.[25] The denomination of a coin was no more than an arbitrary name for a certain weight of silver and not a value in its own right. Reducing the amount of silver in a coin by a devaluation reduced the amount of silver owed under a contract (but not the number of shillings) and so to his mind necessarily adversely affected the creditor or landlord. All prices would automatically rise to compensate for this loss. In any case, the 'intrinsic' value of silver had been 'set by general consent' and it was not open to any King or Government to change it. Locke's view was that the problem was due to clipping and people unwisely being prepared to take the clipped coins at face value — described as 'people who know not how to count but by current money'.[26]

Locke was also strongly opposed to bankers and other financiers profiting from any devaluation, which he believed they had caused by their clipping activity. He was sure that they had been deliberately hoarding full weight coins in order to benefit from such a devaluation and he wanted to prevent this. He was against providing any compensation for those in possession of clipped coins because he thought that would benefit the bankers who had most of them, and any taxes to pay for that compensation were likely to be raised from the landed gentry whom he wished to protect. His solution was to issue a proclamation without notice requiring all clipped coins to be valued at their weight rather than face value. He was not swayed by what Lowndes had described as:

> Great contentions do daily arise amongst the King's Subjects in Fairs, Markets, Shops ... Persons before they conclude in any bargains, are necessitated first to settle the Price of Value of their Money they are to receive for their Goods.[27]

While Locke was no doubt correct that most clipped coins were held by the financiers, his proposal would still have affected the poor most since the value of their money would have been halved overnight, and they had no other reserves.

Apart from the considerable practical problems in securing enough equipment to weigh coins, allowing them to pass by weight would have meant a substantial reduction in the money supply. Locke had argued in previous writing that such a reduction would cause damage to domestic trade and reduce prices. He believed that it was better to allow coins to pass gradually to reminting rather than to demonetize them all at once; the Mint would then be more able to cope with the demand for new coins. He may have hoped that implementing his proposal would encourage quick release of full-weight coins from hoarding but in practice this did not happen for at least two years, and he took no account of the further reduction in the money supply arising from the fall in the price of guineas.

Locke's intervention was entirely consistent with his overall intellectual approach. He was supporting a cause that he believed in, both as regards opposition to devaluation in principle and his wish to prevent bankers and goldsmiths from making a killing. He was hurt by suggestions that he was so rich that he would not be affected by the hardships he was advocating for the common man.[28] He did indeed own a small estate, although not of great worth, but his mindset was very much to maintain the interests of the landowning class, at least those not in debt.[29] He was keen to respond to the requests of his former friend, now patron, the Lord Chancellor Lord Somers, who was one of the main opponents of devaluation within government. Locke was looking forward to being appointed to the Council of Trade at a salary of £1,000 a year[30] and he also insisted that Somers put his name forward towards the end of 1695 as Comptroller of the Mint, knowing that he was in competition with his friend Newton, whose patron was Charles Montagu, and who had written in favour of devaluation.[31] A further irony is that it was Locke who had enlisted Montagu in trying to find a post for Newton a few years earlier and had suggested that very post as a possibility.[32] Newton became Warden of the Mint in May 1696 and Master some three years later.

A Discourse concerning coining the new money lighter

Barbon's intervention in the debate on recoinage and devaluation came early in April 1696, following agreement in the Commons to reducing the price of guineas to 22s. This took the form of a lengthy pamphlet entitled *A Discourse concerning coining the new money lighter in answer to Mr Lock's considerations about raising the value of money.* He explicitly contested Locke's arguments and supported devaluation. An MP and supporter of land banks, Sir Richard Temple, produced a pamphlet at the same time, also supporting devaluation.[33] Kleer has argued, following the contemporary writer of *Decus et Tutamen*, that these two supporters of the Land Bank entered the argument because the reduction in the price of guineas had removed the ability of financiers to use them as subscriptions to the Land Bank at their inflated value.[34] A devaluation was therefore required to provide an alternative windfall for the financiers to use as their subscription for the Land Bank. Maintaining the price relationship between silver and gold would then push up the price of guineas.

There may be some force in this, at least in the case of Richard Temple whose pamphlet included the claim that reducing the price of guineas was a mistake. He had indeed voted against the reduction of the price of guineas to 22s., as had other supporters of the Land Bank, such as the Foleys and Robert Harley.[35] Barbon, on the other hand, had voted with the majority of MPs in favour, although his pamphlet argued that reductions in the price of guineas, whether to 25s. or 22s., would do nothing to keep silver in the country and would have the further disadvantage of reducing the money supply.

Locke did not like being challenged and declined to enter into any further debate with those who disagreed with him. He had drafted the beginning of a response to Richard Temple which did no more than accuse him of failing to pay sufficient attention to Locke's argument, on the basis that what was written was self-evident to anyone who would take the trouble to read the work carefully.[36] An annotated copy of Barbon's book remained in Locke's library but the individual annotations do little more than highlight particular words or numbers and contain no comments to suggest his detailed views. A letter from Locke to Edward Clarke recognizes that 'Sir Richard Temple and Squire Barbon have it seems singled me out [...] I wonder anybody should be at all wrought on by them unless it be such as are of their minds for other reasons than their arguments'.[37] The meaning of the term 'Squire' is unclear but may be an example of the general term that Locke used to refer to MPs. It was not meant as a compliment.

Barbon himself accepted that one of the difficulties of the discussion was that 'Gentlemen are jealous of the arguments, lest they should be biased by private Interest'.[38] He argued in his introduction to *A Discourse concerning coining the new money lighter* that bankers would gain whether or not the coin was revalued and therefore 'so that if I were to consider my private interest, I ought to be of the contrary opinion to that I argue for'. No doubt this assertion can be taken with a pinch of salt, but Barbon himself, of course, was extremely unlikely to have had large stocks of silver waiting to benefit from revaluation. He would certainly have benefited as a shareholder if either the united or his own Land Bank had succeeded, but by his standards it would not have been a great financial advantage. In practice, the status of the Land Bank by the middle of 1696 meant his own interest was as much in being seen, yet again, as a successful projector rather than in securing any great financial advantage. Any equity he had in property would have benefitted from maintaining coin at the old standard but, insofar as a largely domestic business was affected, his debts would have weighed more heavily, and a large reduction in the money supply would have caused great practical difficulties for his property dealings.

John Evelyn recorded in his diary not long after the publication of Barbon's *Discourse concerning coining the new money lighter*: 'Money still continuing exceedingly scarce, so that none was paid or received, but all was on trust', and a little later 'Want of current money to carry on the smallest concerns, even for daily provisions [...] such a scarcity that tumults are every day feared, nobody paying or receiving money'.[39] A London correspondent of the Duke of Beaufort wrote on 5 May 1696, that, due to the lack of circulating coin in the City, 'the common people begin to grow a little mutinous'.[40]

Living and working in London, Barbon will already have experienced for himself these very immediate problems and it does not seem unreasonable to suppose that, even if he might have secured some small advantage from devaluation, a large part of his motive for intervening was, as he himself wrote, to oppose a policy 'when the Consequence of it, in my Opinion, will be so fatal to [my] Countrey; which will be no less than the want of the species of Money, a stop of Trade, and a general Complaint and Poverty all over the Nation'.[41] In the same way that John Locke was keen to reiterate views contained in his previous writings, so Barbon explained he had produced his *Discourse concerning coining the new money lighter* because otherwise 'by my silence I might seem to renounce my own Opinion, having some time since wrote a Discourse of Trade, wherein the definition of Money differs from what Mr. Lock asserts'.[42]

Barbon had indeed already covered the definition of money in his *Discourse of Trade* and Chapter IX has dealt with his general economic arguments. Much of this was repeated in his last work: he set out his view of money in the Preface to *A Discourse concerning coining the new money lighter* in a series of propositions. He stated that silver has no intrinsic value, let alone one set by 'common consent'; that money, not silver, is the instrument and measure of commerce; that it differs from silver by Government having certified its value; and that it is money and not the quantity of silver that is contracted for and by which the value of other things is measured.

He ridiculed the idea that a country's wealth depends on the amount of silver or gold present and rejected the idea that the balance of payments is all-important in determining whether a country gets richer. He pointed out that it is difficult, if not impossible, to calculate exactly what is the balance of payments at any time, and that it is perfectly possible to pay for goods by anything of the right value, not just gold and silver. Moreover, manufacturing can add value to raw commodities without the need for any bullion. In the same way, Barbon saw general advantage to economies in increasing trade, while for Locke, the only point was to secure a net import of silver. For Barbon, Locke's mistake was that 'because money is made from gold or silver, [he] does not distinguish twixt gold and silver and money'.[43] Barbon saw the monetary standard as the current shilling, liable to change its weight if the currency deteriorated, while for Locke it was at all times a fixed weight of silver.

Barbon's conception of money was much closer to modern ideas than that of Locke, but he did concede that silver had some value of its own and that that could affect how silver money was valued. However, he went much further than Lowndes, who thought that silver was rightly regarded as money although its value in coin could, and indeed should, be adjusted to reflect external circumstances. Barbon answered Locke's question that if the government was free to vary the value of money by 20 per cent, why not 50 per cent or even more, by recognizing that making the value of coin too high would result in counterfeiting while valuing it too low would merely promote its melting down into bullion.

Given these different views of the concept of money itself, it is not surprising that Barbon took a different approach to the question of devaluation. He was clear that if the old standard were maintained, silver coin would continue to be melted down so that 'the Nation be left without money: The Consequence whereof will be; That Trade will be at a stand; The prices of all Commodities will fall; And a general Poverty and Clamour over the whole Nation ensue'.[44] That is, he forecast a serious deflation.

Like Lowndes, he pointed out the large number of times that currencies had been devalued in the past, going as far back as the Assyrians, before giving extensive examples from the Romans as well as more recent history. He argued that devaluation is an inevitable response to the growth of the economy which produces upward pressure on the value of gold and silver.

> The cause of raising the Money here in Europe will always continue, as long as the Europeans continue in Traffick and Commerce; for Trade makes a People rich, and Gold and Silver are Badges of Riches; and therefore as the People grow rich, the price of Gold and Silver will rise, because the occasions for Gold and Silver will still increase.[45]

He observed that devaluation in England almost always followed devaluation elsewhere in Europe and that France had devalued in 1689, only a few years before. He also argued that domestic prices would not rise as a result while exports would become cheaper, reducing any pressure on the rate for bills of exchange and with it the opportunities for arbitrage (see p. 216, n. 7) that had forced up the exchange rate. On top of this, devaluation would reduce the costs of the recoinage by a million pounds, reflecting the greater value of the clipped coins.

He summed up the *Discourse concerning coining the new money lighter* in very clear language:

> To conclude this Discourse: If nothing in itself has a certain Price or Value; If Gold and Silver are Commodities of uncertain Values. If Money has its Value from the Authority of the Government, which makes it currant, and fixes the price of each piece of Metal; Then the Money will be of as good Value, to all intents and purposes. when it is coin'd lighter. For, the Authority being the same, the Value will be the same. It will buy as much Goods: The Landlord will have as much Rent; And the Nation will save a Million of Money at a time when they have so great occasion for it. Besides the preventing those fatal Consequences that follow the Coining the Money too weighty; As, The Loss of the Money; Decay of Trade; The Fall of Rents; And a general Poverty and Clamour all over the Nation.[46]

Barbon was not the only person who wrote in favour of devaluation. We have already seen that Richard Temple had produced a pamphlet at the same time, but others included James Hodges and Barbon's former banking colleague John Briscoe.[47] Although Hodges in particular gave a very cogent refutation of Locke, his book appeared in 1697 sometime after the House of Commons had decided against devaluing and Briscoe's did not appear until 1698.

Outcome and Commentary

One of the odd things about the arguments at the time was a basic assumption that the effects of the two proposals, that is revaluation and devaluation, were symmetric and opposite. This was not so. Even Lowndes' proposals for a 20 per cent devaluation would have resulted in the coins having more silver than those circulating at the time of the recoinage. Lowndes did point this out but drew no conclusions from it.[48] A detailed calculation has shown that the effects of restoring the coin to its previous level would have produced a deflation of about 20 per cent and the 'devaluation' proposal would have produced a deflation of about 6 per cent. Import prices would have been left unchanged by 'devaluation' and would have been reduced by 20 per cent by restoration. Landlords and recipients of fixed incomes would have benefited a little from devaluation and rather more from restoration.[49]

These calculations are borne out by events: recoinage at the old standard led to a severe monetary squeeze that particularly affected the poor. Over the summer of 1696, a whole series of events demonstrated the problems faced by the common people. In Newcastle, Derbyshire, Lancashire and Westmorland, crowds numbered in hundreds threatened 'the Ministers of State & their [parliamentary] Representatives', including Sir John Lowther, a prominent government spokesman in the Commons. The menace of popular violence also hung over Locke's Whig MP, friend and neighbour in Somerset, Edward Clarke, and his family, where talk of a plot to raise 'the mob' to burn down his house and tear him 'in pieces' convinced a cousin to withdraw to a safer residence.[50]

The final cost of the operation, including both the losses on receiving clipped money and the costs of reminting, was about £2.7m, corresponding to more than 25 per cent of annual public expenditure. Silver kept on being exported and it was recognized two years later, including by Locke, that the price of guineas had been set too high; it was reduced further to 21s. 6d. These changes paved the way for the eventual transition to the adoption of the gold standard. One historian of the Mint commented, 'The great recoinage was an expensive fiasco.'[51]

Barbon and Locke started from completely different concepts of money and both found the other's position hard to comprehend. They argued at cross purposes. For Locke, money was silver, and the weight and fineness alone determined how much it was worth. Mankind had accepted that silver performed the functions required by money and, having put a value on it, by whatever means, it was no longer open to governments to change it. The government's stamp merely gave assurance that the amount of silver in a coin was what it was supposed to be. Wealth was determined by the quantity (weight) of silver. All contracts were based on weight of silver. The denomination was no more than a name for the relevant amount of silver. If someone received less silver by weight than they had contracted for, they were being defrauded. If people accepted clipped coins at full value, they clearly did not understand what they were doing. Devaluation would put prices up. A country only became wealthier by increasing its stock of silver, which for England meant exporting more goods than were imported.

For Barbon, money was a measure and a unit of account. Contracts were made for the amount of money stated, not the weight, content or any other property of the coin, a position endorsed by English case law. The government's stamp on a coin was confirmation of its value, and the amount of metal in a coin did not of itself have to be worth the denomination of the coin; indeed, money did not have to be made of gold or silver. Governments were free to set the value of the coin, although they would be constrained within a range that removed or minimized any advantages of melting the coin for bullion on the one hand or counterfeiting on the other. He noted that this had been done on many occasions in the past, usually where there had been a shortage of money or when neighbouring countries had devalued. Devaluation would not have a short-term effect on prices. Wealth stemmed from the value of goods in a country, not just silver. The balance of trade, even if it could be established in practice, was not a measure of addition to the country's wealth.

Barbon's definition of money meant that he was bound to consider the effects of contributions to the money supply other than silver. He recognized that reducing the price of guineas would also reduce the money supply, thus making a further contribution to deflation, a point apparently missed by Locke. Locke also failed to include the effects of any increase of paper money through bills of credit, saying they were 'nothing else but the expectation of Money in some short time'.[52] Although Barbon says nothing about paper bills in his *Discourse concerning coining the new money lighter*, he does refer to them in his *Discourse of Trade* where he recognizes that they can act like money: 'Credit is a Value raised by Opinion, it buys goods as Money does.'[53] Newton would make a similar point a few years later when he said, ''Tis mere opinion that sets a value on money.'[54]

On this basis Barbon comes out rather better than Locke, at least as far as his prescription for change is concerned, although it could be argued that Barbon concentrated on the issues within the English economy and did not take sufficient regard of the international trading aspects. While Locke was overturning established legal precedent, he was essentially returning to past bullionist principles and supporting the cause of the landed classes which he identified with the public good. It was Barbon who was the revolutionary. Just as his promotion of the macroeconomic benefits of luxury consumption was a radical change from the past, so was his vision of the unit of account essentially being established by the authority of government, and changeable when necessary or to suit. He was the first writer to set this out clearly and systematically.[55] He reflected a more flexible view of society and economic activity, departing from ideas of inherent worth and the preservation of hierarchy to the vitality and disruption of the market.[56]

The verdict of history has changed as well. During the time of 'sound money', devaluation was viewed as a sign of weakness, both moral and economic. The recoinage was first characterized by Thomas Macaulay (with a degree of misrepresentation) as a triumph of Whig history.[57] Going into the twentieth century, as devaluation was adopted more frequently by British politicians, Lowndes became more favoured. This is ironic because, as Kleer has argued, Lowndes' arguments were not strong and had no theoretical backing.[58] It was Barbon who marshalled a much better case against Locke and who laid much of the ground for future monetary economics.[59] It certainly gives the lie to the comment in a nineteenth-century French dictionary of political economy about Barbon's idea that it was the mark of government rather than an intrinsic value that gave money its worth: 'Cette lourde et inconcevable erreur enleva toute autorité à l'ouvrage de Barbon, et fut probablement la cause de l'oubli dans lequel ill tomba bientôt.'[60] That seems a bit extreme, even if one disagrees with Barbon, and ignores the fact that his proposal amounted to a de facto deflation of 6 per cent rather than a devaluation. After all, he was in the same company as the Secretary to the Treasury and Sir Isaac Newton, and his concept of government setting the value of a coin was upheld by English case law.

CHAPTER XII

BARBON AS DEVELOPER — SITES AND DESIGN

Previous chapters have concentrated on telling the story of Nicholas Barbon's individual development activities and have touched on many of his operational methods. This chapter and the next draw these together and consider in more detail how he conducted his business and the extent to which he operated differently from others. The first chapter considers the land he acquired and the buildings he put on them, and the next covers his financial and legal operations. While they draw heavily on Roger North's pen portrait of Barbon, North's descriptions are reinforced by examples using the detail from the mass of litigation in which Barbon was involved as well as other contemporary comments.

Site Acquisition

As we have seen, Barbon started his career after the Fire of London by buying a large number of sites where houses had been burnt down. Most of these involved only one or two houses, often small, and were rebuilt relatively quickly, allowing him to recycle his capital. Praise God appears to have given his son the lease for his own house, the Lock and Key, and as a rich man may well have provided more funds. This phase of Nicholas Barbon's development was profitable and could easily have been self-financing. Few, if any, of its buildings are left standing now.

Identifying these sites was easy for Barbon. They were mostly in the four parishes where he had worked as a doctor during the Plague, which included the parish where he had been brought up and where his father had held a variety of offices in the vestry. He, or his father, probably knew the original owners, many of whom may not have wanted the trouble or expense of rebuilding, even if they could afford it. It is not surprising therefore that he was the second most frequent user of the 'Surveyors' Setting Out' by which surveyors appointed by the City defined the sites to be built on after the Fire, and also had the widest geographical spread.[1] Two of the top four users were Aldermen whose properties were essentially concentrated in one street each; even the largest user of all, Richard Frith, had two thirds of his property in one street near St Paul's.[1] Barbon's experience of using the Fire Court to improve the terms of the lease for his father's property was a good introduction to the use of the law to further his own interests (see p. 19–20).

By the mid-1670s Barbon was well enough known to be approached by those wanting to sell individual properties in the City, including lawyers and scriveners acting on their behalf. He was also beginning to appreciate what might be possible with larger-scale activity. His development of both Crane Court in 1670 and Mincing Lane from 1672 onwards had required him to put a larger site together from a variety of sources, including sites belonging to rich livery companies: he would sell parts he did not need and replace the buildings which had been burnt or destroyed by ones more appropriate for the time.[2] These projects had been very profitable and for the future he would be concerned only with larger sites. Roger North had asked him why he overtraded and so was forced to make everyone unhappy and be perpetually harassed with lawsuits: his answer was, 'it was not worth his while to deal little; that a bricklayer could do'.[3]

The extent to which the purchase and redevelopment of existing buildings for sale to third parties was a new idea is a genuine question. The Dissolution of the Monasteries in London had certainly led to new uses for their land but this consisted largely of sale (or gift) to individual owners who either adapted the site for their own use or let plots to others to build. The construction of the squares at Covent Garden and Southampton, later Bloomsbury, Square took place on what were largely green field sites, although in all cases the motivation of the original freeholder (the Earl of Bedford and the Earl of Southampton respectively) was to increase the ground rent of the site for their own benefit. Indeed, this was the principal meaning of the word 'improvement' in the early seventeenth century. One 1613 dictionary gave the only meaning of 'improve' as 'to raise rents', and in practice mostly for agricultural land.[4] Arguably, this is conceptually different from recognizing that a piece of land, whether or not it had existing buildings on it, could be more valuable used in a different way and, equally importantly, of understanding how that value could be extracted without having to remain as permanent owner. One of the early complaints about Barbon at Essex House says in a rather surprised tone, 'he has propounded unto himself great profit and advantage by building on the premises'.[5] Whether or not it was a new idea, there is no doubt that Barbon seized on it and made it his own.

He may have been helped by another development. The Duke of Buckingham was finding the upkeep of York House, his house on the Strand, very expensive, and was in any case short of funds. He decided to sell the site, which included many individual small houses, and new streets were laid out in 1674. However, the complicated layers of mortgages on different parts of the site produced considerable and continuing litigation. This meant that it was sold in a large number of individual lots; even those who bought the largest shares of the site had plots scattered over the whole site, preventing any common approach.[6] Contrary to some accounts, Barbon was not involved in the redevelopment of York House, possibly because it came too soon for him, but he will have noted the difficulties caused by the piecemeal ownership as well as the opportunities that would have been missed. He would go on to redevelop many large houses,[7] but in every case he made sure that he had overall control of the whole site, with the ability to decide the layout of the streets and the planning of the houses and other facilities, including being able to dispose of parts of it when that made economic sense or was necessary for tactical reasons.

Control of the site did not always come easily since they often contained some small houses with lessees or tenants who did not want to be moved. Roger North makes clear that all Barbon's presentations focused on the financial benefits for all concerned; 'all other arguments and wheedles he esteemed ridiculous and vain loss of time'.[8] He used a combination of pressure, cajoling and force to bring the necessary deals to conclusion; again, Roger North gives a good description of Barbon's approach:

> Another time I asked him how he did take off opposition when he was upon a design that concerned many, whom it would be very chargeable to buy off directly, as when a hundred or more old houses were to be pulled down to accommodate a building design. He said he never bought off all, but only some few of the leaders and most angry of them, and that his method was this. He appointed a meeting. They would certainly be early at the place, and confirm and hearten one another to stand it out, for the Doctor must come to their terms. So they would walk about and pass their time expecting the Doctor, and enquiring if he were come. At last word was brought that he was come. Then they began to get towards the long table (in a tavern dining room for the most part) for the Doctor was come! Then he would make his entry, as fine and as richly dressed as a lord of the bedchamber on a birthday. And I must own I have often seen him so dressed, not knowing his design, and thought him a coxcomb for so doing. Then these hard headed fellows that had prepared to give him all the affronts and opposition that their brutal way suggested, truly seeing such a brave man, pulled off their hats, and knew not what to think of it. And the Doctor also being (forsooth) much of a gentleman, then with a mountebank speech to these gentlemen he proposed his terms, which, as I said, were ever so plausible, and terminated in their interest. Perhaps they were, at this all converted in a moment, or perhaps a sour clown or two did not understand his tricks, or would not trust him, or would take counsel, or some blundering opposition they gave; while the rest gaped and stared he was all honey, and a real friend; which not doing he quarrelled, or bought off, as I said, and then at the next meeting some came over and the rest followed. It mattered not a litigious knave or two, if any such did stand out, for the first thing he did was to pull down their houses about their ears, and build upon their ground, and stand it out at law till their hearts ached, and at last they would truckle and take any terms for peace and a quiet life.[9]

We know from some of his court cases that he did meet his interlocutors in inns such as the White Hart in Bishopsgate, the Mitre Tavern in Fenchurch Street, the Rose Tavern without Temple Bar and The Three Cups in Holborn as well as at Garraways' coffee house. North gives a further indication of his skill at manipulating his audience and of his control of his own emotions:

> If he could not work them all together he would allure them singly by some advantage above the rest, and if he could not gain all, divide them, for which purpose he had a ready wit, and would throw out questions most dextrously. If anyone was fierce against him he quarrelled, then that the man's objections were charged upon the affronts that passed, and not the reason of the thing. And he would endure all manner of affronts and be as tame as a lamb. If it was proper to his end to be so, he would be called rogue, knave, damned

> Barbon, or anything without being moved; then some others, seeing him treated so scurvily, would take the man's part, which advantage he failed not to improve [...] He had good address and could express himself cunningly, and being master of (for none is free from) passion, was never forward to speak importunely, and then made his design the centre of all he said and did. He knew that passion and heat wear off, and as he regarded it not when rashly used by others, he never used it himself but as an engine to work with.[10]

Essex House, the first of Barbon's redevelopments, demonstrates very well all the points in North's piece. Over time he became more sophisticated and the development of Holborn, with its complicated ownership pattern, forced him to use the courts himself to endorse, and then enforce, division of the property between the various owners, so creating unencumbered title to the part that he needed for his plans.[11]

Barbon made an enormous profit on his first large-scale redevelopment. This was variously estimated at between £5,000 and £9,000, on an initial investment of £13,000, a good return by any account. That such a high return was available stemmed from his being the first to recognize what value might be achieved from a project of this kind. Although he developed at least five other large houses, he was never able to secure as good a return again, suggesting that in these later cases he had to share some profit with the previous owners who, by then, were more aware of what might be achieved.

As well as Barbon's redevelopment of large houses, he built extensively on green field sites on the edges of the cities of London and Westminster or on former military grounds. These were concentrated on Soho, Holborn and in the East End at Spitalfields and Well Close Square. He often bought land, or leases, from corporate owners who had little emotional attachment to the sites but were keen to improve their income from them. His purchase of the lease of the Harpur estate from Bedford Corporation at a time when it needed money for a new Charter is a good example of this (see p. 125). It is even possible that, when Barbon acquired a lease from Bedford Corporation or from St Clement Danes for a capital sum, it meant that he could get a better deal on the ground rent he had to pay, thereby increasing his potential profit. He certainly claimed to have the skills and knowledge to make greater improvement than others and this may have allowed him to pay more for sites than others.[12] We only know of one site which he attempted unsuccessfully to purchase when another was successful: Soho Fields developed by Richard Frith. Summerson describes this phase of London's development as 'the scramble for freehold properties'.[13] While perhaps largely true, Barbon was prepared to buy leases when that provided the only way forward, as for example in the Exeter House, Red Lion Square and Holborn developments. He, or those who sold or leased land to him, made little effort to control the layout and development of sites. Apart from retaining the equity of redemption where he could, Barbon had little or no interest in retaining long-term ownership. Greater control as a tactic for maximizing long-term value would only become prominent in the development of entailed and trust property in the eighteenth century, as described by Summerson and Olsen.[14]

Barbon's third major building activity was in the Inns of Court where he was a repeated contractor for the Middle Temple, and also built for Lincoln's Inn. Although neither of these were free from controversy, they were much less development projects than building contracts. Roger North argues that his great knowledge of lawyers and being 'himself full of law' made him an obvious developer for lawyers to turn to.[15] He seems to have managed the rebuilding after the Middle Temple fire in 1679 largely by himself, since one complainant says that Barbon 'contracted with various bricklayers, masons, carpenters, and other artificers, brick makers, lime man and other workmen and labourers'.[16] For later building there he employed individual builders, particularly John Foltrop, whom he paid 'above the usual price because he was to be paid when they were sold'; that is, Foltrop financed the work himself, only receiving funds after the sale of the building.[17]

We know little about the extent to which Barbon prepared his sites before building started. Clearly, demolition of a large house was necessary for its redevelopment, and he always tried to make the best use of any materials already on the site or which became available from demolition. The materials from Essex House were worth some £3,000; he also disposed of the materials from Newport House and even sold the grass from the nearby Military Ground for hay before he built there.[18] We know that he acted as quickly as possible to establish his presence and facilitate his development; examples include his speedy demolition of Essex House and of a number of other properties that stood in his way when developing other sites.

Many complaints cite his digging of trenches: the archaeological investigation of the Spitalfields site suggests that these were shallow setting-out trenches, two feet wide and six inches deep, to mark out house plots.[19] Other complaints, for example in connection with Red Lion Square, concerned the amount of rubbish produced. A standard solution to this issue for many decades was to put rubbish in front of the house so that the eventual level of the street was raised. When there was a lot of rubbish, it might be placed at the rear as well so that what became the basement or cellar was built straight onto the original level of the ground. Again, one example of this is highlighted by the archaeological investigations in Spitalfields where, in the case of Fort Street, the new ground level was over six feet higher than the old. This is shown in Figure 102. The material was mostly fire debris which the archaeologists suggest might even have stemmed from the Great Fire seventeen years earlier.[20]

Fig. 102. View of a section through material dumped to raise ground level at rear of No. 28 Fort Street.
© Museum of London Archaeology

Design

In his *Apology for the Builder* Barbon makes clear that he is not concerned to write about architecture, saying that buildings in London 'are generally so well finished that almost every House is a little Book of Architecture'.[21] He knew both Wren and Hooke well, dining with them on a number of occasions, and also in their roles as regulators, Wren as Surveyor General and Hooke as one of the three City surveyors, but there is no evidence he collaborated with them on any building. While the bricklayer and architectural writer, Venturus Mandey, took a building lease from him and the surveyor, Isaac Rowe, may have worked with him on the layout of Well Close Square as well as taking leases, there is no documentary evidence that he worked with any architect. As we shall see in the next chapter, these grants of building leases were possibly in payment for other work done.

As far as individual houses were concerned, he was content to let his builders build, sometimes, but not invariably, prescribing some degree of uniformity and of course being required to obey the post-Fire regulations within the City of London. We have his drawings for the Middle Temple Cloisters (Figs 43–45), but otherwise only know of two drawings that may have been of proposed buildings, the Royal Mews (Fig. 56) and the Temple chambers (Fig. 82). The Royal Mews was never built, and the chambers in the Temple were built to a very different pattern from the drawing. There are also references in litigation to his 'models' and it is clear from the records of the Middle Temple that he produced a 'model' for the chambers he built in 1688.[22] However given that he was asked to produce it within two days, it is unlikely to have been very elaborate.

Only three of his buildings have any specific architectural treatment, the Watergate at the bottom of Essex Street, which was forced upon him by the purchasers of the freehold of Essex Street, Exeter Exchange, and the gates of the College Hill houses (Figs 22, 27, 76). The first two are ordinary productions of their time, but both the drawing of the Royal Mews and the decoration on the College Hill houses might be due to a craftsman/designer such as Edward Pearce.

That is not to say that he had no plans of his building. Figures 20 and 26 show his original plans for the Essex House and Exeter House developments, neither of which was built to them. In both cases the changes took account of alterations that were advantageous to him, but this was not always so and in Red Lion Square he complained that he had been forced 'to break his model'.[23]

However, he must have done at least sketches of his sites, if only to establish the frontages and hence the potential ground rents, using them to encourage both investors and builders.[24] Formal plans for Charles Street, Westminster, and Devonshire Square near Bishopsgate were attached to the relevant deeds (Figs 54 and 57), while Figure 103, from a proposed sale of houses at the Piccadilly end of Rupert Street, is in fact little more than a sketch setting out the various ground rents.

This leads naturally to his design of the sites themselves and the mix of buildings on them. These days, maximizing the financial return on a site is one of the most important skills of a property developer. Such a skill was relatively, if not completely, unknown in Barbon's time but one that was important to him, and one he was not afraid to declare to others: in buying Red Lion Fields he said, 'that by his skill and knowledge in building he could make a greater improvement than could have been made by Sir Richard Fisher or the said Neale or the said Hinde'.[25] His skill and knowledge included making sure that he put the maximum number of houses on the site or secured the best balance between the more attractive (and expensive) frontage and those less well placed. In his early developments this was less important because he was essentially building a more modern house where an older one had burnt down. But even for his own home in Crane Court, he took the opportunity to create a striking residence at the end of the Court, and he made the most of his site in Mincing Lane.

The first big development that called for an imaginative approach was Essex House. He began by facing down the Privy Council by creating 'facts on the ground' through rapid demolition of the house itself. But he realized he could not adopt this approach for all his opponents. He recognized the need to minimize opposition to his development, or even to create support. He got the Benchers of Middle Temple on board by selling them a small part of the site (see p. 31) which set him on the path to a profitable continuing relationship with them that lasted almost twenty years. He recognized the practical and political need to keep the large new house formerly of Sir Orlando Bridgeman,

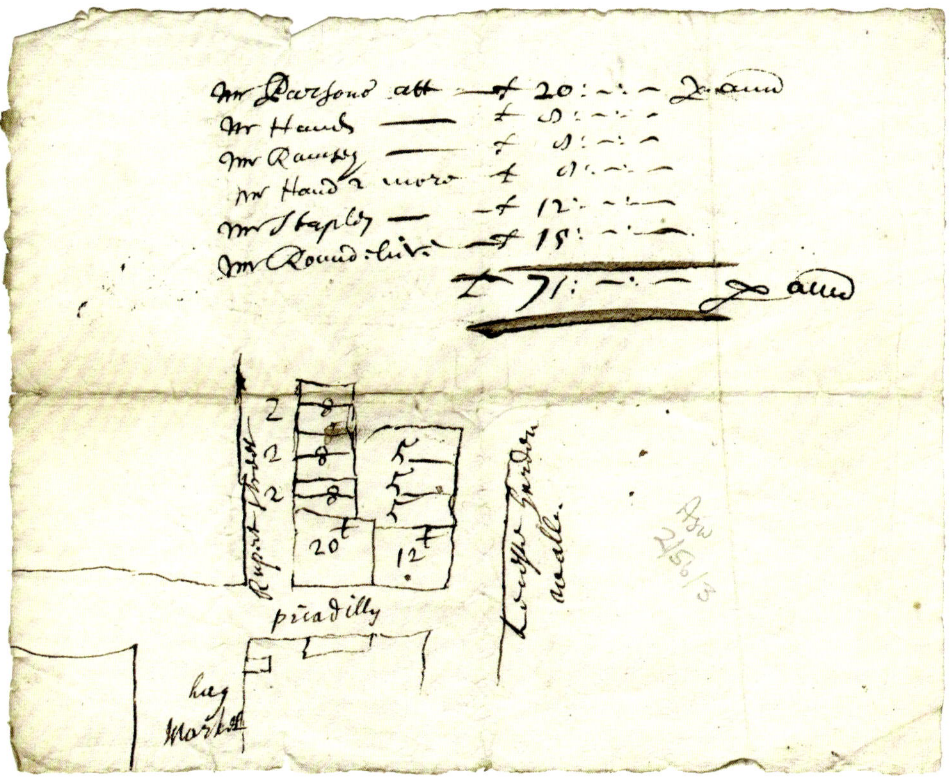

Fig. 103. Plan of Rupert Street houses with ground rents.
© Lincolnshire Record Office, Aswarby 2/56/3

prominent lawyer and judge, but then of his widow, Dame Dorothy. However, he was ruthless in dealing with the other smaller houses: he eventually knocked them down, having done deals quickly with all but two of the tenants. He also came under pressure to make other changes that would enhance the site. The first was blocking off the wharves and riverside from the more expensive houses in Essex Street by creating the 'ornamental arch' which still stands, and the second was creating a larger entry from Essex Street into the Strand and by improving access raising the value of his investment. This improved access would only be possible by knocking down two houses but he had refused to give a covenant to do so on the grounds that it would have only encouraged the owners of the houses to 'advance their price'.[26] He argued for a long time about who should pay for both these improvements and it resulted in one of the few Court decisions that remains — requiring him to widen the passage out of Little Essex Streeet into the Strand (see pp. 35–38).[27] Meanwhile he had already taken the potential value in ground rents.

Essex House is an example of his ability to press on determinedly but to be flexible when necessary. As North wrote:

> He never despaired of a design if it were sound at bottom., but would endure repulse after repulse, and still press his point. If a proposition did not relish one way he would convert it to another, and adapt himself, as well as his designs, to the caprice as well as the interest of those he was to deal with.[28]

His approach to the design of sites demonstrated four elements. First, he was always prepared to sell off bits that he did not need to develop. So he sold some land to the Middle Temple, he acquiesced in the sale of a piece of land for the Fleet Ditch for almost £1,500 which would anyway have been very difficult to develop, and he sold off two inns, one near Crane Court and one on Red Lion Field, both of which would have been contentious to demolish. Second, he was very happy to build facilities where that was helpful to secure support for the site. Examples are allowing land for the Nonconformist chapel in Devonshire Square, and for a Huguenot church in Gerrard Street. There was also a proposal to create a new parish to serve the Essex and Arundel House schemes, and one for what eventually became St George the Martyr, Queen Square, which he promoted in Parliament. Third, he was very conscious of the need to shield the better housing from the main roads and other sources of noise and disruption with barriers of various kinds, including less expensive houses. The arch in his Essex House development shielded Essex Street from both the river and downmarket Milford Lane. Red Lion and Well Close Squares were sheltered from the main roads near to them, and the planning of Red Lion Square made sure that the walks of Gray's Inn were not threatened.

Barbon's approach developed as he gained experience. Whereas his development for Rupert Street did not bother to match up all his roads with those being built outside the site, he had a clear and ambitious vision for the Holborn development from the mid-1680s, even though it started with three different owners. The north–south axis of Lamb's Conduit and Red Lion Street runs through all three parts of the site.

He also looked for ways to raise the status of the development which would allow him to charge higher ground rents. His creation of squares with relatively larger houses was one way of achieving this and the assumption must be that he chose this for commercial reasons. This is borne out by a comparison of the ground rents for houses on Well Close Square with those in the nearby streets and by his statement on Red Lion Square, claiming he would build 'fair large houses for persons of estate and value, before which this defendant intends to leave a very large open square unbuilt with pleasant walks therein'.[29]

He attempted further improvement by encouraging prestige occupiers, particularly the Devonshire family with whom he had a continued relationship, starting when he laid out Devonshire Square near Bishopsgate. The 4th Earl lived in a house built by Barbon on the Military Ground in Soho; there was a suggestion of a proposed Devonshire House on the north side of Great Ormond Street and Barbon may also have had plans for a large house for the Earl nearby in Queen Square, originally Devonshire Square (see p. 131).

Barbon did not only develop housing. He was particularly keen on markets as a potential source of considerable income. His first was the Exeter Exchange, a shopping mall of its time based on the model of the Royal Exchange, but he also created markets on Newport Ground in Soho and Brookfield, east of Hyde Park, in both cases putting them in places near to centres of population which would otherwise have been relatively underserved. He included shops in his building for the Middle Temple.

He was always prepared to choose the mix that maximized the return for him while working within the constraints of what was possible. This provides the substance to his assertion that 'by his skill and knowledge in building he could make a greater improvement than could be made by either [his potential competitors]'.[30] Apart from his success in persuading other developers to give him priority in developing sites, further confirmation of his claim is given by North who wrote, 'His talent lay more in economising ground for advantage and the little contrivance of a family than the more noble aims of Architecture, and all his aim was profit.'[31]

Houses

Although not the only buildings in Barbon's portfolio, he is most remembered for his houses, particularly in squares or as terraces in streets, a layout designed to maximize potential ground rents. It is tempting to refer to the 'Barbon House', but in fact there is no such thing since it was rare for Barbon to take control either directly or indirectly of the design of houses in his developments. While he may have done so with his early rebuilding in the City after the Fire, from Essex Street onwards his ideal was to sell a building lease to a builder and let him get on with it. He made this clear to potential collaborators in development, telling one as early as 1676 that 'he did not intend to build all the ground himself, but to let out the greatest part to other persons to build at a valuable ground rent'.[32] Nevertheless, conditions were occasionally applied to the overall quality of the work. Barbon's houses in Red Lion Square were required to be 'as good as or better than the houses built on the west side of Brooke Street in nearby Brooke Garden', while Barbon himself required John Foltrop to build houses in Westminster 'as firm and well built as those which Foltrop had previously built for one Kent in Lamb's Conduit Fields'.[33]

It was then up to the builder to do any necessary design and to source the materials. While it was possible that the builders may have used materials produced or procured by Barbon, there is limited evidence for this except when reusing material from demolished houses, and we do know that he was involved in brick making. He preferred to leave the eventual lessee or resident to choose the details of the interiors of the houses, even where he employed the builder directly, as for example in his houses in Mincing Lane. We must assume, however, that he did choose the interior for his own house in Crane Court which we have seen was full of elaborate plasterwork (Figs 10, 11, 12).

Left to themselves, builders built as they had done on previous occasions, following innovation or fashion rather than leading it. On this basis we would expect houses in Barbon's developments to reflect building elsewhere, including any changes and developments in building practice in the last quarter of the seventeenth century. Builders, too, would have preferences and it was they not Barbon who had to let or lease the final construction. All things being equal they would prefer a layout which did not impose unnecessary expense, and which created the maximum amount of usable interior space so as to attract the customer. Given that the houses were part of a terrace, whether in street or square, the relationship of a house to its next-door neighbour was important. There needed to be clear rules about party walls and such like and probably some degree of confidence that other builders would build to a comparable quality standard.

Inside the jurisdiction of the City of London, the post-Fire regulations provided for much of this, specifying the storey heights for each category of house, the rules for paying for party walls and a variety of fire protection matters including building with bricks and no, or very limited, jetties. These rules did not have legal force outside the City's jurisdiction, which was where virtually all Barbon's houses were located.

This meant that Barbon did need to set some constraints, one of which was a desire for a degree of uniformity, achieved through a building agreement, a precursor to a full lease. One of Barbon's building agreements survives and is shown in Figure 104; because of its importance it is transcribed in full at the end of this chapter. It is notable that Barbon was content to enter into this agreement some four months before he had finalized the settlement with the owner of the land, Sir Richard Fisher, but no doubt he was confident by then that it would all go through. Because the year (both calendar and regnal) was filled in by hand, the printed agreement could have been used any time from 1680 until 1688 and it is possible that it was used for many other sites as well. One such might have been Well Close Square, where the leases were all dated 1 October 1683; Barbon may have found it helpful to have printed building agreements to add some degree of confidence to those looking for greater certainty that building there would actually take place and so deliver the ground rents for the fire insurance trust.

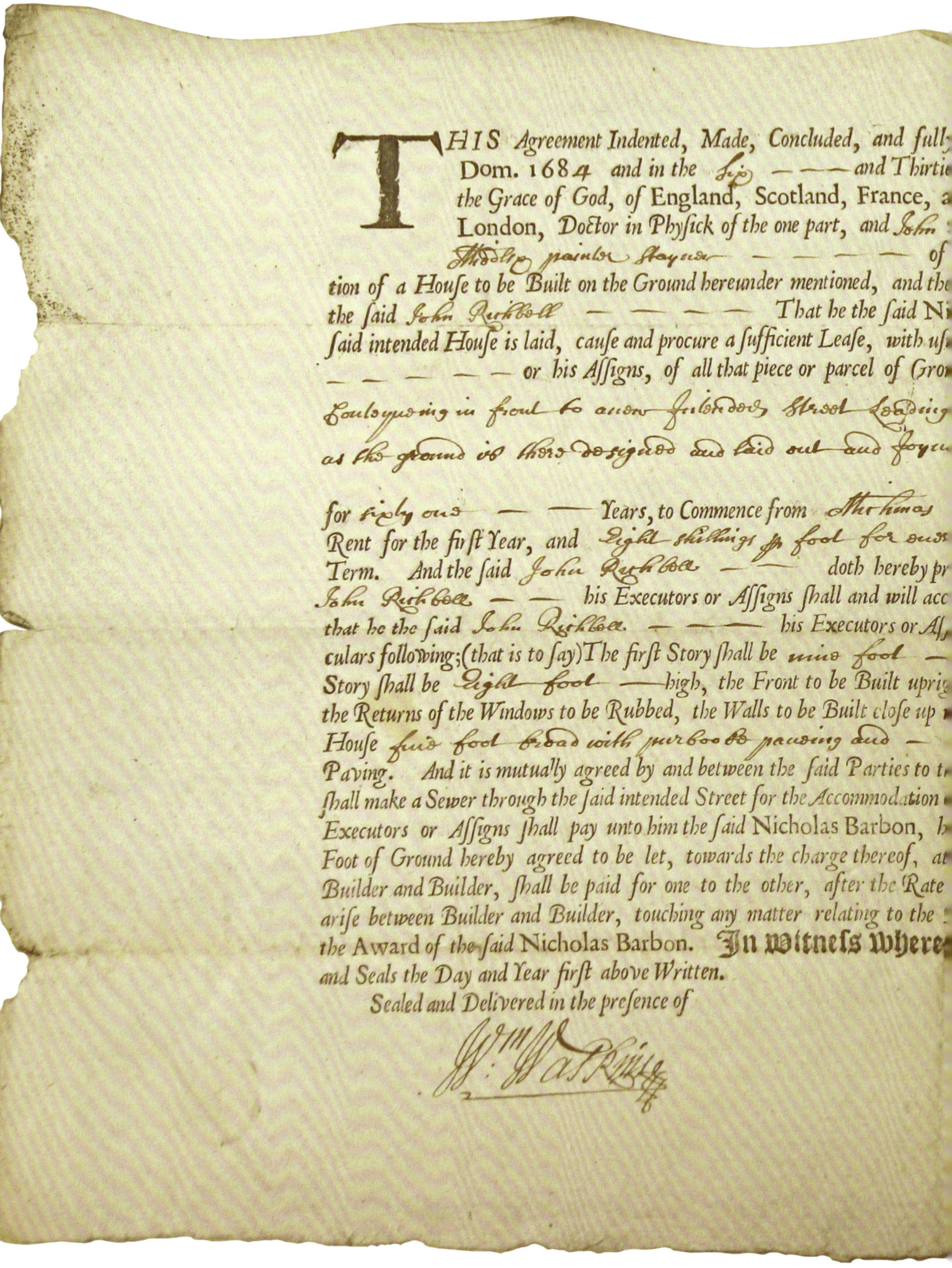

THIS Agreement Indented, Made, Concluded, and full
Dom. 1684 and in the Six ——— and Thirti
the Grace of God, of England, Scotland, France, a
London, Doctor in Physick of the one part, and John
Shadley painter stayner — — — — — of
tion of a House to be Built on the Ground hereunder mentioned, and the
the said John Richbell — — — — That he the said N
said intended House is laid, cause and procure a sufficient Lease, with us
— — — — — — or his Assigns, of all that piece or parcel of Gro
Containing in front to a new intended Street Leading
as the ground is there designed and laid out and
for sixty one — — Years, to Commence from Michaelmas
Rent for the first Year, and Eight shillings per foot for ever
Term. And the said John Richbell — doth hereby pr
John Richbell — — his Executors or Assigns shall and will acc
that he the said John Richbell — — — his Executors or As
culars following; (that is to say) The first Story shall be nine foot —
Story shall be Eight foot —— high, the Front to be Built uprig
the Returns of the Windows to be Rubbed, the Walls to be Built close up
House five foot broad with purbeck paving and —
Paving. And it is mutually agreed by and between the said Parties to t
shall make a Sewer through the said intended Street for the Accommodation
Executors or Assigns shall pay unto him the said Nicholas Barbon, h
Foot of Ground hereby agreed to be let, towards the charge thereof, a
Builder and Builder, shall be paid for one to the other, after the Rate
arise between Builder and Builder, touching any matter relating to the
the Award of the said Nicholas Barbon. In witness where
and Seals the Day and Year first above Written.

Sealed and Delivered in the presence of

Wm Watkins

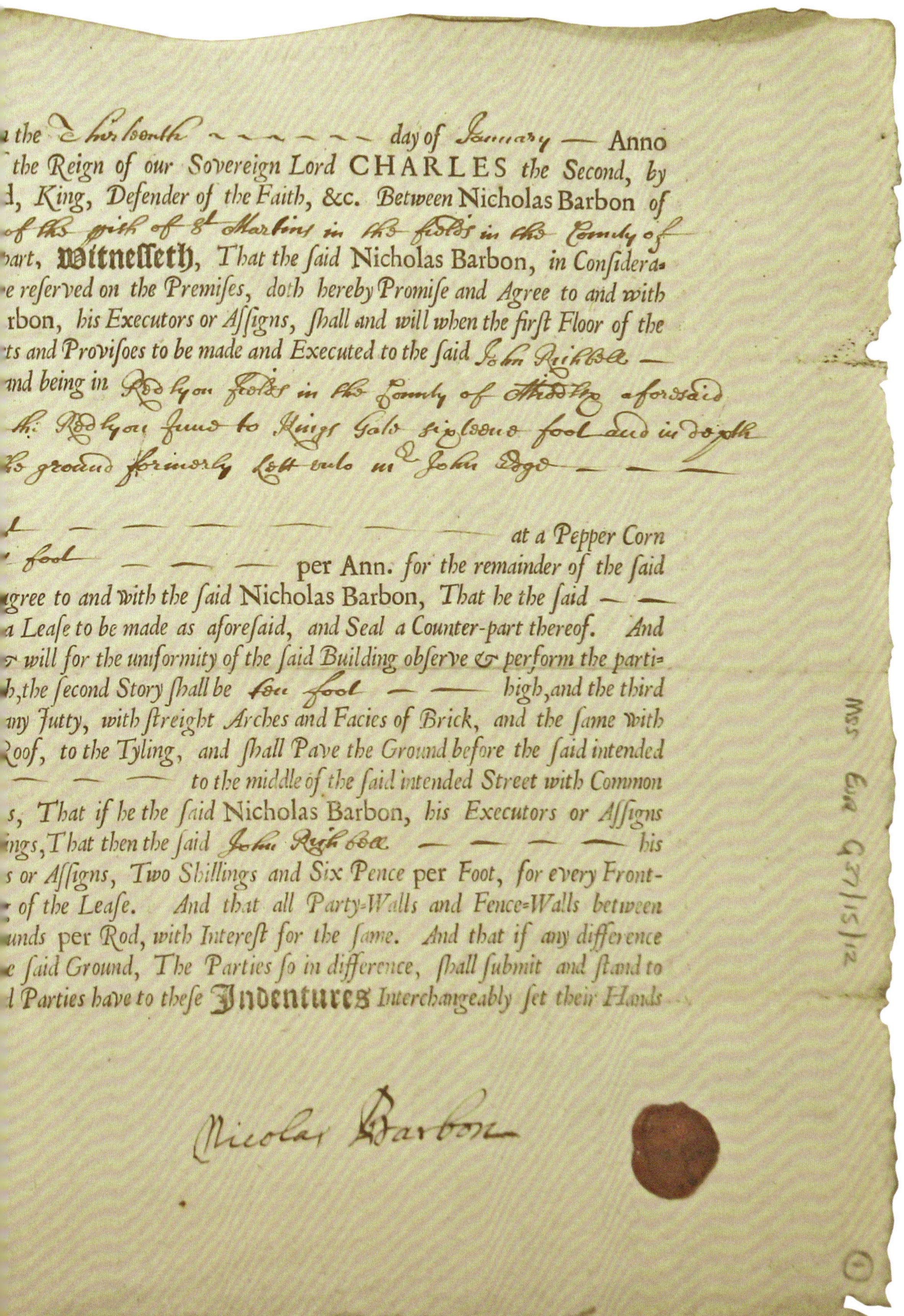

the thirteenth — — — — — day of January — Anno
the Reign of our Sovereign Lord CHARLES the Second, by
d, King, Defender of the Faith, &c. Between Nicholas Barbon of
of the p[ar]ish of St Martins in the fields in the County of
part, **Witnesseth**, That the said Nicholas Barbon, in Considera-
e reserved on the Premises, doth hereby Promise and Agree to and with
rbon, his Executors or Assigns, shall and will when the first Floor of the
ts and Provisoes to be made and Executed to the said John Richbell —
nd being in Redlyon fields in the County of Middlesex aforesaid
the Redlyon frunt to Kings Gate sixteene foot and in depth
the ground formerly lett unto Mr John Edge — —

— — — — — at a Pepper Corn
foot — — — per Ann. for the remainder of the said
gree to and with the said Nicholas Barbon, That he the said — —
a Lease to be made as aforesaid, and Seal a Counter-part thereof. And
will for the uniformity of the said Building observe & perform the parti-
h, the second Story shall be ten foot — — high, and the third
ny Jutty, with streight Arches and Facies of Brick, and the same with
oof, to the Tyling, and shall Pave the Ground before the said intended
— — — to the middle of the said intended Street with Common
s, That if he the said Nicholas Barbon, his Executors or Assigns
ngs, That then the said John Richbell — — — — his
s or Assigns, Two Shillings and Six Pence per Foot, for every Front-
of the Lease. And that all Party-Walls and Fence-Walls between
unds per Rod, with Interest for the same. And that if any difference
e said Ground, The Parties so in difference, shall submit and stand to
l Parties have to these **Indentures** Interchangeably set their Hands

Nicolas Barbon

MSS Eur G37/15/12

Fig. 104. Barbon's Building Agreement as used for Red Lion Square.
By permission of the British Library, MS Eur G37/15/12

The agreement illustrated as Figure 104 refers to a house built by John Richbell next but one to the Red Lion Inn in Eagle Street.[34] It is one of the first that he built in the area but he was also active in both Bedford Row and the original of Richbell Court. After specifying the detailed location of the building, it sets out constraints on how 'uniformity' of the houses should be achieved. The financial part of the agreement will be covered in the next chapter but the printed parts relating to construction required

> the Front to be Built upright without any Jutty, with Streight Arches and Facies of Brick, and the same with the Returns of the Windows to be Rubbed, the Walls to be Built close up within the Roof, to the Tyling.

Apart from the reference to the window returns, which is an aesthetic point, these reflect the requirements of the Rebuilding Act of 1677, although not in the same detail. The only parts of the construction detail not printed as standard but filled in by hand are the storey heights and the extent of purbeck paving in front of the house. Common storey heights are obviously needed for 'uniformity', a concept for the design of new building in London which goes back at least to the proclamations issued by James I. In this connection it is noticeable that the storey heights do not match up to those specified in the Rebuilding Act. The storey heights of the 'second sort of house' in the Rebuilding Act are set at ten, ten and nine feet respectively, while those for the Barbon house in Eagle Street are set at nine, ten and eight.

The building agreement refers to uniformity but that is confined only to those matters set out in the agreement. There is perhaps a supposition that all the houses in a Barbon terrace were identical, but this is not necessarily so, and in some cases less so than in the agreement above. This is particularly noticeable in Essex Street where even apart from variations in the frontage, and notwithstanding the refronting that took place in later centuries, the street clearly consisted of different independent houses built by a range of builders. This is also true of Bedford Row, as illustrated by Figure 94 which includes the effect of a 1965 refronting.[35] Figure 34 also shows variation in fronts from a drawing of Hayes Court. This relative lack of uniformity was not unique to Barbon; the Bloomsbury estate south of Great Russell Street allowed variations of both frontage and facades.[36]

But even while the uniformity achieved was not complete, it was sufficient to raise the issue of standardization and it is often claimed that Barbon was one of the first to achieve economies of scale in house building by standardizing supplies such as ornamental bricks, doors, windows and so on. For example, Summerson wrote:

> The houses he built were all very much alike, economically planned to the point of meanness, with coarse ornaments which repeated themselves over and over again. The design of the panelling and the staircases of his houses never varies, and his carpenters must have turned out thousands upon thousands of the twisted balusters whose slick modernity was calculated to engage the eye of the bumpkin in search of his first town house.[37]

The irony is that, quite apart from the vast majority of Barbon's houses being lived in by existing Londoners or those with long connections there, many surviving Barbon houses began with turned rather than twisted balusters; Barbon himself built relatively few houses after the Essex House development (and not many there) and probably had little or nothing to do with the internal decor. Having let the building lease, he had little interest in whether the house was built as cheaply as possible, although it was in his interest that the builder completed the house quickly so that he was not forced to take back the building lease. It is very unlikely that he had any particular interest in standardizing parts, except possibly for his construction of chambers in the Middle Temple.

Once the building agreement had set the constraints, the design and construction costs were for the builders themselves and any benefits would have accrued to them rather than Barbon himself, while any procurement would only have increased the pressure on his scarce capital. Thus we know that John Foltrop, Barbon's contractor for his house in Westminster, made bulk purchases of doorcases and doors at his own initiative.[38] What is much more likely is that the enormous growth in demand following the Great Fire had led to large-scale manufacture of much carpentry and other material off site with corresponding standardization which the builders naturally took advantage of. Barbon's own building may well have helped to stimulate this further.

The only area where Barbon may have been involved in some degree of vertical integration was bricks. Their supply was critical to the success of a builder and ideally the source should not be too far from where they were to be used. Fields that had the right kind of earth were sought after, particularly if they were conveniently located. Sometimes the earth would be dug for bricks before building, as on the Rugby School site where four acres was identified as appropriate for this use (see p. 129). The right to make bricks was a valuable asset and Barbon was able to sell this right, again demonstrating his ability to make the most of any opportunity.[39] He also bought a brickfield from Thomas Barnes in east London, took an interest in another near Red Lion Square, and bricks were made on his estate at Osterley Park.

Although the Tylers' and Bricklayers' Company had lost their monopoly of the supply of bricks within the City of London after the Fire, they retained the supervision of the quality of bricks including size, type of earth, and how well they had been fired. From time to time many of the larger builders had the bricks supplied by or to them broken by the inspectors as a result of failing the tests: these included Richard Frith, even though he was not only a bricklayer by trade but one of the members of the Court of the Company. Unsurprisingly, Barbon was also of that number, although mostly for bricks which had been supplied to him rather than from his own London brickworks. On a number of occasions, his bricks at Osterley Park were found not to meet the standards, although there is no evidence that he had made them himself.[40]

Interiors

Houses in Barbon's development were, within the constraints set by him in any building agreement, designed and fitted out by his builders or contractors. Further, interiors were often chosen by the eventual occupiers, so it does not seem sensible to try to analyse them in any detail. We do not have unambiguous evidence about whether the houses were sold or leased as carcasses with the occupier choosing the finishing. This has been the assumption previously, at least for the houses for which Barbon himself took responsibility, but recent work suggests this was less usual by the end of the first quarter of the eighteenth century.[41] In any case, the evidence from existing houses would be limited because there have usually been extensive changes to those that remain, and we have limited information about original interiors. One exception to this is a block of nine houses in Essex Street where there is a complete list of the changes made at the end of the first lease in 1736.[42] This shows that, as one would expect, the original windows were casements later replaced by sashes, and staircases were also changed. However, the top flights of the original staircase remain in No. 32 Essex Street, illustrated in Figure 105.

Fig. 105. Top flights of staircase at No. 32 Essex Street, photograph, 1971.

Image © London Metropolitan Archives (City of London), no. 135641

This raises a general question about staircases in houses in Barbon developments. While the traditional placing of the staircase in eighteenth-century terrace houses is at the back along the party wall, those in Essex Street are between the front and rear rooms in the centre of the house,[43] as are found in the slightly earlier Buckingham Street. The floor plan is illustrated at Figure 106. A number of house plans including staircases were published in 1667 in a pricing guide for builders, and both these types were included (among others) suggesting that both were in use (Fig. 107).[44]

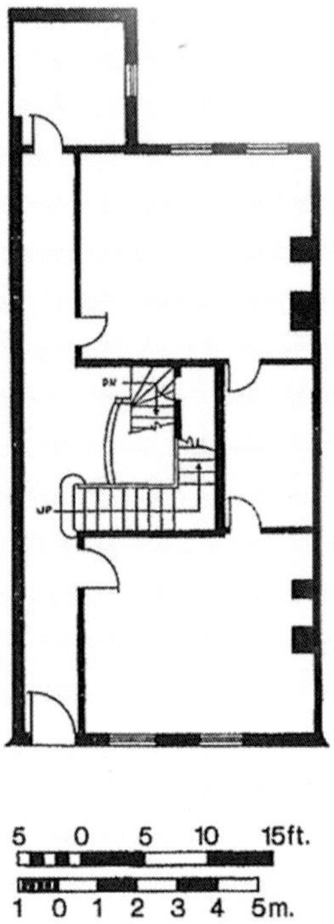

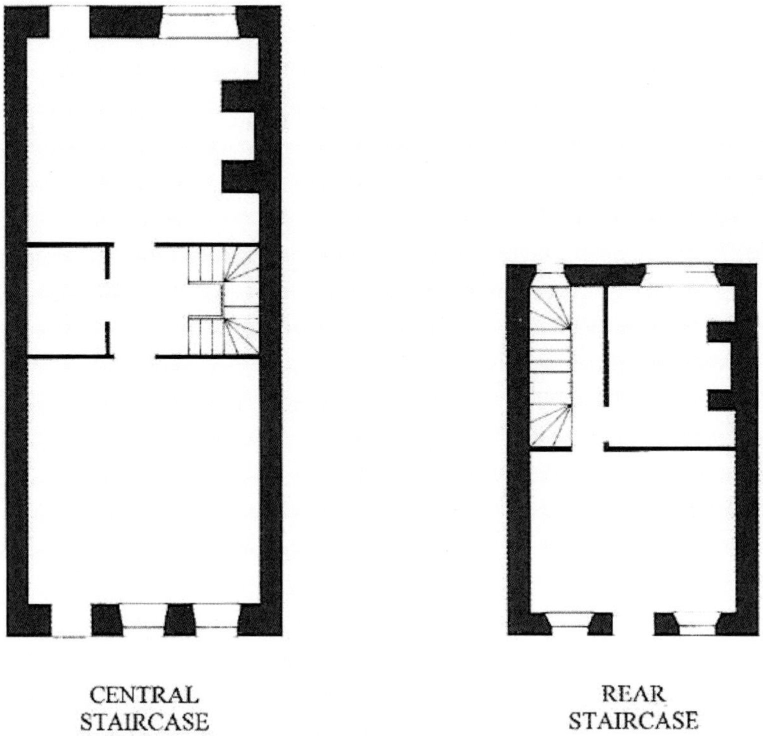

Fig. 106. Ground-floor plan of No. 34 Essex Street.
Drawing by Robert Weston

Fig. 107. Two house plans with staircases.
Drawing by Andrew Donald © Historic England

One of the present authors has argued that the central staircase represents an earlier approach, perhaps reflecting its use in timber-framed rather than brick houses, and it seems to have been common at the top end of the speculative market in the 1660s and 1670s.[45] In this case the period after 1670 represents a transition when all types of staircase were being used and the change was probably made to provide greater economy of space and materials and avoid problems caused by top lighting. Figure 108 shows the staircase for 42 Bedford Row, built in 1693 and clearly at the side.

Both types of staircase have advantages and disadvantages, considered at length in Peter Guillery's book on small houses in London.[46] While Roger North considered that the side staircase 'was the common forme of all late built houses' by the 1690s, Guillery is less sure that this was so and believes that the middle staircase continued well on into the early eighteenth century, though with great variability according to districts within London.[47] It seems likely that this was true also for houses in Barbon's developments. This is confirmed by site plans from the St Clement Danes estate for which Figures 109 and 110 show both forms. The plot width may also have been a factor in the location of the staircase, particularly for houses of less than sixteen-foot width.

Of course, it is possible that any particular expertise of the contractor would affect the external design or internal decoration. What we have been describing as 'builders' covers a range of specialists. After the Fire of London there were insufficient tradesmen in the City to do the necessary rebuilding and monopolies of the livery companies were removed with many artisans coming in from outside the City and its immediate surroundings, some of them living in the surrounding villages such as Clapham.[48] According to North, the design of houses was left to the craftsmen, such as bricklayers, carpenters and glaziers: 'all is done by profest builders, and the gentry hire or buy of them [...] they pay for ground and then cut it out to the advantage of their trade'. Barbon claimed to be able to identify the craft of a builder from the way he had constructed a house, thus:

> As some being set out with fine brickwork rubbed and gaged, were the issue of a master bricklayer; if stone coyned, jambed and fasciaed, of a stone mason; if full of window, with much glass in compass, and relieve, a glazier; if full of balcone and balustring, a carpenter; and so others.[49]

Fig. 108. View from the half landing on the stairs at No. 42 Bedford Row, Holborn, looking towards the front entrance, photograph, 1975.

Image © London Metropolitan Archives (City of London), no. 69623

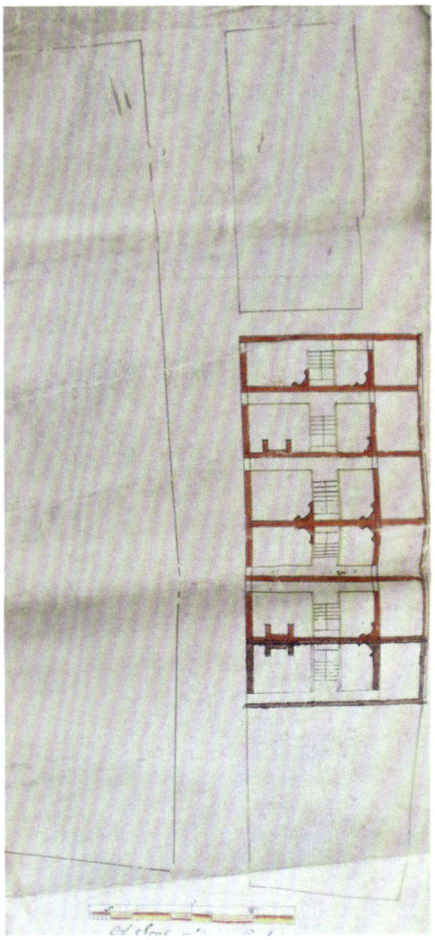

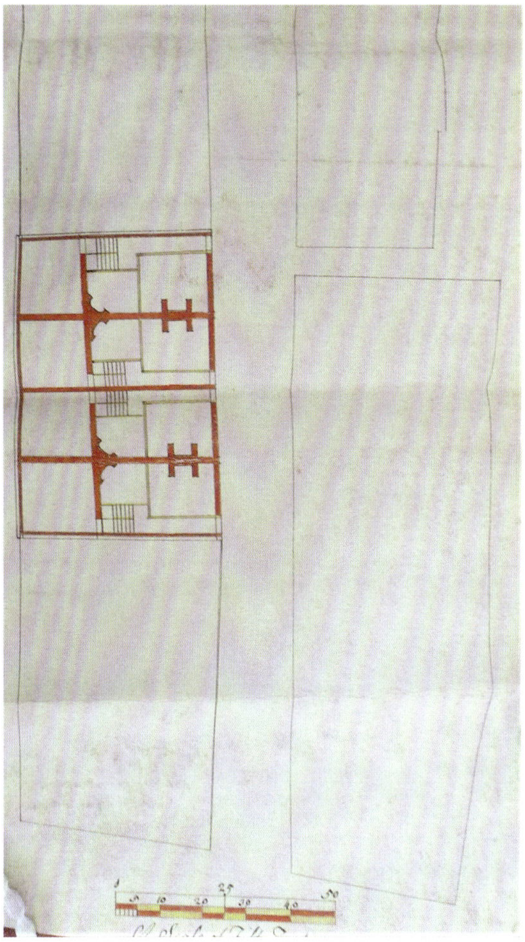

right
Fig. 109. St Clement Danes estate, Dane Street, east side.

© Trustees of the St Clement Danes Holborn Estate Charity. City of Westminster Archives Centre, 1576/Box70

far right
Fig. 110. St Clement Danes estate, Dane Street, west side

© Trustees of the St Clement Danes Holborn Estate Charity. City of Westminster Archives Centre, 1576/Box70

While Roger North was convinced by this argument, it is difficult to see how such individuality could be expressed within the uniformity asked for in building agreements and the changes to any remaining houses since that time make it impossible to conduct the same analysis now. In any case, while it is tempting to characterize contractors by their own expertise, even those builders taking overall responsibility for the whole construction subcontracted to other skills where appropriate. By now, we often have nothing but membership of a livery company to identify a man's craft, but these did not necessarily correspond. While Richard Frith was indeed a member of the Tylers' and Bricklayers' Company, and John Foltrop of the Carpenters', William Edge was actually a member of the Fletchers' Company, which ostensibly made bows and arrows, and John Richbell was a Painter Stainer. In addition, when cash was particularly short, Barbon sometimes paid his builders by granting them a lease of a house built, or part built, by another, thereby weakening even further the linkages.

As we have seen, Barbon only provided other than minimal interior decoration when specifically requested by the client and some examples of these have been shown in previous illustrations. Figures 10 to 12 display plaster ceilings in Nos 5–6 Crane Court, while Figure 33 shows the elaborate staircase built in Gerard House, now demolished.

Conclusions

Much of the argument relating to design in this chapter is based on the contention that there is no such thing as a 'Barbon House'. Even though Barbon did place some constraints on design to secure a degree of uniformity this did not mean that the houses were identical and existing houses developed by him demonstrate this. Not only was he not an architect, neither was he really a builder, except by default. He was a developer.

But more than that he was driven by his financial model, which will be explored in more detail in the next chapter. Even though he was dependent on the builders constructing houses and finding occupiers for them in a timely fashion, his interest was in the ground rents. He needed the builders, or occupants, to pay him ground rent after the year's peppercorn, and was able to persuade lenders to give him a mortgage against the value of the ground rents from the fully developed property before building was completed. Indeed, his preferred option was to take out the mortgage immediately after agreement was reached to purchase the property. He could then pocket the difference between the original and developed value, or more usually use it to pay off the most pressing of his debts. Given the lengthy time taken to effect a transfer of property, this could even be before he had paid any money himself.

His mortgage was secured on the future ground rents and, if they were not paid, he failed to pay the interest on the loan; the only recourse the mortgagee had was to foreclose, thereby having all the problems of managing the various builders. Against this background, the detailed design of the houses was not Barbon's problem. There seems little financial point to his promoting any standardization of supply, although there could have been advantages in relations with those who had taken his building leases. Problems would only arise for him if it became difficult to unload the building leases, or if the builders collapsed, and he was forced to take on the leases himself. This was true for Well Close Square, and he avoided the problem by passing it on to the trustees of the Fire Office. The slow take up of leases for Red Lion Square prevented him from buying its freehold and similarly led to major issues with the Holborn development.

TEXT OF BARBON'S PRINTED BUILDING AGREEMENT (MANUSCRIPT ADDITIONS IN BLUE)

This agreement indented, made, concluded, and fully agreed on the sixteenth day of January Anno Dom 1684 and in the five and thirtieth year of the reign of our Sovereign Lord Charles the Second, by the Grace of God, of England, Scotland, France and Ireland, King, Defender of the Faith &c. Between Nicholas Barbon of London, Doctor in Physick of the one part, and John Richbell of the parish of St Martins in the Fields in the County of Middlesex painter stainer of the other part Witnesseth, that the said Nicholas Barbon, in consideration of a house to be built on the ground hereunder mentioned, and the Rent to be referred on the premises, doth hereby promise and agree to and with the said John Richbell that the said Nicholas Barbon, his executors or assigns, shall and will when the first floor of the said intended house is laid, cause and procure a sufficient lease, with usual covenants and provisoes to be made and executed to the said John Richbell or his assigns, of all that piece of ground, lying and being in Red Lyon Fields in the County of Middlesex aforesaid contayning in front to a new finished street leading from the Red Lyon Inne to Kings Gate sixteene foot and in depth as the ground is there designed and laid out and joyning to the ground formerly let unto John Page for sixty one years, to commence from Michaelmas last past at a peppercorn rent for the first year, and eight shillings per foot for every front foot per ann. for the remainder of the said term. And the said John Richbell doth hereby promise and agree to the said Nicholas Barbon, that he the said John Richbell his executors or assigns shall and will accept of such a lease to be made as aforesaid, and seal a counterpart thereof. And that he the said John Richbell his executors or assigns shall and will for the uniformity of the said building observe and perform the particulars following; (that is to say) The first story shall be nine foot high, the second story shall be ten foot high, and the third story shall be eight foot high, the front to be built upright without any jutty, with streight arches and facies of brick, and the same with the returns of the windows to be rubbed, the walls to be built close up within the roof, to the tyling, and shall pave the ground before the said intended house five feet broad with purbeck paving and to the middle of the said intended street with common paving. And it is mutually agreed by and between the said parties to these presents, that if the said Nicholas Barbon, his executors or assigns, shall make a sewer through the said intended street for the accommodation of the buildings, that the said John Richbell, his executors or assigns, shall pay unto him the said Nicholas Barbon, two shillings and six pence per foot, for every front foot of ground hereby agreed to be let, towards the charge thereof, at the sealing of the lease. And that all party-walls and fence-walls between builder and builder, shall be paid for one to the other, after the rate of five pounds per rod, with interest for the same. And that if any difference arise between builder and builder, touching any matter relating to the building the said ground, the parties so in difference, shall submit and stand to the award of the said Nicholas Barbon. In witness whereof, the said parties have to these indentures interchangeably set their hands and seals the day and year first above written.

CHAPTER XIII

BARBON AS DEVELOPER — FINANCE AND LEGAL

The previous chapter highlighted the implications of Barbon's approach to development for the design of the houses. This chapter considers the financial and legal issues related to his approach in more detail.

Finance — Ground Rents

Once Barbon moved away from developing small individual houses, he no longer had the capital to purchase sites outright and needed to borrow the necessary funds as well as obtain money for further activity on site. His essential problem was that he was grossly undercapitalized for the scale of development that he aspired to. Solving this required him to make the best use of the system of leasing. Broadly speaking, a freeholder would issue a lease, most often at the end of the seventeenth century for sixty-one years at a ground rent that was usually an improvement on the rent from the earlier agricultural or other use, but did not reflect the value of the building still to come. At the end of the term of the building lease, the land and any buildings on it reverted to the freeholder who could then take the full value.

Unlike small-scale investors, Barbon did not aim to make his return from renting individual houses; he preferred others to do the building if at all possible and told one potential collaborator that he did 'not intend to build all the land himself, but let out the greatest part to other persons to build at a valuable ground rent'.[1] His margin came from the increase in value produced by the ground rents set out in the building leases. He could then sell or mortgage the land for a capital sum based on the new ground rent. While the official maximum interest rate, used for mortgages and personal loans, was 6 per cent, the return on land was a little bit less to reflect its presumed higher security. and was usually calculated at twenty years' purchase — that is, twenty times the ground rent, although lower values might be used to reflect any adverse factors, such as location or uncertainty about title.[2] Barbon's interest was therefore to grant building leases as quickly as possible and with as high a ground rent as possible. Where the site was attractive, this would cause no problems, although he would usually allow up to a year at a peppercorn rent to encourage their take up. He could then mortgage those ground rents, thereby generating a capital value greater than he had paid for the original property. We have already seen the increase this produced on the site of Essex House; for Newport Ground he produced £1,000 of annual ground rents (£20,000 of capital) on a site for which he originally paid £9,500;[3] for Little Tower Hill ground rents of £125 (£2,500 of capital) were generated by an outlay of a few hundred pounds.[4] Obviously the difference was not all profit since he had to clear and lay out the site and there would have been interest charges, but it gives an estimate of their potential profitability.[5] Where Barbon was not able to buy a freehold he also, as head lessee, had to pay a rent. The problem for the lender was that the security was based on the developed value of the site, which could take a long time to be realized. At least one mortgagee found that he could not dispose of the loan before development was completed.[6]

Despite trying to find builders to take leases on most of the individual sites, he was prepared to take responsibility for some himself, sometimes through the agency of his lawyers who would act for him. John Bland, a lawyer and scrivener, was the most common such but throughout his career there are many cases of his sister-in-law, Rebecca Hayes, taking leases and building houses. (Her father and brother had both been involved in arranging finance for building.) While Barbon was extremely determined to bring sites to development, he was prepared to be patient; indeed, Roger North said he 'had an inexpugnable pertinacity of pressing it through' and 'if he got into an undertaking he mattered not time, for some would depend many years, and if money failed he would stand stock still, whatever ruin attended his works'.[7] There was, however, one site which he did give up: Old Devonshire House, near Bishopsgate. He had knocked the house down and laid it out as a Square by 1679 and calculated that he would obtain annual ground rents of over £700, which he proposed to use as security for his fire insurance in 1680.[8] Pamphleteers pointed out that very few houses were anywhere near to being built, so he sold the site for £7,300, not much more than he had paid for it, and looked elsewhere for suitable ground rents.[9] Ironically, Barbon Alley, one of the only two existing London streets named after Barbon, is probably in about the same place as the alley he laid out to connect his creation of Devonshire Square with Houndsditch. (The other, Barbon Close, off Great Ormond Street, is not contemporary with him.)

We have a good example of how Barbon used to work because a copy of his proposal to the Treasury in February 1681 to build a new Royal Mews still exists, and includes his calculations.[10] He proposed building on an available site near the existing Royal Mews at Charing Cross, probably somewhere on the edge of St James's Park, which, as he points out, would be 'nearer His Majesty's Palace and nearer the Thames and fields for the breathing and watering of horses'.[11] His design contained 403 square feet of building costed at £50 per square foot (a total of £20,150) and provided more room for horses and coaches than previously, as well as larger apartments for those who needed to live in the Mews. Adding the cost of the new ground as £6,500 and interest for eighteen months of £2,400, the total cost would be £29,050, which he said was more than anyone would give for that piece of ground. His proposal was that he should be paid by being given the existing Mews site, thereby saving the Crown the £20,000 rebuilding costs.

He calculated the value of the new building that he would put on the old Mews site as follows. The plan contained 3,360 feet of frontage, on average, worth 10s. a foot ground rent and so producing £1,680 per annum, capitalized over twenty years at £33,600. He estimated that the old materials would be worth £1,500, so making the total income £35,100. He argued that the risks, not least the likelihood that it would be three years or more before it would all be let, with consequent interest cost, meant that no one would be prepared to give £30,000 in the hope of gaining only £4,000 or £5,000. As he wrote:

> But that the exchange being made by building it is found advantage to the builder though it is the same thing to His Majesty, be it paid in money or in building, because it will cost His Majesty as much money to build.

Although the proposal was referred to the appropriate authorities, it was not taken up. The Mews remained on its site until the metropolitan improvements of the 1820s saw the construction of Trafalgar Square and the removal of the Mews to a site near Buckingham Palace. Barbon's proposal confirms his approach as that of a speculative property developer and emphasizes the scale of his thinking. He was offering to arrange finance for the £20,000 cost of building the new Mews as well as the £40,000 or more for building the houses on the old site. It would have been equivalent to three times the work on Essex House, and the financing and organizational burden may well have been the reason for it not being taken up.

The need to find sites with sufficient potential ground rents to provide security for his fire insurance concentrated Barbon's mind and he quickly bought three sites just east of the City from the Crown. One of these, Little Tower Hill, was clearly profitable for him but the other two, the Artillery Ground and Well Close, both caused difficulties. He seems to have overpaid for the Artillery Ground, at least by his standards, but it did meet his need for ground rents. Well Close had been relatively cheap but the problem was establishing the ground rents on a site that was not yet well connected. Barbon was forced to adopt radical methods (see pp. 86–87 and 94–95).

It would not have been credible for him to claim, even with his partner John Parsons, that he would complete all the building himself and so those leases that he could not dispose of were given to one of his servants, William Prideaux. Prideaux took seventeen in all, but there was no chance that he would either build or pay the ground rent. He was later described as 'a person of mean circumstances in the world, either dead or insolvent',[12] and a litigant described him twelve years later as 'being a servant, workman or else under some dependency for Barbon', characterizing the leases as

> so designed only for the benefit of the said Mr Barbon, and contrived to countenance the greater valuations of the premises whereby to enable him to raise money thereupon afterwards of other persons and not really expected from the said William Prideaux [...] which would have required a very great and considerable sum of money [...] and more than the said William Prideaux was capable on his own account of disbursing.[13]

Well Close was an extreme example, but the approach was one that Barbon had used elsewhere.

There was one other technique that Barbon needed in order to be able to dispose of his leases at an early stage. He wanted to set ground rents long before the houses were built and needed a formula for doing so. North believed that Barbon was the inventor of the method which calculated the rents by so much per foot frontage on the street and was clear that this contributed to 'making ground rents high for the sake of mortgaging with others taking it up'.[14] This approach allowed flexibility because different rates could be used depending on the attractiveness of the individual streets. Since it would have been unlikely to have been used on any of the pre-1670 developments it is entirely possible that North was correct.

This discussion has been based on the assumption that Barbon purchased the freehold of sites. This was indeed usually so, but in some cases he was prepared to rely on having a head lease, as for Exeter House, where the freeholder, the Earl of Exeter, agreed to grant leases directly to the builders when the houses were nearly finished. In Red Lion Square, Fisher had granted Barbon an option to purchase the freehold, but he was never able to find the funds to do so. For Lamb's Conduit Fields, Barbon owned half of Conduit Close freehold, with one third on lease from the Rugby trustees. Ownership also gave him the equity of redemption, that is the right, even when in default on the interest, to pay off the mortgage and outstanding interest to regain the asset which had been mortgaged. Clearly, this was only worth doing if the value of the site had risen, or there was a good prospect of it doing so, but it was an asset in its own right and could sometimes be valuable. Barbon used it as security for further borrowing of £2,000 on Newport Ground, and his executors later sold the equity of redemption for Newport Market for £2,000.[15] His will listed the many sites for which he still retained the equity of redemption, further evidence of their potential value.

Finance — Sources of Funds

The leases defined the structure of the assets, but Barbon still had to find the funds from somewhere. His early rebuilding of burnt houses was largely financed from his own or his wife's resources, from retained profits, and possibly with assistance from his father. He raised money by mortgaging properties from time to time with the same lawyer, Thomas Fountaine, but these were repaid relatively quickly after the new houses were sold. He also mortgaged his own house in Crane Court and nearby property to a widow from Battersea; this debt was sold on in turn to a number of lawyers, demonstrating the market for such debt. In principle, individuals might have been a source of funds for Barbon since they often purchased single or small groups of property to provide themselves or their children with an income (or dowry) but these sales did not provide sufficient funds to finance Barbon's later large-scale investments.

Broadly speaking, there were three categories of person who had access to large sums of money for investment. The first were the goldsmiths who were beginning to operate in a way that we would recognize as banks; some of whom kept cash balances for or on behalf of their clients. The second category were people who acted as middlemen, putting together sums from a variety of people to create larger loans. The Usury Acts entitled them to charge up to 0.25 per cent of the loan as a fee.[16] These loan brokers included goldsmiths, lawyers and also scriveners who wrote the contracts and were often a first port of call for financing land and building deals, even becoming known as 'money- scriveners'.[17] Barbon was supposed to have 'had always a bank of credit with a scrivener and goldsmith or two'.[18] The third category covered those dealing with large amounts of cash, chiefly the tax farmers who collected the taxes for government, or brewers whose industry was a large generator of cash. Barbon borrowed from all of these at various times and a number of the complaints in litigation pay tribute to Barbon's ability to secure offers of finance 'by the much persuasion and importunity'.[19]

Conversely, merchants, that is those engaged in international trade, were much less commonly involved in investment in property in London and Westminster, except for their own homes or, as John Pollexfen put it, 'for children's portions which they are most willing should continue till such occasion call for it'.[20] They knew the difficulties of ensuring a clear title to property in or near the City, and did not want to have to spend much time on managing the rents. Similarly, country landholders preferred to invest in other country properties rather than the riskier London market. Country estates were preferred as a more stable source of income. Nevertheless, Barbon did from time to time enter into financial arrangements with merchants, such as Peter Vanderput or Jeremy Whichcott, usually through some kind of middleman.

One scrivener he worked with on many occasions was John Adams, who helped him raise the money for Essex House in 1675. Adams was also involved in College Hill and St James's Square around the same time, Newport Ground in 1681, Derby House in 1682 and Dean Street in 1684. In all cases Adams approached others as potential sources of funds, in particular two men who would be regular lenders to Barbon, Sir James Ward and Roger Jackson. These two often shared the total loan between them, including funding the purchase of Osterley Park. No more information is available about Sir James Ward, but a Roger Jackson was agent for the Earl of Devonshire and, given Barbon's previous involvement with Old Devonshire House, it is possible that this was the same person. Another of Barbon's scriveners was John West, who became enormously wealthy, and was a friend of Sir John Moore, another Barbon client. West was also Samuel Pepys's scrivener for many years and witness to his will. The most famous scrivener of all, Sir Robert Clayton, who developed a substantial moneylending business alongside his activities in land transactions, also lent money on Essex House with his partner John Morris.[21] This was a short-term loan for only three months of the kind Clayton made on his own account using funds deposited with him; it was intended to be repaid with the proceeds of the sale of Essex House.[22] Interestingly, Barbon claims that it was arranged in such a hurry that 'Clayton and Morris did not have time to examine the securities proposed', a rare departure from the careful checking of land-based securities that made them very rich.[23]

Building up large loans from smaller ones was clearly a common feature of the time, as shown by Thomas Browne, another scrivener who acted for Barbon; he had been apprenticed to Robert Clayton and was related to John Morris.[24] Browne was approached by Barbon in connection with raising money on the security of Exeter House: 'after much importunity' he lent £1,000 of his own money and said that he would lend more 'as monies should come in'; soon afterwards a number of merchants got in touch asking for 'good security' for their money, in two cases £1,500 and another £7,000. They were all recommended to Barbon.[25]

As might be expected, many lawyers were active on Barbon's behalf. George Bradbury, later a distinguished judge, often acted as a trustee on his behalf, signed off some of his evidence to Chancery courts and in one case was described as 'Mr Barbon's Counsel'.[26] Like scriveners, these lawyers would put together larger loans from a number of sources: John Duckett of Lincoln's Inn was party to many such loans while Edward Noel arranged for Robert Breedon, a brewer who was quoted earlier as complaining about Prideaux, to lend Barbon £5,000 for Well Close together with a distiller William Jarman.[27] Perhaps the most commonly involved was John Bland, variously described as lawyer of the Middle Temple, scrivener or measurer, who was nominated as one of the executors of Barbon's will. It was Bland who normally drew up Barbon's contracts and let many of Barbon's leases, for which he would have been paid. Even five years after Barbon's death, Bland sued Francis Child, claiming that he had done all the work on the leases for the Exeter House development and that Francis Child, who had then been the agent of the Earl of Exeter, had used the results without paying the £40 or so allegedly due to Bland.[28]

Barbon's first involvement with goldsmiths was with Thomas (later Sir Thomas) Cooke and Nicholas Cary who lent him funds for Essex House. Goldsmiths lent to him on many occasions, including for his developments in the Strand in 1679, and much later Cooke was a partner of Barbon in developing Ficket Field near Lincoln's Inn. Thomas Price financed Charles Street and Newport Ground. Michael Scrimshire, as well as Francis Child and his partner Robert Blanchard, all lent to Barbon, and a number of other goldsmiths were involved in the Fire Office, including Bernard Turner and John Hinde. Chapter VI on fire insurance showed how brewers and tax farmers such as Samuel Vincent, Felix Calvert, Sir John Parsons and Robert Breedon invested in the insurance project. Vincent was the only one of them who had previously invested in ground rents (he had bought Essex Street from Barbon) so the others were compelled to buy from Barbon to get their share(s) in the business.

Business did not always end happily for these goldsmiths and many of them went bankrupt. For Price and Hinde this was largely because of their large debts to the Crown, although Hinde had been involved in some housing development activities. For Scrimshire there was a variety of causes, although he claimed that 'he would not have had to leave his shop and trade' if Barbon had paid the £10,500 that he owed.[29] The bankruptcies of Price and Hinde gave rise to much litigation over many years to establish who was entitled to claim the ground rents of the lands which they had financed. This was exactly the kind of problem that merchants looked to avoid by not investing in mortgages or ground rents in London. The solvency of goldsmiths was important for other builders and Richard Frith lost his money because of the collapse of Bernard Hinton.[30]

The next section will show how Barbon used various legal devices to avoid or delay payments of his debts. He usually mortgaged the property for the maximum possible amount with the result that he could afford to walk away from the debt by giving up the site which had provided the security for the loan. This happened on many occasions, although he would retain the equity of redemption as a further asset. Certainly, he was never made bankrupt, although he had a few skirmishes with debtors' prison, once because he had underwritten a bond by John Rowley, one of his partners who was made bankrupt and died shortly after.[31] Nevertheless, Barbon's reputation was well enough known and people did have worries about dealing with him, as the pamphleteering about fire insurance made clear (see p. 78).[32]

Thomas Barnes was trying to sell his brick field and agreed the price with the scrivener John West acting for someone he described as 'an able and honest man'. Barnes agreed, but when it was revealed that man was Barbon and 'after hearing of the manner of dealings of the complainant', possibly as a result of the fire insurance pamphlets issued about the same time, he insisted that Barbon should get the landlord's agreement to his tenancy. The deal later fell apart acrimoniously.[33]

However, many experienced and sophisticated money men clearly continued over very long periods of time to lend Barbon money or to partner with him, and many small builders worked with him on many occasions. It seems very unlikely that they would have continued to do so if they believed there was little chance of getting their money back. Indeed, the vast majority of the legal cases reported in Chancery involving Barbon do not appear to have gone to trial. Both sides may have used them to delay when it suited them, and at least some others appear to have been more concerned with establishing site boundaries, as in the division of Lamb's Conduit Fields or in connection with goldsmith bankruptcies affecting Newport Ground.[34]

We can end with a story quoted in a mid-eighteenth-century biographical miscellany:

> [Barbon] had drawn a gentleman in the city into a building project there, by which he had lost a considerable amount of money. To make him amends, he engaged him in another scheme of building in the fields, where he buried the rest of his fortune. Whether the gentleman had really any foul play, or whether his misfortunes rendered him suspicious, so it was, that meeting Barebone in Leicester Fields, he clapped his hand upon his sword, and bid him draw. 'Draw', said the Doctor calmly, 'Why, where would you have me draw you, I had already drawn you from one end of town to the other.'[35]

Legal Devices

Legal manoeuvres were an important weapon in Barbon's negotiations. He had three basic tactics: delay, complication, not to say obfuscation, of the leases, and daring his opponents to go to law in time to stop him. On the first, it is hard to do better than Roger North's full description:

> He said his trade would not afford to borrow on such disadvantage as he must, for want of sufficient security, be at, at ten per cent at least; so he was forced to take the other way of being in debt, which he said was very much cheaper to him than borrowing, for his way was to put men off from time to time by fair words, as long as were current, and so he got one, two, and sometimes three years. And then perhaps they would begin to threaten most fiercely to arrest him, which at last they did. So he put in bail, for which end he had always a bank of credit with a scrivener and goldsmith or two. Perhaps for some carelessness of the plaintiff's attorney the suit baffled at first, but if it came so far as a trial he defended stoutly, if he had colour, if not let it go by default, then brought a bill in Chancery, and perhaps got an injunction, and at the last, when the injunction was dissolved, and the judgement affirmed upon a writ of error (which was one delay seldom omitted) and execution ready to come out, he sent to the party, and paid the money recovered, and costs, which might amount to three four, or even five per cent, and seldom more than half the charge of borrowing, and thus he maintained a gang of clerks, attorneys, scriveners, and lawyers, that were his humble servants and slaves to command.[36]

North points out that, when awarding interest on unpaid loans, the Courts used significantly lower interest rates than those at which Barbon would have been able to borrow, a very strong incentive for him to delay payments until forced to pay by a court.

As North wrote, his overtrading 'exposed him to great and clamorous debts, and consequently, to arrests and suits, wherein he would fence with much dexterity, with dilatories and injunctions'.[37] Barbon appeared in the Chancery Courts very many more times than any of the other developers of the time with at least twice as many cases involving him as those involving all the other main builders, Richard Frith, Cadogan Thomas and Thomas Neale, put together. Unlike the others, many of his cases had Barbon as the plaintiff, confirming his proactive use of the law. One example concerned the disputed ownership of a brickfield where, having gained possession by force, Barbon threatened to 'keep the said Proby in suit in Chancery about two years and in that time will make out and convert all the brick earth on the premises' (for details of the case, see p. 184).[38]

In cases brought under Common Law, the procedures ensured that the pleading was confined to a single, narrow issue: ability to prove the debts, whether by documents or witnesses, meant that the claimant could normally expect to recover what was owed. However, these awards could be overridden by injunctions from Chancery reserving the matter to be heard in its own jurisdiction. Complaints to Chancery were more likely to set out the whole story, often with much elaboration of circumstantial detail and ideally with insinuations of other misdemeanours to give colour to the complaint; these were not taken under oath. The defendant responded with answers, which were under oath. It was then open to the plaintiff to take exception to the 'insufficiency' of the answer, and indeed to continue to do so as long as the Court would permit.[39] A counterclaim in Chancery would require the original plaintiff to submit his answer under oath, thereby revealing how much he was prepared to stand by his original complaint. It was only after the process of complaint and answer had been completed to the satisfaction of both sides that the case would proceed to the taking of formal depositions and, eventually, to a court hearing. Very few cases involving Barbon got this far, let alone to a court decision.

Extended legal processes of this kind helped to buy him time to pay: the pleadings give ample confirmation. One lawyer who had met Barbon 'in several taverns and other places' said Barbon made 'one excuse or another' and did nothing but 'trifle and delay'.[40] Jeremy Whichcott complained that he had been 'put off by Barbon's fair speech [...] and at length being wearied and tired out with the said Nicholas Barbon's shifts, breaches of promise and delays, which he of purpose used and contrived to tire out your orator';[41] one plaintiff complained that Barbon removed a bill of indictment for nuisance by *certiorari*, 'hoping that the plaintiff's witnesses, who are very ancient and infirm, would die and not to be able to give evidence';[42] another complained that Barbon had been able to get a Chancery injunction striking down a King's Bench judgment for his arrest after his partner John Rowley had gone bankrupt, leaving Barbon to meet his bond;[43] a third complained early on in Barbon's litigation career that his tactics of bringing repeated Writs of Error meant that 'in [...] all judgements the said complainant at law may be enervated by a sidewind in a Court of Equity'.[44]

Sometimes he did no more than neglect to draw up his accounts, although it is clear that he kept detailed books.[45] He would claim that he had 'mislaid his receipts' or had 'paid the tradesman when they were alone or before witnesses who could not easily be found'.[46] As Roger North put it:

> He hated to make up accounts with anyone, and seldom failed to sink in his own profit a considerable balance, which the interested would lose rather than go to law on an intricate account. This article brought good profit.[47]

Barbon's tactics depended on having sympathetic judges in Chancery, but once he complained he had lost only through 'the neglect of this defendant's clerk or solicitor in not getting the [plea] filed in due time'.[48] One of the judges that caused Barbon difficulty was Roger North's brother, Lord Guilford, who was strongly opposed to attempts to circumvent the Court of Common Law by going to Chancery which, in his view, had been 'very liberal in the matter of injunctions to stay suits at law'. This caused Barbon to tell North that 'his Lordship had not sat long enough to be a good Chancery Man', although others too have argued that Guilford 'did not shine with superior lustre in the Court of Chancery'.[49] There was certainly no love lost between Guilford and George Jeffreys who succeeded him as Lord Chancellor in 1685.

There are a number of intriguing connections between Barbon and Jeffreys, who had made a point of having good contacts with the City business community.[50] Jeffreys had spoken up unusually strongly in support of Barbon's application for a patent for his fire insurance, and he also intervened in Barbon's dispute with Gray's Inn over Red Lion Square, his mediation effectively allowing Barbon to proceed against the wishes of Gray's Inn. George Jeffreys had bought an estate in Bramber as early as 1675 and this was inherited by his son, John, giving him and Barbon the two principal parliamentary interests in Bramber at the time of Barbon's election as MP. Relations between Barbon and Jeffrey's son were good enough for Jeffreys to be a commissioner for collecting subscriptions for Barbon's land bank. This was not the only connection between the Jeffreys and Barbon. The John Jeffreys who purchased Gerrard Street from Barbon was from a Welsh family near to the family home of George Jeffreys. Although they may not have been directly related, they were known to be good friends and George Jeffreys was godfather to John Jeffreys' son, yet another John Jeffreys and an MP at the same time as Barbon.[51] It is tempting to speculate that there was some deeper connection between Barbon and the Jeffreys families, but as yet there is no clear evidence for it.

Barbon's second legal tactic was the construction of complicated leases, although this was often the inevitable result of the layers of mortgages superimposed on complex ownership arrangements. Sometimes this had the effect, whether or not intended, of making it difficult for the lessee to know who to deal with. Some of the lessees of the small houses on the Essex House estate complained that 'the diverse conveyances and insurances had been made on purpose to perplex your orators and weary them out of their said leases'.[52] In fact all but one or two of the lessees sold out to him quickly. Once Barbon had sold the head lease, these kinds of complications could be helpful to Barbon by making it much harder for its new owner to gain access to the property, essential if tenants/lessees were to be evicted, or in some cases to allow the collection of rents. Barbon often issued leases for different parts of the property or several different leases for different sums and terms on the same property. These complicated the establishment of the real security underpinning the mortgage and for Essex House he would be accused of seeking to 'entangle or perplex or otherwise make invalid or lessen your orator's said security'.[53] In principle all transfers of ownership and existing mortgages should have been recorded in a court of record such as on the Close Rolls which were available for examination, but there were inevitably delays in doing so, and not everyone was as persistent in establishing the facts as Robert Clayton.[54] Multiple mortgages inevitably led to disputes about title and the basis of the security offered, as for Little Tower Hill where an extra lease in the chain was described as 'a mere contrivance between the said Doctor Barbon and Humphrey Ambler to intangle and imbarace the title and to out this defendant'.[55]

Layers of leases obscured who had responsibility for building on site, important if the declared ground rents were ever to be collected. When ground rents for Well Close were used to underpin the fire insurance regime, Barbon and Parsons covenanted to build the necessary houses within twelve months (see p. 82). However, once Barbon had sold the head lease, he argued that it was the new lessee who was bound by that covenant. By the time that the shares in the Fire Office had been sold on yet again, there were countless law cases brought to try to define who exactly had that responsibility.

His third tactic was to take whatever action he wished and dare his opponents to take him to law. The first example of this was his purchase of Essex House. Even when the Earl of Essex tried to buy the house back, and the King himself intimated that he did not want to see it developed, Barbon went ahead and knocked it down. He was confident that 'facts on the ground' would be enough for him and shared the view of the Privy Council that 'if the houses once get up a jury will not easily find it a nuisance' and require them to be knocked down.[56] The smaller houses on the Essex House site also provided the well-known example whereby Barbon was accused of threatening 'to set workmen at work who shall untile the house and pull the same down over your orator's head', although in the end that complainant accepted that Barbon had the right to pull the house down. Exactly the same words were used in a complaint by another lessee about different houses seven months later, but he too found himself ejected legitimately from those houses. In both cases Barbon only knocked the houses down some years later.[57] Other examples include his development of the Bedford Corporation estate in Holborn, where he needed to get rid of tenants holding underleases so that he could proceed. Allegedly, he dug trenches across the ground and removed a music house, selling the materials for £40.[58] He would proceed even when the title was unclear, confident that his position would not be overturned. One such was when he had pulled down the old houses on a site in Charles Street, Westminster, and destroyed the ancient boundaries so no one could tell how the new houses mapped on to the previous ownership.[59]

We have seen that Barbon went ahead with the Red Lion Square development in the face of opposition, sometimes forcible, from Gray's Inn (see pp. 101–02), and whenever the Gray's Inn lawyers got injunctions from the magistrates in the Middlesex Sessions he stayed them by *certiorari* in the Exchequer Court, so much so that the magistrate sought support for his legal fees. There were other occasions when Barbon appeared to take the law into his own hands. Two years earlier, he had been involved in a dispute about the purchase of some land in Stepney that was used for brick making. He thought the owner had sold it to him, while the owner claimed to have sold it already to a Mr Proby. Barbon claimed that his servants had been molested in the making of bricks and had been arrested, while Proby claimed that Barbon

> by force and in a hostile manner, with guns, took possession of one empty house by breaking open the doors, and then putting padlocks thereon, and he continues in possession, threatening to shoot or kill Proby's workmen.[60]

However, this may well have been common practice and in one case Barbon himself complained to Chancery that his putative landlords 'threaten violence against Barbon and his tenants, which they ought not to be allowed to do'.[61]

Chancery was not the only court used by Barbon to secure delays. A frequent issue affecting new building was how to connect their drains to the waste-water sewers; Barbon would usually include a provision in the lease which required the lessee to pay their share for the street sewer, but there remained the question of joining it to the main sewer. Although he would often apply, and be granted, permission to build a sewer or to join his sewer to the main one, there were often complications. Residents in St Martin's Lane complained that the alterations he had made caused flooding. He was ordered to make good the damage, failed to do so, failed to appear before the Sewer Court and was fined £100 before he made good the damage. In the next two years he was forbidden to connect his sewers from both Newport Ground and Charles and Duke Streets to the main sewer and it would be five years before residents of Newport Ground finally paid £49 to link their sewer. Other times he would claim that he was using the route of a pre-existing sewer until that was proved not to be the case. Other large builders were just as guilty: Richard Frith and Thomas Neale both appeared before the Court for the same kind of offences.[62]

Barbon's final method of avoiding lawsuits was to take advantage of the immunity given to a Member of Parliament, who could not be sued in the civil courts. He had told Sir Thomas Draper as early as 1681 that he intended to become a Member of Parliament and 'did intend to pay no rent to this defendant'.[63] In fact, he did not become an MP until almost ten years later, thereafter repeatedly using his position to refuse to answer attempts to recover debts in the courts.[64] This was thought to be worth £1,000 a year to him. Many examples have already been given and he also used his parliamentary privilege in 1693 with his partner, Sir Thomas Cooke, himself shortly to become an MP, to ignore a grand jury finding that their building in Ficket Field was blocking ancient lights; they even threatened to proceed with construction during the long vacation so that no case could be brought.[65] Sir Nathaniel Curzon also complained wearily of the lack of progress of his legal actions which were 'by the said Nicholas Barbon delayed by insisting on his privilege being then a member of Parliament'.[66] Finally, parliamentary privilege allowed him to remain in continued occupation of Osterley Park despite his accumulating debt and judgments against him.

In all these cases and for all kinds of litigation, Barbon sought to avoid or delay paying what was due as a means of reducing the problems for his cash flow. It is hardly surprising that one weary creditor explained 'what trouble this defendant was put unto before he could recover his rent from the complainant'.[67] There is even a record of him being taken to court for failing to pay his £15 poor law rate at Osterley.[68]

Relations with Builders/Contractors

The removal of the monopoly for livery companies after the Great Fire brought an influx of artisans from outside the City and stimulated new ways of working with more emphasis on payment for measured work rather than by a daily wage. John Bland was often Barbon's 'measurer'.

There were essentially three ways that Barbon would arrange the building on his sites. First he could take responsibility himself, entering into contracts either directly with the workforce or with a number of builders who would organize the whole construction of their part themselves. The detailed contracts were usually on a piece-rate basis, requiring the measurement of work done. Second, he could grant a lease to investors who would themselves manage the construction on their site(s). Third, he could grant a lease to a builder who would then construct the house; in this case the builder was effectively acting as an investor himself. There was always a wish to see the houses built as quickly as possible and a number of techniques were used for this purpose: the ground rent could be reduced to a peppercorn for the first year, or even eighteen months while building was underway; the lease itself would not be granted until a substantial part of the building was complete, often when the roof was in place; or there could be a series of penalty payments if the work was not completed to a deadline. Barbon was adept at using his powers of persuasion to find builders and investors to take up his leases and would paint an optimistic picture of the scope for profits, sometimes offering to help them in selling or letting the properties they would build.[69]

Where the lease was only offered on a delayed basis, or sometimes merely because it would take some time to issue, work would proceed on the basis of a building agreement setting out what was required. This could be extremely detailed, and one such that became the subject of litigation covered not just the need to follow the regulations for City houses, the number of storeys and height of the ceilings, the material for the fireplaces, the type of wood to be used — spire oak and yellow fir — but 'the need for ceilings to be rendered with one coat and trowelled when dry, not with a coat of fine stuff'.[70] This was a house next to the ones Barbon had built in Mincing Lane and they were required to be 'agreeable to the outward ornaments' of his houses.

The building agreement for a house in Red Lion Fields set out in the last chapter provides that the lessee will pay his share of any sewer that may be built and sets out the regime for party walls. The ground rent is a peppercorn the first year and then 8s. a foot for the proposed sixteen feet frontage, that is £6 8s. per annum altogether, and Barbon's undertaking is 'to cause and procure a sufficient lease' once the first floor is laid. The language about 'cause or procure' a lease reflects the fact that Barbon would sometimes arrange that the lease went directly from the freeholder, Sir Richard Fisher. In some cases this is what the builders asked for, as in Exeter House where they made clear that they wanted a lease directly from the Earl of Exeter rather than from Barbon,

> not wanting to become undertenant to Barbon or to adventure such vast and great sums of money [...] upon no better title than by or under particular leases from Dr Barbon derived out of the aforesaid original lease which might become void and voidable by his default.[71]

Exeter House was at a relatively early stage in his career and it is not clear whether this reflected on their previous experience of dealing with Barbon or was their normal practice, although it was also adopted in his Devonshire House development in the City.

Just as investors and lenders were not put off from lending again and again to Barbon, so builders and contractors worked for him on many occasions. Allen Weaver, a Painter Stainer, worked for Barbon on most of his sites over a period of at least six years, from the chambers at the Middle Temple to houses in the Military Ground, Devonshire Square near Bishopsgate and Duke Street, Westminster. Weaver also painted houses for Barbon's associates including his sister-in-law, Rebecca Hayes, and one of the first lawyers to finance him, Thomas Fountaine.[72] William Edge and his son took leases on the sites of Essex House, Exeter House and Red Lion Square. John Foltrop, a carpenter, worked on many occasions for Barbon, including at the Middle Temple in 1689, in Lamb's Conduit Street, the Artillery Ground and Duke and Charles Street, Westminster. He operated both as a contractor and by taking houses in his own right, and in Well Close Square did both, providing carpentry services for nine houses while building two on his own account.[73] He seems to have been particularly successful in managing his relations with Barbon, probably because he had enough capital to finance the scale of building that he undertook, although lack of payment sometimes led him to stop work. Further evidence of this is that Barbon employed Foltrop on the Middle Temple chambers at higher rates than usual because Foltrop was to be paid only when the chambers were sold.[74] Foltrop's will demonstrates that he had retired to a house in Putney and was able to leave a large estate with many houses and substantial legacies to his children.[75]

Sometimes a contractor for Barbon struck out on his own. The eminent carver, Thomas Young, a member of the Joiners' Company, was one of the workmen employed by Richard Frith and his partner, Cadogan Thomas, to finish the Duke of Monmouth's house in Soho Square in 1681–82. Three years later Young worked on the slating of Sir Samuel Grimston's new house in Soho Square, and in Gerrard

Street he and another building tradesman were granted the lease of a house in partial payment for work undertaken for Nicholas Barbon himself.[76] Young laid out Kensington Square starting in 1685 but later went bankrupt and spent ten years in the Fleet Prison.[77]

Barbon was careful to control his accounts with contractors, and Allen Weaver's son revealed:

> it being the normal practice and way of dealing used by the said Nicholas Barbon with workmen employed by or under him when he paid any money to his workmen upon account of work done by them to take their bond for the same until their work was viewed, measured and adjusted and their accounts stated.[78]

Possession of these bonds put Barbon in a very strong position in negotiations, and there were, of course, the usual problems with payment, as reported by Roger North:

> Bricklayers etc could tease for money when employed, and if not paid knock off. I have seen his house in a morning like a court, crowded with suitors for money. And he kept state, coming down at his own time like a magnifico, in deshabille, and so discourse with them. And having very much work they were loath to break finally, and upon a new job taken they would follow and worship him like an idol, for then there was fresh money, as I observed upon his undertaking in the Temple. And thus he would force them to take houses at his own rates instead of money, and so, by contrivance, shifting, and many losses, he kept his wheel turning.[79]

As North recognized, one of Barbon's tactics was to pay for building work by giving the leases to the builder. In some cases, as with Foltrop in the second Middle Temple building, this was planned from the start, but very often it was to deal with his cash-flow problems. There are even cases where he transferred the lease of another house entirely so that one cannot necessarily assume that a house leased by a builder was built by him. One example is where he transferred two small houses, worth £100, to Allen Weaver, his normal painter.[80]

As we have seen, Barbon preferred not to take responsibility for building himself, but it could not be avoided completely and failure to pay contractors often caused difficulties. Two merchants who had bought houses from Barbon in Mincing Lane obtained a declaration against him in King's Bench for a debt of £5,000 because the houses which they had paid for were not completed. He countered it with a complaint in Chancery claiming it was all their fault, but their answer asserted that they knew Barbon 'to be very needy and bare of money', with the result that 'several of the complainant's workmen complained of their want of pay and would not come to finish the work for want thereof'.[81] Similar accusations were made by those opposing his fire insurance company (see Chapter VI).[82]

It is clear that, as is very common with deal makers, Barbon disliked getting a bad bargain and was particularly averse to losing out. We have already seen the example of the brick field where Barnes decided to sell the field elsewhere after Barbon thought he had done a deal (see p. 181). In that case Barbon took possession by force. On another occasion, Barbon had paid William Stephens, the joiner fitting up the Great House in Gerrard Street, partly in cash and partly by the lease of another house in the street. Unfortunately, the Great House burned down while still under construction. This left Stephens with the lease of the smaller house but without the work that he had completed in the Great House, and so owing Barbon money. Barbon clearly believed that Stephens was responsible for the fire even though, according to Stephens, other of Barbon's workmen had been there when the fire started. Accordingly, Barbon pursued him in the courts and Stephens spent five weeks in Newgate before persuading Barbon to accept back the lease and whatever he had paid so far. Stephens claimed to have had to give up £300 worth of other work as a joiner, as well as his credit and reputation. He sued Barbon for wrongful arrest and imprisonment and even, albeit only temporarily, won damages of £240 chiefly because Barbon claimed not to have known of the action.[83]

The final example is of a deal done by Barbon under considerable pressure to find purchasers of leases for Red Lion Fields, but then regretting it. Jeremiah Whichcott claimed that Barbon realized he had conceded too much over the sale to him of some of these leases by adding in the possibility of alternative purchases of leases on Barbon's Bedford Corporation development. Barbon then tried to buy himself out of it. It is ironic to hear Barbon claim

> the complainant being a merchant [...] conceived no other design in this agreement than to return his money with great profit [...] which agreement the complainant seemed very well pleased with, he being likely thereby to make a greater profit of his money than by an East India voyage.[84]

Payment

Some of the sums involved in Barbon's transactions were extremely large for the time; for example, the sales of Essex House or Newport Ground were worth £20,000 or more. It is interesting to speculate how these were actually paid, since it is unlikely that the buyers could easily have put their hands on so much cash, which would have required about 2.5 tonnes of silver or 160 kilos of gold, or indeed that the vendor would have wanted it. Generally, people avoided moving large amounts of money in cash and there were very few cases.

As we have seen, whenever Barbon received large sums, he used them to pay off other debts and mortgages, although not always on the same property, so he would have needed some way of making funds available to his chosen creditors. Although there was no fully fledged banking system operating at the time, scriveners and goldsmiths were certainly equipped to handle this kind of transaction. The goldsmith Edward Blackwell frequently cleared amounts of £3,000 a day from other goldsmiths such as Bernard Hinton; Barbon's financiers Thomas Cooke, Bernard Turner and Francis Child all had accounts with him.[85] There is little information from the records of Barbon's litigation about the mechanics of payment although it is noticeable that a number of meetings took place at the houses of scriveners and on one occasion Barbon makes clear that he had brought a goldsmith's note rather than cash.[86]

Commentary

Barbon's lack of capital meant that he had to manage his cash flow very carefully and he was not afraid to use all the tricks of the law to achieve this. This was his reputation, yet it did not stop people working for him or lending him money. The Chancery material about Barbon is consistent with this reputation, and with the comments made by Roger North. It is reasonable to suppose therefore that the Chancery records give an accurate picture, while accepting that because the complaints were not given under oath, they may well be exaggerated. The requirement that complaints were signed by the complainant's lawyer was supposed to reduce frivolous actions: for example, the claims that Barbon threatened to knock down houses over the heads of tenants were not made under oath and nothing of that kind appears in any answer given under oath to a complaint.

It is instructive to compare Barbon's approach with that of his contemporaries. He was by a long way the largest developer of his day and was generally recognized as such. The Tory MP Sir John Lowther reckoned that Barbon had achieved 'not less than £200,000 in building; for which [...] he deserves more of the public than any subject in England'.[87] As we have noted before, the developer most like Barbon was Richard Frith. Although not as well known at the time as Barbon, he was described as,

> in his lifetime a great builder of houses or a great undertaker in or for the finishing of many dwelling houses, as well upon his own proper account as for others [...] so much so that for sundry years before his death he had left off his trade of a bricklayer and was generally taken or reputed to be a man of very considerable estate.[88]

Even as late as 1710, fifteen years after his death, Frith was described as 'a great (and once rich) builder.'[89] He built in St James's Square, and on the garden of Leicester House, as well as in Soho Fields where he is commemorated by Frith Street. He also built in Arlington and Bennet Streets and was one of a syndicate who redeveloped the site of Clarendon House.[90]

Frith was not involved in as many lawsuits as Barbon, but there are enough to get some idea of how he worked. It is evident that he employed exactly the same approach as Barbon. Having got possession of some land, he would mortgage it and then parcel it out in lots, building some himself and subcontracting the rest to other tradesmen.[91] He sometimes paid them by giving them leases rather than cash; he even paid a scrivener who had been working on his contracts by offering to build him a house. He was sued by his subcontractors for non-payment, fined by the Commissioners for Sewers for joining his sewer to an existing one without permission, and even fined by his own livery company for producing substandard bricks. There are only two cases recorded where Frith himself brought cases in Chancery, but both were designed to overturn suits brought against him.[92]

Frith and his partner Cadogan Thomas had borrowed some £30,000 from the goldsmith Bernard Hinton to develop Soho Fields, and when Hinton went bankrupt in 1683, this brought them down as well. A Chancery case of about that time describes Frith as 'declined in his estate'.[93] He managed to continue as a builder but died in 1695 in so much debt that his executor refused to prove the will and his wife had to be granted its administration.[94] Cadogan Thomas, who was originally a timber supplier, also died in debt early in 1690. Property speculation was an uncertain business and even the great projector and developer of Seven Dials Sir Thomas Neale died insolvent, having got through two fortunes and having been ejected from Parliament for buying the votes of his constituents.

One must recognize that delay or even refusal to pay debts was a characteristic of the rich and powerful of the time and an occupational hazard for the tradesman. Moreover, Barbon's use of the law was not unique and his former partners, Vincent and Tookie, also brought Writs of Error to delay or frustrate judgements against them.[95] Barbon's *modus operandi* was no different from the other large-scale property speculators of the time. For the last eight years of his career, he had the advantage over Frith and Thomas of being an MP and so was protected from civil suits, but before that and even though his scale of operation was far greater, he had been able to avoid insolvency when his creditors such as Hinde, Scrimshire and Price went bankrupt. His use of Chancery was on a far greater scale, nineteen suits compared with Frith's two, just over 40 per cent of the cases that Barbon was directly involved in as defendant or plaintiff. The conclusion must be that, while his reputation as a whole is justified, he was no different from his contemporaries save in the scale at which he operated and his success in deploying the various, and commonly used, mechanisms for his own benefit.

CHAPTER XIV

LAST YEARS

The 1690s were a difficult time for Barbon's business activity. His involvement in Holborn absorbed more and more of his capacity without making much progress, except for the New Square of Lincoln's Inn. For most of the other sites that he had developed, he had either sold up, forfeited most or all of his interest by defaulting on a loan, or retained either a limited equity of redemption or residual rights from being one in a complicated layer of leases and subleases. Only a few sites would have continued to generate an income for him; indeed, if he had secure title to such income and it was of any substance he would probably have capitalized it and sold it, applying the results to put funds to his Holborn activities.

As far as projects were concerned, he had largely sold or given up his interest in the Fire Office that he had launched in 1681; his new fire insurance launched in 1694 had not got anywhere, despite Tory grandees being its trustees; and while his land bank limped on making a few loans it was clearly not a success, being wound up shortly after his death.

His position as a Member of Parliament protected him from civil suits meaning, among other things, that he could not be sued successfully for debt. The number of Chancery cases involving him in the 1690s was correspondingly reduced dramatically, amounting to only about 10 per cent of the total number during a period comprising about a third of the time since his first case. Many of these cases were devoted to sorting out the various layers of leases either on the insurance sites or on Red Lion Square, although one or two of the latter were brought by Barbon himself.

There was, however, one personal project that absorbed him: his country house at Osterley which he had bought in March 1684. He immediately raised £12,000 on a mortgage also including as security Exeter Exchange which he had recently built in the Strand. The two principal mortgagees were Roger Jackson on behalf of the Earl of Devonshire and Christopher Cratford on behalf of Francis Child. Both these lenders were well known to Barbon: he had begun the development of the Exeter House site under leases from the Earl of Exeter in 1676 and had bought Devonshire House, Bishopsgate, from the Earl of Devonshire in 1678. Child must have known what Barbon was buying because he had been one of those who had drawn up an inventory of the house at Osterley after the death of a previous owner, Sir William Waller, in 1668.

Barbon may well have been attracted to Osterley because it had been built by Sir Thomas Gresham, the Elizabethan financier who had built the Royal Exchange. Barbon's Fire Office was based near the Royal Exchange and his recently built Exeter Exchange was mortgaged with it. To a man who wished to cut a figure in London's financial world Osterley had resonance. After his purchase of this country property, he sold the house in Crane Court which had been his London home since the Great Fire and thereafter seems to have lodged in chambers he had built, first in Middle Temple and then in Lincoln's Inn. From 1684 Barbon is increasingly described in deeds as 'of Osterley' rather than 'of London'. It was not a development site but intended to be his great house. The Court rolls of Osterley Manor had 'Nicholas Barbon esq.' as Lord of the Manor for the first time on 24 September 1684 and continued to do so until his death, retaining the same steward who had served his predecessor.[1] The estate may have been worth up to £600 pounds a year and there is certainly evidence that Barbon let parts of it from time to time and presumably enjoyed the income from it.[2]

In 1733 Barbon's executor John Asgill claimed that Barbon had spent £15,000 in building and plantations at Osterley.[3] The extent of Barbon's works is borne out by an action in the Court of Exchequer in the late 1690s, his having neglected to pay the interest on the loans. This shows that in 1689 Sir Francis Child, through Christopher Cratford, sought to gain possession for non-payment of his mortgage. Child got a judgment in his favour and it was later claimed that he had been able to seize £2,000 of household goods towards satisfaction of his debts, plus income from the manor of Heston. Child's answers say that by February 1690 he had received nothing apart from £50 worth of hay.

Jackson had got a writ of ejectment against Barbon but, after finding that he had pulled down part of the house and his alterations were so great that it was unfit to live in unless Barbon went on to finish, it was agreed that Barbon should hold the house, gardens, warren-house and tile kilns, with any clay then dug, but not the cherry plantations, as Jackson's tenant-at-will. Jackson would then let the rest of the estate.[4] Thereafter Barbon fended him off by claiming his privilege of parliament, presumably doing enough work to be able to live there. Barbon's will referred to his equity of redemption in Osterley House 'in which I now live'. Both Barbon and his wife were buried at St Leonard's, Heston, Osterley's parish church. Child did not get his money and in 1713 decided that he would make the property his own. The house remained in his family's ownership until it was given to the National Trust in 1947.

The reference to a tile kiln and clay at Osterley is borne out by searches made by the Company of Tylers and Bricklayers in the early 1690s, the search of August 1691 noting 'good stuffe but thin'. This material was probably for Barbon's own use at the house. But any description of the effect of his works on the appearance of Osterley must be conjectural. It seems almost certain that he built two of the square towers at the corner of the present house, those at the south-west and north-west, shown in Figure 111, and these only make sense if he changed the roof line with dormers, which can be seen in an early view of Gresham's house, into a full square second storey; the staircase in one of these towers remains, but substantially rebuilt, and there is a second altered staircase in the south range which remains *in situ*. Elsewhere there is moulded panelling which dates from Barbon's time, but it appears to have been altered and moved. While the amount of evidence of Barbon's work in the surviving fabric at Osterley is small it is sufficient to support the documentary evidence that his changes to the house were extensive but may not have been complete by his death. It seems likely that by the 1690s much of the money that Barbon derived from his property speculations in central London was spent not on completing developments there, but on an ambitious scheme for his own house.

Fig. 111. West side of Osterley Park with Barbon's towers, photograph by James Shaw.

Barbon was re-elected unopposed for Bramber in the general election of November 1695 together with the son-in-law of Judge Jeffreys, William Stringer, who had failed to get elected in 1690. One of Barbon's first parliamentary actions was to promote a bill to have his Red Lion Square development made into a separate parish. A petition to this effect from the inhabitants had already been presented to the Commons early in 1694 and was repeated on 13 December 1695. Barbon was named to a drafting committee for a bill, which he presented on 11 February 1696, but it fell at the committee stage.

Much of his time in Parliament in 1696 was taken up with the issues of land banks and recoinage, and these have been covered in previous chapters. Unlike many Tories, he immediately signed the Association, a declaration supporting William III after a Jacobite plot was discovered in February 1696. In contrast, he had been forecast as a probable opponent of the Court in the divisions on 31 January 1696 over the proposed Council of Trade, thereby supporting Parliamentary rather than Royal control of appointments to the Council of Trade. This was possibly because he favoured Parliament as a place to resolve conflicts between the various mercantile interests; Royal control of appointments was likely to favour the monopoly trading companies which Barbon had opposed in both *A Discourse of Trade* and *A Discourse concerning coining the new money lighter* and indeed voted against in 1693. This illustrates that, as for many if not most of the MPs of the time, his votes were not consistently for one party or faction.

Barbon does not appear to have been particularly active in the 1696/7 session although he started with two actions related to his banking interests. At the end of 1696 he presented a written proposal to the House for reforming the administration of tallies and increasing their value by setting up a transfer office to deal with them. The proposal received favourable attention, but nothing further came of it. On 3 February 1697 Barbon demonstrated his opposition to the Bank of England by acting as a teller against the successful move to enlarge it by a new subscription. His only other recorded activity is membership of two Bill committees, one on Highways and one on paving the Haymarket.

The final session of the Parliament started in December 1697. Early in the new year Barbon spoke against the standing army and was then put on the committee to consider army arrears. His opposition to the army, which reflected the growing view in England at the time, probably explains his classification as a Country supporter in a comparative list of the old and new Parliaments of September 1698. A few days later he indulged one of his longstanding prejudices and brought in a bill to lower the rate of interest, although it went no further. He was appointed to a committee to investigate the fraudster William Chaloner's complaint about the Mint, but must then have fallen ill because, at the beginning of April several writers reported his death, including Secretary of State James Vernon and Narcissus Luttrell who described him as 'the famous builder'.[5]

He had not died, but recovered enough strength to return to the House of Commons in May, complaining to the House that 'his goods have been taken in Execution by *George Howard*, a Bailiff, and *John Smith* and *John Bunting*, his Followers, in Breach of the Privilege of this House'. He was presumably successful in this complaint and seems to have been well enough to work, because the same day he was first-named to a second-reading committee for a bill to explain the Recoinage Acts.

But Barbon did not last much longer. His wife Margaret died in the second week of May and was buried on 17 May 1698 at St Leonard, Heston.[6] He wrote a new will the next day, whether to change it in the light of his wife's death or because he too feared illness. (A transcript is at Appendix II.) Parliament was dissolved on 7 July and Barbon clearly intended to fight the subsequent election, voting for which would continue until after the middle of August. His lack of presence at Bramber was attributed by some to his having been intercepted by bailiffs with the result that he had been obliged to withdraw.[7] In fact he had died, and was buried in the same churchyard as his wife on 31 July 1698, duly reported by Nicholas Luttrell and *The Post Boy*, where he was described as 'the famous projector'.[8]

After his wife's death, Barbon had no immediate family and there is no record of any monument or headstone to his grave. Originally his main beneficiaries were his 'loving' sister-in-law, Rebecca Hayes, and long-time lawyer, John Bland, but Bland withdrew and was replaced by John Asgill. Asgill, a Middle Temple lawyer, had been Barbon's principal colleague in the creation of their land bank, and would in the future display eccentric views, sufficient for his writing to be declared blasphemous and his book ordered to be burnt by the hangman.[9] Following his expulsion from the House of Commons in 1707 he was committed to the Fleet and King's Bench prisons for debt largely incurred from mismanagement of estates he had purchased in Ireland. He lived on for a further thirty-one years.[10]

One of the myths about Barbon is that his will decreed that his debts should not be repaid. On the contrary, it required explicitly that his assets should be sold 'to pay and satisfy what shall be justly due and owing on the said estates'.[11] The remainder was to be used for paying what he owed his sister-in-law, including a bond of £700 and any deficit from the sale of his goods which he had 'made over to his sister long since by bill of sale' for £600, presumably as an additional precaution to avoid them being seized by bailiffs. Following that, priority was to be given first to two specific debts and any of his bonds in which his sister-in-law was also bound, second to any remaining debt for his wife's funeral, and then to 'all such debts as at the time of my decease I shall justly owe'. After that he left £50 to each of his executors together with half the remaining estate, with the other half to be divided between his relations and those of his wife at the discretion of the executors. A legacy of 20s. was left to his cousin, John Barbon (the one he had earlier been asked to look after, see p. 9) in full of all claim to his estate, that is he was excluded from any further share.

Of course, the will could not be implemented until its validity had been proven, and even this became the subject of litigation. Robert Breedon and William Jarman, who owned a share in the Fire Office, had tried to take Barbon to court in 1693 to try to sort out responsibility for building houses in Well Close. They failed because of parliamentary privilege but returned to the battle a few months after his death to ensure that his will was proved and progress could be made with their case.[12]

The scale of Barbon's debts is unknown. He borrowed to the maximum possible for a site on the assumption of speedy completion of the building. Where this did not occur, or took longer than envisaged, the lender had no recourse other than to foreclose on the mortgage and take possession of the land with its partially developed or unbuilt houses, a process that could only take place once he had lost parliamentary privilege, in practice after his death. A Chancery case in 1702 reveals that one of Barbon's regular investors, Arnold Browne, estimated that he was owed £11,904 but described the debt as 'desperate and unrecoverable'.[13] Sir Nathaniel Curzon claimed that he was owed £23,344.[14] William Milman was owed £2,844 and Sir Francis Child £12,000. Often the debts included accrued interest or even associated bonds, but the capital had been secured against attractive development sites. It was now up to their new owners to develop them in the hope that they would eventually be worth as much as they had lent.

This was not always as easy as it might appear, and it could take some decades to complete the development. One pair of creditors admitted that, while they had an 'absolute security in law therein, yet the same being in the nature of a security only and redeemable in equity', meant that their title was uncertain.[15] This was exacerbated by the various layers of leases that Barbon had built up, particularly on the Holborn sites. In one case Milman went to court just to obtain discovery of the several estates and interests so that those who had leases might agree to becoming his tenants and Barbon could formally be decreed to have redeemed the mortgage or have been foreclosed on.[16] In other cases the creditors did a deal with the executors who either gave up their interest or agreed to be bought out by a token sum.[17] Sir Nathaniel Curzon claimed that he had spent much on 'improving the premises, discharging incumbrances, prosecuting and defending suits, and perfecting the title'.[18] This desire to establish a clear title meant that, even as late as 1733, John Asgill managed to extract a payment of £100 from Francis Child's son for Barbon's residual interest in Osterley, even though there could have been no possibility of redeeming the mortgage.[19]

We do not know what assets were available to Barbon's executors, the extent to which they were unencumbered, and whether there was enough to meet his debts, let alone the various legacies. Certainly, where debts were secured, at least theoretically, against the developed value of the site, Barbon's estate might well have no residual liability. Indeed, his will lists the estates which he believed had some residual value. These are set out below, together with an estimate of what they might have been worth. They fall into five categories, properties held for his personal use, ones that may still have been delivering some income, those related to his insurance, his most recent developments in Holborn, and finally a miscellaneous category.

There was clearly some value in these assets, if only because Barbon had been receiving income and because the executors were able to sell at least one equity of redemption for a substantial sum. John Asgill was able to inherit the Bramber property assets and, in due course, the parliamentary seat, while there is evidence that Rebecca Hayes was able to continue with her own various property transactions despite the number of Barbon's bonds she had been party to.

PROPERTY MENTIONED IN BARBON'S WILL

Property	Outcome
Personal	
Osterley House	Repossessed by Francis Child. John Asgill secured £100 for residual interest in 1733.[20]
Bramber	John Asgill inherited and took the parliamentary seat in due course
Income	
Newport Ground Market	Barbon had some rent for 'market house'.[21] Equity of redemption sold to Sir Nathaniel Curzon by executors for £2,000.[22]
Exeter Change	Barbon may still have been collecting rent but his leasehold interest had been mortgaged to the Earl of Devonshire and Francis Child and was repossessed.
Great/Little Brookfield	Once Barbon was dead, parliamentary privilege could no longer protect the market. The City won the battle to stop it and so the residual value was reduced.
Insurance	
Manor of East Smithfield	This was Little Tower Hill, part of the fire insurance package, but Barbon continued to receive rents until his death.[23] The final equity in Barbon's insurance share was conveyed to the insurance trustees after his death.
Well Close	Executors claimed most of the debt had been paid. They agreed an extension of the lease but asked for a share of any future proceeds.
Holborn	
New Square, Lincoln's Inn	Barbon's executors released their equity of redemption in April 1699.[24]
Bedford Ground	Barbon had already mortgaged the equity of redemption.[25]
Conduit Mead leasehold Conduit Mead freehold	Asgill admitted these had little or no residual value. The executors' interests were bought out for token sums.[26]
Other	
Queen Street, Westminster	Kirk's inheritance was the site of Liquorish Garden which became Old Queen Street. This was leased by Thomas Sutton in June 1698, after Barbon's will was written, but before his death.[27]

What was not left after Barbon's death was a substantial estate to carry his name or to provide clear evidence of his thirty years of activity. Profits — or positive cash flow — had always been invested in his next project(s). Part of the reason for this was the precariousness of his business and Roger North's estimate that he overtraded by £1,000 a year was almost certainly too low.[28] But there may have been another reason — he had no children to inherit, and this might have affected his whole approach. Apart from Osterley and Crane Court for his own personal use, he made no effort to create an estate to pass on to future generations and Crane Court had been sold by 1690. Others with no obvious descendants often did the same: the financier and Barbon's contemporary, Sir Stephen Fox, lost interest in his estates when he thought he would have no male descendants.[29] Generally, all Barbon was able to keep was the equity of redemption, which would only be worth anything if the value of the development had increased above what he had borrowed against it. This was true for his market in Newport Ground, but elsewhere it seems that the most that could be realized was a relatively small sum to buy out what was no more than a minor irritant to the title. That is not to say that Asgill did not try to maximize the return, as shown by his determination over Osterley.

The failure of Barbon to make more progress with his Holborn estates has left many to conclude that his life ended in failure. Sir Nathaniel Curzon, who picked up many of the pieces commented, perhaps a little sadly, in one of his Chancery suits after Barbon's death:

> He lived many years after the purchase and could not or did not effect his designs and purposes [...] to the undoing and utter ruin of the undertakers, which is no uncommon fate to great projectors and unthinking builders.[30]

Barbon's overall legacy is covered in the next chapter, but even for his building Curzon is too one-sided. Barbon was a great promoter of London, its growth and success. Holborn was eventually developed, albeit not completely until about 1730, but very much as Barbon had envisaged it when he first began to put the site together in 1684. His other developments were also completed and, although few of his houses remain untouched by later changes, he left his physical mark on two of the Inns of Court, parts of Holborn, Westminster and Soho, and the two squares, Red Lion and Well Close. Equally important, his methods formed the basis for development ever after. A fairer comment perhaps comes from Sir John Lowther, his contemporary and fellow MP, who himself did business with Barbon, and who wrote that Barbon had invested 'not less than £200,000 in building; for which [...] he deserves more of the public than any subject in England'.[31]

CHAPTER XV

CONCLUSIONS

Barbon undoubtedly overstretched himself financially in the 1690s, although his re-election for Bramber in 1698, if he had lived, would have allowed him to avoid the fate of his fellow speculator and projector, Sir Thomas Neale. Neale faced insolvency the next year after being stripped of his parliamentary seat for bribing his voters too obviously. It was not for nothing that the satirical poem grouped Neale and Barbon together saying,

Be silent now, and for the public weal
Give ear to learned Barbon, prudent Neale! ...
For, who can help so well at a dead lift
As those who always live by shark and shift
Most members in vacation take their pleasure,
Or waste their time upon their private treasure;
Whilst these great public souls, humbly content
With the bare privileges of being pent,
And safe ensconced within their forts at home,
Against the assaults of dun and dreadful bum.[1]

One suspects that Barbon did not object to his inclusion in satirical verse; at least it kept him in the public eye, albeit generating adverse stories. However, as this book has shown, some of the well-known charges against him do not stand up to investigation. He was not a slum landlord, nor was he the developer of insalubrious property, as alleged by the disgruntled Nathaniel Chyle in 1680.[2] Indeed, some of the most celebrated coffee houses were in his buildings; he did not start the fighting with the young lawyers of Gray's Inn, although he was perfectly happy to take up arms against his attackers, and he was supported by the courts; Roger North seems to have been wrong in attributing to him the collapsed houses in Mincing Lane, although there were indeed cases where his houses needed early repairs. Finally, his will did not instruct that his debts should not be paid, in fact the contrary, although many of his creditors will have had to take ownership of the sites which they had accepted as security for his borrowing.

While we have little personal information about Barbon, apart from the comments of Roger North who certainly knew him well, two characteristics stand out from both his actions and his writing. The first is his preparedness to think and act on the basis of his own views, not giving priority to what others thought; he was genuinely an individual mind. The second, not always consistent with the first, concerns how he wanted to be seen by others. He wanted to cut a dash, he wanted to be seen as special, and from time to time he took steps to reinforce this image.

Barbon eschewed Praise God's Puritanism but did inherit his father's independence of thought. He was one of the first of the stream of Englishmen with a Puritan connection who studied medicine in the Netherlands after the Restoration. He was also attracted to the new ways of thinking there, not least the emphasis on using evidence, and he adopted the most up-to-date medical ideas in his doctoral thesis. Unlike many, even most, doctors he stayed in London and tried to help with the Plague in 1665. He was not afraid to promote development in London both in writing and by taking on vested interests. He argued, against the orthodoxy of frugality, that luxury and consumption were good for the country. He relished developing fire insurance and a new bank, both against opposition. His writing on trade and the status of money was innovative and reflected his practical experience.

Barbon was not only attracted to new ideas, he also used them and made them work. People before him were dividing land up into lots and selling leases, but he was the first to do so repeatedly, on a large scale and, most significantly, to borrow on the security of future ground rents. He was not the first to use the courts to delay and confuse his creditors, but did so more often than any other property developer. He was not the first to propose fire insurance, but was the first to make it operational. He was not the first to propose a bank, or even a land bank, but again secured legislation for it, only for it to be dealt an almost mortal blow by the recoinage.

In Parliament, he voted sometimes Tory, sometimes Whig, sometimes country and sometimes court. He was one of only 10 per cent of MPs between 1690 and 1715 who defy classification as Whig or Tory.[3] Certainly, later in his parliamentary career one of his criteria was using his vote to gain supporters for his projects. Some have assumed that he was a Tory because he supported the land bank.[4] However, his involvement in what started as a land bank was purely a means of allowing him to gain support for his bank which ended up having very little to do with land.

Barbon had a developed sense of his own importance. As a young man at Oxford, he chose to identify himself as 'armiger' rather than the usual 'pleb'. This gave him more status but involved more expense, presumably underwritten by his father, but there is no record of him or his family ever having been granted a coat of arms. He dressed extravagantly, at least when it suited him, and he probably spent considerably on his furnishings: according to North, he lived splendidly.[5] Francis Child denied having obtained a judgment against Barbon that allowed him to enter Osterley and remove some £2,000 of household goods.[6] This would have been an extraordinarily large amount, equivalent to two years' income for a rich merchant. Even the sum of £600 for which his will showed he had sold his household goods to his sister-in-law was large, three times the average value of the household goods of contemporary merchants with wealth of over £5,000.[7]

While there are few details about his social life, we know that he dined from time to time with Wren and Hooke as well as having numerous professional exchanges with both of them. He clearly had a continuing relationship with Judge Jeffreys who intervened on at least two occasions to assist Barbon in legal arguments and may have been instrumental in helping him purchase the property in Bramber that allowed him to become an MP. His frequent interactions with the Earl, later Duke, of Devonshire also point to some continuing relationship.

He wanted to distinguish himself from others in his field. The image on his seal, at least on his early deeds, was unusual, consisting of the backbone and ribs of a skeleton.[8] His support of luxury consumption was not just theoretical; he practised it himself. Although he gave up practising as a doctor, he continued to use the title, almost flaunting the fact that he was not a member of a normal livery company and so 'a foreigner' in the City of London. After his first housing projects he only wanted to be involved in large developments; he said, 'it was not worth his while to deal little; that a bricklayer could do'. Undoubtedly, he wanted his developments to leave his mark on London's environment but he had other ways of making his presence felt. On at least two occasions he owned, or had purchased deliberately, a piece of land that was key to someone else's development and held out for large sums of money to release it (pp. 55 and 139).[9] He was also unforgiving when he felt he had been done down in a deal.

His published writings were also a way of making his presence felt and their timing reflected issues of current political interest. In the 1690s at least half the writing on economic matters was published anonymously, with a small proportion having initials only.[10] Barbon maintained this approach. Like many other publications, his included large numbers of classical allusions and tags, drawing on his Oxford education. Of his pamphlets on fire insurance or banking, only one on each subject even has his initials, although the authorship would have been obvious to anyone who read them: *A Discourse of Trade* had his initials, while *A Discourse concerning coining the new money lighter* was the only pamphlet published under his name and is one of his rare uses of the title 'esquire'.

While it is true that Barbon secured considerable financial advantage — and protection — by becoming an MP, it also brought status and contact with a wide range of politicians. His published writing was an important means to influence his fellow MPs. His *Discourse of Trade* published not long after he became an MP was designed to announce his presence as well as arguing for those things he believed in: a flourishing London with open trade and buildings to support it. He did not like leaving the last word to others and, when criticized, felt compelled to reiterate his views on interest rates in 1694, and later produced a proposal for improving the regime for tallies.[11] His *Discourse concerning coining the new money lighter* in 1696, which restated and developed the views in his previous *Discourses*, was written in part explicitly to avoid anyone believing 'that by my silence I might seem to renounce my own opinion' in favour of Locke. He foresaw, correctly, the practical difficulties that would arise from what was effectively the large revaluation proposed by Locke and others. Four publications in under six years were more than most of his counterparts and, whatever their content, were all extremely political.[12]

Cutting a dash naturally implied either a country house or at least one on the outskirts of London. It was no chance that Barbon bought Osterley Park, the former home of Sir Thomas Gresham. Gresham was one of the most successful merchants and financiers of the Elizabethan age. He was responsible for the construction of the Royal Exchange, the first building in England designed as a commercial centre that served as a model for Barbon's own Exeter Exchange. Buying Osterley, even though he was only able to stay there by virtue of his parliamentary privilege, reinforced his sense of being Gresham's natural successor. Barbon's first residence in Crane Court was the location for many of his negotiations, but the same could not be said of Osterley Park, some thirteen miles out of London. He purchased the estate in 1683, but by 1690 it was described as uninhabitable because of his unfinished alterations.[13] By that stage he had sold Crane Court and was living in chambers in Lincoln's Inn, perhaps explaining why the satirist claimed 'he hadn't a hut which he dares to call his own'.[14] And yet he voluntarily spent money on improvements to the house, with no obvious commercial return; these must have been for his own personal pleasure. Towards the end of his life, he began to refer to himself as Nicholas Barbon of Osterley.

Barbon was not the only one developing property in London in the late seventeenth century. Most aristocrats, such as the Earls of Essex and St Albans or Lord Gerard, were content merely to sell their land, ideally having first secured permission from the King. The only ones to do differently, retaining income from development of their properties, were the Earl of Southampton in Bloomsbury and the Earl of Exeter with the Exeter House development. Brewers and tax farmers such as Samuel Vincent, John Parsons and Felix Calvert looked for places to put their cash flow but relied on others to do the organization. Small investors developed a few houses at most. Those already in the building industry such as the brickmaker Richard Frith, the timber merchant Cadogan Thomas, or the joiner and carver, Thomas Young, took on larger individual sites. All went bankrupt. Goldsmiths such as Thomas Price, Michael Scrimshire, Bernard Hinton or John Hinde provided the funds for the purchases of large sites but rarely developed themselves. They too all went bankrupt in the end, although not always because of their property deals. It is hardly surprising that an anonymous critic commented in 1695, with a sideways reference to Barbon himself, 'Pray let us reflect on the vast number of projectors in and about this city, how bare-bon'd they are, that is, how few of 'em are rich.'[15]

Like Barbon, his contemporaries also used the aggressive tactics associated with at least some property developers throughout the ages. At the same time, it is noticeable how often tradesmen would come back to work for him again, and the same goldsmiths, lawyers and scriveners would lend him money repeatedly. Despite the problems Barbon caused his creditors, it was still worth working with him, reinforcing his own maxim 'Credit is a value raised by Opinion'.[16] Equally, his failure was also typical of property developers throughout time. As Roger North commented,

> had not his cash failed, which made his works often stand still, and so go to ruin, and many disadvantages grow, in all probability he might have been as rich as any in the nation.[17]

Whether or not, as Roger North claimed, Barbon was the first with 'the new method of building by casting the ground into streets and small houses and selling the ground to workmen by so much per foot front', he certainly made the most of it.[18] A much higher proportion of his building leases than in earlier developments went to building tradesmen.[19] He mortgaged the sites immediately against the security of the maximum anticipated ground rents after development, allowing him to give up ownership of the site to the mortgagee rather than repay what was owed, while retaining the equity of redemption in case the site were to rise in value. Others often left it too late, waiting until their cash was low, as recorded by John Strype for the redevelopment of Clarendon House some thirty years after it had begun:

> The undertakers [...] not being in a condition to finish so great a work, made mortgages, and so intangled the title, that it is not to this day finished, and God knows when it will be, so that it lyeth like the Ruins of Troy, some having only the foundations begin, others carried up to the roof, and others covered, but none of the inside work done [...][20]

Not only did Barbon survive, but he was successful in that all his sites except Holborn were largely developed during his lifetime and along the lines, if not the timetable, that he had originally envisaged, producing attractive properties. He had been able to extricate himself from all his developments before

Holborn — which Strype also likened to the Ruins of Troy — reserving to himself some rents and the equity of redemption, and if necessary allowing the mortgagee to take over the site. Proceeds of any development were recycled into current schemes. Despite North's comment that Barbon's only aim was profit, he does not appear to have been interested in building up a large portfolio to live off, perhaps because there were no children who might inherit. It was only Osterley Park that he retained purely for his own pleasure. North commented that Barbon's talent lay elsewhere 'than the more noble aims of architecture'.[21] He was certainly no architect, nor is there evidence that he used architects. No building can be identified as his solely from its style or appearance. There is no such thing as a 'Barbon house'. His various chambers for the Inns of Court could have been built by anyone in the last quarter of the seventeenth century. Most of his houses were put up by tradesmen, acting under leases or building agreements. Summerson and others have proposed that he achieved economies by standardization of components, but that was not the case as he sold building leases to many different builders.[22] While the front elevations had a degree of uniformity, stemming from the regulations following the Great Fire, many of the terraces in his developments varied with the builder. This variation was even more marked for the interiors, which Barbon left to be chosen by the client when he was the builder and with which he was not involved when he had already given a building lease. Everything was still made manually and there was no mass production, although there may have been benefits from giving a large order for, say, windows or balusters which could then be made off site. Even so, it is unlikely that Barbon would have used his own capital on behalf of those acting under building leases.

He did not leave great buildings for posterity. The few elements that had architectural effects, such as the arch at the bottom of Essex Street or the columns on Exeter Exchange, hardly show great aesthetic creativity. Only one London street in roughly its original location bears Barbon's name, a rebuilt Barbon Alley off Devonshire Square, but his name did linger on during the eighteenth century. His last building on Middle Temple Lane was referred to as Barbon's (or sometimes Barebone's) Building into the mid-eighteenth century and John Rocque included a Barebone Square near Newport Court in his map of London published in 1747. Many of his houses were remodelled in subsequent centuries, often more than once, and it can be often difficult to see them as they once were. His were some of London's first terrace houses, and those that do remain relatively untouched demonstrate a pleasing appearance to modern eyes, although his sale of leases to many builders mean they lack the uniformity more common in the eighteenth century. His concentration on terrace houses stemmed from his financial approach rather than anything architectural or related to the creation of townscapes. This model came to dominate London's development.

While Christopher Wren wrote about architecture, Barbon wrote about building. His *Apology for the Builder* has a sole, brief, reference to architecture in its first paragraph, but merely to make two points. The first that there is no need to 'transcribe a Folio from Vitruvius', that is to copy out a textbook, and the second to claim that:

> In a place where Buildings are generally so well finished, that almost every House is a little book of architecture [...] so the Artists of this Age have already made the City of London the Metropolis of Europe, and if it be compared for the number of new Houses, for its many and large Piazzas, for the richness of Inhabitants, it must be allowed the largest, best built, and richest City in the world.

There is nothing here about design, aesthetics or planning. One cannot imagine Barbon being in favour of any top-down planning for the City after the Fire as envisaged by gentlemen such as Wren, North or Evelyn. He recognized all too well the commercial imperative to redevelop the City quickly, and understood the constraints imposed by the complications of layers of leases and mortgages. Barbon was also very happy to develop outside the walls of the original City and argued in his *Apology for the Builder* that this would increase the value of houses closer to the centre. His role in enlarging the built-up area was again picked up by the satirist,

> The amphibious doctor (who more years hath spent
> In making mortar than medicament)
> Many fair palaces and fields defaced
> And stately nothings on the same spots placed,
> Has made the suburbs to outswell the town
> Yet hasn't a hut which he dares call his own:[23]

He was quite content for London to expand with the market deciding when land became available and how it was developed, a bottom-up consumer-driven approach in keeping with his ideas of promoting competition and innovation.

Naturally, this approach did not command universal support and Hawksmoor referred to the houses in the post-Fire redevelopment of London as so much 'rubbish' or 'a chaos of dirty rotten sheds'. He described the workmen, in rather exaggerated terms if applied to Barbon, in a letter in 1715:

> The Workmen so far from skill or honesty that the general part of them are more brutal and stupid then [*sic*], in the remotest part for Britain and the longer they work the worse they grow, as you may see in all the additional scoundrel streets they are continuously cobbling up, to sell by wholesale and this is not all in London, for this sort of vermin has run, and spread over all the country, and as they have ruined the capital so have they all the other cities and towns in England.[24]

Despite comments such as these, Barbon's methods set the model for the future of London's building, dominated by private developers using land as it became available for uniform terraces. Londoners do not perhaps realize how much this represents English exceptionalism and is so different from that in continental Europe. This was captured well by the German architect, Hermann Muthesius, who was sent by his government to London in 1900 to study the 'English House'. He wrote:

> Each developer in England lays out the streets for himself. The planning of the whole city is thus handed over to the lowest order of intelligence. The result has been the English cities of today, the sorriest product that English culture has produced [...] The terrace house [...] is usually built in long uniform rows, the effect of which is in most cases dreary in the extreme.[25]

Although Muthesius was commenting largely on the houses of eighteenth- and nineteenth-century London, this pattern was started in the seventeenth century. Barbon took the leasehold system and created financial mechanisms to exploit it which became the norm for speculative building for the next two centuries. In doing so, he also laid out a number of squares, Devonshire Square, Red Lion, Well Close, and effectively Queen Square, although he did not build that himself. All retain at least a vestige of green.

Barbon's business would only thrive when London thrived, and he recognized the importance of making a wider case for its continued development. His pamphleteering over a twenty-year period was important in promoting his vision of London and the building which went with it. Development was not an end in itself. It was required to help London, and so the English, fulfil their destiny. His vision of the nation expanded 'not only to preserve its Antient Sovereignty over the Narrow Seas, but to extend its Dominion over all the Great Ocean'[26] would indeed be realized in the nineteenth century. It was picked up by Tennyson's poem, *The Fleet*:

> [...] the mightiest Ocean-power on earth
> Our own fair isle, the lord of every sea.

When he wrote his *Apology for the Builder* in 1685, Barbon claimed that London was the best city in the world, his *Discourse of Trade* five years later described it as 'the largest, richest, and chiefest City in the world for Trade', and his *Discourse concerning coining the new money lighter* pointed out in 1696 that an infallible symptom of a nation getting richer was 'when they enlarge and new build their cities and towns'.[27]

For Barbon, building and fashion were the two main drivers of the economy; both of these were stimulated by emulation 'which is seen by Out-vying one another on Apparel, Equipage, and Furniture of the House', and in turn this was most manifest in a city, the larger the better.[28] International trade was a further stimulus, so was immigration, which had the further advantage of bringing new skills. Seen in this light, his economic writings are not merely special pleading, they were part of a coherent view of the world which saw England's economic success as dependent on a vibrant, growing London with vigorous open markets stimulated by trade and supported with the building needed to house the different degrees of people.

It is often claimed that Barbon's economic writing was not widely read at the time and had little influence, but it was not an age when writers carefully cited previous authors. His writing on London helped to prevent taxes on new housing and his pamphlets on fire insurance and banking stimulated considerable response from the economic interests opposed to his proposals. Neither his fire insurance nor his bank would have come into existence without his supporting pamphlets. One writer, E. H., supported his arguments for lowering the interest rate and quoted extensively and explicitly from the *Discourse of Trade*.[29] Barbon was one of a number who wrote on the recoinage and at least one pamphlet was produced specifically to rebut his views, as it happens by the same man, E. H., who had supported him on interest rates.[30] John Locke annotated his own copy of Barbon's *Discourse concerning coining the new money lighter*, although the comments shed no light on his detailed views of it.

While Barbon was only one of the first to identify the potential for conspicuous consumption in promoting the economy, he was the first to identify emulation as a way of promoting that consumption and to point out that it would be greater, and therefore yet more advantageous, in cities. He first made the point in 1678 in his *Discourse shewing the great Advantages that New Building and the enlarging of Towns and Cities do bring a Nation*. It was repeated in his subsequent *Discourses* and gradually became more widely acceptable. Even a conventional balance-of-trade writer like John Cary advocated the growth of pride and luxury as the principal quickener of trade and some of Barbon's ideas were picked up by his younger contemporary Henry Martin.[31] Writing in 1724, Defoe would place this change of attitude as having taken place 'in the years 1684 to 1688', just at the time of Barbon's *Apology for the Builder*.[32]

His writing also influenced Bernard Mandeville (another doctor) who wrote the poem *The Grumbling Hive*, expanded a few years later into *Fable of the Bees: or Private Vices, Publick Benefits*, which shocked the public with its assertions that it was precisely through men pursuing their material self-interest — including greed and human pleasure — that all improvements in society come about.[33] Barbon would surely have been amused that Mandeville's book was convicted as a nuisance by the Middlesex grand jury in 1723, and by Keynes asserting that it stands out in the history of the moral sciences for its scandalous reputation.[34]

His *Discourse of Trade* was certainly read by David Hume who used Barbon's phrase describing trade as 'an Affair of State' in his essay '*Of Civil Liberty*'.[35] Hume's notebooks also contain a reference to Barbon's point that Machiavelli's writing contains no reference to trade even though his city had become rich by it, and this thought is also included in Hume's essay. Hume was not one to reveal his sources, and in any case his view of the world was very different from Barbon's vision of a commercial empire. Nevertheless, what has been described as 'Hume's blatant borrowing from Barbon' demonstrates that his work was indeed read and used, allowing Hont to argue that 'it was a sophisticated and extensively argued pamphlet, and probably had more influence than usually assumed'.[36]

Otherwise, we do not know how widely he was read by eighteenth-century writers, partly because only his writing about the recoinage appears under his full name.[37] His four major publications were all part of the collection of economic tracts collected by Joseph Massie, but he only appears in Andrew Kippis's *Biographica Britannica* as an adjunct to the piece on John Asgill; this was probably the source for the false story that his will instructed that his bills should not be paid.[38]

The nineteenth century appears to have been largely uninterested in Barbon's economics. The standard mid-century compendium of economic texts only referred to his *Discourse concerning coining the new money lighter*, claiming that it very soon fell into oblivion.[39] Despite this, Karl Marx not only read it but quoted it favourably in *Das Kapital* with a reference to 'old Barbon'.[40] Barbon's other works were only rediscovered in 1890 by an Austrian economist during a postdoctoral year spent in the British Museum, where he had spotted that the *Discourse of Trade* had been misattributed to a 'Nicholas Berber'. Stephen Bauer's findings were published in an article that became the source of most knowledge about Barbon's economics for many decades.[41] In his *General Theory*, Keynes quoted from *Discourse of Trade* that 'Prodigality is a Vice that is prejudicial to Man not to Trade [...] Covetousness is a Vice, prejudicial both to Man and Trade', but in the twentieth century Barbon's writing was mostly of interest to economic historians.[42] Many of these were looking for anyone who might have anticipated Adam Smith, thereby missing the point that Barbon's writings were as much about politics as what we would call economics, being designed to influence MPs, usually in connection with legislation.

What, then, was Barbon's legacy? In most of what he did, Barbon is a controversial figure. His economic writing, often of a polemic nature, was directed at politicians to influence legislation, rather than to create a body of economic thought. He was at least partially successful in this. He undoubtedly contributed to the acceptance of increased building in London and its then suburbs, and played an important part in gaining acknowledgement that luxury consumption was an aid to the economy, reducing, if not removing altogether, the adverse moral connotations of so doing. This was picked up shortly afterwards by Bernard Mandeville and, in the twentieth century, by Keynes.

He is universally regarded as the father of fire insurance and, ever since he started his company in 1681, fire insurance has been on offer in London. Such insurance increased the value of the land used to underpin his insurance company as well as increasing the value of houses generally. He argued for the creation of banks in London long before the creation of the Bank of England and he got close to a successful launch himself. The coinage crisis put paid to that, although the bank limped on until after his death, lending to a number of his builders and associates. Although he had used the language of a land bank to gain support for his proposals, the final version approved by legislation was not a land bank. It certainly cannot be held to prove he was a Tory.

All these activities were important and constitute a worthwhile legacy in themselves. They have an underlying connection, which is a view of London which puts it at the centre of a trading empire, with a vibrant open and competitive economy driven by consumer demand based on fashion and building. This leads back naturally to Barbon's legacy in London's housing, but it is important to see his projects as a whole and treat them accordingly. All his activities were linked together and these links have been a constant theme of this book.

After Barbon's time there was little question of the state or the City undertaking development themselves. Development would be led by the private sector and move out to the suburbs; there would be no sustained centralized planning. His terrace houses became the model. Building would be speculative, based on leases; profits would be made, developers would go bankrupt. Even now the country's economy is more dependent on housing than that of most other European countries. Barbon would approve of that.

REFERENCES

Abbreviations

TNA The National Archives
LMA London Metropolitan Archives

CHAPTER I INTRODUCTION

1 Paul Slack, 'Politics of Consumption', *The English Historical Review*, 122, Issue 497 (1 June 2007), p. 616; English Heritage, *London Terrace Housing 1660–1860. A Guide to Alterations and Extensions* (London, 1996); Robert Bucholz and Joseph Ward, *London A Social and Cultural History 1550–1750* (London, 2012), p. 327; Terence Hutchinson, *Before Adam Smith* (London, 1988), p. 78; Courtney Weiss Smith, 'A Foundation in Nature', *The Eighteenth Century*, 53 (2012), p. 219; Peter Dickson, *Sun Insurance Office, 1710–1960* (Oxford, 1960), p. 7; Deborah Valenze, *Social Life of Money in the English Past* (London, 2006), p. 41; Francis Sheppard, *London: A History* (London, 1998), p. 180.

2 *The Correspondence of Sir John Lowther of Whitehaven, 1693–1698: A Provincial Community in Wartime*, ed. by D. R. Hainsworth (London 1983), pp. 510–11.

3 Edward Hatton, *New View of London: or an Ample Account of that City* (London, 1708), p. 604.

4 Karl Marx, *Das Kapital* (Berlin, 1867), ch. I, p. 1; John Maynard Keynes, *The General Theory of Employment, Interest and Money* (London, 1936), pp. 324–25; Joseph Schumpeter, *History of Economic Analysis* (London, 1954), p. 294.

5 John Summerson, *Georgian London* (London, 1945), p. 29; Douglas Vickers, *Studies in Theory of Money 1690–1776* (London, 1959), p. 74; https://oll.libertyfund.org/person/nicholas-barbon [accessed 29 November 2019], Donna Bohanan, *Fashion beyond Versailles. Consumption and Design in Seventeenth-Century France* (Baton Rouge, 2012), p. 31; Peter Groenewegen, 'Introduction' and Marina Bianchi, 'The Infinity of Human Desires and the Advantages of Trade', in *Physicians and Political Economy: Six Studies of the Work of Doctor Economists*, ed. by Peter Groenewegen (London, 2001), pp. 3, 51.

6 Emma Rothschild, *Economic Sentiments: Adam Smith, Condorcet, and the Enlightenment* (Cambridge, MA and London, 2001), pp. 40–41. She calls this tendency 'processionalism'.

7 Ingine in Ben Jonson, *The Devil is an Ass* (first printed 1631).

8 Daniel Defoe, *An Essay on Projects* (London, 1697), p. 27.

9 Insurancehalloffame.org/nicholas-barbon [accessed 29 November 2019]; John Clapham, *The Bank of England*, 2 vols (London, 1958), I, p. 14.

10 Roger North, *Autobiography*, ed. by Augustus Jessop (London, 1887), p. 53.

11 A picture that has been identified as a portrait of Barbon in recent decades was included in the International Insurance Society's Insurance Hall of Fame in 1965: https://www.insurancehalloffame.org/nicholas-barbon [accessed 22 September 2021]. It does not appear to be a seventeenth-century painting and no provenance is available. It seems very unlikely to have anything to do with Barbon.

12 Nicholas Barbon, *A Discourse of Trade* (London, 1690), p. 29.

13 Jeremy Boulton, 'London 1540–1700', in *Cambridge History of Urban Britain*, II, ed. by Peter Clark (Cambridge, 2000), pp. 316–17; Jeremy Boulton, *Neighbourhood and Society* (London 1987), p. 19.

14 Daniel Defoe, *A tour through the whole island of Great Britain* (1724), ed. by G. D. H. Cole and D. C. Browning, 2 vols (London, 1962), I, pp. 314–15.

15 Derek Keene, 'Migration, Mobility, and Cultural Norms, London 1100–1700', in *The Development of Standard English 1300–1800*, ed. by Laura Wright (London, 2010), p. 97.

16 For a full discussion, see Linda Peck, *Consuming Splendor: Society and Culture in Seventeenth-Century* England (Cambridge, 2005).

17 Lisa Margaret Bowers Isaacson, 'The Building Society: Speculative Building in the West End of London, 1660–1760' (doctoral thesis, Princeton University, 1992).

18 D. W. Jones, *War and Economy in the age of William III and Marlborough* (London 1988), pp. 279–83.

19 North, *Autobiography*, p. 54.

20 Ibid., p. 55.

21 Elizabeth McKellar, *The Birth of Modern London* (London, 1999).

22 Nicholas Barbon (attributed to), *A Discourse showing the great advantages that New Buildings and the Enlargement of Towns and Cities do bring to a Nation* (London, 1678), p. 5.

23 Nicholas Barbon, *A Discourse of Trade* (London, 1690), p. 20.

24 Nicholas Barbon, *An Apology for the Builder* (London, 1685), p. 30.

25 Barbon, *Discourse of Trade*, preface.

26 North, *Autobiography*, p. 56.
27 Barbon, *Discourse of Trade*, p. 33.
28 Paul Slack, *The Invention of Improvement* (London, 2015) gives a good overview of this topic.
29 Barbon, *Discourse of Trade*, p. 22. The tag is [Res tantum] valet quantum vendi potest.
30 Nicholas Barbon, *A Discourse concerning coining the new money lighter* (London, 1696), p. 42.
31 Ibid., p. 59.
32 Barbon, *Discourse of Trade*, p. 17.
33 Ibid., p. 33.
34 Samuel Grascome's List of Placemen, 1693 (University of Oxford, Bodleian Library, MSS Rawl. D. 846, ff. 1–2).
35 Barbon, *New money lighter*, pp. 9, 93, 94 and 96.
36 Vickers, *Theory of Money*, p. 75, n. 7; Valenze, *Social Life of Money*, pp. 41–43; Weiss Smith, 'Foundation in Nature', pp. 210–28.
37 Narcissus Luttrell, *A brief historical relation of state affairs from September, 1678 to April 1714*, 6 vols, (Oxford, 1857), IV, p. 364; *Post Boy*, 20 July 1698.
38 *The Times*, letters 3, 8, 11, 15 and 31 October 1929.
39 Istvan Hont, *Jealousy of Trade: International Competition and the Nation-state in Historical Perspective* (Cambridge, MA, and London, 2005), pp. 8–9; see also Istvan Hont, 'Hume's Knaves and the Shadow of Machiavellianism' (paper given at conference, 'Pact with the Devil: the Ethics, Politics, and Economics of Anti-Machiavellian Machiavellism', Centre for Intellectual History, University of Sussex, 28–29 May 2010 (https://arts.st-andrews.ac.uk/intellectualhistory/islandora/object/intellectual-history%3A153/datastream/OBJ/view [accessed 29 November 2019]).
40 Barbon, *New Buildings*, p. 5.

CHAPTER II EARLY LIFE AND FAMILY

1 North, *Autobiography*, p. 53. There is some confusion about the first name 'Unless-Jesus-Christ-Had-Died-For-Thee-Thou-Hadst-Been-Damned' in the Barbon family, often paired with the alternative 'Christ came into the world to save'. In some accounts the first of these was given to Praise God, while others claim that the two were the names of two other brothers (i.e., not Fear God). Yet others attribute the name to Nicholas, although Roger North's *Autobiography* clearly attributes it to Praise God. None of the relevant baptismal records survive: Praise God's because the records of Charwelton parish for that time have been lost and Nicholas's because his father would not have baptized him in the parish church. Such first names were not uncommon at that period, although it is also possible in this case that they were invented by those wanting to mock Praise God. Whatever their source, both father and son were sometimes referred to as 'Damned Barbon' or 'Damned Barebone'. See 'The History and Antiquity of Dissenting Churches, etc', in *The Monthly Repository of Theology and General Literature*, 11 (1816), p. 239, and Charles W. Bardsley, *Curiosities of Puritan Nomenclature* (London, 1880), pp. 156–58.
2 Nicholas Tyacke, *Aspects of English Protestantism c1530–1700* (Manchester, 2001), p. 95.
3 British Library, Harleian MS 7332, ff. 41, 47v, 48, 49; Ian Frederick Moulton, *Before Pornography: Erotic Writing in Early Modern England* (Oxford, 2002), pp. 64–67.
4 http://landedfamilies.blogspot.co.uk/2014/08/138-andrews-alias-andrew-of-charwelton.html [accessed 2 December 2019].
5 Will of John Barbon, Northamptonshire Archives Service, Archdeaconry of Northampton, 3rd series, N.36.
6 Calendar State Papers Domestic, 25 July 1649, p. 249.
7 Stephen Wright, 'Praise God Barbon', *Oxford Dictionary of National Biography*, https://www.oxforddnb.com [accessed 26 January 2022].
8 Praise God Barbon, *A Discourse Tending to Prove Baptism ... to be the Ordinance of Jesus Christ* (London, 1642).
9 Tai Liu, *Puritan London* (Delaware, 1986), pp. 113, 185–86.
10 Wright, *ODNB*.
11 Samuel Pepys, Diary, 11 and 21 February 1660.
12 Calendar State Papers Domestic, Charles II 1661–62, 27 July 1662, p. 447.
13 John Guillim, *A Display of Heraldrie* 5th edn (London, 1679). The blazon is: Argent, on a Fess engrailed Gules, three Leopards Heads Or.
14 Communication from Windsor Herald of Arms in Ordinary, 13 December 2019. These arms are associated with the Lee and Freston families.
15 Calendar State Papers Domestic, Interregnum, 1652–53, p. 386.
16 Stephen Porter, 'University and Society', in *The History of the University of Oxford*, ed. by Nicholas Tyacke (Oxford, 1997), p. iv.
17 Quoted in G. G. Meynell, 'John Locke and the Preface to Thomas Sydenham's *Observationes Medicae*', *Medical History*, 50 (2006), p. 94.
18 William Birken, 'The Dissenting Tradition in English Medicine of the Seventeenth and Eighteenth Centuries', *Medical History*, 39 (1995), pp. 197–218.
19 E. Peacock, *Index to English speaking students who have graduated at Leyden University* (London, 1883); R. W. Innes Smith, *English-speaking students of medicine at the University of Leyden* (London, 1932); William Munk, *The roll of the Royal College of Physicians of London*, 2 vols (London, 1861), I, p. 345.

20 Sanjay Saint, Thomas Cogswell, Eliot Siegel and Philip Mackowiak, 'Oliver Cromwell's Fatal Ague', *American Journal of the Medical Sciences*, 353/4 (2017), pp. 398–401.
21 David Stewart, 'Some early military hospitals', *Society for Army Historical Research*, 28/116 (1950), pp. 174–79.
22 North, *Autobiography*, p. 53.
23 Andrew Wear, *Knowledge and Practice in English Medicine, 1550–1680* (Cambridge, 2000), pp. 353–98.

CHAPTER III FIRST STEPS IN BUILDING

1 Norman Brett James, *The Growth of Stuart London* (London, 1935), passim.
2 Quoted in W. Maitland, *History of London* (London, 1759), I, p. 264.
3 Sheppard, *London*, p. 126; Boulton, 'London 1540–1700', pp. 316–17; Roger A. P. Finlay and Beatrice Robina Shearer, 'Population Growth and Suburban Expansion', in *London 1500–1700: The Making of the Metropolis,* ed. by A. L. Beier and Roger A. P. Finlay (London, 1986), pp. 37–59; Boulton, *Neighbourhood and Society*, p. 19; Slack, *Improvement*, p. 12.
4 Quoted in Louis Landa, *Essays in Eighteenth-Century English Literature* (Princeton, 1980), p. 220.
5 British Library, Cotton MS Titus B.v, f. 213.
6 Thomas Hobbes, *Leviathan* (London, 1651), part 2, chapter 29.
7 Peter Heylin, *Cosmographie* (London, 1652).
8 Thomas Slaughter, *Ideology and Politics on the eve of the Restoration* (Philadelphia, 1983), p. 6.
9 John Graunt, *Natural and political observations mentioned in a following index, and made upon the bills of mortality* (London, 1662), pp. 320–21.
10 The only evidence for this is that he was present at the death of his wife's brother-in-law, Edmund Lenthall, on 16 August 1676. See TNA, C7/254/26.
11 LMA, COL/CA/01/01/074.
12 S. D. Clippingdale, 'A Medical Roll of Honour', *British Medical Journal* (6 February 1909), p. 293.
13 W. G. Bell, *Great Fire of London* (London 1920), p. 137. See also Ian Doolittle, *London Topographical Society Newsletter*, November 2016, p. 4.
14 Ian Doolittle, 'Who Owned the City of London in 1666?', *London Topographical Record*, 32 (2021), p. 235.
15 T. F. Reddaway, *The Rebuilding of London after the Great Fire* (London, 1940), p. 65.
16 Brett James, *Stuart London*, p. 303.
17 Timothy Walker, *The First Clapham Saints* (London, 2016), p. 182.
18 Peter Mills and John Oliver, *The Survey of Building Sites in the City of London*, ed. by P. E. Jones and T. F. Reddaway, London Topographical Society vols 97–99, 101 and 103 (1962–67).
19 Michael Cooper, *Robert Hooke and the Rebuilding of London* (London, 2003), p. 139.
20 Bell, *Great Fire*, p. 276.
21 Samuel Roll, *London's Resurrection* (London, 1668), pp. 91–98.
22 LMA, CLC/522/MS02827.
23 Mills and Oliver, *Survey.*
24 North, *Autobiography*, p. 53.
25 TNA, PROB/11/306/316, PROB/11/317/221, C 8/310/145.
26 Barbon, *New Buildings*, p. 16.
27 TNA, C 8/219/41,42.
28 Ibid.
29 John Strype, *A survey of the cities of London and Westminster*, 2 vols (London, 1720), I, Book III, Chapter XII, p. 277.
30 TNA, CP/25/2/785/3/4JASIIHIL.
31 Richard Westfall, *Never at Rest; A Biography of Isaac Newton* (Cambridge, 1983), pp. 675–77.
32 Robert Hooke, Diary, 24 March 1674 (unpublished edition of his diary courtesy of Felicity Henderson).
33 Hustings Rolls 341, no. 65; 342, no. 22; 343, nos 24, 28.
34 Hustings Rolls 348, no. 21; 348, no. 28.
35 City Lands Committee Orders, I, ff. 42r, 46r.
36 Hooke, Diary, 6 November 1674.
37 Strype, *Survey*, II, Book IV, Chapter VII, p. 277.
38 See London Metropolitan Archives, John Wykeham Archer, *The House of John Dryden, Fetter Lane*, hand-coloured etching, 1851 (Catalogue: q4026901; London Picture Archive no. 3091) after a watercolour by Archer in the British Museum, 1874,0314.29.
39 TNA, C 8/219/41,42.
40 Cooper, *Hooke*, p. 139.
41 State Papers Domestic, Car. II Proclamations, vol. 3, p. 286.
42 F. H. W. Sheppard (ed.), *Survey of London*, vols 31 and 32*: St James, Westminster* (London, 1963), part 2, p. 1.
43 See collection of petitions in British Library, Add. MS 32471, f. 687.
44 Charles Hull, *The Economic Writings of Sir William Petty* (Cambridge, 1899), vol. 1, pp. 40–41.
45 Anchitell Grey, *Debates of the House of Commons, 1667–1694* (London, 1763), II, p. 301.
46 J. K. Horsefield, 'The Stop of the Exchequer Revisited', *Economic History Review*, 35/4 (1982), pp. 511–28; H. Roseveare, *The Financial Revolution 1660–1760* (Harlow, 1991); M. A. Milevsky, *The Day the King Defaulted* (London, 2017).
47 Bell, *Great Fire*, p. 265.

48 Londonophilos, *Proposals moderately offered for the full peopling and inhabiting the City of London, etc.* (London 1672), British Library, 1103.f.37.

49 Bell, *Great Fire*, p. 286; *Reasons humbly offered to Parliament for the abatement of the proportion of the assessment upon the City of London* (London, 1667), British Library, 10350.g.11.(6.).

50 Reddaway, *Rebuilding*, pp. 300–01.

51 Ibid., p. 303.

52 *The Grand Concern of England explained in several proposals offered to the consideration of the Parliament* (1673), British Library, RB.31.b.1.(8.).

53 G. H. Gater and E. P. Wheeler (eds), *Survey of London*, vol. 18: *St Martin-in-The-Fields II, The Strand* (London, 1937), pp. 51–60.

54 Fire Court, 14 July 1674; Chamberlain's Posting Book, 1 January 1674/5.

55 Corporation of London Repertories, vol. 79, ff. 6, 16, 24, 30b, 44; Hustings Roll, 344, no 36.

56 TNA, C 7/543/52.

57 TNA, C 10/181/4. 'Agreeable' to contemporaries implied uniform and conforming with each other.

58 TNA, C 7/543/52.

59 North, *Autobiography*, p. 53.

60 Corporation of London Repertories, vol. 76, f. 37b, 15 December 1670.

CHAPTER IV REDEVELOPMENT OF LARGE HOUSES

1 TNA, Privy Council: Registers PC 2/44, p. 189. For the history of Essex House before Barbon, see C. L. Kingsford, 'Essex House', *Archaeologia*, 73 (1922), pp. 243–77, and Manolo Guerci, *London's Golden Mile: The Great Houses of the Strand 1550–1650* (London, 2021), pp. 17–31.

2 Grey, *Debates*, II, pp. 336–37.

3 TNA, PC 2/64, f. 383.

4 TNA, PC 2/64, f. 394.

5 Arthur Capel, Earl of Essex, *Essex Papers*, ed. by Osmund Airy, Camden Society (Great Britain) Publications, New Series, 47 (1890), p. 311.

6 Ibid., p. 312.

7 TNA, PC 2/64, f. 398.

8 Arthur Capel, *Essex Papers*, p. 323.

9 TNA, C 54/4600, No. 2.

10 *Middle Temple Records: Minutes of Parliament of the Middle Temple*, 4 vols, ed. by C. T. Martin (London, 1904–05), 26 January 1677, 25 January 1678, 19 April 1678.

11 *Middle Temple Records: Minutes of Parliament*, 24 May 1677.

12 William Baer, 'The Institution of Residential Investment in Seventeenth-Century London', *Business History Review*, 76 (2002), pp. 515–51.

13 TNA, C 8/241/22.

14 The exact date of this petition is not clear but was before the end of 1675. It is one of the 'memoranda of statutes, etc. to restrain building in London as a nuisance;, British Library Add. MS 32471, f. 687.

15 North, *Autobiography*, p. 56.

16 The Treasury auctioned the right to collect a particular tax or duty to individuals or groups of individuals, who took the risk that tax might not materialize or take longer to collect. Such individuals or groups were called 'tax farmers'. The Treasury would have greater certainty about the payments in the contract but would inevitably pay a price for this. Samuel Vincent was involved in collecting excise duties.

17 TNA, C 8/203/95, C 8/269/79, C 9/74/112.

18 A. F. Kelsall, 'The London House Plan in the Later 17th Century', *Post-Medieval Archaeology*, 8 (1974), pp. 80–91.

19 TNA, C 10/481/99.

20 TNA, C 5/491/65.

21 North, *Autobiography*, p. 56.

22 TNA, C 5/491/85, C 8/255/116, C 6/77/19, C 10/481/99, C 8/241/13, C 8/269/79, C 78/1210.

23 TNA, C 10/128/17.

24 TNA, PC 2/63, p. 341. Anthony Geraghty, *The Architectural Drawings at All Souls College, Oxford: Wren and Hawksmoor*, https://iiif.bodleian.ox.ac.uk/iiif/viewer/1cd06d7a-1bf3-4ebc-a09c-e8b8461d64a0#?c=0&m=0&s=0&cv=462&r=0&xywh=-1481%2C0%2C10599%2C6165 [accessed 20 June 2020].

25 The material on Exeter House is drawn from the following cases. TNA, C 8/263/91, C6/280/107, C8/279/140, C8/263/71, C8/263/81, C8/281/55, C5/226/43. For the history of Exeter (alias Burghley) House before Barbon, see Guerci, *Golden Mile*, pp. 89–103.

26 The builders included William and John Edge, Nicholas Durant, Henry Ford, William Hobbs, Robert Dowton, John Sheppard, John Turbervill, John Badler, William Bates, John Greene, George Pawley and John Rowley, together with Barbon's representatives and family including John Bland, George Bland and Rebecca Hayes.

27 John (Johannes) Hunyades (*c.* 1621–96), son of the Transylvanian alchemist Johannes Banfi Hunyades, was a wealthy moneylender. For his elaborate tomb in St Leonard's Church, Shoreditch, see James Bird (ed.), *Survey of London, vol. 8: Shoreditch* (London, 1922), p. 112 and pls 37–41.

28 Jouvin de Rochefort, *Le Voyageur d'Europe* (Paris, 1676), p. 440.
29 François Colsoni, *Le Guide de Londres Pour Les Etrangers Dedié & Offert Aux Voyageurs Allemands & Francois* (Paris, 1693).
30 F. H.W. Sheppard (ed.), *Survey of London*, vols 29 and 30, *St James, Westminster* (London, 1960), I, pp. 88–89.
31 Stephen Inwood, *The Man who Knew Too Much. The Strange and Inventive Life of Robert Hooke* (London, 2002), p. 251; Hooke, Diary, 26–30 October 1677; TNA, C 8/23/11.
32 TNA, C 54/4508, No. 22.
33 Brett James, *Stuart London*, p. 327.
34 Nathaniel Chyle, *History of Wells Cathedral* (1680), in H. E. Reynolds (ed.), *Wells Cathedral: its foundation, constitutional history and statutes* (Leeds, 1881), p. 67. The *OED* gives 'bawdy house' as one meaning of 'vaulting-school'.
35 Strype, *Survey*, II, Book IV, Chapter VII, p. 117.
36 Ingrid Rima, *Development of Economic Analysis*, 7th edn (London 2008), p. 44.
37 Nicholas Barbon (attributed to), *A Particular of the New Buildings within the Bills of mortality, and without the City of London* (London, 1678), British Library, 491.k.4.(4.); *The grand concern of England explained* (London, 1673).
38 Brett James, *Stuart London*, pp. 504–06.
39 Nicholas Barbon (attributed to), *Arguments concerning the New Building in the Parishes within the weekly Bills of Mortality, without the City of London* (London, 1678), British Library, 491.k.4.(5.)
40 *Journals of the House of Commons*, IX, p. 444.
41 A. B. Grosart, *The Complete Works, in verse and prose, of Andrew Marvell*, 4 vols (London, 1872–75), II, pp. 590–91.
42 Hertfordshire Archives and Local Studies, Cowper (Panshanger) Collection C4252.
43 *Journals of the House of Commons*, IX, p. 505.
44 Barbon, *Discourse showing the great advantages that New Buildings ... do bring to a Nation*, p. 6.
45 Ibid., p. 7.
46 Ibid., p. 11.
47 A. H. Maslow, 'A Theory of Human Motivation', *Psychological Review*, 50/4 (1943) , pp 370–96.
48 Graunt, *Natural and Political Observations*, 5th edn (London, 1676).
49 Extracts from Dr Henry Sampson's day-books transcribed by Ralph Thoresby, British Library, Add. MS 4460.
50 Graunt, *Natural and Political Observations* (1676), p. 62.
51 Barbon, *Discourse showing the great advantages that New Buildings ... do bring to a Nation*, pp 18–19.
52 Paul Slack, 'Perceptions of the Metropolis in Seventeenth Century England', in *Civil Histories; Essays presented to Sir Keith Thomas*, ed. by Peter Burke, Brian Harrison and Paul Slack (Oxford, 2000), pp. 161–80.
53 Slack, *Improvement*, pp. 142–53.
54 Barbon, *Discourse showing the great advantages that New Buildings ... do bring to a Nation*, p. 5.
55 Slack, *Perceptions*, p. 144.
56 North, *Autobiography*, p. 56.
57 John Houghton, *England's Great Happiness; or a Dialogue between Content and Complaint* (London, 1677), pp. 6–8.
58 John Locke, *Political Essays*, ed. by Mark Goldie (Cambridge, 1997), pp. 221–22.

CHAPTER V EXPANSION

1 North, *Autobiography*, p. 55.
2 TNA, C 7/225/4.
3 TNA, C 8/510/40.
4 Ibid.; Lincolnshire Record Office, Aswarby 2/56/1.
5 Strype, *Survey*, II, Book VI, Chapter VI, p. 84.
6 TNA, C 8/248/10.
7 G. H. Gater and F. R. Hiorns (eds), *Survey of London*, vol. 20: *St Martin-in-the-Fields* (London, 1940), III, pp. 104–05.
8 F. H. W. Sheppard (ed.), *Survey of London*, vols 33 and 34: *St Anne Soho* (London, 1966), p. 383.
9 TNA, C 6/86/78.
10 The family name was Gerard and Gerard House maintained the same spelling. By the middle of the nineteenth century, the street was called Gerrard Street.
11 Sheppard, *St Anne Soho*, p. 384.
12 Strype, *Survey*, II, Book VI, Chapter VI, p. 86.
13 TNA, C 6/86/78.
14 Ibid.
15 TNA, C 6/259/81.
16 St Martin's Vestry Minutes, 7 December 1681.
17 Strype, *Survey*, II, Book VI, Chapter V, p. 69.
18 Source: https://www.middletemple.org.uk/archive/archive-month/june-2020-great-fire-london-%E2%80%93- narrow-escape-middle-temple [accessed 26 October 2020].
19 North, *Autobiography*, p. 43.
20 Ibid., pp. 57–61.
21 Ibid., p. 52.
22 John Fitch was the brother of Thomas Fitch, the prime contractor for the Fleet Ditch. He also worked on three buildings

designed by Robert Hooke and later on major works such as docks at Portsmouth Dockyard. He and his brother were also principal contractors in 1663–65 for the new Kingston Lacey built by Sir Ralph Bankes. William Ettrick's father had been steward to Ralph Bankes's father, Sir John Bankes.

23 Charles Worsley, *Master Worsley's Book on the History and Constitution of the Honourable Society of the Middle Temple* (1732), ed. by A. R. Ingpen (London, 1910), p. 274.

24 Middle Temple Archive, MT/6/RBW/343, p. 10; *Middle Temple Records: Minutes of Parliament*, 4 July 1679; North, *Autobiography*, p. 60.

25 *Middle Temple Records: Minutes of Parliament*, 27 April 1683. The date on the sundial may be why the Middle Temple dates the whole of No. 1 Essex Court to 1685, instead of just after the fire, that is in 1680. The Royal Commission on Historical Monuments ascribes this building to 1784, but that is presumably a typographical slip.

26 *Middle Temple Records: Minutes of Parliament*, 8 February 1684.

27 *Middle Temple Records: Minutes of Parliament*, 19 May 1704.

28 Sir Aston Webb, 14 October 1908, Middle Temple Archive, MT.1/MPA/21; J. B. Williamson, *Notes on the Middle Temple in the Nineteenth Century* (London 1936), pp. 25–27.

29 F. A. Inderwick (ed.), *A Calendar of the Inner Temple Records* (London, 1896–1901), vol. III, p. 132, 19 May 1679.

30 *Middle Temple Records: Minutes of Parliament*, 4 July 1679.

31 *Middle Temple Records: Minutes of Parliament*, 24 May 1677.

32 Middle Temple Archive, MT/6/RBW/343.

33 Inderwick, *Calendar of the Inner Temple Records*, vol. III, p. 145.

34 Ibid., p. 158; General Account Book, p. 168.

35 Middle Temple Archive, MT.6/RBW, 17.

36 Middle Temple Archive, MT.6/RBW 18, 6.

37 Middle Temple Archive, MT.6/RBW 18, 7.

38 Middle Temple Archive, MT.6/RBW 18, 1–7.

39 Timothy Daniell, *The Lawyers: The Inns of Court: Home of the Common Law*, 2nd edn (London, 1976).

40 *Middle Temple Records: Minutes of Parliament*, 11 February, 13 May 1825.

41 TNA, C 8/230/72.

42 *Middle Temple Records: Minutes of Parliament*, 8 February 1684.

43 TNA, C 10/270/21, C8/555/84.

44 TNA, C 54/4715 No. 4.

45 Joseph Georgirenes, Archbishop of Samos, *An Account of his building the Grecian Church in So-hoe Fields* (London, 1682), British Library, 816.m.9.(118.).

46 Sheppard, *St Anne Soho*, p. 279.

47 Strype, *Survey*, II, Book VI, Chapter VI, p. 86.

48 Defoe, *A tour through the whole island*, p. 40.

49 TNA, C 8/388/7, C8/404/23.

50 TNA, C 8/404/23.

51 Strype, *Survey*, II, Book VI, Chapter VI, p. 63.

52 City of Westminster Archives Centre, 0021/001.

53 TNA, C 6/318/30.

54 TNA, C 8/555/84.

55 Calendar of Treasury Books, VIII (1685–89), p. 323.

56 TNA, C 6/318/30.

57 Letter from Robert Roper to Roger Kenyon, 13 December 1681, Lancashire Archives, DDKE/acc.7840 HMC/424.

58 TNA, C 7/169/26.

59 TNA, C 7/365/27, C10/260/44, C10/294/65.

60 Letter of John Graham to Lord Dartmouth, 22 October 1683, Historical Manuscripts Commission, Dartmouth MSS, vol. III.

61 LMA, CLC/521/MS01994.

62 Westminster Sewer Records, 26 November 1686, 15 December 1687, 8 March 1688.

63 TNA, C 8/570/15.

64 B. H. Johnson, *Berkeley Square to Bond Street*, London Topographical Society publication, No. 86 (1952), p. 117. Frith was buried at St Clement Danes on 20 November 1695.

65 Strype, *Survey*, II, Book VI, Chapter V, p. 64.

66 TNA, WORK 30/6465/1.

67 Margaret Sefton Jones, *Old Devonshire House by Bishopsgate*, (London 1923), p. 139.

68 Lisa Bowers Isaacson, 'The Building Society: Speculative Building in the West End of London 1669–1760' (doctoral thesis, Princeton University, 1992), p. 103.

69 Winston Churchill wrote that No. 10 was 'shaky and lightly built by the profiteering contractor whose name they bear', Hector Bolitho, *No. 10 Downing Street — 1660–1900* (London, 1957), p. 20.

70 Chyle, *Wells Cathedral*, p. 67.

71 North, *Autobiography*, pp. 54–55.

CHAPTER VI FIRE INSURANCE

1 Walker, *Clapham Saints*, p. 115.
2 The history of fire insurance is covered in Cornelius Walford, *The Insurance Cyclopaedia*, 6 vols (London, 1871–80), III; Henry Raynes, *A History of British Insurance* (London, 1960); Frederick Haines, *Chapters of Insurance History* (London, 1926); F. B. Relton, *Account of the Fire Insurance Companies* (London, 1893); Dickson, *Sun Insurance Office.*
3 State Papers Domestic, Car I, vol. 139, 1 May 1638.
4 L. R., *A Second Letter to his honoured friend Mr M.T. one of the Committee chosen by the Common Council of London for the insuring of house from fire* (London, 1682), British Library, 816.m.10.(80.).
5 William Petty, *A Treatise of Taxes and Contributions* (London, 1662).
6 Bell, *Great Fire*, p. 137; see also Ian Doolittle, *London Topographical Society Newsletter*, November 2016, p. 4.
7 Londinophilos, *Proposals moderately offered for the full peopling and inhabiting the City of London* (London, 1672).
8 A. Newbold, *London's Improvement and the builder's security asserted* (London, 1680), British Library, 816 m.10.(64.).
9 *Protestant Domestick Intelligence*, 2 April 1680.
10 Nicholas Barbon, *Propositions for Insuring Houses from Fire* (London, 1680), British Library, HS.75/1042/35.
11 British Library, 816.m.10.(67.)
12 *Protestant Domestick Intelligence*, 7 May 1680.
13 *Mercurius Civicus*, 12 May and 4 June 1680.
14 Nicholas Barbon, *Arguments for Insuring Houses from Fire* (London, 1680, reprinted in Walford, *Cyclopaedia*), pp. 444–45.
15 TNA, C 45/4556.
16 *An Advertisement from the Insurance Office for Houses*, British Library, 816.m.10.(68.); *A Table of the Insurance Office at the Backside of the Royal Exchange*, British Library, 816.m.10.(73.).
17 TNA, C 103/157.
18 Luttrell, *Brief Historical Relation*, I, p. 135.
19 Nicholas Barbon, *An Enquiry whether it be in the interest of the City to insure houses from fire and what advantages the insured may expect, more from the Insurance Office already settled* (London, 1681), British Library, 816.m.10.(65.).
20 *A letter to a Gentleman of the Insurance Office, concerning the Cities insuring houses*, British Library, 816.m.10.(79.).
21 British Library, 816.m.10.(70.); 816.m.10.(69.); 816.m.10.(71.).
22 Nicholas Barbon, *Observations on the Proposals of the City, to insure Houses in case of Fire* (London, 1681), British Library, 816.m.10.(66.).
23 Minutes of the Court of Common Council, December 1681, quoted in Walford, *Cyclopedia*, p. 453.
24 L. R., *To my honoured friend Mr M.T. one of the Committee chosen by the Common Council of London for the insuring of house from fire*, British Library, 816.m.10.(72.); L. R., *A Second Letter.*
25 Barbon, *An Enquiry whether it be in the interest of the City.*
26 Barbon, *Observations on the Proposals.*
27 Barbon himself, although an honorary fellow of the Royal College of Physicians, was not a freeman of the City of London and few of his colleagues were. Non freemen were sometimes referred to as 'foreigners'. The term 'outlying deer' refers to a deer outside the main herd.
28 H. M. Colvin and John Newman (eds), *Of Building: Roger North's Writings on Architecture* (Oxford, 1981), p. 7.
29 Court of Aldermen, 13 November 1682; Relton, *Fire Insurance Companies*, p. 56.
30 In 1682–83 the King's Bench issued a writ of Quo Warranto against the City of London which led to the Charter of the City being forfeited and the Corporation of London being dissolved, reducing the city to the legal status of a small village. Quo Warranto writs had often been used to regulate liberties and franchises, such as the right to hold a fair or a market. It was claimed that the City of London had breached its Charter by allowing the collection of tolls at market and by publishing a seditious petition against the King and Government — these abuses of the ancient liberties of the City were enough to justify issuing the writ. The overall aim of the King, Charles II, was to control the personnel and the government of the Corporation of London. After the Charter was forfeited, the King issued a new one giving him the right to appoint and remove officers, including the Mayor, Sheriffs, Recorder, Common Sergeant, Justices of the Peace and Coroner, thus allowing him direct control over the government of the City. Between 1683 and 1688 the City of London was governed by a Royal Commission.
31 Quoted in Walford, *Cyclopedia*, p. 455.
32 When a freeman of the City died with children who were underage, his executor was obliged to report the death at the Guildhall and produce an inventory of the dead man's estate. The court of orphans appointed guardians to care for the orphans and their inheritance until the orphan reached the age of majority. Those inheritances were increasingly deposited with the City Chamberlain, who used the money to help shore up the City's worsening finances.
33 Strype, *Survey*, I, Book I, Chapter XXVIII, p. 240.
34 Quoted in Walford, *Cyclopedia*, p. 455.
35 M. Goldie *et al.* (eds), *The entring book of Roger Morrice*, 7 vols (Woodbridge, 2007), 21 November 1682, III, p. 333; Luttrell, *Brief Historical Relation*, I, p. 238.
36 *London Gazette*, 20 November 1682.
37 J. R. Tanner (ed.), *A Descriptive Catalogue of the Naval Manuscripts in the Pepysian Library at Magdalene College, Cambridge*, 4 vols (London 1903–23), I, p. 165.
38 TNA, C 10/531/31, C10/338/14.

39 Calendar of Treasury Books, VII (1681–83), p. 626.
40 Daniel Defoe, *A Tour through England and Wales* (Everyman edition, 1928), I, p. 328.
41 TNA, C 7/148/37.
42 TNA, C 10/337/19.
43 TNA, C 54/4600.
44 John M. Sims, 'The Trust Lands of the Fire Office', in *Guildhall Miscellany* (London, April 1972), pp. 88–113.
45 TNA, C 10/236/48.
46 TNA, C 9/245/3.
47 *An Advertisement from the Insurance Office for Houses*, British Library, 816.m.10.(68.); *A Table of the Insurance Office at the Backside of the Royal Exchange*, British Library, 816.m.10.(73.); Lawrence Wulcko, Review of 'The Trust Lands of the Fire Office' in *Journal of the Fire Mark Circle*, IV (1974), p. 52.
48 TNA, C 54/4760 No. 18, C54/4832 No. 20.
49 *The Friendly Society*, British Library, 816.m.10.(77.).
50 *The Friendly Society Settled*, British Library, 816.m.10.(78.); *Breviate of the Establishment of the Friendly Society*, British Library, 816.m.10.(76.).
51 Barbon, *A letter to a Gentleman in the Country giving an account of the Two Insurance Offices* (London, 1684), British Library, 816.m.10.(74.).
52 *An answer to a letter to a Gentleman in the Country giving an account of the Two Insurance Offices*, British Library, 816.m.10.(75.).
53 *London Gazette*, 6 July 1685, 8 July 1686.
54 David Garrioch, '1666 and London's Fire History: A Re-Evaluation', *Historical Journal*, 59/2 (2016), pp. 319–38.
55 Barbon, *Arguments for Insuring Houses from Fire*, p. 444.
56 Goldie, *Morrice*, III, p. 481.
57 Charles Corbet, *Blanket Fair, or the History of Temple Street* (1684).
58 TNA, C 7/169/99.
59 Edward Chamberlayne, *Angliae Notitia* (London, 1687).
60 TNA, PC 2/72, f. 432.
61 Goldie, *Morrice*, 30 April 1687, IV, p. 30.
62 Goldie, *Morrice*, 24 December 1687, IV, p. 200.
63 TNA, PC 2/72, ff. 554, 563, 580, 586, 609, C66/3301 No. 12.
64 *London Gazette*, 1 October 1688.
65 Calendar State Papers Domestic, 1702–03, p. 445.
66 TNA, C 6/309/18.
67 Defoe, *Projects*, p. 54.
68 TNA, C 54/4806 No. 25.
69 TNA, C 10/236/48.
70 TNA, C 7/337/40, C 6/326/51, C 10/236/48.
71 TNA, C 7/148/37, C 7/245/3.
72 TNA, C 10/337/19, C 54/4760 No. 16, C 54/4760 No. 14.
73 TNA, C 10/337/19, C 9/244/60.
74 TNA, C 10/531/31, C 10/338/14, C 66/33.
75 *London Gazette*, 20 November 1693.
76 TNA, C 66/3374 No. 5.
77 TNA, C 54/4776 No. 20.
78 Nicholas Barbon, *An advertisement being a proposal by Dr Barbon and partners for insuring houses and goods from fire* (London, 1694).
79 'The Settlement of the Land Bank' (1695) in *A Collection of Scarce and Valuable Tracts*, ed. by John Somers, Lord Somers, 2nd edn by Walter Scott, 13 vols (London, 1809–15), vol. XI, pp. 16–34 (1814).
80 TNA, C 5 4/4832 No. 19.
81 *Post Man and Historical Account*, 14 July 1698.
82 TNA, PC 1/1/274.
83 British Library, 816.m.10.(99.).
84 *London Gazette*, 21 June 1694.
85 British Library, 816.m.10.(107.).
86 Wulcko, 'Trust Lands', *Fire Marks*, MLR 1712/4/95.
87 British Library, 816.m.10.(100.).
88 Cecil Wall, *History of the Worshipful Society of Apothecaries, 1617–1815*, ed. by E. Ashworth Underwood (London, 1963), p. 152.
89 *Daily Courant*, 18 August 1718.
90 TNA, C 54/5159 No. 8.
91 *Evening Post*, 29 November 1720.
92 Miranda Clow, *The Design of Trust, Past and Present: A dialogue between the 'design for trust' in contemporary design practice and the fire insurance industry 1680–1914* (Doctoral thesis, School of Arts and Humanities, Royal College of Art, 2020).

CHAPTER VII MORE BUILDING

1 British Library, Sloane MS 1048, ff. 62, 63.
2 F. H. W. Sheppard (ed.), *Survey of London, vol. 27: Spitalfields and Mile End New Town* (London, 1957), pp. 24–38.
3 P. Guillery (ed.), *Survey of London*, vols 54 and 55: *Whitechapel* (forthcoming 2022).
4 TNA, C 9/124/85.
5 TNA, C 10/230/7, C 9/457/109.
6 TNA, C 9/294/7.
7 TNA, C 8/420/53.
8 TNA, C 7/126/93, C 8/523/28.
9 R. J. Fletcher (ed.), *The Pension Book of Gray's Inn, Records of the Honourable Society. 1569–1669 and 1669–1800*, 2 vols (London, 1901 and 1910), II, pp. 71, 73, 77–79.
10 John Verney letter of 9 June 1683 to Sir Ralph Verney, Historical Manuscripts Commission, 7th Report, p. 481.
11 Ibid.
12 Luttrell, *Brief Historical Relation*, I, p. 309.
13 TNA, PC 2/70, p. 208.
14 Goldie, *Morrice*, 12 June 1684, II, p. 481.
15 John Verney letter of 16 June to Sir Ralph Verney, HMC, 7th Report, p. 481.
16 TNA, C 9/92/3.
17 Ibid.
18 TNA, PC 2/70, p. 208.
19 TNA, PC 2/70, p. 236.
20 George Keeton, *Lord Chancellor Jeffreys and the Stuart Cause* (London, 1965), p. 238.
21 Fletcher, *Pension Book*, II, pp. 92–97.
22 TNA, C 9/92/3.
23 TNA, C 9/461/173.
24 TNA, C 9/457/109, C10/230/7.
25 Strype, *Survey*, I, Book III, Chapter XII, p. 254.
26 https://www.thebarbonbuildings.london [accessed 28 March 2020].
27 Graunt, *Natural and Political Observations* (1662), pp. 320–21, and 5th edn (1676).
28 Barbon, *Apology for the Builder*, p. 21.
29 Ibid., p. 30.
30 Ibid.
31 Ibid., p. 31.
32 Ibid., p. 40.
33 LMA, CLC/L/SE/B/001/MS30708/005; LMA, CLC/L/TF/G/003/MS03803.; TNA, C 54/4457, No. 12; TNA, PROB11/567/161.
34 Philip Norman, 'Buckingham House, College Hill', *Notes and Queries*, 8th series, XI, 13 February 1897; *Litany of the Duke of Buckingham*, British Library, C.20.f.2.(313.); Hatton, *New View*, p. 624.
35 LMA, ACC/0436/001.
36 *Middle Temple Records: Minutes of Parliament*, 15 and 22 June 1687.
37 TNA, C 5/144/1; Middle Temple MSS, former reference LOFTMS92.
38 Middle Temple Archive, MT/6/RBW/343.
39 *Master Worsley's Book*, p. 80.
40 The Royal Commission on Historical Monuments of England, *An Inventory of the Historical Monuments in London*, 5 vols (London, 1924-30), IV, The City, p. 155.

CHAPTER VIII PARLIAMENT AND *A DISCOURSE OF TRADE*

1 TNA, C 8/238/19.
2 Defoe, *A Tour Through the Whole Island*, I, p. 188.
3 D. Hayton, E. Cruickshanks and S. Handley (eds), *History of Parliament: The House of Commons 1690–1715*, 5 vols (Cambridge, 2002), II, Constituencies: Bramber.
4 *Journals of the House of Commons*, 19 November 1690.
5 I. F. Burton, P.W. J. Riley and E. Rowlands, *Political Parties in the Reigns of William III and Anne* (London, 1968); Steve Pincus, *1688: The First Modern Revolution* (New Haven and London, 2009); Henry Horwitz, *Parliament, Policy and Politics in the Reign of William III* (Manchester, 1977); Dennis Rubini, *Court and Country 1688–1702* (London, 1967).
6 Hayton *et al.*, *House of Commons, 1690–1715*, III, Members: Barbon.
7 Narcissus Luttrell, *The Parliamentary Diary of Narcissus Luttrell, 1691–1693*, ed. by H. Horwitz (Oxford, 1972), 22 December 1692, 2 February 1693.
8 TNA, C 10/337/19.
9 TNA, C 8/352/47.
10 *Journals of the House of Commons*, IX, 28 February 1700.
11 TNA, C 9/245/3, C9/244/60.
12 Grascome, Placemen, ff. 1–2.

13 'On Squire Neale's Projects', in *Poems on Affairs of State: Augustan Satirical Verse, 1660–1714*, ed. by George Lord, 7 vols (London, 1963–75), v, pp. 493–96. The King's Bench and Fleet were both prisons, while the Mint and White-Friars were sanctuaries; Alsatia was a slang term for White-Friars and hence an asylum for criminals.
14 Sheppard, *St Anne Soho*, p. 256.
15 H. M. Colvin (ed.), *The History of the King's Works* (London, 1976), v, pp. 401–03.
16 Barbon, *Discourse of Trade*, Preface, pp. 6–7.
17 Barbon, *New money lighter.*
18 Barbon, *New Buildings*, p. 5.
19 Barbon, *Discourse of Trade*, p. 72.
20 Ibid., p. 6.
21 Andrea Finkelstein, *Harmony and the Balance: An Intellectual History of Seventeenth-Century English Economic Thought* (Ann Arbor, Michigan, 2000), pp. 205–34.
22 Barbon, *Discourse of Trade*, p. 4.
23 Ibid., p. 20.
24 Ibid., p. 37.
25 Ibid., p. 27.
26 Luttrell, *Parliamentary Diary*, 24 January 1693
27 Barbon, *Discourse of Trade*, p. 34.
28 Ibid., p. 63.
29 Ibid., pp. 67–68.
30 Ibid., p. 69.
31 Luttrell, *Parliamentary Diary*, 17 February 1693.
32 *Journals of the House of Commons*, 20 March 1694.
33 Barbon, *New money lighter*, p. 43.
34 Barbon, *Discourse of Trade*, p. 78.
35 Barbon, *New money lighter*, p. 59.
36 Ibid., p. 40.
37 See discussion in Vickers, *Theory of Money*, p. 91 *et seq.*
38 Barbon, *Discourse of Trade*, p. 32.
39 Ibid., pp. 31–32.
40 The pamphlet is attributed to Barbon by both Stephen Bauer, *Dictionary of Political Economy*, ed. by R. H. I. Palgrave, 3 vols (London, 1894), I: *Nicholas Barbon*, and Tyler Cowen, 'Nicholas Barbon and the Origins of Economic Liberalism', in *Research in the History of Economic Thought and Methodology*, 4 (1986), pp. 67–83.
41 E. Harris and N. Savage, *British Architectural Books and Writers 1556–1785* (London, 1990).
42 Emma Rothschild, *Economic Sentiments: Adam Smith, Condorcet, and the Enlightenment* (Cambridge, MA, 2001), pp. 40–41.
43 See for example the discussion in Joyce Appleby, *Economic Thought and Ideology in Seventeenth Century England* (Princeton, NJ, 1978), and Joyce Appleby, *Liberalism and Republicanism in the Historical Imagination* (Cambridge, MA, 1992).
44 Thomas Mun, *A Discourse of Trade from England unto the East Indies* (London, 1621).
45 Thomas Mun, *England's Treasure by Forraign Trade or the Balance of Forraign Trade is the Rule of Our Treasure* (London, 1664).
46 Barbon, *Discourse of Trade*, p. 5.
47 Josiah Child, *Brief Observations concerning Trade, and Interest of Money* (London, 1668); Josiah Child, *A Discourse about Trade* (London, 1690), p. 161; Josiah Child, *A New Discourse of Trade* (London, 1693).
48 E. H., *Reasons for the abatement of interest to four in the hundred and the objections against it fairly stated and briefly answered* (London, 1692), British Library T.1593.(4).
49 Dudley North died on 31 December 1691. His *Discourses* were published shortly thereafter in what would be 1692 by the modern calendar but was then still the year 1691 (which ended on 24 March).
50 Dudley North, A *Discourse concerning the abatement of Interest* (London, 1691), p. 4; Dudley North, *A Discourse of Coyned Money* (London, 1691), pp. 13 and 15.
51 Dudley North, *Coyned Money*, p. 22.
52 Roger North, 'Preface to Sir Dudley North's *Discourses on Trade*', in *The Life of the Honourable Sir Dudley North* ..., ed. by Montagu North (London, 1744), p. 9.
53 See discussion in William Letwin, *The Origin of Scientific Economics* (London, 1963), Appendix IV.
54 Matthew Walker, *Architects and Intellectual Culture in Post-Restoration* England (Oxford, 2017), p. 9.
55 Barbon, *New money lighter*, p. 43.
56 'As defence, however, is of much more importance than opulence, the act of navigation is, perhaps, the wisest of all the commercial regulations of England', Adam Smith, *An Inquiry into the Nature and Causes of The Wealth of Nations*, 2 vols (London, 1776), II, Book IV, p. 46.
57 Barbon, *Discourse of Trade*, p. 61.
58 TNA, C 66/3374 No. 5, C 54/4776 No. 20; Barbon, *An Advertisement being a Proposal.*

CHAPTER IX NEMESIS IN HOLBORN

1 TNA, C 5/292/68.
2 Joyce Godber, *The Harpur Trust 1552–1973* (Bedford, 1973), pp. 8–10.
3 Godber, *Harpur Trust*, pp. 163–64.
4 TNA, C 5/72/88; Godber, *Harpur Trust*, p. 10.
5 TNA, C 8/302/60, C 8/337/139.
6 TNA, C 5/144/7.
7 TNA, C 5/178/4, C 5/187/61, C 5/187/67.
8 C. F. Farrar, *Harpur's Bedford Charity* (Bedford, 1930), pp. 8–10.
9 TNA, C 5/187/67, C 5/72/88; Godber, *Harpur Trust*, pp. 11–12.
10 TNA, C 5/72/88, C 5/292/68, PROB11/449/217.
11 Farrar, *Harpur's Bedford Charity*, p. 12.
12 Camden Local Studies and Archives Centre, M1390.
13 Farrar, *Harpur's Bedford Charity*, p. 14.
14 R. J. B. Pooley, *The History of St Clement Danes Holborn Estate Grammar School, 1552–1952* (London, 1960).
15 City of Westminster Archives Centre, B1060 and B1296; TNA, C 10/225/12.
16 This may have been John Prince 'junior' (d. 1748) who worked in Marylebone and Covent Garden in the early eighteenth century, or perhaps his father (H. M. Colvin, *A Biographical Dictionary of British Architects, 1600–1840*, 4th edn (London and New Haven, 2007).
17 TNA, C 7/152/40; City of Westminster Archives Centre, B1296 and St Clement Danes Holborn Estate Trustees Papers 1576/Box 70.
18 Philip Norman, 'On an Ancient Conduit-head in Queen Square, Bloomsbury', *Archaeologia*, 56 (1899), pp. 251–66; Philip Norman, 'On the White Conduit, Chapel Street, Bloomsbury, and its Connexion with the Grey Friars' Water System', *Archaeologia*, 61 (1909), pp. 347–56.
19 Philip Norman, 'Queen Square, Bloomsbury, and its Neighbourhood', *London Topographical Record*, 10 (1916), facing p. 3.
20 Henry A. Harben, *A Dictionary of London* (London, 1918), p. 303; Ben Weinreb and Christopher Hibbert, *The London Encylopaedia* (London 1983), p. 441; Guy Thompson and Amanda Fairman, 'Muddy Fields, Litigation, Disputes and Ditches: The Story of a Site at Roger Street, Camden', *London Topographical Record*, 32 (2021), pp. 203–23.
21 W. H. D. Rouse, *A History of Rugby School* (London, 1898), pp. 10–18.
22 Rouse, *Rugby School*, pp. 384 and 404; David Flintham, *The English Civil War Defences of London* (Bristol, 2014), p. 31; Norman, *Ancient Conduit-head*, p. 263; TNA, C 7/92/93.
23 Luttrell, *Brief Historical Relation*, I, p. 263.
24 Rouse, *Rugby School*, p. 88; Camden Local Studies and Archives Centre, M0163 and M0521a.
25 Camden Local Studies and Archives Centre, M0615 and M0663–0664.
26 TNA, C 113/202 Part 2; Camden Local Studies and Archives Centre, M0615.
27 Philip Norman, *Ancient Conduit-head*, pp. 251–66.
28 LMA, ACC/2558/MW/C/15/059, ACC/2558/MW/C/15/322.
29 TNA, C 7/92/93.
30 TNA, C 5/113/70 and C 5/148/21.
31 TNA, C 5/148/21, C 113/193 Part 1; McKellar, *Birth of Modern London*, pp. 124–25 and 225–28.
32 Camden Local Studies and Archives Centre, M0663.
33 TNA, C 5/251/11, C 5/218/38, PROB11/449/217, C 5/203/51.
34 TNA, C 5/151/43, C 5/251/11.
35 TNA, C 5/155/66, C 113/191 Part 1, C 113/192, C113/202 Part 2; British Library, Maps Crace Port. 15.27; the extent of Milman's property holdings elsewhere can be seen in a 1720 settlement of his estate in TNA, C 113/191 part 1.
36 TNA, C 113/191 Part 1, C 113/192, C 113/193 Part 1.
37 TNA, C 113/203 Part 2, C 5/203/51, C 5/218/38, C 113/202 Part 2.
38 *Journals of the House of Commons*, XI, pp. 97, 250, 359, 438, 440; Farrar, *Harpur's Bedford Charity*, p. 13.
39 Lambeth Palace Library, MS2735; LMA, P82/GEO2/047/01–03; M. H. Port (ed.), 'Minutes of the Commission for Building Fifty New Churches', *London Record Society*, 23 (1976).
40 See above p. 189.
41 TNA, C 54/4700 No. 43, C 5/155/41; RIBA, British Architectural Library, Talman Drawings; John Harris, *William Talman: Maverick Architect* (London, 1982), p. 24; Great Ormond Street is called Kent Street in some of the leases scheduled in TNA, C 5/251/11.
42 Camden Local Studies and Archives Centre, M1390.
43 TNA, C 7/258/75.
44 TNA, C 54/4777 No. 20.
45 TNA, C 54/4789 No. 8.
46 TNA, C 105/21.
47 TNA, C 8/614/9, C 6/345/61.
48 LMA, CLC/522/MS01898; TNA, C 5/251/11, C 54/4700 No. 43.
49 TNA, C 5/155/66, C 10/244/50, C 113/202 Part 2; Frank Kelsall, 'Why 99 Years?', *London Topographical Society Newsletter*, 76 (2013), p. 10.

50 TNA, C 54/4700 No. 43, C 5/144/1, C 5/155/41.
51 David Pearce, *London's Mansions* (London, 1986), pp. 44–48; W. Edward Riley and Laurence Gomme (eds), *Survey of London*, vol. III: *St Giles in the Fields* (London, 1912), 1, p. 116; National Library of Wales, Powis Castle Estate Records, 12732; LMA, MDR/1713/002/99.
52 Christopher Clay, *Public Finance and Private Wealth: The Career of Sir Stephen Fox, 1627–1716* (London, 1978), passim.
53 Strype, *Survey*, 1, Book III, Chapter XII, p. 254; for the dating of the compilation of this edition see Stanley Rubinstein, *Historians of London* (London, 1968) and L. Worms, 'A Note on the Maps and Plans contained in the Eighteenth-century Editions of Stow's *Survey*', in Ralph Hyde *et al.*, *London Parish Maps to 1900* (London Topographical Society publication, No. 183, 2020), pp. 30–33.
54 Defoe, *A Tour through the whole Island*, 1, pp. 328–29.
55 Riley and Gomme, *St Giles* (London, 1912), 1, pp. 1–10; Brett James, *Stuart London*, pp. 152–60; A. Saunders, P. Barber and R. Hyde, *The A to Z of Charles II's London, 1682* (London Topographical Society publication, No. 174, 2013), pl. 20, p. 30.
56 TNA, C 54/4849 No. 18.
57 TNA, C 10/214/19, C 10/224/3; British Library, Add. MS 33576, f. 66; E. Fairfax Taylor and Felix Skene (calendared by), *Manuscripts of the House of Lords, 1678–93*, 4 vols (London, 1887–94), 1, pp. 59–61 and II, pp. 304–05; W. P. Baildon (ed.), *The Records of the Honorable Society of Lincoln's Inn: the Black Books*, 6 vols (London, 1897–2001), III, 18 May 1680, 5 and 28 November 1681, 28 June 1682, 5 July 1682, 17 November 1684, 27 April 1686, 9 May 1688, 19 June 1689.
58 Private Act 2, William & Mary Session 2, c.17, 1690; TNA, C 8/379/4; Calendar State Papers, Domestic: James II, February–December 1685, pp. 183 and 238; LMA, WCS/332/021; *Black Books*, III, 13 and 20 May 1685.
59 *Black Books*, III, 2 January 1691, 3, 9, 12 and 17 February 1691; TNA, C 54/4738 No. 21, C 54/4739/ No. 2.
60 *Black Books*, III, 1 July 1691, 6 November 1691, 12 and 17 February 1692; https://rictornorton.co.uk/though12.htm [accessed 31 August 2021]; University of Oxford, Bodleian Library, MS Carte 76, f. 185; Lincolnshire Archives, Fane 3/1/D/5; Hampshire Archives, 15M50/1360; Huntingdonshire Archives, CON/3/6/1/3–4; TNA, C 5/599/23, C 8/352/47.
61 *Black Books*, III, 21 June 1692; LMA, MDR/1726/3/198; TNA, C 54/4760 No. 15, C 54/4819 No. 7, C 54/4849 No. 18, C 6/336/7.
62 *Black Books*, III, 13 and 20 November 1696.
63 Shepherd's Market was later built on the southern part of Brookfield; see plan in Johnson, *Berkeley Square*, facing p. 240.
64 TNA, C 54/4685 Nos 17 and 18, /4687 No. 4, C 5/151/43; LMA, 4019/B/07/011.
65 TNA, PC 2/71 f. 10.
66 Gater and Hiorns, *St Martin-in-the-Fields*, p. 95; Sheppard, *St James Westminster, Part 1*, 1, pp. 215–16; Sheppard, *St. Anne Soho*, 2, pp. 365–66; Johnson, *Berkeley Square*, p. 64; TNA, C 54/4685 No. 17, C 54/4687 No. 4.
67 Parliamentary Archives, HL/PO/JO/10/6/7/1570.
68 Johnson, *Berkeley Square*, pp. 64–65.
69 Ibid., p. 163.
70 LMA, 4019/B/07/010, 011 and 040; Johnson, *Berkeley Square*, pp. 74–75, 113 and 163.

CHAPTER X LAND BANKS

1 Richard Kleer, 'Fictitious Cash: English Public Finance and Paper Money, 1689–97', in *Money, Power and Print*, ed. by Charles McGrath and Chris Fauske (London, 2008), pp. 70–114; John Brewer, *The Sinews of Power* (London, 1988).
2 Clapham, *Bank of England*, p. 19.
3 Defoe, *Projects*, p. 67.
4 The detailed history of the Land Banks is dealt with by J. K. Horsefield, *British Monetary Experiments 1650–1710* (London, 1960), pp. 125–79; Dennis Rubini, 'Politics and the Battle for the Banks', *English Historical Review*, 85/337 (1970), pp. 691–714; Richard Kleer, 'Fictitious Cash'; Steve Pincus and Alice Wolfram, 'A Proactive State? The Land Bank, Investment and Party Politics in the 1690s', in *Regulating the British Economy 1660–1850*, ed. by Perry Gauci (Farnham, 2011; London, 2016). The most recent, and fullest, description is Richard Kleer, *Money, Politics and Power* (London, 2017).
5 John Briscoe, *A Discourse on the Late Funds of the Million Bank, Lottery Act, and Bank of England, showing that they are Injurious to the Nobility and Gentry and Ruinous to the Trade of the Nation* (London, 1694).
6 Clapham, *Bank of England*, p. 34; David Kynaston, *Till Time's Last Stand. A History of the Bank of England 1694–2013* (London, 2017), p. 15.
7 Thomas Macaulay, *The History of England from the Accession of James II* (London, 1848).
8 Kleer, *Money, Politics and Power.*
9 Barbon, *Discourse of Trade*, pp. 21–22.
10 Luttrell, *Parliamentary Diary*, 24 January 1693.
11 Leopold von Ranke, *History of England*, 6 vols (Oxford, 1875), VI, p. 259. James Vernon letter to Lord Lexington, 18 December 1694, British Library, Add. MS 46527, ff. 33–34.
12 'On Squire Neale's Projects', pp. 493–96. Gabel is a tax, particularly on salt, while a cully is a fool who gets cheated.
13 John Asgill and Nicholas Barbon, *A Proposal for a Subscription to raise £100,000 for circulating the credit of a Land Bank* (London, 1695).
14 The Treasury constantly needed short-term loans. These were secured against specific future tax revenue and incurred

interest. The Exchequer issued its lenders a wooden proof-of-payment, called a tally, and repayment was made in the same order as the original loan. Tallies were made payable to bearer and fully transferable.
15 John Asgill and Nicholas Barbon, *An Account of the Land Bank* (London, 1695).
16 John Briscoe, *The Freehold Estates of England* (London, 1695).
17 Nicholas Barbon and John Asgill (attributed to), *The Freeholders Answer to Mr John Briscoe's Proposals for a National Bank* (London, 1695).
18 John Briscoe, *Mr Briscoe's reply to a Pamphlet intituled the Freeholders' Answer to Mr John Briscoe's Proposals for a National Bank* London, 1695).
19 John Briscoe, *Proposals for raising Money for the National Land Bank* (London, 1695).
20 Edward Harley to Sir Edward Harley, 1 August 1696, British Library, Add. MS 70018, f. 17.
21 John Briscoe, *Advice to the Freeholder* (London, 1695).
22 John Asgill and Nicholas Barbon, *A Letter from a Citizen of London to his Friend in the Country* (London, 1695).
23 John Briscoe, *Advertisement* (London, 1695).
24 Pincus and Wolfram, 'A Proactive State?', pp. 56–57; Anne Murphy, *The Origins of English Financial Markets* (Cambridge, 2009), pp. 150–53.
25 TNA, C 6/331/64. This is the complaint for a civil case brought by those who had deposited cash with Briscoe's bank, attempting to claim payments both from those subscribers who had (allegedly) actually committed themselves to support the bank and those subscribers of specie who had not paid. It gives their version of events, revealing the amount of the losses and the fact that only about half of those who subscribed cash actually paid up even the first ten per cent.
26 Pincus and Wolfram, 'A Proactive State?'. Their study was based on those they could identify through linking them with wills, which only allowed them to identify a small proportion. The proportion of Barbon subscribers that they identified was small. In particular, the suggested high proportion of subscribers from the West Midlands arises solely from their small sample and the relatively large number of Harleys, Foleys and their associates who came from Worcestershire and Herefordshire. The Chancery complaint cited in note 25 above gives the county of every land subscriber to Briscoe's bank who actually committed funds to the bank.
27 Walker, *Clapham Saints*, ch. 7.
28 TNA, C 6/318/30.
29 TNA, C 113/201.
30 Minutes of the National Land Bank, September 1695–January 1696 (University of London, Senate House Library, MS61).
31 TNA, C 6/331/64.
32 John Asgill, *Several Assertions Proved, in order to create another species of Money than Gold and Silver* (London, 1696).
33 John Asgill, *An Argument, proving, that the Reason given by the Directors of the Bank of England, against Settling any other Bank, viz. because they are already settled, is the highest Reason for it* (London, 1695).
34 William Atwood, *A safe and easy method for supplying the want of coin* (London, 1695).
35 Kleer, *Money, Politics and Power*, p. 103.
36 *Reasons against a Land Bank contained in a Dialogue between a Yeoman, a Merchant and a Land-Banker* (1696).
37 Ibid.
38 John Briscoe (attributed to), *Mr J Asgill his Plagiarism detected* (London, 1696), p. 42.
39 Hugh Chamberlain, *An answer to a Libel* (London, 1696).
40 John Asgill, Nicholas Barbon and John Briscoe, *A Scheme for a National Land Bank* (London, 1696).
41 Robert Price to Duke of Beaufort, 11 February 1696 (University of Oxford, Bodleian Library, MS Carte 130, f. 359).
42 Ibid.
43 *The Trial and Condemnation of the Trustees of the Land Bank at Exeter Exchange for murdering the Bank of England at Grocers Hall* (London, 1696).
44 *A Second Discourse about Banks; Between a Brigadier, a Lawyer, a Merchant, and a Goldsmith* (London, 1696).
45 William Tindall, *Some remarks upon the Bank and other pretended banks* (London, 1696).
46 *Mr B---coe's Reply to the Almanack, being Land and money United; or B----coe and the B-k of E---nd joined* (London, 1696).
47 Horsefield, *British Monetary Experiments*, p. 207.
48 Barbon, *New money lighter.*
49 TNA, C 6/331/64.
50 Nicholas Barbon, *A proposal for Raising the Public Credit, by Setting up an Office for Transferring and Discounting Tallies* (London, 1696).
51 Letter of Francis Gwyn to the Marquess of Halifax, 3 August 1696 (British Library, Add. MS 75370).
52 TNA, C 6/331/64.
53 *The Postman*, p. 558, *The Post-Boy*, p. 584, *The Flying Post*, pp. 570, 3–5 January 1699.

CHAPTER XI MONEY, MONEY, MONEY

1 William Lowndes, *A Report Containing an Essay for the Amendment of the Silver Coins* (London, 1695).
2 John Locke, *Some Considerations of the Consequences of the Lowering of Interest and Raising the Value of Money* (London, 1692); *Some Observations on a Printed Paper, Intituled For Encouraging the Coining Silver Money in England, and after keeping it there* (London, 1695); *Further Considerations Concerning Raising the Value of Money* (London, 1695).

3 Barbon, *Discourse of Trade*, p. 21.
4 Locke, *Some Considerations.*
5 Some of the more recent include Kleer, *Money Politics and Power*; Christine Desan, *Making Money: Coin, Currency, and the Coming of Capitalism* (Oxford, 2014); Daniel Carey (ed.), *Money and Political Economy in the Enlightenment* (Oxford, 2014). Others include Murphy, *English Financial Markets*; Thomas Sargent and François Velde, *The Big Problem of Small Change* (Princeton, NJ, 2002); Patrick Kelly, *Locke on Money* (Oxford, 1991); Jones, *War and Economy*; Appleby, *Economic Thought*; P. G. M. Dickson, *The Financial Revolution in England: A Study in the Development of Public Credit, 1688–1756* (London, 1967); Minh-Hsun Li, *The Great Recoinage of 1696–9* (London, 1963); Horsefield, *British Monetary Experiments.*
6 Arbitrage is the simultaneous purchase and sale of the same asset in different markets in order to profit from tiny differences in the asset's listed price.
7 Stephen Quinn, 'Gold, Silver, and the Glorious Revolution', *Economic History Review*, 49 (1996), pp. 473–90.
8 Economic modelling work by Sargent and his collaborators has demonstrated that the effect of a shortage of small coins is to cause them to depreciate, in time causing the content of the coin to be worth more as metal than coin: Sargent and Velde, *Small Change*; Thomas Sargent and Brian Smith, 'Coinage, Debasement, and Gresham's Laws', *Economic Theory*, 10 (1997), pp. 197–226; François Velde and Warren Weber, 'A Model of Bimetallism', *Journal of Political Economy*, 108 (2000), pp. 1210–34; Angela Redish, *A Model of Commodity Money with Minting and Melting* (Minneapolis, 2011). It has been argued that Sargent and Velde's model is too simplistic and there are other important factors, but while this may have been so for a range of mediaeval coinages, the model's assumptions appear reasonable enough for England's economy in the late seventeenth century: Isabel Schnabel, 'Review of Sargent and Velde, *Small Change*', *Financial History Review*, 12/2 (2005), pp. 311–13; Oliver Volckart, *The Big Problem of the Petty Coins and How It Could Be Solved in the Late Middle Ages*, Economic History Working Papers, London School of Economics, No. 107 (2008); Oliver Volckart, *Premodern Debasement: A Messy Affair*, Economic History Working Papers, London School of Economics, No. 270 (2017).
9 Minh-Hsun Li, *Great Recoinage*, p. 54.
10 Jones, *War and Economy*, p. 231.
11 Minh-Hsun Li, *Great Recoinage*, p. 31.
12 Kleer, *Money, Politics and Power*, p. 154.
13 Jones, *War and Economy*, pp. 240–41.
14 A. E. Feavearyear, The Pound Sterling. A History of English Money (London, 1931), pp. 109–33; Clapham, *Bank of England*, pp. 45–46.
15 Luttrell, Parliamentary Diary, 31 December 1692.
16 Colley Cibber, *Love's Last Shift; or, The Fool in Fashion* (London, 1696); see also Mattie Burkert, 'Virtue is as Much Debased as Our Money: Generic and Economic Instability in Love's Last Shift', *Modern Philology*, 114 (2016), pp. 59–81.
17 Lowndes, *Amendment of the Silver Coins*, p. 84.
18 Newton's paper is reproduced in Ming-Hsun Li, *Great Recoinage*, Appendix III, pp. 217–23. See also Thomas Levenson, *Newton and the Counterfeiter* (London, 2009), pp. 109–21.
19 Kleer, *Money, Politics and Power*, pp. 115–35, 171–86.
20 Patrick Kelly, 'Monkey Business: Locke's College Correspondence and the Adoption of the Plan for the Great Recoinage of 1696', in *Locke Studies*, 9 (2009), pp. 139–65.
21 Kelly, *Locke on Money*, table 6, p. 119. See also Richard Kleer, '"The Ruine of their Diana." Lowndes, Locke and the Bankers', in *History of Political Economy*, 36/3 (2004), pp. 533–56.
22 Locke, *Further Considerations*, in *Works*, IV (London, 1824), p. 144.
23 Ibid., p. 179.
24 David Fox, *The Case of Mixt Monies*, University of Cambridge, Faculty of Law, Research Paper, No. 70 (2014).
25 Locke, *Further Considerations*, p. 140. This comment of Locke drew the response from a later commentator: 'this is undeniably true in every instance except that to which the author applied it, namely the currency; for as the money was fixed at five shillings and two pence the ounce, by law, it was impossible that it should be at all times of the same value as an equal quantity of bullion, which must be liable to perpetual variations of price, according to the quantity, and the demand in the market'. Rogers Ruding, *Annals of the Coinage of Great Britain and its Dependencies*, 6 vols (London, 1817–19), II, p. 42.
26 Locke, *Further Considerations*, p. 194.
27 Lowndes, *Amendment of the Silver Coins*, p. 115.
28 Kelly, *Locke on Money*, p. 35.
29 Ibid., p. 103.
30 John Locke letter to William Molyneux, 30 March 1696 (E. S. de Beer (ed.), *The Correspondence of John Locke*, 8 vols (Oxford, 1976–89), IV).
31 Lord Somers letter to Duke of Shrewsbury, 4 November 1695.
32 Levenson, *Newton*, pp. 45, 120.
33 Richard Temple, *Some Short Remarks on Mr Locke's Book in Answer to Mr Lounds and Several Other Books and Pamphlets Concerning Coin* (London, 1696).
34 Kleer, *Money, Politics and Power*, pp. 160, 181; E. H., *Decus et Tutamen; or our New Money as now coined in full weight proved to be for the Honour, Safety, and Advantage of England — written by way of answer to Sir Richard Temple and Dr Barbon* (London, 1696).
35 Samuel Grascome, *An Account of the Proceedings in the House of Commons in Relation to the Recoining the Clipp'd Money, and Falling the Price of Guineas* (London, 1696).

36 University of Oxford, Bodleian Library, MS Locke b.3, ff. 114–18.
37 John Locke letter to Edward Clarke MP, 8 April 1696.
38 Barbon, *New money lighter*, Preface.
39 John Evelyn, Diary, 13 May 1696, 11 June 1696.
40 Quoted in Henry Horwitz, *Parliament, Policy and Politics in the Reign of William III* (Manchester, 1977), p. 180.
41 Barbon, *New money lighter*, Preface.
42 Ibid., Preface.
43 Barbon, *Discourse of Trade*, p. 18.
44 Barbon, *New money lighter*, Preface, p. 92.
45 Ibid., p. 80.
46 Ibid., p. 96.
47 James Hodges, *The Present State of England, as to Coin and Public Charges* (London, 1697); John Briscoe, *A Discourse of Money &c in Historical and Political Essays or Discourses on Several Subjects* (London, 1698).
48 Lowndes, *Amendment of the Silver Coins*, p. 81.
49 Horsefield, *British Monetary Experiments*, pp. 23–36.
50 Quoted in Brodie Waddell, 'The Politics of Economic Distress in the Aftermath of the Glorious Revolution, 1689–1702', *English Historical Review*, 130 (2015), pp. 541–70.
51 G. Findlay Shirras and J. M. Craig, 'Sir Isaac Newton and the Currency', *Economic Journal*, 55 (1945), pp. 217–41. See also Thomas Levenson, *Money for Nothing* (London 2020), pp. 52–65.
52 Locke, *Further Considerations*, p. 148.
53 Barbon, *Discourse of Trade*, pp. 18–19.
54 Isaac Newton, *Observations on Mr Pollexfen's reply*, Part 3, 1701 (TNA, MINT 19/2/631-2).
55 Vickers, *Theory of Money*, p. 75, n.7.
56 Valenze, *Social Life of Money*, pp. 41–43; Weiss Smith, 'Foundation in Nature', pp. 210–28.
57 Thomas Macaulay, *History of England from the Accession of James II*, 5 vols (London, 1848), IV, chapters 21 and 22. Macaulay was unaware that Newton had supported devaluation and he grossly underestimated the effect of recoinage on the poor.
58 Kleer, 'Ruine of their Diana'.
59 Vickers, *Theory of Money*, pp. 74–93.
60 J. R. McCulloch, 'BARBON (Nicholas), esq.', in *Dictionnaire de l'Économie politique*, ed. by C. Coquelin (Paris, 1852), vol. I, p. 145. This was a translation of the comment in J. R. McCulloch, *Literature of Political Economy* (London, 1845), p. 157, which said, 'This gross and unaccountable error destroyed the influence of Barbon's tract; and was most probably the cause of the oblivion into which it very soon fell and of its never having attracted that attention to which, on other accounts, it was entitled.'

CHAPTER XII SITES AND DESIGN

1 Mills and Oliver, *Survey.*
2 Mills and Oliver, *Survey*, vol. 97, p. xxvi.
3 Goldsmiths (Crane Court), Grocers (Mincing Lane) and Skinners (College Hill).
4 North, *Autobiography*, p. 53.
5 Slack, *Improvement*, pp. 4–5.
6 TNA, C 6/77/19.
7 Gater and Wheeler, *St Martin-in-the-Fields II, The Strand*, 2, pp. 51–60.
8 Essex House, Exeter House, Old Devonshire House, Newport House, Trevor House, Derby House, Carew House.
9 North, *Autobiography*, p. 54.
10 Ibid., p. 55.
11 Ibid., p. 54.
12 Rouse, *Rugby School*, p. 88.
13 TNA, C 9/124/85.
14 Summerson, *Georgian London*, 3rd edn (1978), p. 35.
15 Ibid.; Donald J. Olsen, *Town Planning in London* (London and New Haven, 1982).
16 North, *Autobiography*, p. 57.
17 TNA, C 8/230/72.
18 TNA, C 5/144/1.
19 TNA, C 8/269/79, C 8/388/32, C 6/86/78.
20 Chiz Harward, Nick Holder and Nigel Jeffries, *The Spitalfields Suburb 1539–1880*, Museum of London Archaeology Monograph 61 (London, 2015), p. 157. The example given is for No. 28 Fort Street.
21 Ibid., p. 158.
22 Barbon, *Apology for the Builder*, p. 1.
23 *Middle Temple Records: Minutes of Parliament*, 15 and 22 June 1687.
24 TNA, C 9/457/109, C 10/230/7.
25 One example is for his Essex House development, see TNA, C 8/269/79.
26 TNA, C 9/124/85.

27 TNA, C 8/269/79.
28 TNA, C 78/1210.
29 North, *Autobiography*, p. 54.
30 TNA, C 9/92/3.
31 TNA, C 9/124/85.
32 North, *Autobiography*, p. 53.
33 TNA, C 8/231/25.
34 TNA, C 8/420/53, C 5/144/1.
35 TNA, C 54/4740 No. 8.
36 https://www.danielwatney.co.uk/knowledge/case-studies/42-43-bedford-row [accessed 18 August 2021].
37 Olsen, *Town Planning*, p. 43.
38 Summerson, *Georgian London*, p. 45.
39 TNA, C 5/144/1.
40 TNA, C 5/148/21.
41 LMA, CLC/L/TG/E/003/MS03047/001 (former reference, Guildhall Library MS 3047).
42 Robert Shepherd, 'Shell or Finished House?', *The Georgian Group Journal*, 29 (2021), pp. 67–82.
43 LMA, ACC/0349/293.
44 Kelsall, 'London House Plan', fig. 5, p. 85.
45 Stephen Primatt, *The City and Country Purchaser and Builder* (1667) as reissued by William Leybourn, British Library, 1043.k.2.
46 Kelsall, 'London House Plan', pp. 80–91.
47 Peter Guillery, *The Small House in Eighteenth-Century London* (London and New Haven, 2014), pp. 63–66.
48 Colvin and Newman, *Of Building*, p. 69.
49 Walker, *Clapham Saints*, pp. 180–84.
50 Colvin and Newman, *Of Building*, p. 25.

CHAPTER XIII FINANCE AND LEGAL

1 TNA, C 8/231/25.
2 Primatt, *The City and Country Purchaser*, pp. 13–14: 'Lands in fee simple in and around London [...] are for the most part valuable at twenty years' purchase.' There was continuing argument about whether the external interest rate affected this calculation. Locke claimed that the return on land was independent of the external rate, while those who argued for lower external interest rates believed they would increase the years purchase, e.g., a 4 per cent interest rate would result in land being valued at twenty-five years' purchase. For discussion of these points see H. J. Habbakuk, 'The Long-Term Rate of Interest and the Price of Land in the Seventeenth Century', *The Economic History Review*, 5/1 (1952), pp. 26–45; Robert C. Allen, 'The Price of Freehold Land and the Interest Rate in the Seventeenth and Eighteenth Century', *The Economic History Review*, 41/1 (1988), pp. 33–50; Asgill and Barbon, *Account of the Land Bank*.
3 Sheppard, *St Anne Soho*, 2, pp. 360–79.
4 Sims, 'Trust Lands', pp. 88–113.
5 Guillery, *Whitechapel*.
6 TNA, C 5/292/68.
7 North, *Autobiography*, pp. 54, 57.
8 Barbon, *Propositions*.
9 See Chapter VI for a full discussion of these transactions.
10 TNA, T 4/1, ff. 212–13.
11 Colvin, *King's Works*, v, p. 207.
12 TNA, C 9/244/60.
13 TNA, C 7/148/37.
14 North, *Autobiography*, p. 55.
15 TNA, C 8/555/84; Sheppard, *St Anne Soho*, pp. 360–79.
16 Frank T. Melton, *Sir Robert Clayton and the Origins of English Deposit Banking 1658–1685* (London, 1986), p. 38.
17 D. C. Coleman, 'London Scriveners and the Estate Market in the later Seventeenth Century', *Economic History Review*, 4 (1951), pp. 221–30.
18 North, *Autobiography*, p. 55.
19 TNA, C 9/245/3.
20 Jones, *War and Economy*, pp. 279–81; John Pollexfen, *A Discourse of Trade* (London, 1696), pp. 72–73.
21 TNA, C 8/203/95.
22 Melton, *Robert Clayton*, p. 39.
23 TNA, C 8/241/22.
24 Melton, *Robert Clayton*, p. 77.
25 TNA, C 8/263/71, C8/263/91.
26 TNA, C 8/263/91.
27 TNA, C 7/148/37.
28 TNA, C 5/226/43.

29 TNA, C 18/236/6.
30 Sheppard, *St Anne Soho*, pp. 27–36.
31 TNA, C 8/248/10.
32 L. R., *To my honoured friend Mr M. T.*
33 TNA, C 8/260/63.
34 TNA, C 8/555/84.
35 Andrew Kippis, *Biographica Britannica*, 5 vols (London, 1778–93), I, p. 290.
36 North, *Autobiography*, p. 56.
37 Ibid., p. 54.
38 TNA, C 8/260/63.
39 Henry Horowitz, *Chancery Equity Records and Proceedings, 1600–1800* (London, 1995), p. 15; Christine Churches, 'Business at Law: Retrieving Commercial Disputes from Eighteenth-Century Chancery', *The Historical Journal*, 43/4 (2000), pp. 937–54.
40 TNA, C 10/227/5.
41 TNA, C 10/336/74.
42 *Certiorari* is a writ or order by which a higher court reviews a case tried in a lower court; TNA, C8/352/47.
43 TNA, C 8/248/10.
44 TNA, C 5/453/29. At that time the legal meaning of 'enervate' was 'to render ineffectual'.
45 TNA, E 112/596/451.
46 TNA, C 8/219/41.
47 North, *Autobiography*, p. 57.
48 TNA, C 6/77/19.
49 Roger North, *The Life of the Right Honourable Francis North, Baron of Guilford* (London, 1742), p. 200; James Granger, *A Biographical History of England* (London, 1779), p. 364.
50 Paul D. Halliday, *George Jeffreys, First Baron Jeffreys*, Oxford Dictionary of National Biography (London, 2004).
51 Keeton, *Jeffreys and the Stuart Cause*, pp. 508–09.
52 TNA, C 10/481/99.
53 TNA, C 8/241/22.
54 Melton, *Robert Clayton.*
55 TNA, C 6/94/7.
56 Arthur Capel, *Essex Papers*, 47, p. 323.
57 TNA, C 8/255/116, C 5/491/85, C 6/77/19, C 78/1210.
58 TNA, C 5/187/67.
59 TNA, C 8/388/7, C 8/404/23.
60 TNA, C 8/260/63.
61 TNA, C 10/413/36.
62 LMA, Westminster and Middlesex Commission of Sewers, Orders of Court (Minutes): WCS/041, vol. 5, f. 159, Saturday 28 January 1682; WCS/042, vol. 6, f. 59, 8 June 1683; WCS/042, vol. 6, f. 61, 12 June 1683; WCS/042, vol. 6, f. 104, 14 August 1684; WCS/042, vol. 6, f. 70, 22 August 1683; WCS/044, vol. 8, f. 24, 5 January 1694.
63 TNA, C 8/238/19.
64 TNA, C 10/337/19, C 9/245/3 and C9/244/60; *Journals of the House of Commons*, IX, 28 February 1700.
65 Grascome, Placemen, ff. 1–2; TNA, C 8/352/47.
66 TNA, C 5/251/11.
67 TNA, C 8/238/19.
68 Middlesex Sessions Book 544, May and June 1697, p. 39.
69 TNA, C 10/270/21.
70 TNA, C 10/181/4.
71 TNA, C 8/263/91.
72 TNA, E 112/596/451.
73 TNA, C 5.144/1.
74 Ibid.
75 TNA, PROB 11/600/523.
76 Sheppard, *St. Anne Soho*, pp. 107, 114n., 384.
77 Hermione Hobhouse (ed.), *Survey of London*, vol. 42*: Kensington Square to Earl's Court* (London, 1986), p. 5.
78 TNA, E 112/596/451.
79 North, *Autobiography*, p. 57.
80 TNA, E 112/596/451.
81 TNA, C 7/543/52.
82 L. R., *To my honoured friend Mr M.T.*; L. R., *A Second letter.*
83 TNA, C 8/309/23.
84 TNA, C 10/336/74.
85 Stephen Quinn, 'Balances and Goldsmith Bankers; The Coordination and Control of Inter-Banker Debt Clearing in Seventeenth Century London', in *Goldsmiths, Silversmiths and Bankers*, ed. by David Mitchell (London, 1993), pp. 53–76; Dorothy K. Clark, 'Edward Blackwell as a Royal Agent', *The Economic History Review*, 9/1 (1938), pp. 45–55.
86 TNA, C 8/260/63, C 10/283/68, C 8/260/63.

87 Hainsworth, *Lowther*, pp. 510–11.
88 TNA, C 10/454/86.
89 Hatton, *New View*, I, p. 31.
90 Johnson, *Berkeley Square*, pp. 87–98.
91 Sheppard, *St. Anne Soho*, pp. 31–32.
92 TNA, C 5/83/15 and C 7/581/69.
93 Sheppard, *St. Anne Soho*, p 36.
94 TNA, C 10/454/96.
95 TNA, C 5/144/1.

CHAPTER XIV LAST YEARS

1 LMA, ACC/0435/M/004–06.
2 TNA, E 112/690/697.
3 TNA, C 11/1503/3.
4 TNA, E 112/690/697.
5 *The Post Boy*, 5–7 April 1698; Luttrell, *Brief Historical Relation*, IV, p. 364; Lexington Papers, Vernon-Shrewsbury letters, 7 April 1698. British Library, Add. MS 46527.
6 Parish Register, St Leonard, Heston.
7 Biscoe Newsletters, 30 July 1698. James Marshall and Marie-Louise Osborn Collection, Beinecke Rare Book and Manuscript Library, Yale University.
8 Parish Register, St Leonard, Heston; Luttrell, *Brief Historical Relation*, IV, p. 409; *The Post Boy*, 20 July 1698.
9 William Cobbett, *Parliamentary History of England*, 12 vols (London, 1806–12), VI, pp. 600–01.
10 Hayton *et al.*, *House of Commons, 1690–1715*, III, Members: Asgill.
11 TNA, PROB 11/449/217.
12 TNA, C 9/245/3, C9/244/60.
13 TNA, C 7/169/26.
14 TNA, C 5/151/43, C 5/251/11.
15 TNA, C 5/72/88.
16 TNA, C 9/440/94.
17 TNA, C 10/413/36, C 6/342/50, C 6/333/41, C 8/564/56, C 5/72/88, C 5/203/51, C 113/203 Part 2.
18 TNA, C 5/72/88.
19 TNA, C 11/1503/3; LMA, ACC/0436/001.
20 Ibid.
21 TNA, C 10/413/36.
22 TNA, C 6/342/50, C 6/333/41.
23 TNA, C 8/564/56.
24 Black Books, 21 June 1692; LMA, MDR/1726/3/198; TNA, C 54/4760 No. 15, C 54/4819 No. 7, C 54/4849 No. 18, C 6/336/7.
25 TNA, C 5/72/88.
26 TNA, C 5/203/51, C 113/203 Part 2.
27 Montagu H. Cox (ed.), Survey of L*ondon, vol. 10: St Margaret, Westminster (London, 1926), 1, p. 62.*
28 North, *Guilford*, p. 100.
29 Clay, *Stephen Fox*, pp. 175–76. Fox eventually married a second time and had two sons who lived to adulthood, one of whom was the famous politician Henry Fox, later Lord Holland.
30 TNA, C 251/11.
31 Hainsworth, *Lowther*, pp. 510–11.

CHAPTER XV CONCLUSIONS

1 'On Squire Neale's Projects', p. 494. 'Bum' refers to bum-bailiff, defined by the Oxford English Dictionary as 'A bailiff empowered to execute writs and warrants, esp. to collect debts or arrest debtors for non-payment'.
2 Chyle, *Wells Cathedral*, p. 67.
3 Hayton *et al.*, *House of Commons, 1690–1715*, I, Introductory Survey: The Politics of the House.
4 W. J. Ashley, 'The Tory Origin of Free Trade Policy', *Quarterly Journal of Economics*, 11/4 (1897), pp. 335–71.
5 North, *Autobiography*, p. 57.
6 TNA, E 112/690/697.
7 Peter Earle, *The Making of the English Middle Class* (London, 1989), p. 291.
8 *Master Worsley's Book*, p. 76.
9 TNA, C 6/86/78; Johnson, *Berkeley Square*, p. 163.
10 Julian Hoppit, 'The Contexts and Contours of British Economic Literature, 1660–1760', *The Historical Journal* 49/1 (2006), p. 89.
11 Nicholas Barbon, *An Answer to a paper entituled Reasons against Reducing Interest Rates to four percent* (London,

1694); Nicholas Barbon. *A proposal for Raising the Public Credit, by Setting up an Office for Transferring and Discounting Tallies* (London, 1696).

12 Barbon, *Discourse of Trade*; Barbon, *Answer to a paper*; Barbon, *New money lighter*; Barbon, *Raising the Public Credit.*

13 TNA, E 112/690/697.

14 'On Squire Neale's Projects', p. 495.

15 Anonymous, *Angliae Tutamen* (London, 1696), pp. 34–35.

16 Barbon, *Discourse of Trade*, p. 27.

17 North, *Autobiography*, p. 57.

18 Ibid., p. 55.

19 Barbon played a significant part in this change. In Covent Garden (and elsewhere, though there is not such good evidence) only about a third of the building lessees were building tradesmen; by the 1670s and 1680s a very much larger proportion of building lessees were tradesmen.

20 Strype, *Survey*, II, Book VI, Chapter V, p. 78; Johnson, *Berkeley Square*, chs 13–18.

21 North, *Autobiography*, p. 53.

22 Summerson, *Georgian London*, 4th edn (1988), p. 30; McKellar, *Birth of Modern London*, pp. 77–79, 148–49.

23 'On Squire Neale's Projects', p. 495.

24 Nicholas Hawksmoor letter to Dr George Clarke, 17 February 1715, in H. M. Colvin and J. S. G. Simmons (eds), *All Souls: An Oxford College and its Buildings* (Oxford, 1989), p. 89.

25 Hermann Muthesius, *The English House* (London, 1979), p. 137 (first published as *Das Englische Haus* (Berlin 1904)).

26 Barbon, *Discourse of Trade*, p. 61.

27 Barbon, *Apology for the Builder*, p. 1; Barbon, *Discourse of Trade*, p. 29; Barbon, *New money lighter*, pp. 51–52.

28 Barbon, *Discourse of Trade*, p. 69.

29 E. H., *Reasons for the abatement of interest.*

30 E. H., *Decus et Tutamen.*

31 John Cary, *An essay on the state of England* (Bristol, 1695), p. 143; Henry Martin, *Considerations upon the East India Trade* (London, 1701), p. 16.

32 Daniel Defoe, *The Great Law of Subordination considered* (London, 1724), p. 50; see also the discussion in Slack, *Improvement*, pp. 150–53, 209–10.

33 Bernard Mandeville, *The Grumbling Hive: or, Knaves Turn'd Honest* (London, 1705); Bernard Mandeville, *Fable of the Bees: or Private Vices, Publick Benefits* (London, 1714).

34 Keynes, *General Theory*, p. 359.

35 David Hume, 'Of Civil Liberty', in *Essays, Moral and Political* (Edinburgh, 1741, reissued in 1758), p. 1; Istvan Hont, *Jealousy of Trade: International Competition and the Nation-state in Historical Perspective* (Cambridge, 2005), pp. 8–9.

36 Istvan Hont, *Hume's Knaves and the Shadow of Machiavellianism*, conference paper, Brighton, 28–29 May 2010, pp. 15-20, https://arts.standrews.ac.uk/intellectualhistory/islandora/object/intellectualhistory%3A153/datastream/OBJ/view (accessed 29 November 2019).

37 Hoppit, 'British Economic Literature', pp. 79–110, claims that *Discourse concerning coining the new money lighter* only appears in one of the major economic libraries of the eighteenth century, but he seems to have omitted the copy in John Locke's library. He also claims that the Joseph Massie collection of economic pamphlets only contains Barbon's *Discourse concerning coining the new money lighter* while in fact it contains all his major publications. These omissions naturally cast some doubt on Hoppit's overall analysis.

38 William A. Shaw, *Bibliography of the Collection of Books and Tracts on Commerce, Currency, and Poor Law, 1557 to 1763, formed by Joseph Massie ... Transcribed from Lansdowne Manuscript MXLIX with historical and bibliographical introduction* (London, 1937); Kippis, *Biographica Britannica*, I, p. 290.

39 McCulloch, *Political Economy*, p. 157.

40 Marx, *Das Kapital*, ch. 1, p. 1.

41 Stephen Bauer, 'Nicholas Barbon. Ein Beitrag zur Vorgeschichte der klassischen Oekonomik', *Jahrbücher für Nationalökonomie und Statistik*, 21/6 (1890), pp. 561–90.

42 Keynes, *General Theory*, pp. 324–25.

APPENDIX I

PUBLICATIONS BY NICHOLAS BARBON

1678 *A Particular of the New Buildings within the Bills of mortality, and without the City of London*

1678 *Arguments concerning the New Building in the Parishes within the weekly Bills of Mortality, without the City of London*

1678 *A Discourse shewing the great advantages that New Buildings and the Enlarging of Towns and Cities do bring to a Nation*

1680 *Propositions for Insuring Houses from Fire*

1680 *From the Insurance Office for Houses on the back-side of the Royal Exchange*

1680 *Arguments for Insuring Houses from Fire*

1680 *A Table of the Insurance Office at the Backside of the Royal Exchange*

1681 *An Enquiry whether it be in the interest of the City to insure houses from fire and what advantages the insured may expect, more than from the Insurance Office already settled*

1681 *A letter to a Gentleman of the Insurance Office, concerning the Cities insuring houses*

1681 *Observations on the Proposals of the City, to insure Houses in case of Fire*

1684 *A letter to a Gentleman in the Country giving an account of the Two Insurance Offices*

1685 *An Apology for the Builder*
(reprinted 1689)

1690 A *Discourse of Trade*

1694 *An advertisement being a proposal by Dr Barbon and partners for insuring houses and goods from fire*

1694 *An Answer to a paper entituled Reasons against Reducing Interest Rates to four percent*

1695 With John Asgill, *A Proposal for a Subscription to raise one hundred thousand pounds for circulating the credit of a Land Bank*

1695 With John Asgill, *An Account of the Land Bank*

1695 With John Asgill, *The Freeholders Answer to Mr John Briscoe's Proposals for a National Bank*

1695 With John Asgill, *A Letter from a Citizen of London to his Friend in the Country ...*

1696 With John Asgill and John Briscoe, *A Scheme for a National Land Bank*

1696 *A Discourse concerning coining the new money lighter: in Answer to Mr Lock's Considerations About Raising the Value of Money.*

1696 *A proposal for Raising the Public Credit, by Setting up an Office for Transferring and Discounting Tallies*

APPENDIX II

WILL OF NICHOLAS BARBON

(The National Archives, PROB 11/449/217)

In the Name of God Amen the eighteenth day of May Anno D[omi]ni one thousand & six hundred & ninety eight And in the tenth yeare of the Reigne of our Soveraigne Lord William the third by the grace of God King of England & Scotland & France and Ireland Defender of the Faith etc I Nicholas Barbon of Osterly in the County of Middx Esqr being sick in body but of sound and perfect memory doe make and publish this my last Will and Testament First I humbly resigne my Soul to the mercy of God and my body to be buryed And I dispose my Estate in this manner I give and bequeath all my Estate right and Equity of Redemption which I have in and to Osterly House which I now live in The Mannor of Heston and the ground and appurtenances thereunto belonging And all my Estate right and equity of redemption which I have in and to Newport ground and Newport Market with their appurtenances in the parish of St Anns Westminster And also all my Estate right title and equity of Redemption of and in the ground called Bedford ground near Redd Lyon Square and near Grayes Inne and the ground adjoyning belonging to Rugby School part of Conduit mead And my Estate right and title to the ground purchased of [blank] Hookings and [blank] Bonny being the West part of Conduit mead containing about twelve acres And all my Estate right title and equity in and to the Mannor of East Smithfeild and to the ground and buildings thereto belonging And all my Estate right title and equity in and to the ground and building in a New Street called Queen Street and places adjoyning in the Parish of St Margarets Westminster formerly the Inheritance of [blank] Kirke And all my Estate right title and claime in and to Lincolns Inn Square in the County of Middx And likewise all my Estate right title and interest in and to the houses and ground in the Burrough of Bramber in the County of Sussex And all my Estate right title and equity in and to the ground called great Brooke Feild and Little Brooke Feild in the Parish of St Martins in the Feilds in the County of Middx aforesaid and the buildings thereon and the Beast Market and sheep market and Fair thereunto belonging kept on the said ground and all other ground thereunto adjoyning belonging to me And all my Estate right title and equity in and to Exeter Change in the Strand and the shopps with the appurtenances thereunto belonging And all other my right and equity of Redemption in or to any ground houses or rents of Inheritance or for any term of yeares And all other my Estate whatsoever both reall and personall To my loveing sister Mrs Rebecca Hayes John Asgill of Lincolns Inne Esqr. and John Bland of the Middle Temple London gent and their Heires Executors and Administrators upon trust that they shall sell the same with all convenient speed and thereout shall pay and satisfye what shall be justly due and oweing on the said Estates and the remainder which shall be raised thereby I desire may be in the first place applyed to pay and satisfye my said sister the remaineing part of six hundred pounds if my goods shall not amount to soe much when sold which were made over to her long since by bill of sale And seaven hundred pounds more I owe her by bond and The remainder I desire may bee applyed towards payment of the rest of my Debts in manner as hereunder is directed vizt. a bond of two hundred pounds and Interest which I owe Mr George Dodson in which bond my said sister is bound and all other Bonds wherein she is bound for me and one hundred pounds and Interest which I owe Thomas Ducket Esqr And afterwards shall pay all such Debts as at the time of my decease I shall justly owe in any manner whatsoever especially that Debt in the first place if any shall be then unpaid for my late wifes Funerall And the rest and residue of my Estate which shall afterwards remaine the Legacyes hereunder named being first paid one moiety or half part thereof I give to my Executors hereunder named The other moiety or half part I give to and amongst my late wifes and my Relations according to the discretion of my Executors I give and bequeath to my Cousin John Barbon twenty shillings in full of all claimes to my Estate And I give my said Trustees fifty pounds apeice And I make my said sister Rebecca Hayes and the said John Asgill and John Bland Executors of this my last Will Witnesse my hand and seale to

each sheete the day and year abovesaid. Nic Barbon. Nic Barbon signed sealed and published by the said Nicholas Barbon in the presence of Witness in the presence of Dr Nicolas Barbon. Alex. Cutting James Smethurst Elizabeth Price
Signed Sealed and published by the above named Nicholas Barbon after the interlineation of John Asgill as a Trustee in the first sheete and as an Executor in the last sheete in the presence of us who have subscribed our names as Witnesses thereunto in the presence of the said Nicholas Barbon Arthur Clay James Smethurst and Elizabeth Price

Probate was granted on 6 February 1699

APPENDIX III

BUILDINGS ON THE NATIONAL HERITAGE LIST FOR ENGLAND WITH LINKS TO BARBON

Middle Temple		
New Court	I	1676 (Fig. 15)
1 Essex Court	I	1679 (Fig. 40)
2 and 3 Essex Court	I	1677 (Fig. 19)
4–5 Pump Court	I	1679 (Fig. 42)[1]
1–11 New Square Lincoln's Inn (including railings)	II*	1690 (Fig. 100)
11 Essex Street	II	1675 19th-century alterations
14 Essex Street	II	1676 refronted in 20th century
19 Essex Street	II	1676 (Fig. 25)
32 Essex Street	II*	1676 rebuilt in 18th century
34 Essex Street	II	1676 18th-century refacing
Gateway	II	1676 rebuilt in 1953 after Second World War bombing
20 Devereux Court	II	1676 originally Grecian Coffee House remodelled as pub 1843
22 Devereux Court	II	1676 rebuilt early in 18th century
23 Devereux Court	II	1676 rebuilt in 18th and 20th centuries
Devereux Chambers	II	1675 altered in 18th and 19th centuries
22a College Hill	II*	1680? (Gateways Fig. 76)
22 College Hill	II*	1680?
18 Newport Court	II	Rebuilt 1778
19 Newport Court	II	1685 19th-century alterations
20, 20a Newport Court (including 12–13 Little Newport Street)	II	Rebuilt 1772–73
21–24 Newport Court	II	1688 modern shopfronts
25 Newport Court	II	Rebuilt 1784–85
26 Newport Court	II	Rebuilt 1784–85
27 Newport Court (including 4–8 Newport Place)	II	Rebuilt 1784–85
12 Gerrard Street	II	*c.* 1695 stuccoed 19th century
19 Gerrard Street	II	Altered 19th century
41 Gerrard Street	II	1683 19th-century alterations
47 Gerrard Street	II	Early 18th-century alterations
5 Crane Court	II	1670 rebuilt in replica in 1971 after fire

6 Crane Court (including 18 Red Lion Court)	II	1670 rebuilt in replica in 1971 after fire
42, 43 Bedford Row (and railings)	II	1693 refronted in replica in 1965 (Fig. 94)
33–36 Bedford Row (and railings)	II	1691 refronted in 18th century
14–17 Red Lion Square (and railings)	II	refronted in 19th century

1 4–5 Pump Court appears in the List with no mention of Barbon, see https://historicengland.org.uk/listing/the-list/list-entry/1193870?section=official-listing (accessed 25 January 2022).

INDEX OF BARBON'S DEVELOPMENT SITES

Page references for illustrations are in italics and for maps and plans in **bold**

ERRATA

Chapter XII endnotes: an additional endnote reference '1' has been inserted on p. 161; this has affected all the subsequent note numbers in that chapter, so that the reference '2' actually refers to endnote 3, '3' to endnote 4, etc.

pp. 101 and 191: 'Nicholas' Luttrell should be 'Narcissus' Luttrell.

GENERAL INDEX

Barbon's development sites are indexed in detail in the separate 'Index of Barbon's Development Sites' on pages 229–30; only major references to development sites are included here.

The following abbreviations are used: NB, Nicholas Barbon; IBDS, Index of Barbon's Development Sites (pages 229–30).

Page numbers in *italic* indicate illustrations. Page numbers followed by 'n' indicate notes.